NOT FREE, NOT
FOR ALL

A VOLUME IN THE SERIES

Studies in Print Culture and the History of the Book

EDITED BY

Greg Barnhisel
Robert A. Gross
Joan Shelley Rubin
Michael Winship

NOT FREE, NOT FOR ALL

PUBLIC LIBRARIES IN THE AGE OF JIM CROW

Cheryl Knott

UNIVERSITY OF MASSACHUSETTS PRESS

Amherst and Boston

ISBN 978-1-62534-178-5 (paper); 177-8 (hardcover)

Designed by Sally Nichols
Set in ITC New Baskerville St
Printed and bound by Sheridan Books, Inc.

Library of Congress Cataloging-in-Publication Data
Names: Knott, Cheryl, 1954– author.
Title: Not free, not for all : public libraries in the age of Jim Crow /
Cheryl Knott.
Description: Amherst : University of Massachusetts Press, [2015] | Series:
Studies in print culture and the history of the book | Includes
bibliographical references and index.
Identifiers: LCCN 2015031827| ISBN 9781625341778 (hardcover : alk. paper) |
ISBN 9781625341785 (pbk. : alk. paper)
Subjects: LCSH: African Americans and libraries—Southern
States—History—20th century. | Public libraries—Social aspects—United
States. | African Americans—Books and reading—History—20th century. |
African Americans—Southern States—History—20th century. | Carnegie
libraries—United States—History—20th century. | Library
architecture—United States—History—20th century. | Architecture and
society—United States—History—20th century.
Classification: LCC Z711.9 .K59 2016 | DDC 027.475—dc23 LC record available at
http://lccn.loc.gov/2015031827

British Library Cataloguing-in-Publication Data
A catalogue record for this book is available from the British Library.

Contents

Preface

Imagine a life without libraries, and without money to buy your own books and magazines. Imagine a life where food, clothing, shelter, and your personal safety were precarious and where no library offered solace or sanctuary. For most African Americans in the southern United States, that's what life was like, at least until the Supreme Court's 1954 *Brown v. Board of Education* decision and the passage of the Civil Rights Act of 1964 and the Voting Rights Act of 1965 began to officially dismantle the structure of white supremacy known as Jim Crow. Although public libraries were said to be "free to all," not all African Americans were free to use them.

During the first half of the twentieth century, millions of African Americans moved off the land and into northern and southern urban areas, where many had their first experience with libraries. In southern cities and towns, that experience was one of restriction. Southern city residents might pass the library building daily yet know, as they knew to step off the sidewalk when a white person walked by, that the life inside the building was not for them. If they were in a town in which white officials wanted to appear to be serving all the taxpayers, they might have an alternative, a separate Negro library, whose inadequate collection represented another kind of restriction. In rural areas, the alternative might be a box of books on a table that a teacher or a librarian occasionally replaced with a box of different books, or it might be a school library with some extra books for the public to borrow.

For literate African Americans in particular, restriction required resistance, and resistance took many forms. In this book, I focus on one of those forms: the creation and maintenance of public library collections and services for African Americans in the south, from the beginning of the twentieth century until the late 1960s. My sources include publications written while the libraries were founded and functioning, secondary accounts published during and after segregation, and archival and manuscript records linked to the creation and administration of segregated libraries. I have worked to concentrate on the libraries and their collections and services without diverting to related topics that other writers have already covered well, such as the segregated education of librarians and the role of the overwhelmingly white American Library Association in tacitly and explicitly supporting racial segregation.

In the course of researching and writing this history of racially segregated public libraries, I have learned four key things that I hope the book clearly documents. First, racially segregated public libraries were not aberrations that belied the free-to-all commitment voiced by white librarians but were routine in the Jim Crow era, particularly as racial segregation intensified in the late nineteenth and early twentieth centuries. Public libraries had a widespread policy of restricting access, whether total or partial, named or hidden. Second, the deep involvement of middle-class white women in founding and using tax-supported public libraries ensured that the newly created structures were white spaces. This suggests that the notion of the library building as a sanctuary supporting common community-wide reading has been inflected with gender and race considerations.

Third, against the odds and counter to their own preference for equity and justice, African Americans created separate libraries for themselves. Those who wanted access to libraries were put in the difficult position of extending racial segregation while creating new collections and services that were potentially of great help to individual readers. In one of the many ironies of the Jim Crow era, the earliest library collections and services specifically designed to meet the needs of black readers developed in the south. Finally, the long, slow movement toward library desegregation proceeded unevenly. In the 1950s and 1960s, it took place in two phases: a quiet lifting of some restrictions, followed by a period of white resistance to changing policies and practices. Yet in the earliest moments of quiet desegregation, new segregated libraries were being established.

I glimpsed all of these events and patterns years ago, when the kernel of this book formed my dissertation on the founding of "colored" Carnegie libraries. Subsequent research, as I have tried to keep up with new publications and newly digitized resources, has made it possible to offer a fuller picture of the past, and Carnegie libraries are only one part of the story. I remain profoundly grateful to my dissertation committee at the University of Texas at Austin—chair Donald G. Davis, Jr., and members Loriene Roy, Philip Doty, Desley Deacon, and the late Shearer Davis Bowman—for their knowledge, guidance, and enthusiasm during the earliest years of this project. George C. Wright encouraged me to study Louisville's libraries and offered very helpful advice that led to my first journal publication, for which I am ever thankful.

At the University of Illinois and now at the University of Arizona I have benefited greatly from the assistance of numerous graduate students, and countless archivists and librarians have helped in my search for information. The University of Arizona Libraries' interlibrary-loan staff members have given stellar service over many years. An Arnold O. Beckman Research Award and a Centennial Scholar grant at the University of Illinois supported my travel to archival collections at various southern libraries. The University of Arizona Social and Behavioral Sciences Research Institute funded my purchase of research material on microfilm, and the University of Arizona International Affairs Office provided funding to attend conferences of the Society for the History of Authorship, Reading, and Publishing, where Ezra Greenspan and other scholars asked questions and made comments that helped me refine my work. I am grateful for the opportunity to have been a Fellow of the Gilder Lehrman Institute of American History, which included a grant for travel to New York City to conduct research at the Schomburg Center for Research in Black Culture. I also received a Franklin Research Grant from the American Philosophical Society to support travel to collections to research the Ella Reid Public Library.

The dean of the University of Arizona's College of Social and Behavioral Sciences kindly granted me a one-semester sabbatical, which gave me time to put the manuscript into a sufficiently finished state to submit it to the University of Massachusetts Press for review. I am indebted to the two individuals who reviewed the manuscript for the press, including Wayne Wiegand, who allowed himself to be identified by name. Their comments and suggestions helped me rethink and rewrite in what I hope have been productive ways.

Louise Robbins read and commented on chapter 3, and I appreciate all her help, both recently and in the past. I thank James Connolly and Frank Felsenstein for their willingness to share relevant passages from their book *What Middletown Read* before publication. Expert editor Brian Halley has been kind and patient, and his wise words have saved me from myself on more than one occasion. I also appreciate the work of Carol Betsch and Mary Bellino at the University of Massachusetts Press and the copyediting of Dawn Potter. Photographer J. E. Syme lent his expertise by preparing some of the photographs for publication, and he has been supportive and enthusiastic throughout the final stages of this project, for which I will always be grateful.

I appreciate having permission to remix and reuse the following: Cheryl Knott Malone, "Louisville Free Public Library's Racially Segregated Branches, 1905–1935," *Register of the Kentucky Historical Society* 93 (Spring 1995): 159–79; "Reconstituting the Public Library Users of the Past: An Exploration of Nominal Record Linkage Methodology," *Journal of Education for Library and Information Science* 39 (Fall 1998): 282–90; "Autonomy and Accommodation: Houston's Colored Carnegie Library, 1907–1922," *Libraries and Culture* 34 (Spring 1999): 95–112; "Books for Black Children: Public Library Collections in Louisville and Nashville, 1915–1925," *Library Quarterly* 70 (April 2000): 179–200; "Quiet Pioneers: Black Women Public Librarians in the Segregated South," *Vitae Scholasticae* 19 (Spring 2000): 59–76; "The Adult Collection at Nashville's Negro Public Library, 1915–1916," in *Libraries to the People: Histories of Outreach,* ed. Robert S. Freeman and David M. Hovde (Jefferson, N.C.: McFarland, 2003), 148–56; "Unannounced and Unexpected: The Desegregation of Houston Public Library," *Library Trends* 55 (Winter 2007): 665–74; and Cheryl Knott, "The Publication and Reception of *The Southern Negro and the Public Library,*" in *Race, Ethnicity and Publishing in America,* ed. Cécile Cottenet (London: Palgrave Macmillan, 2014), 51–76.

As a white woman raised in a working-class neighborhood in a rapidly growing and slowly desegregating southern city, I may have made errors of commission, omission, assumption, and interpretation, which I acknowledge as mine alone.

NOT FREE, NOT
FOR ALL

INTRODUCTION

Questions of Access

In the early 1950s, the city of Houston opened its central public library to African Americans after fifty years of denying them access. As word of the new policy spread, teenager Gloria Dean Randle entered the library for the first time and made a point of browsing among the stacks, walking up and down between the rows of shelves on several floors of the building, defying the racist past. What she saw were the thousands and thousands of books that, till then, had existed for her only in theory. Before her lay material evidence of the texts that white city officials and librarians had deliberately kept from her and her fellow black Houstonians.[1] Randle's experience of restricted access was common across the south until the last official public library barriers fell in the 1960s.

Public libraries are fixtures in U.S. cities and counties of all sizes; if they weren't, we would feel that something was essentially amiss. Today, even as they rethink their roles and reposition themselves in the information age, public libraries persist as community institutions. Theories about public libraries as "arsenals of a democratic culture" (to use Sidney Ditzion's 1947 phrase) and "cornerstones of liberty" (to use Nancy Kranich's 2001 words) emphasize the institution's enduring role as what Redmond Kathleen Molz and Phyllis Dain call a "civic space" in which community members find entertainment, education, and information.[2] A striking reference to libraries in John Willinsky's *The Access Principle*, which advocates making research openly available on the Internet rather than in for-profit databases, echoes such sentiments:

> Opening the research literature's virtual door to the public . . . bears a certain kinship to the nineteenth-century public library movement. . . . The public library . . . has long been a beacon of self-directed and deeply motivated learning on the part of common readers. It is not only a vital cornerstone of democracy, but a public site of quiet solace, intellectual inquiry, and literary pleasures.[3]

Such theories understand the institution as both a collection and a place, but they do not take into account an important part of the public library's past: the decades when many tax-supported libraries refused service to African Americans or provided service in segregated buildings. However libraries themselves are conceptualized, it is clear that African Americans value reading and writing. Duke University professor Karla F. C. Holloway has used the memories of libraries and reading recorded by authors such as Richard Wright, Ralph Ellison, and Maya Angelou to discuss her own experience of the relationship between race and reading. She is especially interested in the booklists that Ellison, Wright, and others compiled and publicized, writing that such lists serve an important antiracist agenda: "Black writers who mark their literary histories in this way indicate that if there remains some lingering skepticism about the authority of their literacy, it might be best contradicted with a lofty list of great books."[4] In particular, Holloway notices that many readers/writers recall their experiences with and in public libraries, which she characterizes as "fragile" locations:

> The habit of the booklist may have emerged as a consequence of black writers' vulnerable relationship to public libraries and as a way to contradict the value that those segregated spaces explicitly assigned. That so many of these writers recall the libraries in which they accomplished their reading, or that denied them access, is not just the occasion of finding the familiar within the expected. Instead, the memories about the locations and the places of the books that made their way onto the reading lists indicated how deeply the authors' relationship with books is related to race—whether the libraries themselves became a hurdle to their reading habits, or a help.[5]

Far from being an uncomplicated relationship, the connections among public libraries, African Americans, and democratic participation have a history that raises questions of access. Separate libraries reserved for black readers set aside public space for private research, information gathering, and educational and recreational reading as well as for group gatherings in assembly halls and meeting rooms. Their existence underlined the significance of access to information in an urban and industrial milieu that was increasingly dependent on new communication technologies. As "universities of the people," public libraries helped create an African American identity, asserting individuals' capacity for intellectual labor in an era when the value of a liberal education for blacks remained a topic for debate. Libraries provided access points for black literacy and intellectualism, confirmation that African Americans were reading, reflecting, striving human beings.

Yet even as they were counterpoints to prevalent racism, separate libraries were part of the institutionalization of oppressive racial policies. They signified the pervasiveness of segregation, which by the early twentieth century was already in place in public facilities such as schools, streetcars, trains, restaurants, and hotels. In the age of Jim Crow, segregated facilities were the model for providing library services to African Americans in cities and towns of the south. As one of the paradoxes associated with racial segregation, the earliest deliberate efforts to create public library collections and services for African Americans occurred in a region identified with white supremacy, poverty, and ignorance—and where public library development in general lagged behind that in the northeast and midwest.[6]

The history of racially segregated libraries has the potential to change our theories of print culture, our assessment of library history and information policy, and our story of the civil rights movement. In a model of print culture history that depicts an endless loop of book production and consumption processes, how do we account for libraries that denied or restricted access to their buildings and collections? In a history of public libraries that relies on sources generated by whites to reconstruct the past, how do the voices and experiences of black activists, librarians, and readers change what we think we know about libraries as institutions and about librarians as champions of intellectual freedom and democratic participation?

In the story of the civil rights movement, how do we understand African American agency in both the creation of Jim Crow libraries and their demise? I explore such questions by examining the history of racially segregated public libraries in the American south from the beginning of the twentieth century to the 1960s. In the process I incorporate the work of historians of the book, of libraries, and of the civil rights movement in an effort to tell a more complex story than could otherwise be told.

Among other goals, I seek to expand the categorization of libraries in Robert Darnton's 1982 model of the "communications circuit," which depicts book processes as carried out by authors, publishers, printers, shippers, booksellers, readers, and binders. Darnton was motivated by the idea that "it might be useful to propose a general model for analyzing the way books come into being and spread through society."[7] The model is based on the assumption that books come into being in order to spread through society—why else go to the trouble of creating books? In Darnton's graphic depiction of the communications circuit, libraries fit into the category he has labeled "readers," as do purchasers, borrowers, and clubs. His accompanying text does not explain why libraries are in that particular category, although he does point out that a scholar can begin to study a book anywhere in the process, including "at the point of its assimilation in libraries."[8] Darnton later compared his model to a subsequent one proposed by Thomas R. Adams and Nicholas Barker, which focuses on the stages a book goes through (publication, manufacture, distribution, reception, and survival) rather than on the people involved.[9] Adams and Barker mention libraries in the distribution, reception, and survival processes, but their discussion emphasizes the rare-book room and the research library rather than the public library.[10] Putting libraries into the same category as readers or identifying them with the various book processes that connect texts to readers reinforces their role as "institutions of reading."[11]

Because models have a tendency to depict what is, they can be difficult aids to understanding what is not. We can see how libraries might help find "every book its reader," one of S. R. Ranganathan's "five laws of library science," but it is difficult to imagine librarians' collusion in the denial of information access.[12] Yet the story of racially segregated public libraries reveals a hidden law of southern library science: every book its white reader. Restricted access to reading material in public libraries and to the spaces enclosed in library buildings is part of the history of libraries and print culture. Restricted access—both the complete denial of service and the provision of small, inadequate collections, services, and spaces—should be understood as a policy instantiated in practice. Drawing on the work of Bruno Latour and others, Geoffrey Bowker has written about the creation of industrial science in the early twentieth-century oil fields and the management of the information produced. Scientific principles discovered in mud and rock were conveyed in scholarly papers that erased the messy history of fieldwork.[13] Likewise, policy is better understood as something that happens "on the run," in the field, at a white library's circulation desk in 1907, when a black teacher walks up to borrow a book. Information policy, formulated at the level of everyday work life, has a history.

Library and information science educators often craft courses on information policy that focus on federal-level intellectual property, publishing, surveillance, privacy, and security. These courses do not consider *Plessy v. Ferguson,* which established a legal basis for so-called separate but equal facilities and services, or *Brown v. Board of Education,* which reversed *Plessy,* or the Civil Rights Act of 1964, which addressed whites' continuing efforts to undercut *Brown.* They do not consider the formal or informal policies that white librarians implemented when faced with actual black readers. Yet as Patterson Toby Graham's important *A Right to Read: Segregation and Civil Rights in Alabama's Public Libraries, 1900–1965* demonstrates, "the exclusion of African-American readers from public libraries undermined intellectual freedom in American libraries more than any other factor during the twentieth century."[14] Incorporating the history of library services and collections for African Americans into library history can and should change our definition of information policy, including our understanding of intellectual freedom and ultimately of libraries as institutions.

Incorporating the history of racially segregated libraries can also change our conceptualization of the periods of American library development. Since at least the 1940s, scholars have been documenting the record of the library profession on race matters and service inequities while highlighting the contributions of individual black and white librarians and the alternative institutions created in the absence of public libraries.[15] Writing in the late 1970s about "Segregation and the Library," Doris Hargrett Clack proposed four periods: no access, segregated access, desegregated access accompanied by white resistance, and free access, which she hoped would arrive soon.[16] The literature of American public library history conceptualizes a different periodization. Failing to incorporate the history of racial segregation makes it possible to place the "free access" period at the end of the nineteenth century, when public libraries began opening previously closed stacks and creating spaces for children. Such an approach whitewashes the ways in which librarians' historical complicity in refusing or restricting service to African Americans while espousing a "free to all" rhetoric undermines the assertion that intellectual freedom and universal access to information have been enduring core values of the information professions.

Additionally, there has been a tendency among some academics and professional practitioners who research their field's history, and I've been among them, to search for heroes and heroines.[17] One might choose to see whites who helped establish library collections and services for African Americans as enlightened torchbearers of the profession's noblest values, especially if one focuses on whites' own words as evidence. Such an approach tends to portray whites as the central characters whose training and commitment led them to do the right thing, or, as one library science educator has put it, to "make the sympathetic white person the hero . . . [of] a Black story."[18]

The search for librarian heroes is pronounced in literature that recounts the profession's role in the history of intellectual freedom. Accounts of the creation of the American Library Association's Library Bill of Rights during the rise of fascism in the late 1930s trumpet the tenet that public libraries have a right to select books for purchase without regarding the race of the author. Yet these accounts do not always note that this policy was addressing collections, not readers. Not until 1961 did the Library Bill of Rights declare that "the rights of an individual to the use of a library should not be denied or abridged because of his race, religion, national origins, or political views."[19] Intellectual freedom is a hollow promise as long as it focuses on what's in the collection and ignores who has access to it. What does it matter what a library holds if up to half of the local population cannot use it? In such a scenario, intellectual freedom is just one more white privilege.

As Grace Elizabeth Hale has argued, racial segregation was an instrument for maintaining white supremacy after slavery, and maintaining white supremacy took constant effort.[20] In the early twentieth century, as fee-based libraries were giving way to tax-supported ones, whites looked for other ways to continue restricting access. In Little Rock, Arkansas, for instance, city leaders asked Andrew Carnegie for money to construct a building that would be used by whites only. As the city worked to secure a building grant, Carnegie's assistant James Bertram and local white banker Samuel Reyburn discussed the matter. Reyburn learned that Booker T. Washington, the former slave who had founded Tuskegee Institute and catapulted himself to international fame by publicly accepting segregation, would be dining with Carnegie. The unreconstructed Reyburn, who told Bertram that he remembered eating with one of his father's favored slaves, said that he would also be willing to dine with Washington. It was his white right to "[choose] the colored people he sat at dinner with or rubbed shoulders with at the library."[21]

Despite the fact that people such as Reyburn denied them access and agency, African Americans took an interest in public libraries and sought to use them. If they could not enter the central facility, then they worked to create and stock another building with books. Although early historians of the civil rights movement tended to ignore public libraries, more recent scholars have included accounts of actions designed to gain access to public libraries. In his study of race relations in Virginia, *Managing White Supremacy*, J. Douglas Smith tells the story of a black sit-in at the newly opened Alexandria Public Library, part of a larger series of actions in the late 1930s and early 1940s.[22] The timing of that direct action in Alexandria coincided with the beginning of "the long civil rights movement," which, according to Jacqueline Dowd Hall, "took root in the liberal and radical milieu of the late 1930s, . . . stretched far beyond the South," and always confronted massive white resistance.[23] Glenda Elizabeth Gilmore pushes the roots of the movement even further back, to the era after World War I, when Communists and blacks were advocating for equal rights.[24]

Actions such as library sit-ins were initiated by educated African Americans who were active in their church and school communities and in voluntary associations such as the National Association for the Advancement of Colored People (NAACP). In some cases such organizations took on segregated public libraries, but not always. They tended to pursue other long-term goals that might have a greater impact because they involved larger institutions and more people: defeating ordinances that required segregated residential areas and transportation, eliminating whites-only primary elections, securing equal pay for black teachers, desegregating public schools. In Petersburg, Virginia, the Reverend Wyatt Tee Walker, head of the local NAACP branch, was shocked when national office officials declined to help him desegregate the city's library because their objectives lay elsewhere. Undaunted, he proceeded without them.[25]

My focus on the south is not intended to imply that blacks in the north enjoyed unfettered access to integrated public libraries. As Clack has shown, racially restricted library access existed in the north, but much of it was perpetrated under cover. Abigail Van Slyck discusses how library exteriors and interiors can be designed to discourage some people from entering a building or staying in it for long.[26] And there were other ways to discourage use: a stern expression on a white librarian's face, an all-white staff and clients, the request that a black library user sit at a table where white users wouldn't sit. Such methods are seldom documented in libraries' standard archival records, yet they were used in places where African Americans lived, particularly during the Great Migration, as blacks moved from their rural homes to towns and cities, leaving the south for what they hoped were greater opportunities in the north.

Between 1916 and 1919, wartime labor shortages in northern industrial cities and the dire economic and political conditions of the rural south combined to encourage nearly half a million southern blacks to relocate. Throughout the 1920s, black southerners continued heading north, and by 1930 another million had made the move.[27] A 1925 survey published by the American Library Association offers glimpses of northern and midwestern libraries as reported by the white librarians in charge of them.[28] Their assertions should be read in the context of entrenched racial segregation in neighborhoods. Cerene Ohr, supervisor of branches of the Indianapolis Public Library, reported that the Paul Laurence Dunbar Branch had opened in May 1922 "to relieve [the] situation at [the] central library. Required great tact at first to convince colored patrons that it was not the first step to debar them from other libraries." The new library was housed in a schoolroom in an African American section of town, but it had a separate entrance so the public did not have to go through the school to enter the library. The branch librarian and assistant librarian had completed a training course run by the Indiana Public Library Commission. The Indianapolis Public Library also provided deposit stations and classroom collections at some of the African American schools.[29]

From Evansville, Indiana, Ethel McCullough reported that "the community's southern point of view would necessitate segregated service." Although the town sat on the northern bank of the Ohio River, it was still south of Louisville, Kentucky. Its Cherry Street Branch for African Americans opened in December 1914 in a $10,000 Carnegie building. The branch librarian working there in 1925 had spent five years taking Indiana Public Library Commission summer courses as well as Evansville Public Library staff training. McCullough asserted that "difficulties met at colored libraries [are] ten times those in public libraries for whites because of meager educational background of Negro group." There's no evidence that McCullough had worked with any "colored libraries" other than the one at Evansville, but she nevertheless felt comfortable generalizing from her limited experience to the entire "Negro group" while failing to analyze or acknowledge the conditions that created educational disparities.[30]

In Minneapolis, head librarian Gratia A. Countryman reported that three branches in the city were primarily used by African Americans but that the system was racially integrated. Her counterpart in Saint Paul reported that his library system was also integrated, noting that the city did not have a large number of African American residents. The Saint Paul Public Library staff included one or two African Americans at any given time, but director Webster Wheelock did not allow them to serve the public directly, "in justice to them and to spare prejudices of public." Kansas City Public Library supervisor of branches Agnes F. P. Greer reported that the system was "open freely to Negroes" but did refer to a "colored branch," which opened in 1914 in a room of the Garrison Field community house and moved in 1922 to Lincoln High School. Similarly, Lillie Wulfekoetter, chief branch librarian of the Cincinnati Public Library, asserted that the system was "freely open to Negroes" but referred to two "Negro branches": Douglass, opened in 1912, and Stowe, opened in 1923. Both were housed in black elementary schools and stayed open until nine o'clock at night to serve the public. Cleveland's public schools and libraries were not segregated, although one library branch had opened in a predominately black area of town in 1923, specifically to serve that population. According to vice-librarian Louise Prouty, Cleveland had no African American librarians or assistants. In the city's integrated library system, African Americans used five of the branches more than the others. The librarians in charge of those branches and the system's supervisor of branches formed a Committee on Work with Colored People to learn more about African Americans and to find ways to serve them better.[31]

Between 1910 and 1920, the black population of Chicago increased from 44,103 to 109,458.[32] In 1924 the Chicago Public Library hired its first African American professional librarian, Vivian G. Harsh, and in 1932 opened its first branch in an African American part of town, Bronzeville. Harsh had originally joined the Chicago Public Library staff as a clerk after finishing high school in 1909. She moved to Boston temporarily, attending Simmons College and earning a degree in 1921 in library science, and then returned to work at the Chicago Public Library. She rotated through different branches, including the Lincoln Center Library, until 1932, when she was appointed director of the new George Cleveland Hall Branch Library. The new branch was situated on land donated by Julius Rosenwald, and Harsh spent more than two decades there building an important collection that documented African American culture and history. She relied on donations because money for her special collection was not forthcoming from the library's managers.[33]

Between 1910 and 1920, the black population of New York City increased from 91,709 to 152,467.[34] Ernestine Rose, head librarian at the 135th Street Branch in Harlem, reported hiring two African American staff members in 1920, a response to the local Urban League's pressure to represent the neighborhood as it changed from a largely Jewish to a predominately black population. By 1925, half the staff at the branch were black, and Rose reported that "colored workers are as satisfactory as white." Noting the diversity of Harlem's population, she wrote, "Experience seems to show that [an] adult Negro waits for tangible proofs of the library's willingness to extend full privileges to him before he takes advantage of its service, then he responds to library service and needs more of it than the library can give. . . . Time is ripe for development of library services for Negroes, but it must not be patronizing or partially informed."[35]

Rose, however, was a relative latecomer to this idea. Southern libraries had already hired the first African American librarians, and they were also providing the earliest apprenticeship training for blacks, mainly at the Western Colored Branch in Louisville. The New York Public Library allowed open access to its collections and focused its services for special populations on the mostly European immigrants moving into its neighborhoods. For years before the demographics of New York's Harlem shifted from white to black, southern public libraries had been experimenting with serving African Americans, although they were always constrained by racist attitudes and racial segregation. Consequently, Harlem's 135th Street Branch could draw on the southern experience as it attempted to respond to changes in its clientele.

During the Great Migration, the New York Public Library began to expand its focus beyond European immigrants to include recent black immigrants from the African diaspora as well as African Americans migrating from the south. This was especially true of the 135th Street Branch. It followed the lead of southern libraries in its approach to providing services for African Americans, in every way but one: New York did not insist on segregation. In fact, the racially mixed staff of the 135th Street Branch were active participants in the 1920s Harlem Renaissance, a phenomenon fueled by modernist, integrationist ideology. As George Hutchinson has argued, the era witnessed a rising interest in American national and regional literature along with a commitment to cultural pluralism. The concomitant belief in black artistic expression as uniquely American helped fuel the Harlem Renaissance and the black-white interaction (if not integration) that characterized it.[36]

Despite their common professional interests, northern and southern librarians did not always understand each other. An active member of the American Library Association, Rose had helped create the Work with Negroes Round Table and had arranged its first formal meeting during the 1922 annual conference in Detroit. The organizing group had met the year before and had decided that it must remain a "round table" rather than a more formal, permanent, and ALA-sanctioned "section" because of the contentious regionalism apparent at that first informal gathering.[37] The group decided to survey 126 public libraries regarding their services to blacks, including whether they hired African American staff members. Ninety-eight responded. Marion P. Watson, one of Rose's employees, compiled the results, which generally revealed that in the far north and in the west (where the black population was minuscule) librarians reported open access and equal service. Responses were mixed for the midwest, but only two southern libraries allowed unrestricted access. The New York Public Library system reported allowing open access but also provided branches in black neighborhoods. Various librarians at the meeting spoke briefly about their policies and practices, and then Rose gave a talk on segregation. According to Rose's own minutes of the meeting, she pointed out that the north was beginning to move toward southern-style segregation. Noting that her 135th Street Branch was the only city branch with an integrated staff, even though other branches served large black neighborhoods, she said, "It is a question whether [the 135th Street Branch] should be made a colored branch or whether colored assistants should be put in other branches. . . . Legally, colored and white are on the same ground, but in many cases there is not a real feeling of equality in the library."[38] The minutes also hinted at controversies in the group: "Miss Rice, Chicago, feels that the Chicago Public Library has no problem to discuss. No separate branches are considered and work does not differ from that with foreigners. The branch in Abraham Lincoln Center has a fast growing colored patronage, with two colored assistants. There was some staff discomfort at first, but that has disappeared.

Colored children do not seem to prefer the colored assistants above the white."[39]

The following spring, in anticipation of the association's annual conference, scheduled for the last week of April in Hot Springs, Arkansas, Morris Lewis, executive secretary of the Chicago branch of the NAACP, wrote a letter to Robert W. Bagnall, the New York office's coordinator of NAACP branches. Lewis stated that two young women from the Chicago Public Library (presumably the two "colored assistants" who had been mentioned at the round table meeting) had told him that Ernestine Rose "interested herself especially along the lines of segregation in the library work; that is, separate libraries for Negroes in northern as well as southern states." Lewis suggested that Mary Pearson of the Cleveland Public Library, who was scheduled to speak to the round table in Hot Springs, be induced to counter Rose's "propaganda" in her talk on "Progress, North." He also thought that Mary White Ovington, chairman of the NAACP board, should send a statement to the American Library Association to be read at the conference. Bagnall evidently passed the letter on to W. E. B. Du Bois, who answered Lewis: "I do not think Miss Rose will say anything that can be interpreted as advocating Negro libraries this year. She did not mean to say it last year, as she explained. . . . I am including a statement made by Miss Rose at my suggestion clarifying her position taken last year."[40]

Apparently sensing her wording's potential to offend, Du Bois had rewritten Rose's statement and returned it to her. At the 1923 round table meeting, Mary Pearson of Cleveland seemed to make no special effort to counter Rose's remarks of the year before, although she did note that "the library is the one real democratic institution which is free to all." No comments are recorded in the minutes from Miss Rice of Chicago. Rose herself did not attend the meeting, but her New York Public Library colleague Harry M. Lydenberg read her report to the group. In it, Rose described a significant development in the city's librarian training program: the acceptance of "a colored applicant on precisely the same terms as the White. . . . Before the practice trip to other libraries was taken, all hotels on the route were asked if they had any objection to admitting a colored woman, and without exception they answered they had none."[41] The *New York*

Amsterdam News received a copy of Rose's Hot Springs paper and reported on it, quoting the part at the end that Du Bois himself may have written: "Miss Ernestine Rose . . . declares herself as being opposed to the purely Negro library. 'It is by the contact of individual with individual, the acquaintance of one person with another,' she says, 'that all prejudice, personal or racial, breaks down.' "[42] The "contact of individual with individual" apparently did not help keep the round table functioning, as southerners continued to defend their approach. Although the estimated one hundred members at the round table discussion agreed to meet again the next year, they never did.[43]

Although New York and Chicago public libraries served all residents, the branch system—wherein smaller libraries were sprinkled through a city to serve the residents of different neighborhoods, particularly children who found it difficult to travel to the central library—mirrored the residential segregation common in both the north and the south. The south was not exceptional in its racism: it is clear that at least some northern, midwestern, and western public libraries thought of themselves as having "colored branches" and did not always provide equitable information access. In fact, the branch library system developed along with the "American apartheid" that Douglas Massey and Nancy Denton have identified as the outcome of residential segregation policies that cities created in response to the Great Migration.[44] At the same time, northern libraries imposed fewer restrictions than southern libraries did. For example, Dorothy Barnett (who grew up to become Dorothy Porter Wesley, the renowned curator of a major Africana collection at Howard University) freely used the Carnegie library as a youngster in Montclair, New Jersey. When she moved to Washington, D.C., to attend school, she was denied full access to the public library in that more southern-oriented city.[45] While more work on the history of public libraries' treatment of African Americans outside the south is needed, my focus on the south emphasizes that public library history remains partial as long as it fails to account for the south.[46] We cannot assume that historical case studies of libraries in the north, midwest, or west are representative of all public libraries or that they provide examples of policies and practices that were more enlightened than those in the south. Information injustices perpetrated on African Americans anywhere reflect on the information professions everywhere.[47]

Race is a social construction rather than a biological fact and public libraries have contributed to the construction of race since their beginnings.[48] Public libraries designated for the exclusive use of African Americans clearly participated in the construction of blackness. Less obviously, public libraries in general helped define whiteness. On one hand was the public library, with its unannounced restriction on access; on the other was the Negro library, with its label of difference sometimes carved into its facade. "As the unmarked category against which difference is constructed," George Lipsitz has written, "whiteness never has to speak its name, never has to acknowledge its role as an organizing principle in social and cultural relations."[49]

The U.S. public library was one of many institutions upholding the systemic racism that enabled white supremacy. In his book-length explanation of how whites and blacks experience systemic racism, sociologist Joe Feagin defines the phenomenon as "white-generated and white-maintained oppression [that] is far more than a matter of individual bigotry, for it has been from the beginning a material, social, and ideological reality . . . manifested in all major societal institutions."[50] It is fantasy to believe that the public library was one of the few institutions not implicated in a system of racism or that separate public libraries for African Americans were just an unfortunate exception to the public library's true democratic nature.

Despite the rich literature available about African American library collections and services, many details remain unknown about separate public libraries for African Americans and about the individuals who raised private funds; secured public support; arranged for the design, construction, furnishing, and staffing of the buildings; and demanded desegregation of libraries, not because they were special but because they were one among many tools in the armory of white supremacy. Many people automatically identify all picturesque old Carnegie libraries with a white clientele, the unmarked category. According to philosopher Charles Mills, a racial contract exists among whites in which they keep full citizenship rights and resources for themselves. Mills asserts that the resulting white-supremacist state oppresses blacks by ensuring differential access to civic and economic opportunities. Much of the power of the racial contract arises from its invisibility to the whites who benefit from it: *"white misunderstanding, misrepresentation, evasion, and self-deception on matters related to race* are among the most pervasive mental phenomena of the past few hundred years."[51]

The surprise that some white people register on learning of the historical existence of separate libraries for African Americans suggests that we need to counter the hegemonic narrative of white public library history. Conceptualizing an unacknowledged underlying racial contract among whites intent on expanding their own material, political, and cultural resources at the expense of non-whites makes differential access to public libraries unsurprising. Mills points out that the oppression of African Americans has never gone unchallenged; blacks have resisted consistently and creatively. In the case of public libraries, they did so by founding their own libraries, by surreptitiously using white libraries, by sometimes refusing to use segregated collections and services, and by agitating for full access.

Chapter 1 establishes a context for understanding the development of racially segregated libraries, interweaving the state of print culture with race relations in the late nineteenth and early twentieth centuries. Chapter 2 recounts the use of Carnegie money to create the segregated branch model in the first two decades of the twentieth century. Chapter 3 follows the spread of the model in the 1920s after the Carnegie Corporation ceased giving building grants. Chapter 4 discusses the use of private and public money during the Great Depression, when librarians worked to extend services to rural areas through county libraries. Chapter 5 focuses on the 1940s, when libraries staffed and used exclusively by African Americans continued to be founded, even as blacks began taking action to dismantle existing segregated services. Chapters 6, 7, and 8 break from the narrative to discuss the buildings, the collections they housed, and the ways in which they were used. Finally, chapter 9 offers an account of library desegregation before and after *Brown*. As African Americans shaped their libraries and the urban landscapes from which those library buildings rose, they participated in a larger project involving literacy and identity. The significance of separate libraries for African Americans lies in the meanings assigned to them by the people who created and used them as well as in what they can tell us about an era that has ended but whose contradictions continue to confound.

CHAPTER 1

The Culture of Print in a Context of Racism

The creation of racially segregated public libraries early in the twentieth century followed two key trends of the age: the amplification of print culture and the attenuation of black civil rights. The amplification of print culture was apparent in the heightened production, distribution, and consumption of all kinds of reading matter throughout the nineteenth and into the twentieth centuries. Evidence of the burgeoning print culture of the late nineteenth century can be found in paper manufacturing, book publishing, the newspaper and magazine trade, the library industry, and the literacy rate. Evidence of the attenuation of black civil rights after Reconstruction ended in the 1870s can be found in the legal system and in daily social practices.

The increase in paper manufacturing is documented in the 1900 *Census of Manufactures*. Data reveal that the 1890s had been a period of consolidation and growth in the paper industry, a response to "the extraordinary development of the newspaper press and . . . the great demand for reading matter which characterizes the American people."[1] The aggregated value of the products published and printed in 1900, including books, pamphlets, music, newspapers, and periodicals, totaled more than $347 million and accounted for more than half of all the goods produced in the printing and publishing category.[2]

Coinciding with the production of reading material was the rapid creation and construction of public libraries as agencies that selectively collected, organized, and distributed printed matter. Carl F.

Kaestle and Janice A. Radway characterize the period between 1880 and 1940 as one of "print in motion," a time when the publishing industry was consolidating as the reading public was expanding and diversifying. In their introduction to a collection of essays about the national book trade, the importance of newspapers and magazines, institutions of reading such as libraries, and related topics, Kaestle and Radway discuss the culture of print in the context of accelerating social change, the rise of the consumer economy, and the emergence of interest groups such as women, ethnic minorities, and African Americans: "We have found the term 'culture of print' a useful short-hand descriptor for this period's social formation, in part because the tensions between social integration and disintegration, between order and disorder, and between incorporation and diversity were themselves played out with the indispensable assistance of proliferating print practices and reading formations."[3]

Technological innovations and other factors made publishing a less-expensive enterprise than it had been before 1880, and the publishing trade became an integrated industry with national sweep and scope.[4] At the same time, cheaper production gave previously marginalized groups access to print as producers and consumers. Evidence of increased access among African Americans includes a rise in the literacy rate: from about 5 percent at the start of the Civil War to almost 80 percent by 1920. Close to 700 black-owned periodicals were in existence at the end of the Civil War, compared to more than 3,000 twenty years later. Organizations such as the NAACP and the National Urban League began issuing their own publications, and by the end of World War I the NAACP's *Crisis* had a circulation of nearly 100,000. Tuskegee Institute's *The Negro Yearbook,* first published in 1912, became a staple reference work, featuring statistics on lynching, home ownership, literacy, and other phenomena and reporting on numerous developments related to African American lives and experiences. Religious organizations, including the National Baptist Convention and its publishing board and women's auxiliary, issued millions of tracts, pamphlets, and books, not all on strictly religious topics. African Americans founded newspapers, including, in 1905, the influential *Chicago Defender,* whose nationwide circulation of about 280,000 helped fuel the Great Migration.[5]

In Philadelphia, newspaper columnist William Carl Bolivar drew on his extensive private library to publicize the history and accomplishments of the city's black residents and make readers aware of other bibliophiles like himself.[6] Black women's clubs undertook a combination of charitable and educational activities in which print culture sometimes played a central role. For instance, the Woman's Era Club in Boston published a newspaper that exhorted readers to expand their intellectual and critical faculties and represent their own interests in their own voices as they engaged with a broad swath of literature discussed in the club paper and at local club meetings.[7] Numerous subscription libraries and reading rooms (as opposed to tax-supported public libraries) offered collections and space for African American readers, particularly those living in northern cities and towns, where a critical mass made such ventures viable.[8] An 1876 U.S. Bureau of Education report counted 257 public libraries. By the mid-1930s, there were more than 6,000. Only 491 were in the south, and among them were 64 separate public library branches for African Americans.[9]

One might assume that the widespread production, distribution, and consumption of reading material would have fostered an era of enlightenment, but it did not, at least not as regards notions about race. Instead, the rights and status of black Americans diminished in the late nineteenth century, in a series of post-Reconstruction legal decisions that signaled what one historian has called a "nadir" in race relations.[10] In 1883 the U.S. Supreme Court declared the Civil Rights Act of 1875 unconstitutional. Thirteen years and a number of state and local segregation ordinances later, the Court's *Plessy v. Ferguson* decision found "separate but equal" facilities to be constitutional. The system of segregation had its greatest impact in urban areas, where it regulated relations among strangers as the south's faltering agrarian economy and brutal sharecropping practices increased black migration to towns and cities.[11]

Until the civil rights era of the mid-twentieth century, racial segregation persisted as a result of laws as well as ingrained customs that made explicit laws unnecessary. Not surprisingly, some African Americans—those who had the advantage of education and the courage of conviction—turned to the communication circuitry of writing, publishing, disseminating information, collecting publications, creating bibliographies, and reading in an effort to lessen the impact of racist policies and practices. Some built and staffed libraries.

Underlying such efforts to participate in the production, distribution, and consumption of print culture was a long-standing reverence for education. African Americans' interest in acquiring and using literacy as a means to a variety of ends had a history long before southern public libraries began opening branches for blacks. But that history intersected with whites' "possessive investment in whiteness," as George Lipsitz has termed it. He argues that European Americans seldom have sustained resistance to racism because they benefit materially from widespread discrimination against blacks and other minority groups. Among his examples are the bifurcation of black neighborhoods by freeways constructed during urban renewal, the undermining of fair housing laws by government officials and real estate brokers and agents, and the placement of landfills and hazardous waste dumps in minority communities. All of these actions have improved whites' ability to own homes where property values increase steadily, leading to the accumulation of personal wealth that accompanies better education, better health, and greater life chances overall—at the expense of members of minority groups, who are consigned to substandard, inconvenient, scarce, and overpriced housing.[12] Similarly, as print culture burgeoned in the United States, there were obvious efforts to limit its associated privileges and profits to whites. Such practices included offering industrial rather than liberal education to African Americans and refusing blacks admittance to printing trade unions. Countering those systems and practices were the group and individual efforts that African Americans employed to gain access to print.

Observers of life in the United States during its first fifty years as an independent nation applauded what they saw as "the general diffusion of knowledge" and a concomitant interest in books and other printed materials. Between 1780 and 1835, reading became "a necessity of life" in the rural northeast, an impetus that gradually spread to other parts of the developing republic.[13] During the 1820s and 1830s African Americans in urban areas of the north began to act collectively on that necessity. In cities and towns in Pennsylvania,

New York, Massachusetts, Connecticut, Rhode Island, New Jersey, Maryland, Ohio, Michigan, and the District of Columbia, black residents gathered to read aloud, participate in debates, share their writings, and borrow and return reading materials. They organized literary societies that offered access to the organizations' collections of books as a privilege of paid membership.[14] Their rationale would be echoed three-quarters of a century later with the founding of public libraries for African Americans in the South. They sought to enrich their intellectual and cultural life, to encourage reading of the "best" literature and the dissemination of information, and to provide wholesome alternatives to what they saw as destructive forms of entertainment, such as visits to taverns.

More significantly, literary societies gave African Americans an opportunity to position themselves as participants in rather than victims of a democratic experiment whose founding documents revered liberty but whose national economy increasingly depended on slavery. Free blacks who joined such societies gained confidence as both consumers and producers in an increasingly influential print culture and hoped their contribution to public life would help overcome racial prejudice. As Elizabeth McHenry has argued in her study of black literary societies, "it was immensely important that the public see black people engaged in the particular activities and discourse valorized by the white majority."[15]

In contrast, the south's participation in and interpretation of print culture was shaped by different economic and social conditions. Over the course of the nineteenth century, the northeast developed the railroads that distributed books, the industries that generated disposable income, the mechanics' institutes and social libraries that promoted reading, the common schools that taught literacy skills, and the developing economy that created a middle class with leisure time.[16] At least until the Civil War, the south had a less diversified, agrarian economy dependent on slave labor. The region consistently reported higher rates of illiteracy, not only because of its different pattern of economic development but also because of deliberate attempts to keep a significant proportion of its population—African Americans, slave and free—uneducated and ignorant.[17]

Despite their disparate skills and practices, however, both north and south, elite and non-elite, linked the idea of literacy with knowledge and knowledge with power. In the south, that underlying formulation drove efforts to prohibit the distribution and circulation of abolitionist pamphlets, newspapers, and books because they had the potential to foment rebellion against the peculiar institution. Such potential could not be averted simply by denying access to printed matter and to the skills needed to decipher it. Instead, a whole system comprising law, economics, politics, ideology, and brutality was at work to preserve slavery. Nevertheless, denying access to printed matter that opposed such a system of oppression was one of several powerful practices for maintaining the status quo.[18]

In the antebellum south, state statutes forbade the education of blacks in slavery, and a slave discovered to be literate faced punishment. Despite the risks, some sought education because they comprehended the advantages of literacy. Consequently, individual slaves did learn to read and write, either teaching themselves, studying with another member of the household, or, like Frederick Douglass, doing both. Occasionally, religious whites were moved to take action. For instance, in the 1840s, two white members of Nashville's First Baptist Church taught several of their black counterparts and reported that their students were "greatly delighted with the privilege of reading the Bible." In a few southern cities, schools were open to blacks, even to slaves who had their owners' permission to attend. For the most part, however, slaves lived and learned in a largely oral culture.[19]

At emancipation, the illiteracy rate among black adults was approximately 93 percent. It was less than half that by the turn of the century, and in 1920 it had dropped to 23 percent.[20] The rapid gain in literacy indicated the value that African Americans placed on schooling and their long-term dedication to securing education for themselves and their children, despite the discouraging conditions that worked against such efforts. Their sense of urgency was apparent in the Reconstruction south, where former slaves became the earliest advocates of universal state-funded public education. At the same time, influential white southerners who recognized the futility of mounting an all-out campaign against black education put their efforts into shaping a special kind of education for African Americans, one that would counter the broad-based education envisioned by the ex-slaves and prepare them instead for a life of subordination and service.[21]

After the Civil War and Reconstruction, racist ideology shaped and was shaped by the economic promise of an alliance between northern industrialists and southern businessmen, who were ready to build what they called the "New South." The desire to improve the southern economy translated into a need to improve the southern educational system for both whites and blacks. In the 1880s, southern newspapermen such as Henry Grady of Atlanta, Richard Hathaway Edmonds of Baltimore, and Henry Watterson of Louisville publicized the New South creed. Grady promoted the cause of north-south reconciliation in an 1886 speech to the New England Society of New York, where he outlined the south's efforts to make the Mason-Dixon line irrelevant, especially for northern commercial enterprises. Among his claims for southern progress he listed education: "We have planted the schoolhouse on the hilltop and made it free to white and black."[22] In truth, however, Grady's speech was a promotional effort rather than a report of actual conditions.

In the 1890s, an alliance of northern industrialists and philanthropists and southern educators emerged. Members were intent on establishing universal education in the south, including industrial training for blacks. They proselytized throughout the region for education as a force for stability and efficiency in an industrializing economy. The alliance promoted black educational approaches such as the Hampton Normal and Agricultural Institute in Virginia (founded by white northerner Samuel Chapman Armstrong in 1868 and sponsored by the American Missionary Association) and its progeny, the Tuskegee Normal and Industrial Institute in Alabama (founded by Hampton alumnus Booker T. Washington in 1881). Among the northerners who financially backed the model known as the Hampton-Tuskegee Idea were Robert C. Ogden, manager of Wanamaker's in New York and head of both Hampton's and Tuskegee's boards of trustees; George Foster Peabody, a Wall Street banker and Hampton trustee; and William H. Baldwin, Jr., general manager of the Southern Railway Company and a Tuskegee trustee. Southern supporters included James Dillard of Tulane University, Charles William Dabney of the University of Tennessee, and North Carolina school superintendent and later U.S. commissioner of education Philander Claxton. J. L. M. Curry and Walter Hines Page, both born in the south but living in the north, were also engaged in the southern education movement. They worked through agencies such as the Southern and General Education boards and the Slater, Rosenwald, and Jeanes funds to foster the spread of schoolhouses and teacher-training programs, including programs for African Americans. Newspapers in several New South cities supported this drive, including the *Atlanta Constitution* and the *Nashville Banner*.[23]

Central to their understanding of how southern educational reform would progress was Curry's assertion at the whites-only first Conference for Education in the South: that it must be at the initiative and under the direction of whites. For Curry and his colleagues, "there was no inherent conflict between white supremacy and the advocacy of universal education."[24] The southern educational movement maintained the practice of separate programs and facilities for blacks and whites. The north-south alliance understood not only that education could fit workers for their role in the economic system but also that black workers had an essential and distinct role within the system. As Andrew Carnegie noted in an essay advocating that black southerners stay put rather than migrate northward, "the negro has become of immense economic value and is indispensable where he is." He continued: "The question to-day is, how more of them and of other workers can be obtained."[25]

Yet the southern education movement faced opposition over the issue of blacks as workers. Most white southerners opposed black education because they knew it would open a wider world for African Americans. In states where blacks were in the majority—Alabama, Florida, Georgia, Louisiana, Mississippi, South Carolina, and Virginia—opposition to education was rooted in the realization that educated blacks would qualify for voting (indeed, would expect to vote) even where literacy requirements had been established specifically to prevent their political participation. All over the south, where most blacks worked as agricultural or domestic laborers, whites understood that blacks who were able to read, write, and make mathematical calculations would have choices beyond those backbreaking, exploitative jobs. If they could read the newspapers circulated by white and black publishers, they could learn that conditions might be better in town or in another state. Whether they voted with their ballots or not, they would be able to vote with their feet by leaving the farms for the promise of opportunities elsewhere.

Overall, the south's per capita spending on education was much lower than the national average. The region's children spent many fewer days in school, and southerners, especially black southerners, had higher-than-average illiteracy rates. In some places where new compulsory school attendance laws had passed, exemptions for black students were allowed, and everywhere in the south black students attended classes for briefer periods each year and left school sooner than white students did. Schools for black children were substandard, a result of the inequitable distribution of tax revenues. In some locales where tax levies for common schools for all came up for a vote, whites balked.[26]

The reform response to such recalcitrance involved a combination of public dollars, philanthropic donations, and the sweat equity of African American parents and grandparents who raised roofs and funds to build schools and hire teachers for their children. Black citizens found themselves in the double bind of having to contribute money, labor, and time to augment the taxes they paid to support the public schools their children attended. Additionally, despite the establishment of numerous public high schools in the south between 1880 and 1930, whites resisted the provision of secondary education for blacks.[27] Nonetheless, the education that some African Americans were able to obtain gave them the skills they needed to become consumers of print culture. It also prepared some to produce books, pamphlets, magazines, and newspapers. Covering topics, issues, and news that most white publications neglected, black publishers were "proud protectors and vindicators of the race."[28] Through a variety of distribution channels, print culture infiltrated African American communities.

Among the book publishers of the period was the American Negro Academy, founded in 1897. As a member, W. E. B. Du Bois proposed, and the group approved, that one goal be "to aid by publication a knowledge of the truth and the vindication of the race against vicious assaults."[29] Members wrote occasional papers that they read at meetings and then published as pamphlets. In 1914, the academy published John Cromwell's *The Negro in American History*, a high school textbook. The academy sent its publications to members, public libraries, and review editors of newspapers and magazines.[30]

Blacks engaged in cultural production often had additional business interests, spreading their influence more broadly than a single endeavor might allow. Writers Pauline Hopkins and Jessie Fauset had steady jobs as magazine editors. *Indianapolis Freeman* publisher George Knox owned and operated barbershops. Religious individuals often combined their spiritual work with news gathering and reporting, and religious organizations were major publishers of material by and about blacks. Among the longest-running periodicals was the *A.M.E. Church Review,* founded in 1884 and reporting a circulation of 2,500 by 1895.[31]

Literary societies also saw a resurgence toward the nineteenth century's end, particularly among women. The members of a literary society formed an interpretive community, reading and discussing a wide variety of classic and popular texts. Some members also produced their own texts: papers they researched and wrote and then read to other members at a club meeting. Such societies were part of the widespread involvement of women in public life, particularly in reform movements, during the late nineteenth century. Reform-minded clubs that organized around issues such as prohibition, sanitation, and child labor operated overtly as Progressive efforts. Others, such as the many self-culture and literary societies that served as alternatives to formal education, intended to reform women themselves. Nonetheless, Anne Firor Scott, who has documented the transformative role of such voluntary organizations in the United States, has criticized women's historians who have taken clubwomen's pronouncements about their own altruism at face value.[32]

For married white women, clubs allowed them to accomplish political goals, even before women had the vote, and to learn without having to leave their home and family to attend one of the new women's colleges. Clubs also offered opportunities for group interaction and personal development.[33] The General Federation of Women's Clubs in the 1890s made the founding of public libraries a national goal, and state federations followed suit.[34] Members were mostly well-to-do or middle-class married women, and they were white, having spurned black women's attempts to affiliate.[35] Their decision to focus on public libraries signaled their interest in the intellectual work of reading, research, and writing as well as the luxury of having access to a space designated for those purposes. They championed the public library, a municipal service whose use was voluntary and whose reform impact, if it existed at all, was indirect and long term. In so doing, they transformed many private, fee-based libraries, founded and frequented by men, into public spaces for women—a result that demonstrated their ability to influence local politics and their determination to occupy a world beyond the home. They showed what could be accomplished by collaboration among middle-class women, a group that had, if not leisure, at least what Scott has called "a margin of time" in which to achieve their goals.[36]

Middle-class black women organized clubs to provide both social welfare services and educational programs. Their activities called attention to the low status and material deprivation of many blacks, even as they provided assistance to ameliorate such conditions. Club members also expended considerable energy on the compatible goal of disproving the popular white stereotype of African American women as licentious and lazy.[37] The overwhelming needs of black communities and clubwomen's own need to reinvent their image meant that black women's clubs served a number of purposes.

Among those purposes was a long-standing interest in and struggle for education and its related agencies.[38] By 1909, organizations such as Boston's Woman's Era Club existed in a number of cities, including Kansas City, Missouri; Saint Paul, Minnesota; Colorado Springs, Colorado; and Portland, Maine. In the 1910s, the Neighborhood Union in Atlanta investigated conditions in the city's black schools and agitated for improvements in sanitary conditions, lighting, playgrounds, and student-teacher ratios. In Guthrie, Oklahoma, a black women's club raised funds to open the Excelsior Library and Industrial Institute and eventually succeeded in convincing the city to appropriate taxes for its support. In Vicksburg, Mississippi, the Phillis Wheatley Club operated a reading room. In Montgomery, Alabama, thirty African American women, as members of the Sojourner Truth Club, established the Free Reading Room to serve black residents of the city who were denied access to the Carnegie Library. The reading room held about five hundred volumes available for home use, and club members hosted "entertainments" and accepted contributions to fund the library.[39]

Unlike the white General Federation of Women's Clubs, the National Association of Colored Women did not declare the creation of public libraries a priority. Instead, clubs wove a commitment to books and reading into their social welfare programs and services. Most black clubwomen pursued individual self-improvement through reading and writing as well as community improvement in a variety of charitable activities. Clubs founded and supported homes for the elderly, refuges for black working women, reformatories, and orphanages, providing social services before the emergence of the welfare state. But they also raised money for kindergartens and other educational institutions.[40]

In Indianapolis, it was common for black clubwomen to combine literary work and charitable enterprises, undertaking reading and writing projects but also conducting food drives for flood victims and providing assistance to families relocating from the south. Inspired by a vision of themselves as dutiful and contributing members of a larger community, black clubwomen's efforts to improve themselves were also efforts to improve their communities.[41] A club in Buffalo, New York, stocked the public library with books by African American authors, agitated for the improvement of city services in African American neighborhoods, and participated in establishing a branch of the NAACP. As Deborah Gray White has written, "patrolling their communities, teaching children to read, improving homemaking skills—there were few things that black women's clubs did not do."[42]

Even as women's club work was creating new civic services, white clubs' deep interest and involvement in founding libraries in the south had the effect of framing libraries as public spaces for white women. In the literature of library history, portrayals of librarians as "tender technicians," clubwomen as altruistic, and female patrons as objects of the male gaze have obscured the agency of white women who deliberately created a place for themselves in the public library.[43] White clubwomen sought in the library a public space in which their own intellectual pursuits would be supported.[44]

Public libraries became acceptable places for women to work at the same time they became appropriate spaces to visit. Teachers of library science courses offered at colleges and universities and at public libraries generated a network of white women students instrumental in the feminization of librarianship in the final quarter of the nineteenth century.[45] The occupation offered an alternative to other socially acceptable feminine occupations such as sales clerking, social work, nursing, and teaching, especially for young women who, after attending college, found their vocational opportunities circumscribed. But in the final quarter of the century, both the transformation of private collections into public libraries and the creation of new public collections accelerated. The growth of libraries in the last quarter of the nineteenth century created positions that women would fill, usually at lower pay rates than men.[46]

Libraries became public spaces for white women (and, by extension, white children) in part because white women had identified themselves so closely with the institution. White women's commitment to public libraries occurred in the context of the "black beast rapist" hysteria thoroughly documented by historian Joel Williamson. False accusations and rumors of black men raping white women fueled the hysteria and gave racist white men a spurious rationale for lynching. Against such a backdrop, a public library construed as a proper place for white women was necessarily constrained by considerations of race and gender.[47] The racially restrictive admission policies of southern public libraries ensured that the new public spaces would not challenge white women's sense of racial superiority and entitlement nor white men's sense that white women needed protecting from a threat manufactured by white men themselves.

Thus, the construction of libraries was implicated in the social construction of race, with concrete consequences. During the Progressive era, racist whites clung to the notion that there were biologically distinctive human races and that membership in a particular racial category determined the individual's economic and social standing. This notion was part of the "social stock of knowledge" that represented both what whites understood about their society and what individuals understood about their predicament within that society.[48] In the schemata of everyday life, most Americans took for granted that there were races, from which a hierarchy of racial categories followed. Caricatured images on postcards, in advertising, and on consumer products represented race as something easily identifiable by physical features.[49] But it took disenfranchisement, lynching, and segregation to enforce a definition of the Negro race as different from and lesser than the Caucasian. Historian Grace Elizabeth Hale has traced the ways in which racial segregation in particular served as a keystone in the reconstruction of white supremacy after the Civil War.[50] Understanding but not accepting their situation, some blacks sought redefinition through their work in churches, clubs, and schools; through an expressive culture of music, dance, poetry, and fiction; through editorial efforts at newspapers and magazines; and, in some instances, by maneuvering to erect public libraries.

Because the establishment of Carnegie libraries occurred during the so-called Progressive era, much of the difficulty in interpreting the meaning of the separate Carnegies for blacks stems from their place in time. Progressivism, characterized by political and social reform impulses in reaction to the problems associated with industrialization and urbanization, took on a distinctive cast in the agrarian south. Historian Dewey Grantham has asserted that "southern progressives looked toward the creation of a clearly defined community that would accommodate a society differentiated by race and class but one that also possessed unity, cohesion, and stability."[51] They sought to transform a rural economy and society accustomed to local control into an efficient system under centralized bureaucratic direction. Southern Progressives exhibited a paradoxical "combination of democracy and hierarchy, of humanitarianism and coercion, and of racism and paternalistic uplift."[52]

One way for whites to create such a community was to restrict black civil rights through segregation and disenfranchisement, reserving democracy for whites. But southern progressivism was hardly a simple matter of excluding blacks from the equation so as to effect a kind of monolithic white progress. African Americans created their own Progressive movements complete with "civic organizations, boards of trade, public welfare leagues, and community betterment groups . . . to extract worthwhile concessions in education and other public services from the white system."[53] The nadir and the Progressive era overlapped. Out of the cacophony could be heard the voices of activist blacks who resisted their victimhood and of southern liberals who would cooperate across the color line without actually trying to erase it.[54]

Given the records of struggle over libraries, these institutions were clearly among the public services that African Americans in some southern towns and cities saw as worthwhile. But where do southern public libraries fit within the phenomenon of early twentieth-century progressivism? Grantham posits three "interrelated but fairly distinct categories" of activism: (1) social control and state regulation, (2) social justice, and (3) efficiency.[55] Among the first category were laws and customs reinforcing the separation of blacks from whites, which helped shape the racial configuration of southern public libraries. But public libraries themselves do not belong to this category of activity, in large part because they lacked the coercive power of state-mandated attendance and use.[56] In the south, public schools also lacked such power. For example, North Carolina and Tennessee did not pass compulsory school attendance legislation until 1913, Alabama and Texas not until 1915.[57] The third category, efficiency, also had an impact on libraries and on the methods applied to managing people and resources.[58]

But the dual system of libraries in the segregated south gave the lie to efficiency, requiring instead a building, furnishings, staff, and collections for whites with duplicates, though on a smaller scale, for blacks. The southern public library movement fits most comfortably into Grantham's social justice category, if we keep in mind the limits of what passed for social justice in the Progressive south. The southern spirit of social justice rested on a recent past that had solved the problems of race relations and party politics by largely eliminating black men, poor white men, and all women, as well as second and third political parties, from the democratic process. From such a delimited social justice arena sprang humanitarian child-labor statutes, women's rights activism, social welfare reform, black and white interest in uplifting "the race," and a sweeping public education campaign. Despite the promise that a widespread dedication to social justice and reform could offer, southern progressivism's undergirding of racialized regulation limited the era's achievements.

This, then, was the discouraging state of affairs in the south as the public library movement proceeded. The atmosphere affected the development of southern public libraries, even in cities that strove to identify with northern business interests by mimicking the northern reverence for "book learning" and libraries. In many cases, rival factions of businessmen, city officials, and clubwomen contested the placement and design of Carnegie buildings for whites. Their negotiations over these cultural institutions revealed the shifting nature of power relations in growing towns and cities.[59] Similarly, the creation of segregated public library systems in the south represented a negotiated settlement between white elites and their less powerful but nevertheless influential counterparts in the black community.

The decade before the founding of the first racially segregated Carnegie public library branch was a breakpoint in the history of race relations in the United States, not least because *Plessy* had established the constitutionality of "separate but equal" public facilities. By advocating an accommodationist approach to race relations, Booker T. Washington had emerged as a national figure, attracting the good will of donor Andrew Carnegie, organizing the National Negro Business League to help blacks become self-sufficient, and, beginning in 1881, serving as principal of Tuskegee Institute in Alabama. In 1895, Washington addressed the Cotton States Exposition in Atlanta, where a separate Negro Building celebrated African American contributions to labor and life. Speaking before an audience of whites and blacks, he delivered a cautious and conservative address that endorsed racial segregation: "In all things that are purely social we can be as separate as the fingers, yet one as the hand in all things essential to mutual progress."[60] He asserted that southern whites and northern philanthropists were friends to his race and that the nation was and should be dependent on the labor of native-born blacks rather than immigrants. Acknowledging the exposition's recognition of black "value and manhood," he celebrated the "man's chance" the south had given to black workers and urged fellow African Americans to make friends "in every manly way" with "the people of all races by whom we are surrounded."[61]

By linking the treatment of African Americans to ideas about masculinity, Washington gave a gendered construction to the dignity of toil and the right to opportunity and fair treatment based on that toil. One scholar has argued that the first chapter of his widely circulated autobiography (published in 1901) sacrificed manhood on the altar of conciliation, erasing the threat of black achievement through the rhetorical act of emasculation. In both the Atlanta address and in *Up From Slavery,* Washington asserted that black men accepted for themselves the political status of nineteenth-century women as disenfranchised and dependent.[62] In his Atlanta address, however, he did not give away manhood so much as redefine it. Black manhood meant accepting a hard lot in life and making the best of it. In compensation, whites were to recognize what such men had given up and accept the conciliation it represented. Black men's power lay in their capacity for work, not in their ability to organize and agitate.

Whites in the audience applauded Washington's reformulation of appropriate male behavior: from demanding rights to accepting paternalistic privileges. Blacks, however, understood the significance of what had transpired. W. E. B. Du Bois, who held a doctorate from Harvard and had launched a promising career as a sociologist and historian, reacted against the speech's tone and content, dubbing it the "Atlanta Compromise." He saw southern whites not as friends but as enemies, and he upheld African Americans' rights to participate fully in American politics, culture, and society. Du Bois championed equitable education rather than a division that prescribed vocational training for blacks and a classical liberal education for whites.[63]

Whereas Washington was an accommodationist, Du Bois was an activist and an assimilationist who helped found the Niagara Movement and later the NAACP as protest organizations designed to counter Washington's philosophies as well as his personal power. For Washington, one of the outcomes of the Atlanta Compromise was his ascendancy to a national role as "the voice of the Negro," which allowed him to bolster his Tuskegee machine of political patronage, philanthropy, and positive publicity.[64] Thus, Washington and Du Bois represented the poles of a continuum ranging from deference to protest. Even college-educated African Americans, the group that Du Bois called the "talented tenth," supported much of Washington's program of self-reliant economic development and racial solidarity, especially around the turn of the twentieth century and always with an eye toward the longer-term goal of Du Boisian assimilation. South-ern lawyers and businessmen, such as Nashville's James C. Napier, supported Washington's conservatism because they depended on political patronage and the support of the similarly conservative black middle class. So did ministers, with their all-black congrega-tions, their emphasis on the rewards of the afterlife, and often their own entrepreneurial sidelines to augment church work. Educators, who depended on white good will, also supported Washington. The members of his National Negro Business League gathered annually to inspire each other with papers on "Making Farming Pay," "Devel-oping a Real Estate Business," and "Negro Success in Medicine."[65] Locally, league members took a role in community organizing and community development, including the creation of public library services.

Despite their differences, both Washington and Du Bois respected and advocated libraries. For all his rhetoric about the education of blacks for manual labor, Washington supported the creation of such institutions, even to the point of urging his fellow black college presi-dents to seek funding for this campus essential. In Atlanta, where the main Carnegie library opened in 1902, Du Bois petitioned officials to make library services available to black Atlantans on the grounds that a publicly funded facility should be available to all taxpayers. But he also argued that blacks needed public libraries even more than whites did because libraries could entice them "from the temptations of the streets."[66]

Carnegie shared this belief in the power of libraries and cred-ited his own success in part to the books and libraries he had been exposed to as a young worker. Although he asserted the importance of free public libraries for workingmen, his first library grant for Afri-can Americans went to an institution of higher education, albeit one dedicated to vocational training. At the turn of the century, Carne-gie began giving grants for college libraries. After hearing publisher Frank N. Doubleday retell Washington's *Up From Slavery* story during a round of golf, Carnegie decided to give Tuskegee a library, despite the fact that he had refused Washington's previous requests for a meeting.[67] Such was the power of the book.

Never one to miss an opportunity to demonstrate the efficiency of black labor and the frugality of black administrators, Washington stretched his Carnegie grant by having Tuskegee students make the bricks from which the building was constructed.[68] He then contacted the president of Livingstone College in Salisbury, North Carolina, urging him to approach Carnegie for a library grant for his campus. Ever the pragmatist, he wrote, "I am very anxious that while Mr. Carnegie is giving away his money that our race be benefited as much as possible."[69] In 1904, Carnegie pledged $30,000 for a library at Atlanta University; it opened in January 1906. After three years of negotiation over a Carnegie library bequest for Fisk University in Nashville, Washington intervened on behalf of his wife's alma mater, and the $20,000 facility opened in 1909. In Marshall, Texas, Washington acted on behalf of his assistant Emmett Scott's alma mater, Wiley College, securing a Carnegie pledge of $15,000 for the school's library in 1906.[70]

By 1910, Carnegie had funded fifteen libraries for black institutions, many of them at Washington's suggestion. Washington's autobiography and Carnegie's response to it had launched a relationship that would shape southern library development in the first decades of the twentieth century. Washington's success as a fundraiser with wealthy northern whites resulted from his ability to convince them, in the words of one scholar, that they were supporting "a bucolic, Christian, exotic black world in the distant south rising up the Darwinian social and intellectual ladder, projected in an aesthetic that matched their own sense of high culture and service."[71]

But another trajectory of library organizing was also shaping the southern movement; and it, too, had roots at the 1895 Cotton States Exposition where Washington had delivered his Atlanta Compromise address in September. In November of that year, the Congress of Women Librarians met in the Woman's Building on the exposition grounds. Arranged by Anne Wallace, who would soon help transform the Young Men's Association Library into the Carnegie Library of Atlanta, the congress featured papers by librarians from outside the south who were determined to nurture the library spirit of their southern sisters. Mary Wright Plummer, librarian at the Pratt Institute in Brooklyn, presented a paper on "library training schools"; and Alice B. Kroeger of the Drexel Institute in Philadelphia spoke about the American Library Association. Nina E. Browne of the Library Bureau delivered a paper on "classification, catalogs, and modern library appliances" and set up an exhibition of her company's products in the model library housed in the Woman's Building. In her report on the event, Kroeger noted that the south had improved its educational system in the past two decades but needed public libraries to improve further: "So from the Congress of Librarians at Atlanta it is hoped will arise new efforts to obtain for every town in the South the opportunity for greater intellectual activity which comes from the possession of a library free to every person in the community."[72]

It is difficult to understand why Kroeger chose to end her report by invoking the "free to every person" idea. Although Atlanta had a black elite, just as her own Philadelphia did, she must have recognized the harsher treatment and lower status of African Americans in the south.[73] Was she casually invoking a phrase that was little more than rhetorical ritual among librarians by the mid-1890s? Or was she attempting to instruct these southern novices about a core value of the profession? Either way, southern public libraries would interpret "free to every person" in a variety of ways that rarely translated into equitable access for African Americans.

Participants fondly remembered the Congress of Women Librarians as launching the development of public libraries in the south, even though it involved no more than a dozen individuals, most from outside the region. Organizer Anne Wallace arranged to have the papers published and distributed, an act that captured the attention of white clubwomen, who began to work on behalf of libraries, and of the American Library Association, which decided to hold its annual meeting in Atlanta in 1899.[74] In 1907, the association met again in the south, this time in Asheville, North Carolina. There a session on "The Southern Library Movement" included a report by Wallace, in which she referred to the Congress of Women Librarians as a crucial event. She identified signs of progress in the south, including the establishment of public libraries, state library commissions, state-level professional associations, and published reports and other publications. But she acknowledged that the southern library movement was still behind those in the northeast and the midwest. Among her rationales for this difference were the fine climate (which encouraged people to enjoy the outdoors instead of reading by a fireplace), the long-term effects of losing the Civil War, and the south's traditional "English conservatism" and obsession with local rather than central control. Moreover, "in addition to the large class of illiterate whites that every section has to carry, the South is burdened with the extra tax of the heaviest negro population of the United States."[75] Her wording suggests that illiterate whites were a concern while all blacks, illiterate or not, were a problem.

Publisher R. R. Bowker, speaking after Wallace, also recalled the 1895 congress. He said that the few who had attended could now be seen as an elite group of pioneers, some of whom could be found among the more than one hundred southern librarians attending the Asheville convention: "If ever you see a badge of a happy little darkey on a cotton bale eating a slice of watermelon, you will recognize a member of that great Library congress, for this was the symbol of the Atlanta cotton states exposition."[76] In other words, he juxtaposed library progress with an offensive image, just as Wallace had contrasted library-related developments with the burden of "the heaviest negro population of the United States." The unexamined assumption in such remarks was that black people were holding back public libraries. The comments blinded white library leaders to another possibility: that keeping the black masses illiterate and ignorant might benefit rather than burden southern whites. It would have been more accurate to say that southern public libraries were held back by white attitudes. Yet in Asheville in 1907, Wallace's and Bowker's remarks went unchallenged. In the series of reports that followed, the association president introduced speakers from Virginia, North Carolina, South Carolina, Florida, Alabama, Louisiana, Texas, Oklahoma, Tennessee, and Kentucky. Only the speakers from North Carolina and Kentucky even mentioned library services for African Americans.

The public library movement had its beginnings in the northeast decades before the south began to consider establishing public libraries. An 1876 government report on public libraries devoted only nine of its more than 1,100 pages to those in the south, noting that "the condition of public libraries in the Southern States presents after all but a barren prospect."[77] The first self-consciously public library had opened in Boston in the mid-1850s, setting a number of precedents that influenced subsequent developments. Passage of the 1848 Massachusetts Act of Authorization endorsed Boston's interest in opening a public library and established the idea that it was properly the purview of the city. Harvard historian George Ticknor formulated the Boston Public Library's approach to collections and services, which he laid out in his 1852 *Report of the Trustees*. The report served as a blueprint for library leaders elsewhere. They followed its advice to allow all residents to use the library's collections and services without charge, to circulate books beyond the building's walls, and to acquire a range of materials for various uses and tastes. The public library was intended to be an alternative and an adjunct to formal education. Before opening a $2.5 million structure in 1895 to replace its outgrown space, Boston city officials inscribed "Free to All" over the new library's front door, reiterating the key concept behind the late nineteenth century's widespread transformation of libraries from private to public entities.[78]

Towns and cities, particularly in the northeast, followed the Boston model, but the Civil War and its immediate aftermath slowed the process. In 1876 librarians founded their own professional association and began publishing a trade journal.[79] As the century waned, the new profession's efforts converged with the volunteer work of women's clubs and the philanthropy of various wealthy individuals. With the founding of the Enoch Pratt Library in Baltimore in 1882, a locale traditionally identified with the south became the site of one of the biggest library events of the period. Pratt, who had made a fortune in iron and banking, had given $800,000 to the city in exchange for a guarantee that $50,000 a year would be spent on the library, and he provided another $400,000 for the building.[80] Baltimore's library followed the "to all" portion of the "free to all" motto, allowing "all residents without distinction" to use the building and its collections. It's not clear how comfortable Baltimore's black readers were at the main library and its branches, however. As late as the 1940s, sociologist Charles Johnson would discover that the library hired African Americans only as janitors and servants. Anyone using any of the library buildings, even in Baltimore's predominately black neighborhoods, saw only white librarians and assistants.[81]

Although much of his inspiration for library philanthropy came from Pratt's example, Carnegie diverged from the Baltimore model in at least one significant way. Whereas Pratt had commanded that the public library in Baltimore would be free to all races and classes, Carnegie shied away from what he considered interference in local customs. Working with his secretary James Bertram, he made other demands on local functionaries, particularly requiring annual city appropriations to maintain Carnegie-funded libraries and brick buildings conforming to a standard set of acceptable architectural designs.[82] Allegiance to the idea of home rule made Carnegie insist that local governments take financial responsibility for maintaining libraries, but it also meant that those officials had the right to follow local customs, even to the point of refusing service to some residents. Carnegie's hands-off attitude corresponded with that of other "New North" industrialists and businessmen, who had decided to let the south deal with race in its own way.[83]

Library development proceeded swiftly after Carnegie decided to begin divesting himself of his self-made wealth in the 1880s.[84] Near the turn of the century, his giving increased dramatically; and by the official end of the library building program in 1917, Carnegie and his foundation, the Carnegie Corporation, had pledged more than $41 million for 1,681 buildings in the United States. The northeast, the midwest, and California were the major beneficiaries, with the south-east receiving only about $3 million in Carnegie building grants.[85] The magnitude of his largesse meant that his attitude had a greater impact than Pratt's. Separate collections and services, rather than the integrated access at the Enoch Pratt Free Library, became the model throughout the south, at least in cities that offered library ser-vices to African American residents. Libraries in the region's border states of Delaware, West Virginia, and Missouri reportedly followed the northern practice of providing services to blacks and whites in the same facilities.[86]

Even in the absence of Carnegie funding, library collections and services for African Americans were created, as Patterson Toby Gra-ham has documented for Alabama. In Birmingham in 1898, teachers used a small collection established in a school for African Ameri-cans, and members of the public were given access for a fee. The city's free library for whites opened in 1909. Black school principals began raising funds for a separate public library branch, an effort applauded by Booker T. Washington in 1913, when he visited the city. The branch, named after Washington, opened in 1918 with city funding. In Mobile, African Americans' activism was also crucial to the establishment of service. White women spearheaded a success-ful effort to pass a bond issue in 1926 to fund libraries for the city. When African Americans asked for a separate room within the main building where they could have access to collections and services, the library board balked. The Davis Avenue Branch was built instead, opening in 1931 with some financial help for staffing and collections from the Julius Rosenwald Fund.[87]

As Louise Robbins has written, the Rosenwald Fund also pro-vided help for schools, distributing almost 1,200 collections of books, including some by African American authors, to schools in 567 southern counties between 1928 and 1948. The presence of a Rosenwald school without library facilities in Saluda County, South Carolina, inspired a white millworker to seek, and receive, donations of books and to work with the local black community to build a log cabin on its school grounds to house them. This first "Faith Cabin" library, which opened in 1932, led to the creation of more than one hundred such libraries serving schools and communities in South Carolina and Georgia. Until the 1940s, Faith Cabin libraries were at least as important as government-supported public and school librar-ies in black communities. It was also in South Carolina that a textile entrepreneur created a demonstration project that eventually led to the establishment of tax-funded libraries, including one opened in 1923 for African Americans in Greenville. In 1927, Susan Dart Butler opened a reading room for African Americans in Charleston, South Carolina, and in 1931 the Charleston County Free Library made it a branch.[88]

By 1916 there were thirty-five library buildings open to southern blacks, according to a government report on black education. Only fifteen were urban public libraries, most in buildings funded by Car-negie. Of 653 schools covered in the report, only 27 provided library collections for their pupils. These collections ranged from 30 to 5,000 books, most "the discarded refuse of garrets and overcrowded storerooms, which should have gone to the paper mill, but was sent to these poor children through mistaken kindness."[89]

Ten years later, the American Library Association documented that only 11 percent of the almost 8.7 million African Americans dwelling in the south lived in areas with access to public library collections and services, compared to 56 percent of the total population of the continental United States and Canada. Only 6 percent of city dwellers lacked library services, compared to 83 percent of rural residents. In fourteen southern states, just 55 of 720 public libraries reported that they served African Americans.[90] A major factor contributing to the inequity was the greater concentration of public libraries in urban as opposed to rural areas. Because the majority of southern blacks continued to live in rural areas, the disproportionate service affected them more than it did whites. Geography worked against blacks in another way: their continuing concentration in the south, where the idea of the public library had not been as enthusiastically embraced as it had in other regions. Rural southerners, disproportionately black, had the least access to library services.[91]

The regional differences identified in the 1870s persisted into the 1930s, despite some improvement. In his landmark study published in 1936, *Southern Regions of the United States,* sociologist Howard Odum documented the economic and cultural lags that characterized the southeast. As his title indicates, he believed that it was misleading to speak of "the South" and argued instead for recognition of the region's complexity and the identifiable and measurable distinctions within it. Considering indices such as the ratio of urban to rural population, the percentage of adults classified as Negro, per capita spending on children's schooling, and the rate of deaths from pellagra, Odum defined the southeast as including Virginia, North and South Carolina, Kentucky, Tennessee, Georgia, Florida, Alabama, Mississippi, Louisiana, and Arkansas. The border states of Missouri and Maryland were not southern, based on Odum's metrics, and Texas was part of the new region known as the southwest, which included Oklahoma, New Mexico, and Arizona.

Throughout the southern regions, Odum perceived a defensiveness and what he called "a general inferiority complex." He wrote: "The cumulative product of historical and geographical incidence appears to characterize the region somewhat as follows: as to resources—superabundance; as to science, skills, technology, organization—deficiency; as to general economy—waste; as to culture—richness, with immaturity and multiple handicaps; as to trends—hesitancy and relative retrogression in many aspects of culture.[92] Given that Odum was a native Georgian who chose to live in the south, he surely recognized that southern inferiority was not so much a "complex" as a reality.

His work helps to explain, in material terms, why the southeast in particular persistently lagged behind other areas of the country in public library development. The area depended on cash-crop farming, often on marginally productive land that yielded only enough for subsistence. It therefore lacked the capital accumulation that could fuel investment in new agricultural methods, industrial diversification, technology, educational institutions, and human development. The result by the 1930s was a drain of brain and brawn as southerners moved out of the region to find opportunities elsewhere. The south lacked leadership to solve its difficult problems, especially the expensive and inequitable racialist system that Odum saw as a major contributor to the region's inability to reform, improve, or progress.[93]

Among the consequences was the dearth of libraries. Some of Odum's most damning evidence appears in comparisons of the southern states to the rest of the nation in levels of literacy and library facilities. The southern states clustered together at the bottom of any ranked list of such measures. For example, in the mid-1930s, the far west spent $1.08 per capita on libraries, the northeast 75 cents, the middle states 73 cents, the northwest 42 cents, the southwest 23 cents, and the southeast 16 cents. Nevertheless, Odum noted that the southeastern states had begun to address the problem through state library commissions and regional library associations.[94]

University of Chicago Graduate Library School professor Louis Round Wilson drew on Odum's work to study libraries more thoroughly. In his report, *The Geography of Reading*, Wilson found that, in 1934, 78.3 percent of the population in the northeast and 72 percent in the midwest lived within a public library service district, compared to only 36 percent in the southwest and 35.1 percent in the southeast. In 1935, 18.44 percent of the black population living in twelve southern states had access to public libraries, an extremely low percentage that nevertheless represented a significant improvement over the 8 percent with library access in 1926. In the state with the highest proportion of black residents—Mississippi, with 50.2 percent—two libraries served blacks. In the state with the lowest proportion of black residents—Kentucky, with 8.6 percent—fourteen libraries served blacks. Wilson cautioned that the figures for the south overall were artificially high. African Americans living in library service districts were counted as part of the population with access to libraries, but in fact many were denied access on the basis of race. Of the 491 library service districts in the south, only 75 allowed African Americans to use the libraries.[95]

The report documented "the relatively backward library development of the South" and offered four explanations. Among them were the region's continued reliance on agriculture, its resulting lack of urbanization, and insufficient capital accumulation to fund libraries or a sound educational system. But another, mentioned at least three times in the study, was the expense of maintaining two separate but similar institutions in a region that required racial segregation.[96] Wilson acknowledged that the turn-of-the-century public library movement had failed to provide services for African Americans, with few exceptions, and he was not encouraged by the little improvement since:

> At present, there are but seventy-five public libraries in the Southeast and Southwest which provide service to Negroes; and that is inferior as compared with the service to whites. The attitude that "book learning" is of little value to the Negro has given way but slowly. This has not only delayed the development of public library service to Negroes, but on account of legal complications, to which provision of certain services to two races within a state gives rise, it has delayed the provision of such generally.[97]

Yet none of the ten recommendations outlined in Wilson's conclusion called for the equalization of separate services and collections, much less the abolition of the dual system.

Following Wilson's work, Eliza Atkins Gleason prepared the earliest in-depth attempt to provide a history and analysis of public library

services for African Americans. She undertook the study in her dissertation for the University of Chicago's Graduate Library School. Her
subsequent book, *The Southern Negro and the Public Library* (published
in 1941 with a foreword by Wilson), focused on quantifying the
"geography of Negro Library Service." Gleason also described and
analyzed the legal and political organization of library services for
African Americans, identifying four categories of service: (1) segregated branches of city or county libraries, (2) small informal stations
maintained by city or county libraries, (3) autonomous libraries for
blacks, and (4) partial or full service at the main library. In general,
though, she found that whenever a southern city erected a new public library, "those who build and control it do not expect the Negro
to enjoy its privileges and benefits. . . . Faced with such a situation
[the Negro] can only travel the road of making the best use that he
can of such library facilities as may be open to him, of making friends
of those who have the power to increase these library facilities, and
of working for the development of more liberal attitudes and public
opinion." Noting that most libraries for African Americans operated
under the auspices of white-run library systems, she described the relatively low number of libraries serving blacks, their inadequate financial support, and the lack of attention given to their improvement.[98]

Gleason addressed the issue of quantifying the denial of services
that Wilson had raised in his earlier work. She wrote that some 6.9
million African Americans, of a total of about 8.8 million living in
the south, did not have access to local public library collections and
services. Of those, almost 2 million lived in areas where libraries
were available for whites' use. Thus, she pointed out, Wilson's figure
reporting the number of persons served by southern libraries was
inflated by 2 million. Gleason also addressed directly the problem
that Wilson had raised, the expense and inefficiency of segregated
libraries, for which he had recommended no solution. She observed
that the south could not afford a dual system in which the separate
libraries for African Americans were "equal" to those for whites and
that it was not likely that the south would provide equal services even
if money were no object. Consequently, she listed desegregation as
her first recommendation. She avoided arguing on the grounds of
access to information as a basic civil right. Instead, she suggested that

some communities would recognize that the monetary expense in a context of blacks' increasing demands for access was too high a price for maintaining separate libraries. "There may be many communities in the South which could be persuaded to see the advantages of providing *one* good public library for all races," she concluded somewhat optimistically.[99]

From the beginning of the public library movement, most southern libraries had a policy of denying service to African Americans. Despite the public library motto "free to all," it was clear that these new institutions were neither free nor available to all. The "free" signified that the new public library was different from earlier forms such as subscription and rental libraries, whose users paid fees for the right to borrow books. The new public libraries were funded by local taxes. They came to be seen as a common good supported by all taxpayers rather than a privilege for those who could afford subscription and transaction fees. For individuals accustomed to the earlier fee-based system, the ability to visit a library without having to prove membership or pay on-the-spot expenses seemed to be a welcome innovation. Similarly, the "to all" in the motto signified that every resident was entitled to take advantage of this common good, this tax-supported institution. Even citizens who chose not to partake of the new service paid for it with their tax dollars. Yet in the south, some citizens who paid taxes were denied access to this "common" good.

Gleason's book documented for the first time the extent of the gap between white librarians' words and their deeds. It revealed the hypocrisy of an institution and a profession that provided access to collections and services as if access were a privilege for whites to bestow rather than a civil right in a democracy founded on the notion of intellectual freedom.[100] Widely reviewed and cited, the book appeared just as African Americans began agitating more forcefully for desegregation, which would slowly and quietly take place in public libraries over the next twenty-five years.

During the first half of the twentieth century, a slowly growing number of southern cities and towns established separate library collections and services for the use of local African American residents. In a 1913 speech at the American Library Association's annual meeting, white librarian William Yust, director of the Louisville Free Public

Library when it opened its first branch for blacks, recommended segregated services. He noted that southern whites refused to use libraries open to blacks, while blacks felt insulted by being limited to the use of a separate room within a library building. A completely separate library governed and administered by African Americans would most likely be doomed by incompetence, Yust asserted. Instead, the most efficient and economical configuration was a separate branch with a black staff working under the authority and supervision of white administrators who also oversaw the main library.[101]

African Americans in the south might be included in the "to all" portion of the public library's motto, but only as long as the ideology of white supremacy remained intact. Southern librarians adapted to "local conditions" and went about their business, seemingly unperturbed by the conundrum.[102] Historian C. Vann Woodward describes the atmosphere in the solidly segregated south:

> Southerners of the present generation who grew up after [Jim Crow] disappeared may well wonder how their elders could have daily made their way back and forth through this anthropological museum of Southern folkways and pronounced its wonders perfectly normal. . . . Everywhere one was assured that this was the way things had always been, that it was because of Southern folkways, that colored people themselves preferred it that way, and anyway there was nothing that could be done to change it.[103]

In their ability to ignore the tension between the professed democratic values of their profession and racist beliefs and practices, white librarians in the south differed little from the white non-librarians they lived among, at least in terms of their perspective on race. If they were to create collections for and offer library services to black patrons, they would conform to the southern code of race relations. Black libraries would be marked as other and lesser by their separateness from white libraries. Southern public libraries would be "free to all," but some buildings—or even parts of buildings—would be free to all whites and others would be free to all blacks. And it was there, in the enclosed space of restricted access, that a burgeoning print culture intersected with a deteriorating racial climate.

In his discussion of the problematics of writing a history of how readers appropriate and interpret the texts they find in books, Roger Chartier has asserted that "the fundamental object of a history . . . of the construction of meaning resides in the tension between the inventive capacities of individuals or communities and the constraints, norms and conventions that limit—more or less forcibly according to their position in the relations of domination—what is possible for them to think, to express, to do."[104] These words apply not only to the history of the book but also to the history of the library. As architectural historian Abigail Ayres Van Slyck has said, "[Carnegie libraries] were always cultural artifacts whose meanings varied with the intentions and experiences of a diverse group of users."[105] Certainly, the establishment of public libraries to serve black readers exhibited the inventiveness against convention that Chartier posits for the interpretation of texts within those libraries. Just as certainly, that inventiveness was limited by a number of factors characteristic of the patterns of domination during the age of Jim Crow, which one historian has deemed "the most violent and repressive period in the history of race relations in the United States."[106] Black Americans had long tested the "constraints, norms and conventions" that governed their access to reading material. Soon after the start of the twentieth century, they had a new venue for contestation: the Carnegie public library.

CHAPTER 2

Carnegie Public Libraries for African Americans

Although the late nineteenth-century south continued to be a rural society dependent on an agricultural economy, by the 1880s a new elite class of businessmen and industrialists was beginning to build cities throughout the region. Their New South looked to the north for inspiration and collaboration; their goals involved not only railroads, factories, and mills but also schools and libraries. Along with investment capital for new enterprises, philanthropic capital for schools and libraries flowed from the north.[1] In southern locales that adopted this New South creed, Carnegie libraries symbolized a progressive spirit.

The last quarter of the nineteenth century was a pivotal era in American library history, for it witnessed the widespread transformation of private institutions into public ones. Private libraries operated by associations or corporations could limit the use of their collections to paying members, subscribers, or shareholders. But the narrow base of financial support that made such exclusivity possible undermined the entire operation in hard economic times. The agrarian and industrial financial panics of the early 1890s had a depressing effect on privately funded libraries. Coinciding with Progressive era reform efforts to counteract the problems of rapid industrialization and urbanization, financial downturns created favorable conditions for the conversion of private libraries into public ones funded by municipal appropriations.[2] Although municipal governments hardly ever provided enough support for public libraries, they usually could offer more stability than a private association could. The availability of Carnegie funding for constructing impressive buildings also eased the financial burden while providing an incentive for cities to promise sustainability. The conversion of private to public, however, made it necessary for racist whites to devise a new method to keep blacks out of libraries that no longer had membership requirements as a reason to restrict access. Segregation would be that method.

The New South ideology promoted cooperation with northern business interests and emulation of northern values such as universal public education. Part of the bargain was the north's willingness to let the south handle race relations as it saw fit. Despite some southerners' urge toward industrialization, the region's economy remained dependent on an eroding agricultural base, and both urban and rural communities had the highest levels of poverty and illiteracy in the nation.[3]

In the late 1890s, Carnegie library grants went to Atlanta; Louisville and Newport, Kentucky; Oklahoma City; and Dallas, Fort Worth, Houston, and Pittsburg, Texas.[4] In the first decade of the twentieth century even more southern communities received such grants. A half-century after Boston had modeled the ideal of an urban library open to all, with a collection serving tastes from popular to erudite, southern libraries were working to follow that model as best they could, given budgetary and racial restrictions. For the most part, the new southern public libraries were free to all whites. Inequitable access did not disappear with the transformation of libraries from private to public; it merely shifted from an economic basis to a racial one. Inability to pay membership and use fees no longer precluded access to library collections and service. Race did instead.

Although many Carnegie libraries lacked sufficient funding, the problem was pronounced in the south. In his study of the effectiveness of the Carnegie library building program, economist Alvin Johnson writes that city appropriations were often inadequate. Carnegie required a city to commit 10 percent of the building grant for maintenance of the institution, but this was insufficient for sustaining a library over time.[5] Some cities increased the allotment, but others felt no compulsion to do more than they had originally promised. In this period of urbanization, the population was growing more rapidly than the library budget. One result was not only fewer new books per capita but also fewer books overall as worn-out volumes were discarded. Another was low salaries, which led to high turnover among staff members and an inability to recruit trained librarians. Municipal libraries competed with all other city services for funding, and in the urban south a lower tax base meant less revenue to distribute among the various agencies. Cities seeking to attract business and commerce devoted dollars to infrastructure, often accompanied by the additional expense of corruption. The construction of new roads and the paving of existing ones, the installation of sewer systems, and the maintenance of police and fire services drained city coffers.

Carnegie's initial American offering went to Allegheny City, Pennsylvania, in 1886, and for the next ten years he provided other Pennsylvania cities and towns with library funding. In 1898, he speeded the pace of his philanthropy, launching what he called the "wholesale" period of library giving. At the turn of the century his giving increased dramatically; in 1903 alone he promised library buildings to 204 municipalities. Southern cities were among the beneficiaries during this period, with Nashville, New Orleans, and Meridian, Mississippi, receiving grants between 1901 and 1904.[6]

Southerners were slower than northerners and midwesterners to approach Carnegie for library funding. In some cities, taxpayers resisted the establishment of public libraries, no matter how they were funded. "Poverty of mind and lack of municipal spirit" kept cities such as Mobile, Alabama; Pensacola, Florida; and Beaumont, Texas, and villages such as Columbia, Tennessee, and Elizabethtown, Kentucky, from accepting Carnegie grants for libraries.[7] Even important southern cities, where one might have expected an outpouring of library support, failed to take advantage of Carnegie's philanthropy. In Richmond, Virginia, the city's limited resources supported competing city services rather than a public library, amid some citizens' fears that a free public library would contribute to the spread of germs and racial integration.[8] Elsewhere, however, in transportation and trade hubs such as Atlanta, Houston, and New Orleans, the library spirit—or some combination of civic pride, pragmatism, and cultural boosterism—animated interest in Carnegie library building grants.

The years immediately following the end of the Civil War were a time of new possibilities regarding race relations. During the early Reconstruction era, southern states passed new constitutions with provisions for fair treatment of African Americans, among them the creation of universal public education. As Reconstruction proceeded, however, whites began redrawing the color line. Although early versions of the legislation that culminated in the Civil Rights Act of 1875 mandated integrated education, the final law left schools out of the list of public accommodations, including hotels and theaters, that were to be integrated. But even that limited commitment to integration did not last: in 1883 the Supreme Court found the law unconstitutional. By the close of Reconstruction in 1877, with the withdrawal of the last federal troops from the south, and the later reversal of the Civil Rights Act, southern whites had reconstructed their old role as superiors in their relationship to southern blacks. A cornerstone of that effort was segregation, and state after state passed laws requiring African Americans to ride in separate railroad cars and in separate sections of streetcars and buses and to occupy separate areas of station waiting rooms and dining areas. State legislatures began dismantling the tax structure that supported universal public education, and local boards of education became responsible for fiscal decisions. The result at the turn of the century was a decline in the amount and quality of free education for blacks.[9]

As schools failed to serve the needs of African Americans, public libraries could potentially take up the slack. This may help to explain African Americans' interest in free public libraries and the collections that could be used to supplement school libraries or to serve in their place where school libraries did not exist. It also helps explain why it was often a school principal or a teacher who tried to use newly opened public libraries and, when barred, worked to establish a public library for African Americans. Public libraries exclusively staffed and used by African Americans were just one more example of segregation mania, which spread to include textile factories, public parks, school textbooks, and telephone booths. In chronicling such laws, historian John Hope Franklin has written, "The supply of ideas for new ways to segregate whites and Negroes seemed inexhaustible." In such a climate, segregation became the norm, whether or not any laws requiring it had passed.[10]

For instance, in 1903, an act of the North Carolina legislature to charter Charlotte's newly forming public library simultaneously required a separate library for Negroes. The city's library history had begun in 1891, with the formation of the private whites-only Charlotte Library Association, whose paying members could borrow books from the association's collection. The fee-based service was not sustainable, however, and soon after the turn of the century the association gave its collection to the school system. Because school commissioners also found it difficult to provide a library for both students and the public, the city of Charlotte turned to Carnegie for help; and in the course of securing a building grant, it also received the state charter establishing the public library and mandating segregated libraries.

Charlotte's Carnegie Public Library opened to whites in 1903. The city appropriated separate funding for a small library for African Americans in a 2,500-square-foot brick building on Brevard Street in a black neighborhood known as Brooklyn. The Brevard Street Library, which opened in 1905, was overseen by librarian Lydia Schencks and had its own board of trustees, including business owner Thaddeus Tate and the Reverend Primus P. Alston of Saint Michael's Church. The library received a city appropriation of $400 and a collection of donated books, and it remained an independently administered public library until 1929, when it became a branch of the Charlotte Public Library.[11]

As in Charlotte, the main library in Guthrie, Oklahoma, constructed with Carnegie money, was open to whites only. But blacks found other ways to create a collection they could use. In 1906, the city became the site of the state's first public library to serve African Americans, thanks to the efforts of Judith Ann Carter Horton. Born in 1866, she had attended school in Saint Louis and, after graduating from Ohio's Oberlin College, worked as a teacher in Kansas and in Guthrie, where she married D. G. Horton, principal of the Favor High School for African Americans. Judith Horton was a founding member of the Oklahoma State Federation of Colored Women's Clubs, and during her five years as president the organization was instrumental in the creation of the state training school for African Americans.

In 1900, Guthrie's whites-only Federation of Women's Clubs began collecting donated books and, through the influence of a local businessman who was a friend of Carnegie, received a $1,000 donation to expand their collection. By 1901, the federation's Carnegie Circulating Library was operating as a municipal service and, with a Carnegie grant of $25,000, it opened in its own building in 1903. After Principal Horton was denied access to the new facility, Judith Horton went into action. She worked with others in the black community to open the independent Excelsior Library in 1906. The city provided $2,000 and local residents donated $1,000 to purchase a building to house the library, and the city then gave organizers an annual appropriation for maintenance.[12]

For eleven years, Horton staffed the Excelsior Library as a part-time volunteer. In 1912 some 8,000 people visited it, and there were 3,296 circulations from a collection of 2,380 books, including 520 added during that year. By the mid-1930s, the independent, publicly supported library held the largest collection accessible to black Oklahomans: some 15,000 volumes, including a special collection featuring black authors, for the city's 1,700 African Americans.[13]

Galveston, Texas, had an Andrew Carnegie of its own in the form of wealthy businessman Henry Rosenberg, a Swiss immigrant who had moved to Galveston in 1843 as a shop clerk and eventually became a wealthy merchant, banker, and philanthropist. He died in 1893, and his will stipulated that assets totaling about $400,000 be used to build a public library and create an endowment providing sufficient income to maintain it. As the new Rosenberg Library was about to open in 1904, the board of directors passed a resolution stating that the building was for whites only but that a separate branch library for residents of African descent would be provided.[14] The board decided to house the library in a two-story addition to blacks-only Central High School; the cost of construction, fixtures, and about 1,000 books totaled $5,000.[15] The library opened in January 1905 and served students as well as the public.[16]

At the request of M. F. Mott, president of the Rosenberg Library's board of directors, E. F. Harris, a state legislator from Galveston County, introduced a statewide bill mandating that African Americans use separate library facilities, if such existed. The bill was introduced just as Galveston's black branch was opening. Black newspaper publisher Henry Noble, Jr., responded with a scathing editorial, noting that the state could keep blacks from using the Rosenberg Library but it could not force them to use the colored branch.[17] Nonetheless, at least some did use the only public library available to them, for in 1930 a visitor reported that it was "small and inadequate for the demands made upon it."[18]

In Durham, North Carolina, women's clubs raised funds to build a public library and secured a monthly appropriation from the city for maintenance. Opened in 1898, the library operated with a staff of volunteer workers until 1911, when Lillian Baker Griggs accepted the position as director, thus becoming the first trained librarian employed by a public library in North Carolina.[19] Because the library was not open to African Americans, black physician Aaron McDuffie Moore took matters into his own hands, opening a library of almost eight hundred volumes in a basement room of the White Rock Baptist Church, where he was superintendent of the Sunday School. Moore and a friend, the entrepreneurial barber John Merrick, solicited funds from other black business owners and professionals and had a small building constructed in the black neighborhood known as Hayti, where they moved the collection in 1916. Such men, as well as counterparts such as the collection's librarian, Hattie Wooten, inspired sociologist E. Franklin Frazier to christen Durham "the Capital of the Black Middle Class." In 1917 the city began giving the library a monthly appropriation, but it also depended on donations from individuals, churches, and women's clubs. Eventually the collection grew to 11,000 volumes under the direction of Wooten's successor, Selena Warren, who became librarian in 1932. Known as the Sanford L. Warren Library, it remained an independent entity with its own board of trustees until it merged with the newly desegregated Durham Public Library in 1966.[20]

African Americans in other southern cities and towns had the same experience of restriction and rejection; but when they pivoted, they turned toward the Carnegie Corporation rather than (or in addition to) local help—at least until the foundation's library giving program ceased. Sometimes, as in the case of Houston, the result was an independently administered, purpose-built edifice constructed

with a Carnegie grant and maintained with a municipal appropriation. At other times, as in the case of New Orleans, Carnegie money
went to construct a branch operated under the control of the white
library's director and board. Between 1905 and 1925, ten racially
mixed cities used grants from Carnegie and his foundation to erect
eleven public library buildings staffed and used exclusively by African
Americans.[21] Those libraries followed one of two models for delivering collections and services to urban blacks: they were independent,
or, more commonly, they were the branch of a main library. While
historians have suggested that a number of conditions precede the
founding of libraries, they have not made any distinctions regarding
the circumstances surrounding the establishment of white versus
black libraries. According to mid-twentieth-century library science
educator and historian Jesse Shera, several "causal factors . . . contributed to the emergence of the public library" in New England:

- Accumulation of individual and community wealth, creating an
  available surplus for funding libraries through private philanthropy and public taxation;

- Existence of a core of individuals interested in history, scholarly
  research, and the preservation of the past who were, in part, fueled
  by nationalistic fervor;

- Civic pride, resulting in competition among cities and towns for
  cultural ascendancy;

- Support for universal public education and an accompanying recognition of the library's potential to promote popular participation in culture and politics;

- Urge toward self-improvement, often involving what we today call
  lifelong learning; and

- Impact of industrialization, which seemed to encourage workers
  to search for information that would help them adjust to the new
  order.[22]

Writing some fifty years after Shera, William J. Gilmore turned his
attention to the spectrum of print culture, in which circulating and
social libraries have been only two of many possible nodes of acquisition and dissemination. In his study of material and cultural life
in one area of Vermont in the late eighteenth and early nineteenth

centuries, Gilmore refers to many of the economic, educational, and social phenomena that Shera discussed. Rather than seeing them as causative factors, however, he construes them as part of a complex web spun out of the processes of commercial exchange and print-culture engagement. In Gilmore's schema, capital accumulation, the ability to read, a desire to improve, a sense of geographic distinctiveness, pursuit of the "wisdom of the ages" as well as "the latest intelligence," and preindustrial commercialization were not necessary to the emergence of libraries. Instead, libraries themselves were part of the infrastructure that helped generate and sustain those conditions. For rural New England families, proximity to transportation and communication modes had more of an impact on their involvement with print culture than class or occupation did. According to Gilmore, "differential access to the basic vehicles of print and written communications was one of the most important distinctions among people in early America." Residents of regions with roads, waterways, postal service, print shops, bookstores, and libraries had the opportunity to exercise their right to know, and many took advantage of it. In areas that lacked such infrastructure, having access to information proved difficult if not impossible.[23]

The early twentieth-century south obviously presented a different temporal and spatial context than the one that existed in the northeast a century earlier. Nevertheless, similar factors affected the development of library services for southern blacks, in part because the south was entering the transition from rural to urban and from agricultural to industrial that the northeast already had undergone. The distinctive circumstances of southern life and culture altered the factors that led to the founding of segregated public libraries, however.

For example, New Englanders applied some of their surplus wealth, collectively and individually, to creating and maintaining libraries. Decades later, the New South commercial and political elite looked to their northern counterparts to help them create and acquire capital—focusing in particular (as northerners also did) on the main storehouse of already accumulated capital, Carnegie and the Carnegie Corporation. Members of the southern black elite, who had even less surplus wealth than their white counterparts did, also sought Carnegie funding. They emphasized the need for libraries not so much as sites for preserving the past but as monuments for ensuring the future. Civic pride was a factor: in the pages of nationally circulated, black-owned newspapers such as the *Indianapolis Freeman* and the *Chicago Defender,* African Americans were learning about new libraries in various southern cities. For black southerners, the library's dual educational roles—to supplement the public schools and to serve those whose schooling had ceased—took on special significance in the context of underfunded, substandard, and (for the older generation) nonexistent public education. Whereas New Englanders had conceived of libraries as resources for helping workers adjust to the new order of industrialization, southern blacks saw them as a tool to help them cope with—and sometimes turn to their own advantage—the new order of post-Reconstruction segregation.[24]

Elizabeth McHenry's interpretation of the benefits that accrued to members of black literary societies applies equally well to the users of black libraries:

> The growing numbers of educated black men and women considered reading and other literary work as essential to the project of refashioning the personal identity and reconstructing the public image of African Americans in the last decade of the nineteenth century. . . . Although most black women's clubs at the turn of the century were not exclusively literary in nature, club membership offered black women a variety of literary and textual means through which to experience and exercise individual and collaborative agency, and a primary impact of the black women's club movement was the increased production, circulation, and readership of printed texts.[25]

Despite the oppression to which African Americans had been subjected throughout their existence in the American colonies, the new republic, the Union and the Confederacy, and the postwar United States, they were able to initiate their own participation in the consumption and production of print culture. One manifestation was the literary society, a voluntary association of individuals who valued reading, writing, and critical thinking. As McHenry has shown, members of early nineteenth-century literary societies in the north saw themselves as intellectually engaged in civic life as citizens in a democracy, while the societies of a hundred years later positioned themselves to construct a complex, valid representation of blackness at a time of deteriorating race relations:

> Historically, black Americans have been denied access to formal educational opportunities, and the public education that has been provided for them has been of inferior quality. They have therefore created and relied on other institutions to supplement and sustain their literary education. To uncover a more nuanced and more accurate history of their interaction with literature, we must look beyond the venues traditionally associated with reading and literary discussions. [26]

When McHenry looked beyond the traditional educational venues, she discovered a wealth of information about literary societies and in so doing traced a long and rich history of African Americans' involvement in reading, writing, and critical thinking. Libraries offer another way of understanding this phenomenon—particularly public libraries because they are further removed than academic libraries are from formal education, even though they often support literary clubs, debating societies, and students by providing meeting space and usable collections.

While societies and clubs provided informal avenues for literary pursuits, public libraries offered formal structures, both as buildings and as tax-supported entities subject to accounting and reporting procedures. A library-mediated interaction with print culture was necessarily different from one mediated by a literary society. The library offered a choice of specific books and periodicals, a certain number of those items, an allotted borrowing period, a standardized catalog system, and predictable hours of operation. It had a staff responsible for applying its policies, spending its money, managing its collection, and serving its users. This staff reported to a higher administrative authority, ultimately the municipal government but often also the administrators of the overall system (for a branch library) or a board of directors (for an independent library). By the time southern towns and cities were opening separate rooms, branches, and libraries for black readers, the closed stacks of the nineteenth century had opened for unrestricted access, making it possible for library users to go directly to the shelves, browse titles on spines, and examine the pages within. But if they wanted to carry materials home, they had to provide personal information such as name and address in exchange for that right.

The library was organized around the needs and desires of individual readers. Once the librarian issued them borrowers' cards with unique identifying numbers, readers followed their own literary tastes (within the limits of the library's holdings), reading paces, and borrowing patterns. In contrast, literary societies were organized around regular meetings, often open to non-members as well as members, which featured the public presentation of a paper written before the meeting and discussed during the session and even afterward. Reading, writing, thinking, and talking were social activities with the potential for political outcomes. A person ventured to literary society meetings in search of spoken words but traveled to the library in search of printed words. The result at both venues could be a meeting of the minds; but at the library, that meeting was silent and invisible, occurring solely between reader and author. The exception was the children's story hour, which public libraries offered regularly in the hopes that youngsters would be inspired by what they heard to borrow books and read the stories for themselves.

Beyond the quiet, unremarked, private acts of library users, the founding of public libraries for African Americans was, like the literary societies, a result of their desire for an intellectual and political life. In the Jim Crow south, these foundings suggest the existence of a condition beyond those identified by Shera and Gilmore: the desire for a place in the network of print. The public library was a common good, a "university of the people," underwritten by public revenue and private philanthropy, and African Americans wanted their share.

The first Carnegie-funded separate public library branch building for African Americans opened in 1908 on the west side of Louisville. Five years later, Carnegie library buildings in Houston and Meridian, Mississippi, opened. In 1914, they opened on the east side of Louisville and in Savannah, Georgia, and Evansville, Indiana. New Orleans opened a Carnegie library for black residents in 1915; Nashville in 1916; Knoxville in 1918; Atlanta in 1921; and Greensboro, North Carolina, in 1924. The dates suggest a measured progression, but each opening was preceded by a period of negotiation and action that revealed the power dynamic among whites and blacks in southern cities. It was no accident that Louisville was the first and, with two branches, the most successful or that Atlanta and Greensboro were the last, opening years after the end of the Carnegie giving program. Carnegie-funded libraries for African Americans defied the pattern that George Bobinski identified in his study of Carnegie libraries, wherein local enthusiasts built on a foundation of preexisting private, subscription, and social libraries. Carnegie "strengthened the strong," as Mary Edna Anders saw it.[27]

That was true for white libraries. Yet even though African American individuals and groups did establish collections and reading rooms in many cities, such preexisting efforts seldom created enough critical mass to convince Carnegie that a library building would be put to good use. Rather, the foundation gave money for separate buildings when it became obvious that African Americans would not be allowed inside the main building bearing Carnegie's name.

Public libraries are necessarily local institutions, and local individuals and conditions affect each library's history. Louisville and Houston were on the edge of the south, and boosters in both places considered their cities to be better homes for African Americans than were other less benign southern locales.[28] Although such assertions were a matter of opinion and did not reflect lived reality for many blacks in Louisville and Houston, they did invoke a widespread understanding that the Deep South constituted a harsher environment. Yet New Orleans and Savannah, located in the quintessential Deep South states of Louisiana and Georgia, were among the earliest cities to establish Carnegie libraries for African Americans. Local people made the difference.

Between 1911 and 1956, some thirty public libraries in Kentucky reported that they did not serve African Americans.[29] In their midst were two others in which African Americans enjoyed the same access as whites did, both located in Kenton County in the state's Bluegrass region. The first was in Covington, across the Ohio River from Cincinnati. Covington formed a library board in 1901, secured a Carnegie building grant of $25,000, and opened the library in 1904. Ten years later, the Women's Club of Erlander, a small town several miles southwest of Cincinnati, opened a one-room library run by volunteers. One of them reported that "Negroes use the library on the same basis as whites and there has never been any discussion as to whether they should or not. Negro borrowers are mostly school children." The capital city of Lexington, about eighty miles south of Covington, opened its public library in 1906 and allowed African Americans to browse among the stacks and borrow books. However, if they wanted to read in the library, they had to use a reading room separate from the one used by whites.[30]

Louisville, about 80 miles west of Lexington and 115 miles south of Indianapolis, created a more substantial monument to segregation, constructing two separate library buildings to serve as black branches and hiring African Americans to staff them. The branches were part of a cohesive plan for a library system that would include a main building and several branches, and city officials asked the Carnegie Corporation for enough funds to turn their vision into reality. The city was willing to commit $25,000 a year to maintain a free public library, and Carnegie pledged $250,000 for the main building. He followed up with another $200,000 to build eight branches, two of which (one on the west side, one on the east) would be for the use of African Americans. The impressive new main building opened in 1908; and the Western Colored Branch, which had been operating out of rented quarters, opened in its own more modest Carnegie building later that year (fig. 1). In 1914, the Eastern Colored Branch opened, marking the end of the Carnegie construction boom in Louisville.[31]

As was often the case, the city had already had a public library, converted from a private institution, before it had a Carnegie library. When Albert Ernest Meyzeek, a transplanted Indiana native who served as principal of the Colored School on the city's east side, took some of his students to that library, the staff apparently allowed them to use the collection, at least a few times. Other white libraries in the south also reported occasionally allowing teachers special access.[32] But at some point it must have occurred to the Louisville library staff that they were establishing a pattern of service that was likely to extend to other African Americans, so they stopped serving Meyzeek and his students. Meyzeek met with the library board and convinced members to use a portion of the newly pledged Carnegie funds to

Figure 1. After opening in its Carnegie building in 1908, Louisville's Western Colored Branch shaped reading and research for local residents and served as a model collection and service for other libraries. Courtesy of Louisville Free Public Library, Photographic Archives, University of Louisville.

construct, first, a library in the black neighborhood on the city's west side and then a second on the smaller, poorer east side.[33]

Virginia native Thomas Fountain Blue, who had served as secretary of Louisville's black YMCA (which Meyzeek had also helped to found), became head of the Western Colored Branch and eventually, during his two decades of library work, director of the system's African American collections and services. Assisting and then succeeding him after his 1935 death was Rachel Davis Harris, who had grown up in Louisville. Meyzeek, Blue, and Harris were able to accomplish a great deal because the city's white elites practiced "polite racism," in the words of historian George Wright, an attitude that allowed them, "with a clear conscience, to exclude Afro-Americans from white institutions."[34] Other cities responded more rudely to blacks' expressed need for libraries. Blue and Harris's work received recognition from the American Library Association, from other public libraries, and in the pages of the NAACP's *Crisis* and Hampton Institute's *Southern Workman*.[35]

The success of library segregation can be interpreted as a positive development. At a time when most southern blacks had no access to libraries, Louisville's African Americans had convenient access to books, story times, and other services, no matter where they lived in town. It can also be seen as a negative development that ensconced racial segregation in a city agency. Only a few years earlier blacks had won the right to integrated buses and streetcars, and only a few years later Louisville's residential restrictive covenants would be struck down. It would be misleading to suggest that public transportation and housing were desegregated just as the library system was being segregated because de facto segregation still existed in the absence of de jure segregation of conveyances and residences. Blacks in Louisville refused to be jimcrowed whenever they could. As early as 1914, they had created the state's first branch of the NAACP and were working to help other towns establish their own branches.[36] The Louisville approach made it possible to claim that a public library *system* served all even as it held the color line within its own operations. It would prove to be a powerful model for public libraries in the first half of the twentieth century.

Booker T. Washington (like Blue, a Hampton alumnus) visited the Western Colored Branch in 1909. Impressed, he wrote to Carnegie's secretary, James Bertram, praising African Americans for using the library and whites for allowing them to.[37] His letter was just one in a series of texts and visits designed to keep Carnegie's money flowing into African American institutions. As discussed in chapter 1, Washington himself was a beneficiary of Carnegie's generosity. After receiving a building grant for Tuskegee's library in 1903, he routinely interested himself in the process of funneling the steel baron's largesse to black colleges and communities for academic and public libraries. Within a few months of his visit to Louisville, Washington began lobbying the Carnegie organization for funds to build a similar institution in Houston, where black elites had leveraged their connection to him to establish a library that, for a time, remained independent from the main whites-only public library.

White clubwomen had been instrumental in the founding of

Houston's public library. They corresponded with the Carnegie organization to get a pledge of funding, worked with city officials to secure an annual appropriation, and raised and gave donations to purchase the site.[38] Texas's schools, trains, and railway stations and Houston's streetcars were already segregated, and in 1907 (the same year that Texas and Houston passed additional segregation laws and ordinances) local black educators were refused service at the newly opened Carnegie Public Library.[39] Although the city did not have a residential segregation ordinance, most black Houstonians were only allowed to inhabit neighborhoods characterized by substandard housing and sparse city amenities. Most of the 23,929 African Americans living in Houston in 1910 were unskilled workers. Yet of black residents over the age of ten, about 86 percent of males and 82 percent of females were literate.[40]

According to the board of the Carnegie Library of Houston, the library was free to all, but trustees did nothing when they were informed that black Houstonians had tried to use the library and had been kept out. In response, high school principal E. O. Smith, Gregory School principal William E. Miller, postal clerk Leonard Henry Spivey, and high school teachers Richard G. Lockett and Walter L. D. Johnson, Sr., created the Colored Carnegie Library Association. They enlisted the aid of Booker T. Washington, whose secretary Emmett Scott was from Houston and who interceded successfully with Carnegie. The association convinced city officials to provide maintenance funds, and members raised enough money to buy the lot on which their Carnegie library was built. They also were able to hire a librarian, Emma Myers, and open the library before construction of the building was completed, operating it in Houston's black high school as a branch of the Houston Lyceum and Carnegie Library from 1909 until 1913. The collection, numbering about 350 volumes when the library opened, was created from the discards (or "duplicates," as they were more delicately called) of the Houston Lyceum and Carnegie Library. Julia Ideson, the director of the Carnegie Library, oversaw the expenditure of the $500 appropriation the city earmarked annually for the branch.[41]

When the new Colored Carnegie Library building opened in the spring of 1913, however, it functioned as an independently

Figure 2. A large crowd attended the opening ceremony for the new library building in Houston, where members of the Colored Carnegie Library Association (left) shared the stage with white city officials (right). Courtesy of the Houston Public Library Collection, Houston Metropolitan Research Center.

administered agency with its own $1,500 annual appropriation (fig. 2). The opening-day collection was close to 4,000 volumes. In its first year of operation, some 1,760 "porters, nurses, cooks and working girls and boys," among others, registered for borrowers' cards, and black residents made more than 11,000 visits to the library. But the new librarian, Bessie Osborne, who had traveled to Louisville to apprentice with Blue and Harris while the library building was under construction, had difficulty stretching the appropriation to acquire a sufficient number of books. Salaries, utilities, coal in the winter, building maintenance, and supplies took most of the funds. Among other problems during the library's first year was a complete lack of chairs in the basement meeting room, so Osborne and the board sponsored a fund-raising picnic, which helped with the purchase of chairs.[42] Eventually, after an increase in the city appropriation in 1915, the library was able to devote a bit of money to book acquisitions.[43]

The Colored Carnegie Library continued to function independently from the Houston Lyceum and Carnegie Library until the early 1920s. Ideson had lost the branch in the same era that William Yust was telling American Library Association members that black libraries needed to be under the control of whites, and for several years she had expressed an interest in taking the black branch back. Finally, with the passage of a bond issue for expansion in 1921, the city library system changed its name to the Houston Public Library and the Colored Carnegie Public Library became a branch. Houston, like Charlotte, had started with a public library not only for African Americans but also governed by African Americans, but in the 1920s both of those independent libraries became branches staffed by African Americans but governed by whites.

Ideson had had direct experience with very few black librarians, but that did not stop her from generalizing about all of them and making negative assessments based on little data. In 1925, she described Bessie Osborne as "a colored woman of refinement and pleasing manner, with highly developed social qualities, . . . [who] has never mastered cataloging or classification." She further asserted that she would not give an African American librarian the same amount of authority and responsibility that she would give a white branch head because the "character of work of colored librarians is superficial."[44] Such an attitude may have been one reason why Houston's black elite had tried to keep the library independent.

It may also have been one of the things that blacks in Savannah were trying to avoid. In contrast to Louisville's, Savannah's library for African Americans did not begin as part of a larger system. In contrast to Houston's, it remained independent until the era of desegregation. And in contrast to almost everywhere else, the customary whites-first chronology did not hold. Savannah's Carnegie library for African Americans opened in 1915, before the Carnegie building for whites, which opened a year later.

Whites in Savannah did have access to a library before either of the Carnegies opened. The Georgia General Assembly in 1839 had granted a charter to the Georgia Historical Society, whose offices were housed in its building, Hodgson Hall. In 1903 the society signed an agreement with Savannah specifying that the city would annually provide $3,000, along with the society's $500, to fund a public library and situate it in Hodgson Hall. The library was open only to white

Savannah residents, who saw the private administration of the public library as an effective way to deny service to "undesirable persons." That loophole later proved to be an obstacle to the city's attempts to secure a library grant pledge from Carnegie, who questioned the historical society's ability and desire to serve the masses.[45]

Early in 1906, twelve men, most of them business owners or educators, met to begin organizing a public library. They formed a seven-member board of curators and elected as president a local attorney and railway mail service clerk, Abraham Lewis Tucker.[46] The members of this founding group no doubt were aware that the public library run by the Georgia Historical Society and partially funded by the city was not open to them. While the historical society and the city were negotiating their agreement regarding the provision of public library services, the president of the board of education, Colonel George A. Mercer, had denied that African Americans wanted or needed access to a public library: "The Negroes [have] not reached the state of advancement where they could be turned at large in such an institution as a public library. If so about half of the books would soon be found in the pawnshops." The *Savannah Tribune,* in a refutation of "his slur upon the race," suggested that "only the better element would take advantage" of library access, and they could be trusted not to steal the books.[47]

The board of curators met regularly throughout the spring of 1906 to plan the opening of the library. Board members donated books and solicited donations from others; by the time the library opened, they had about 350 volumes, more than a third of them by Charles Dickens. The library also subscribed to the *Savannah Morning News,* a white-owned daily newspaper, and the *Savannah Tribune,* a black-owned weekly.[48]

President Tucker's 1909 annual report to the mayor noted that the board of curators of the Colored Public Library had contacted Carnegie to request a building grant. In addition to needing a building, the library also needed more children's books, subscriptions to more black-owned newspapers, and, "by all means, as they are printed and are accessible and reputable, all the books by colored authors."[49] In 1910, Carnegie agreed to give Savannah $12,000 for a library building for African American residents, and the city agreed to appropriate $1,200 annually for its maintenance.[50] The board of curators solicited donations to buy a site for the Carnegie building and eventually acquired land at 537 East Henry Street, paying $3,000 cobbled together from gifts, revenues from entertainments, and a bank loan.[51]

In May 1914, the board was incorporated as a legal entity, meaning that it was now capable of receiving municipal revenues. Members held a dedication ceremony on August 14, 1914, and the building opened in 1915. P. A. Denegall, a graduate of Atlanta University who had recently completed a library course on technical services at the University of Chicago, was the librarian in charge. In 1924, he reported having 822 registered borrowers and a circulation of 3,386. Because Savannah's public schools for African Americans had no libraries, circulation among the 504 juvenile borrowers outnumbered that of adults.[52] But what was perhaps most striking was the library's name. In what might be interpreted as a gesture of one-upmanship, the board of curators took the liberty of naming its institution the Carnegie Library—without any other signifier.[53]

Likewise, in New Orleans, the name of the library branch for African Americans, which opened the same year as Savannah's, did not carry a racial signifier. The city's branches were named for the areas or streets in which they were located. The Dryades Branch, for blacks, opened a few years after the Royal, Algiers, and Napoleon branches opened for whites.

As with many urban public libraries established in the last decade of the nineteenth century, the New Orleans Public Library had its roots in existing private and subscription libraries. In April 1896, the city council had established a free municipal public library, passing an ordinance that merged the Fisk Free Library and the Lyceum and Library Society collections. The Fisk Free Library dated back to the 1840s, when Abijah Fisk had willed his home to the city to house a library. At the same time, his brother, Alvarez Fisk, had acquired a 6,000-volume private collection, which he gave to the city to fill his brother's house.[54] Operated by the Mechanics Institute, the library was not used much and in 1884 moved to the University of Louisiana (now Tulane University). The Lyceum and Library Society collection also dated back to the 1840s, when the American sector, operating as a semi-independent municipality, had established the Public School Lyceum and Library Society. The society's library merged with its counterparts in two other semi-independent municipalities in New Orleans to form the Lyceum and Library Society Library, which most people referred to as the City Library. When the city built a new courthouse, Mayor John Fitzpatrick worked with the city council to pass an ordinance early in 1894 allowing the old building, known as Saint Patrick's Hall, to house what the ordinance described as "a great library thoroughly equipped and centrally located." A second ordinance, in 1895, merged the Fisk and City libraries. When the new institution opened in January 1897, its combined collections totaled approximately 30,000 volumes.[55]

In 1906, after the federal government bought Saint Patrick's Hall to house a post office, the collection moved to temporary quarters. The city secured a Carnegie grant of $250,000 and opened the new building in October 1908. Situated on Saint Charles Avenue at Lee Circle, it featured an exterior design inspired by the Roman temple at Mars Ultor. The main floor consisted of a single vaulted room with glass and steel bookshelves, a delivery desk, reference alcoves, a periodicals area, a separate children's room, and tables and chairs to accommodate readers. Architects Diboll, Owen, and Goldstein situated the building near the front of the lot to make room for renovations at the back, should demand and the collection increase.[56]

Over time, city officials secured another $100,000 from Carnegie for branch libraries. The first three—the Royal in the French Quarter, the Algiers on the city's West Bank, and the Napoleon in a park setting—opened in 1907 and early 1908, before the new central building itself had opened. Each could hold between 5,000 and 6,000 volumes. In 1911, the city opened the Canal Branch, in relatively close proximity to two high schools and designed to hold 12,000 volumes; and in 1915 it opened the Dryades Branch, with a capacity of 10,000 volumes, for the exclusive use of African Americans.[57] As in other southern cities, the ability of the local black elite to work cooperatively with one or a few white officials made the library branch possible.

In June 1912, library board president John Hardy Dillard had announced that he had visited Carnegie and secured a pledge of

$25,000 for an extension of the children's room in the main building and another $25,000 for a separate building for African Americans.[58] Dillard was a white man who was sympathetic to the cause of black education in the context of continuing segregation. Born into a Virginia planter family in 1856, he traced his conversion to the cause of racial justice to an act of injustice he had experienced as a child, when an African American boy was punished for a situation that young Dillard had created. His devout Christianity also influenced his commitment to what he called "the fair opportunity." By 1877, Dillard had completed his bachelor's and master's degrees at Washington and Lee University and had entered the field of educational administration. After stints at two different institutions in Norfolk and a third at Washington University in Saint Louis, he moved to New Orleans in 1891 to teach Latin at Tulane, where he soon became dean of the College of Arts and Sciences. He developed a record of service in his adopted state that included his work not only with the public library but also with the Child Welfare Association and the anti-lynching movement as well as trustee positions at various institutions of higher education for African Americans. Booker T. Washington lured him away from university life by recruiting him to preside over the Anna T. Jeanes Negro Rural School Fund, established in 1907. Dillard soon became head of the John F. Slater Fund as well. Until his retirement in 1931, he used both positions to further the cause of black education.[59]

Beginning in 1912, Dillard consulted with "several of the leading colored people" about the site for the new branch library. They suggested that it should be located near the Colored YMCA on Dryades Street, but Dillard was unable to find a lot that would cost less than $6,500.[60] To underscore their continuing interest in this vicinity, black organizations began petitioning Dillard about the importance of opening the library in the neighborhood.[61] Early in 1913, the library board's site committee announced that it had selected a lot on Dryades between Jackson and Philip streets and had turned in their recommendation to Mayor Martin Behrman for his approval. Robert E. Jones of the *Southwestern Christian Advocate* endorsed the committee's selected site, and committee chairman Albert Baldwin, Jr., paid a visit to the mayor.[62] Committee members also met with local community representatives, who were not satisfied with their choice of lots.[63] By late summer, however, the mayor had introduced an ordinance to allow purchase of the site for $5,300.[64]

In spring 1915, the library board approved the librarian's recommendation to hire library assistants Delia L. Allen at $40 per month and Adelia N. Trent at $35 per month.[65] But Allen resigned in 1919, and in a subsequent annual report, head librarian Henry Gill wrote, "I regret to report the [1921] death of the young woman, Adelia Trent, who was in charge of the Colored Branch. She was a distinct loss to the library. Her loyalty to her work, her conscientious devotion to her duties and her pride in her position won from her readers consideration and respect for herself and her Branch."[66] Miss A. L. Johnson was hired as assistant in charge and Miss D. Guichard as assistant.[67]

In Tennessee, the founding of Nashville's and Knoxville's branches followed an emerging pattern. In the nineteenth century, Nashville, which considered itself a cultural hub, had had numerous social and academic libraries. Confederate veteran and newspaperman Gideon H. Baskette had served as a board member of the private Howard Library, which he worked to convert into a tax-supported public library. He was involved in the hiring of Mary Hannah Johnson as head librarian and the acquiring of a Carnegie grant for a central building, which opened in 1904.

Like many in Tennessee and throughout the south, Johnson advocated for increasing the number of public libraries available to whites before doing the same for blacks.[68] Once the central library was fully functional, Johnson began in 1909 to advocate for an addition to the building and for several branches, including one to serve African Americans. Instrumental in the creation of the branch was a group of members of the Negro Board of Trade, including businessman, attorney, and politician James C. Napier and undertaker and newspaper publisher Andrew N. Johnson, both of whom had had long and useful associations with Booker T. Washington. As in Houston, library advocates in Nashville used a multipronged approach, working locally with municipal officials and nationally with Carnegie and Washington to create the Negro Branch, which opened in 1916, some four years after Carnegie's pledge of funding.[69]

With the exception of Louisville, which had, from almost the beginning, planned to open two black branches on either side of town, the proper site for a black library posed a special challenge for cities. Because it was usually the only collection freely available to a city's black residents, it needed to be convenient to the neighborhoods in which they lived. Differences of opinion often arose within black communities regarding the ultimate location of the library. Much depended on affordability, of course, and in Nashville the chosen site at Twelfth Avenue and Hynes Street cost $1,000 more than the city had earmarked, which meant that donations from African Americans had to make up the difference. In addition, Nashville's black elite argued about whether the working-class population around that site would frequent the library or whether the library should be situated in the more educated and prosperous neighborhood around Fisk University, which itself had a Carnegie library building on campus housing nearly 10,000 volumes. The original site prevailed. In 1915, when the budget of the Carnegie Library of Nashville had dropped to $15,000 from a high of $22,000 in 1913, head librarian Margaret Kercheval proposed keeping the $2,500 that was supposed to go to the Negro branch—in other words, not opening the building that Carnegie had funded. But the library's board rejected that idea.[70]

Whereas blacks in Nashville tended to develop their own independent institutions and organizations, their counterparts in Knoxville tended to involve whites in their municipal projects. But in the case of public libraries, African American communities in both Nashville and Knoxville worked with local white officials to accomplish their goal. Like Louisville, Knoxville was a small city with a proportionately small black population. In 1906, whites and blacks had cooperated on the creation of a black YMCA, and several years later they worked to found two public parks for African Americans.[71]

Although Knoxville had subscription libraries throughout the nineteenth century, it did not have a free public library until 1917. The original Lawson McGhee Library was erected in 1885 with money provided by Charles McGhee in memory of his daughter, who had died in 1883 at the age of twenty-four. To maintain the institution, trustees charged modest membership fees and rented out space in the new building. After a fire in 1904, the library moved into rented quarters, but the original building was renovated and rented out to other enterprises. In 1914, library trustees negotiated a contract with the city, agreeing to construct a new library building (with money raised by first renting and then selling the original building) on a lot they had purchased for $25,000 and then to turn it over to the city. The city agreed to take over the library's maintenance, at not less than $5,000 annually, making it Knoxville's first public library supported by municipal revenues rather than private subscriptions.[72]

The new Lawson McGhee Library opened in January 1917 with a collection of about 20,000 volumes. The opening-day ceremonies featured a speech by Colonel L. D. Tyson, president of the board of trustees, who presented the deed to Mayor John E. McMillan. Tyson recounted the history of the institution and exhorted members of the audience to use the library and send their children there. Knoxville was a progressive city, he said, and the library would help it achieve its dreams: "We want the library to be the center of culture and happiness for all the people of the city."[73]

Although Mayor McMillan had not been in office when the trustees had offered the library to the city in exchange for its upkeep, he indicated his enthusiasm in his speech accepting the deed to the structure. As mayors are wont to do, he evoked civic pride, praising McGhee, who had died in 1907, as a local man with a vision and the means to accomplish it. Calling him the town's own Carnegie, McMillan said:

> Few people probably realize all that the great iron master, Mr. Carnegie, has done to bring these stores of knowledge within the reach of all, scattered as they are through the length and breadth of our land; but we of Knoxville have had no reason to call upon the generosity from an outsider, since in our midst we have had a beloved citizen who in his life time realized what a library meant to a community and who did not count the cost in pennies, but who built not only for the generation of his day, but for those who are yet to come.[74]

Notwithstanding Tyson's and McMillan's "free for all" assertions, the Lawson McGhee trustees stipulated in their contract with the city that only whites would be allowed to use the library. Charles W. Cansler, the principal of Austin High School for black students, had already been turned away, as had some of his colleagues. As construction of the new Lawson McGhee building was nearing completion, Cansler met with Mayor S. G. Heiskell to request that library services be provided for the city's African American residents. Heiskell, despite his reputation as "a friend of the Negro," was indifferent to the suggestion. Cansler returned for a second visit, in which he urged the mayor to ask Carnegie for a building grant for a separate library for black Knoxville residents. He recalled that the mayor "tried to take refuge in the remark that he did not know Andrew Carnegie, but I quickly retorted, 'If I had been Mayor of this city twelve years as you have been, I would make Andrew Carnegie know me.' " The mayor reportedly smiled and quickly dictated a letter to the Carnegie Corporation.[75]

In March 1916, Heiskell (no longer mayor but now president of the city's board of education) wrote to Carnegie to request a $25,000 grant. He estimated that Knoxville proper and its suburbs had a population of about 70,000, of whom 10,000 to 12,000 were African American. Heiskell cited a relatively high rate of home ownership among black residents as indicative of their diligence and prudence and, he implied, of their eligibility to enjoy municipal amenities such as public libraries. As further evidence of the city's fairness toward its African American residents, he noted the recent construction of a new high school for blacks. (Cansler had been instrumental in moving the existing black high school from its location in a vice district to a more suitable site.) Heiskell also informed Carnegie that the impending opening of the Lawson McGhee Library made it necessary for the city to establish a library for blacks, given the state constitution's prohibition against discrimination.[76]

Bertram, Carnegie's secretary, had learned to routinely challenge his southern correspondents, who tended to give him optimistic projections of overall growth rather than actual population figures for blacks and whites. In the case of Knoxville, his query uncovered a trend that Heiskell was not likely to reveal on his own initiative. In the early twentieth century, Knoxville's black residents were decreasing in proportion to its white residents. Whereas, in 1870, 30 percent of the city's population had been black, in 1910, only 21 percent was.[77] In response to Heiskell's letter, Bertram requested population figures for the municipality proper, divided by white and black, and asked how much the city had agreed to appropriate annually for upkeep of the new public library for whites.[78] Heiskell answered that, of Knoxville's 36,346 residents, 7,638 were black, according to the 1910 census. He also told Bertram that the city had appropriated $5,000 annually for maintenance of the new Lawson McGhee Library. When Heiskell reiterated his appeal for $25,000, Bertram countered that, with such a small population of potential users, only a $10,000 building would be needed. Moreover, Knoxville would have to agree to an annual appropriation of 10 percent of that amount for the Carnegie board to consider the gift.[79]

Disappointed, Heiskell pressed Bertram to consider a larger, more expensive building. He was hoping for something more in keeping with the soon-to-open Lawson McGhee building (which had cost, including the site, close to $90,000) or the Brownlow School (constructed for $20,000 while Heiskell was still mayor). He enclosed a pledge from the city's five commissioners to appropriate an annual maintenance fund at 10 percent of the Carnegie gift.[80] Bertram replied with his usual letter, requiring the city council to pass a resolution committing to the 10 percent annual appropriation and the purchase of the site and requesting a copy of the proposed plans; but he cautioned that no expenditures should be made until the corporation could review and approve the plans.[81] Heiskell secured and sent the resolution and then removed himself from the process, which was now officially in the hands of the commissioners, who would select and acquire a site and hire an architect.[82] In November 1916, city commissioners approved the purchase of a lot on the corner of Nelson Street and East Vine Avenue for $3,000.[83]

White and black leaders shared the podium at the opening exercises for the Carnegie building on May 6, 1918. The ceremonies, which attracted close to 1,000 spectators, were held at nearby Mount Zion Baptist Church because the library's basement auditorium could hold only two hundred people. Cansler and a committee composed of Reverend S. A. Downer, Dr. S. M. Clark, Cal F. Johnson, and William L. Gamble arranged the event, including a reception at the library after the program at the church. Speakers included former mayor Heiskell, who emphasized the importance of working hard, saving, and expressing thanks for help received.[84] Cansler opened his own speech with expressions of appreciation to Heiskell, Mayor McMillan, the commissioners, and the Lawson McGhee library trustees and its current head librarian, Mary Utopia Rothrock. (Rothrock, a native of Tennessee, had completed her degree at New York State Library School at Albany before joining the library in 1916, just in time to help plan and implement the branch for African Americans.)[85] Noting the progress that southern blacks had made in the decades since emancipation, Cansler said : "To those who have lived in that other world, who walked the streets of Knoxville when the statutes of our state provided a penalty for Negroes being found with books in their possession, how great must seem the transformation of things as they view our beautiful new Carnegie library with its ample and splendid equipment for the members of their race."[86]

Such a transformation took much longer in Atlanta and Greensboro, where, for years, local wrangling, ineptitude, and bad faith combined in varying degrees to delay the building of Carnegie libraries for African Americans. In 1904, Carnegie promised Atlanta a grant of $10,000 for a branch for African Americans, but the building did not open until 1921. Similarly, in 1905, he offered Greensboro $10,000 for a building for African American residents, but almost twenty years passed before the building was finally erected and opened. In Atlanta a deep and abiding racism underlay the long evolution of library services, while in Greensboro local rivalries within the black community and white foot dragging contributed to the long, slow creation of the library.

The development of public libraries in Atlanta followed the usual southern pattern. Carnegie first pledged $100,000 for the main library in 1899. Walter M. Kelley of the Carnegie Steel Company Limited (he had moved to Atlanta from Pittsburgh in about 1892) had written to Carnegie, describing the existing Young Men's Library Association over which Kelley presided. The association's modest building held 20,000 volumes and took in $2,200 in membership fees. The library had only about $30 a month for new acquisitions. Kelley wrote that northerners' donations for educational purposes had benefited black rather than white Atlantans; as a result, the city was home to Spelman Clark, and Atlanta universities as well as

Gammon Theological Seminary. Acknowledging that these institutions contributed to the uplift of the race and therefore benefited the south, Kelley mentioned them as evidence that "the Negro has received all the attention."[87] He did not ask for a building grant, only funding of $1,500 to $2,000 annually to expand his members-only library's work. Carnegie replied with a much more generous offer, throwing the Young Men's Library Association into a state of turmoil over the implications of the municipal library that Carnegie suggested. Specifically, association members felt that the time was not right "to inaugurate a system where all barriers are removed and the whites and blacks meet upon one common footing."[88] Kelley noted the presence in the city of 40,000 Negroes, and asserted that northerners, whose cities held many fewer blacks, could not fathom the necessity of maintaining the color line in the south, where "the negro is nearer the primitive state with all the crudities resulting therefrom." Therefore, he concluded, the library association would accept Carnegie's gift as long as it was understood that the result would be a library "free to the white public."[89]

Meanwhile, Atlanta attorney Hoke Smith, who had served as president of the association's board, wrote a letter to Carnegie, assuring him that the city would support an annual appropriation in exchange for a donation to construct a public library building.[90] In the spring of 1899, the city accepted Carnegie's gift; and by the end of the year, he had donated another $25,000 for the project. In 1901, he added $20,000 for furnishings and equipment. The building, on the corner of Forsyth and Church streets (the latter was renamed Carnegie Place), opened in 1902.[91]

As soon as the newspapers announced Carnegie's initial pledge, African Americans in Atlanta began lobbying for library services. Carrie E. Young, a former Atlanta University student employed by the *Appeal*, a black-owned newspaper, wrote to Carnegie to ask that he intervene "to help us in this mighty effort . . . to lift up others as we climb by having it so arranged that we too may come in for some share of your magnificent gift."[92] A few days later Carnegie received a letter from Reverend R. M. Cheeks, editor of the *Southern Christian Recorder*, asking him to indicate his intention that the new library should be open to black Atlantans.[93] A week later, J. W. E. Bowen of Gammon

Theological Seminary wrote yet another letter, asking Carnegie to let the city know that its African American residents should be allowed to use the collection "in a reading room for colored people" and to borrow books for home use.[94] The *Southern Christian Recorder* ran an editorial calling for Carnegie to issue a statement supporting library access for all Atlantans.[95]

W. E. B. Du Bois, who at the time was on the faculty of Atlanta University, led a group of African American men to a meeting with the library board of directors, where they presented their "Petition of Negroes to Use the Carnegie Library." The petition read, in part: "It seems hardly necessary in the twentieth century to argue before men like you on the necessity and propriety of placing the best means of human uplifting into the hands of the poorest, the lowest and the blackest." What right did the city have to tax African Americans for a municipal service it then denied them?, the petition asked. A library board member replied by asking the group to agree that allowing the races to mix in this new public space would spell doom for the library. One of the petitioners said that blacks did not insist on equal access to the same space but that they would appreciate an arrangement that provided some kind of library service to them. The board reiterated its exclusionary stance regarding the new library but promised to create an alternative for black Atlantans.[96]

In the summer of 1904, the president and secretary of the board wrote to Carnegie, asking for $10,000 for a separate building for African Americans. In the fall, Bertram replied that Carnegie would donate the sum requested.[97] But nothing happened. Members of the professional library world understood that the library board had been so annoyed by the petition for library access that it had deliberately blocked the building of the promised branch.[98] At midcentury, Du Bois—the smartest man in the room at the library board meeting—recalled that he had pointed out to board members the unfairness and absurdity of the situation: the books he had written were in a library that he himself was not allowed to enter. "Some of the trustees were quite angry. . . . The result of the visit was that we not only got no rights in the Central Library but for ten years no branch library was established."[99]

Contributing to the delay was a major race riot in 1906. That summer gubernatorial candidates Clark Howell and Hoke Smith used inflammatory racist rhetoric to appeal to white voters, and the local newspapers provided coverage of their political battle and published spurious accounts of black men accosting and raping white women. In September, Atlanta erupted as whites rampaged through the Brownsville neighborhood, destroying lives and property. During the five-day riot, white mobs attacked blacks wherever they could be found, killing and wounding many. It took years for black Atlanta to rebuild.[100]

In 1914, librarian Delia Sneed brought up the matter of the branch with Carnegie. Like most southern whites, she dropped polite terms of address when referring to black men. In her letter, she wrote that "the colored clergyman, Proctor," had told the library board president that he had secured a new Carnegie pledge of $25,000 for a black branch. In fact, Henry Hugh Proctor had a doctorate of divinity from Clark University and led the First Congregational Church. An ally of Booker T. Washington, he played a leadership role in creating Atlanta's interracial committee to restore order after the riot.[101]

Although white library board members apparently felt more kindly toward the smooth-talking pastor than they did toward the prickly academic, the project stalled when Sneed resigned as librarian. Her replacement was Tommie Dora Barker, who in April 1916 picked up the thread again, writing to Bertram that the city was thinking of acquiring a lot but wanted some assurance that the Carnegie offer still stood. Bertram's two-sentence reply offered nothing but did ask what the 1910 census showed Atlanta's black population to be. In an equally brief response, Barker informed Bertram that the figure was 51,902. At that, Bertram replied that a $10,000 building would be insufficient for 52,000 people and asked Barker to propose another amount. She countered with a suggestion from the board of trustees that $40,000 or $50,000 might be appropriate. Bertram rebuffed her, noting that the largest Negro buildings, those in Louisville, Nashville, and New Orleans, had cost only $25,000. Barker took the bait, asking for a $25,000 building. Bertram said in June 1916 he would bring the request to the Carnegie board for consideration but warned her that the board would not meet for a while. In September, Barker pressed her case, notifying Bertram that two black Atlantans had offered to buy a lot available through a forced sale and donate it to the city for a black branch library. He replied that a meeting would be held "shortly." Early in November, Barker finally received the formal Carnegie offer of $25,000, but it apparently came too late for the library to take advantage of the proffered gift of the lot.[102]

In February 1917, an editorial appeared in the *Atlanta Constitution* urging the city council to approve purchase of a lot so as not to lose the Carnegie pledge again. Agreeing with the general policy, the writer noted,

> The colored people should be excluded from the white people's library, but that does not mean that they should be excluded from library facilities altogether. . . . If Atlanta stops to reckon the cost to which it is put annually in the prosecution of negroes for crime which library facilities would have a great tendency to correct; to think of the battle against disease and insanitary [*sic*] conditions among the colored people which patronage of a library would have a great tendency to minimize, it would realize that a few hundred dollars spent in the necessary lot upon which a $25,000 library would immediately be constructed, would be a mighty profitable investment.[103]

Although the library board decided not to pursue construction during the Great War, Barker wrote to Bertram in late November 1918 to verify that the Carnegie offer was still good. Bertram replied in the affirmative, with the stipulation that the building be completed within four years of the offer made on November 9, 1916. On the first day of March 1920, the city issued a resolution stating its intention to acquire a lot and to appropriate $2,500 annually in exchange for the Carnegie building grant. In April, former librarian Delia Sneed Lee contacted Bertram to see if the Carnegie Corporation would increase its donation; and in June, Barker followed up with another attempt, writing to Bertram that the 1920 census would probably show an increase in the black population sufficient to justify the extra expense. The tone of Bertram's reply was impatient and discouraging. In late September, Barker sent Bertram the architect's plans for the Negro branch. Noting that the plans were for a $50,000 building, Barker assured Bertram that appropriations of $10,000 each from Atlanta and Fulton County and subscriptions totaling $5,000 would

supplement the Carnegie gift.[104] The foot dragging that had characterized the white role in the project had driven up the price, forcing
whites to invest more in the library than they would have needed to
fifteen years earlier.

The contract for the library construction project was finalized
just a few days before Bertram's deadline for completion, but he
said nothing about that, perhaps because only three weeks before
he had informed Barker that Carnegie would release no money for
the Atlanta project until after the $15,000 from the city and private
donors had been spent. Finally, in June 1921, Barker sent Bertram
photographs of the completed branch. He called it "a very dignified
and practical building." In charge of the branch was Alice Dugged
Cary, an influential educator and a leader in the Georgia Federation
of Colored Women's Clubs.[105]

Bertram's Atlanta letters convey weariness about the relentless
compliance with racial segregation and the complications it created.
Greensboro was one of the cases that had made him weary. In 1905,
a white businessman and library advocate, E. P. Wharton, wrote to
Carnegie to ask for $10,000 for a library building for Greensboro's
African Americans because the city's $30,000 Carnegie building
was open only to whites.[106] Bertram's response implied that, had he
known the building would be for the use of only 7,500 white people,
the grant would have been for a lesser amount. He asked whether
the city could afford to continue appropriating $3,000 a year for
that building and another $1,000 for the new building.[107] Wharton
assured Bertram that the city would appropriate the requisite 10
percent of the Carnegie gift for the colored library and added that
the president of the local Agricultural and Mechanical College for
the Colored Race would appropriate another $500 annually from its
state fund to help maintain the library so that its students could use
it. He also reported that some Greensboro citizens had raised $3,000
for books and furniture and additional funds for a lot.[108] In November, Carnegie promised the requested amount, as long as the city
appropriated $1,000 annually and provided the site.[109] Apparently
city officials saw the college's interest as a way to cut its own commitment to the project. A few days after Wharton received Carnegie's
pledge, he followed up with a query regarding whether it would be

acceptable to Carnegie if the city appropriated $500 and the college made up the difference.[110] Bertram's answer was no; Carnegie expected the city to be solely responsible for the required 10 percent of the building grant.[111]

A decade elapsed before the city commission appointed a board of trustees for the proposed library and charged them with the task of finding a site. In their search for an accessible location, they received and rejected free offers from the Agricultural and Mechanical College and from Saint Matthew's United Methodist Church in the black community of Warnersville. Three of the six trustees were members of the Methodist Episcopal Church, and they became chairman, secretary, and treasurer of the board, to the chagrin of the other three members. After Bennett College, affiliated with the Methodist Episcopal Church, offered a free site on its campus, Mayor T. J. Murphy wrote to ask whether the $10,000 pledge still stood.[112] He said that blacks in Greensboro had acquired a site and that the city would comply with the maintenance requirement.[113] Bertram dryly noted that a promised building grant that had not been acted on for ten years could be assumed to have lapsed, but he eventually did renew the pledge.[114]

The renewal of the project brought renewed conflict as some African American churches and individuals mobilized against the Bennett College location. They expressed concern that the college campus was not conveniently located for the majority of the town's black residents. They also predicted that putting a public library on private land held by the Methodists would discourage not only city residents but students at the Lutheran College and A&M from using it. Two city council members took the side of Bennett College, but others advocated for situating the library on East Market Street, located in the heart of the city's African American neighborhood and one of the few such streets that was paved and thus likely to have streetcar service in the future.[115] Dozens of black clubwomen and business and professional men signed a petition against the site on the Bennett College grounds, declaring "that the location of a public institution on private property will tend to make said institution a private one."[116]

As in Atlanta, the war delayed library progress in Greensboro. Between 1915 and 1920, architect F. A. Weston drafted plans, sent them to Bertram, received criticism and suggestions, and repeated the process. In the spring of 1920, Bertram notified the mayor via registered letter that the Carnegie Corporation would consider the building grant to have expired unless construction were about to begin. The mayor blamed the delay on the high cost of building materials during and after the war and asked for a one-year extension on the pledge.[117]

A couple of weeks later, on the first of June, Bertram sent Mayor Stafford another registered letter, this time rebuffing the request for an extension.[118] The Carnegie Corporation board did not meet during the summer, but late in September Bertram sent Stafford another registered letter, giving Greensboro a last chance before officially withdrawing Carnegie support for the library project.[119] But Bertram seemed reluctant to abandon Greensboro's African Americans, who had raised $1,000 to supplement what had become an inadequate building grant.[120] He wrote to Robert R. Moton, who had become principal of Tuskegee Institute after Washington's death, and to James Dillard, president of the Slater Fund, asking each to visit him; although he did not name Greensboro, he indicated that there was a situation in North Carolina about which he needed their advice.[121]

Dillard met with Bertram and then traveled to Greensboro, where he met with the mayor and the superintendent of education. He asked Bertram if the corporation might increase the grant to $15,000, and he assured Bertram that the argument over the library's location had been settled and that one of the winners of that argument had become chairman of the library board. (Dillard didn't name him or have time to meet with him but said he was "the principal of the main city colored school.")[122] Not surprisingly, Bertram replied quickly that an increase was unthinkable: all that would save the project was Dillard's endorsement and the $1,000 supplement provided by Greensboro's African American citizens. Dillard replied that he would write to the mayor to move quickly to save the pledge. But two months later, neither Dillard nor Bertram had heard from anyone in Greensboro.[123] Dillard concluded cryptically, "I fear there were two lions in the way. When opportunity offers I would be glad to tell you briefly more about it."[124]

On April 21, 1921, Bertram sent a registered letter to the city rescinding the Carnegie pledge of $10,000 for a library for Greensboro's African Americans.[125] The mayor signed for it but did not reply. He apparently also did not inform the chairman of the proposed library board, W. B. Windsor, of the loss of the money, for in January 1922, Windsor wrote to Bertram that a contract had just been signed with the architect to build the $11,000 building. Bertram responded by sending Windsor a copy of the letter from the year before, withdrawing the offer of $10,000.[126]

Calling news of the revocation a "distinct surprise," Windsor wondered whether the Carnegie Corporation had been as misinformed about events as he and his board members had been. He outlined for Bertram the history of the project. The local board of trustees had arranged for the Bennett lot to be deeded to the city on April 20, 1916. The city had passed a resolution on June 21, 1916, to appropriate $1,000 annually for maintenance of the proposed library for African Americans. The city commissioners had then selected Weston as the project architect, and Windsor began consulting with him on the design of the building. Weston had also received Bertram's criticisms of his design and had made modifications, assuring Windsor that all was well. The war and its aftermath interrupted the project; but when prices returned to normal, Windsor and his board had secured a reasonable bid for construction and had submitted it to Bertram. Windsor offered to travel to New York to talk with Bertram about the situation.[127]

Also registering surprise at the rescission was hardware store owner and chairman of the county board of education, Charles H. Ireland. Writing on his company letterhead, he told Bertram that Windsor had showed him his letter, which Ireland attested was accurate. He, too, pleaded for a reinstatement of the pledge. Asserting that Greensboro had sent a disproportionately high number of men to war, making construction work impossible, Ireland told Bertram, "It doesn't look right that these people should be made to suffer from conditions over which they have had no control."[128] In yet another letter from Greensboro, this time from I. Garland Penn on letterhead of the Board of Education for Negroes of the Methodist Episcopal Church, Bertram read that the war had caused the delay in using the Carnegie grant. Penn pointed out that his board had given land on the Bennett College campus, which he described as centrally and conveniently located, and had raised $1,750 in donations to cover the shortfall caused by postwar construction prices. He, too, expressed surprise that the corporation had withdrawn its offer and pleaded for reconsideration.[129]

Bertram replied to Penn. Noting that the Greensboro case had caused him more trouble than any of the other Carnegie library projects, Bertram suggested that, because Penn knew so little of what had transpired, he might want to read the entire sixty-six-item file in Bertram's office and contact James Dillard for verification. Penn took him up on both suggestions.[130] After Penn returned from perusing the files in New York, he told Ireland that Bertram might be willing to ask the Carnegie board to consider Greensboro one more time, but only if local library advocates took the initiative. Ireland, Wharton, Weston, former mayor Stafford, and Dr. Frank Trigg, president of Bennett College, wrote to Bertram to assure him they would do everything necessary to convince the board to grant the donation for the building: "As interested citizens in the welfare of our negro citizens we want to give our unqualified approval of this movement and to assure you of our interest in the matter."[131] Bertram's two-sentence reply promised nothing.[132]

Within a week, Windsor, writing on the letterhead of the Greensboro Public Schools for the Negro Race, sent Bertram a packet of materials, including a new resolution by the members of the city commission committing to the 10 percent annual appropriation for maintenance, a bid of $11,000 for construction of the building, a bid for installation of a heating system, and a statement from the city promising to devote $250 toward construction. He sent Weston's plans separately.[133] Bertram asked for a map of the site, saying he had heard criticism of the Bennett location, and Windsor assured him that the proposed site was quite desirable and that the streets around it were being paved.[134]

Meanwhile, Penn sent a somewhat defensive letter to Bertram, acknowledging that some of Greensboro's African American residents were against the selected site but dismissing them as obstructionists and naysayers. He assured Bertram that the college had deeded the property to the city in 1916 so that the public library would be on publicly held ground. "If, however, after this explanation, which can be corroborated by leading White and Colored citizens in Greensboro, you do not regard the library as a public library for the Colored people, simply because of the fact that our school donated the ground and contributed financially to its erection, the matter is a closed question so far as we are concerned, for we will be powerless to do anything else toward helping the matter."[135] Penn sent a copy to Ireland, who attested to its accuracy in his own letter to Bertram but added his own opinion that blacks in Greensboro who were not affiliated with Bennett College would never have mustered the wherewithal to secure a library for themselves. In reply to both, Bertram asked for a copy of the deed.Within a few weeks, he had all the documentation he needed, and the construction project got underway. In October 1924, the library building opened with about 150 books and a zealous librarian, Martha Sebastian, who spent the next two decades increasing the size of the collection and the rate of its circulation in Greensboro's black community.[136]

CHAPTER 3

Solidifying Segregation

The death of Booker T. Washington in 1915 and the cessation of Carnegie Corporation library building grants in 1917 did not slow the establishment of libraries for African Americans in the 1920s. Throughout the decade, the creation of libraries for blacks in the south was an urban phenomenon as African Americans moved from the countryside into towns and cities. Between 1910 and 1930, the number of African Americans living in rural areas decreased by 10 to 13 percent in Alabama, Georgia, Kentucky, Louisiana, North Carolina, Oklahoma, and Texas.[1] By the middle of the decade about 10 percent of the southern black population had access to public libraries, and a 1929 survey indicated that thirty-one southern public libraries offered segregated branches.[2] The founding of public libraries was a local grassroots effort abetted by, but not dependent on, internationally known leaders such as Washington and Carnegie. Even during the Washington-Carnegie era, whites and blacks had created collections for African Americans without recourse to Washington's influence or Carnegie's money; and in the 1920s, they had no other option but to look to local philanthropists and community leaders.

As Carnegie funding was winding down, a new philanthropic organization, the Rosenwald Foundation (also known as the Rosenwald Fund) was being established in Chicago. Founded by Sears, Roebuck president Julius Rosenwald, it focused on African American health and education initiatives. In 1927, Edwin Embree left the Rockefeller Foundation to join Rosenwald. The Rosenwald Foundation's library program began with Embree's tenure. In 1948, when the foundation intentionally spent its last dollar and ceased to function.

Like Carnegie, Rosenwald insisted on commitments of resources from recipient communities. For example, counties hosting Rosenwald library demonstration projects had to supply space and staff and sustain the effort when foundation money ceased after five years of support. Unlike the Carnegie Corporation, however, which had routinely provided building grants for libraries that refused service to African Americans, the Rosenwald Foundation officially required demonstration libraries to provide equitable service to all county residents.[3] The decade of the 1920s began with the destruction of a black library in Tulsa, Oklahoma, and ended with the creation of new city-funded library services in that city as well as new Rosenwald-funded countywide library demonstration projects in the southeast.

Violence against African Americans was a mainstay of the Jim Crow era. In Atlanta, some whites and blacks had begun working across racial barriers after the city's 1906 riot, and some white southern universities had sponsored activities and promoted research on African American life and work. But their efforts were neither broad nor deep enough to squelch the rise of racial tensions. In 1919, the peak year of the violence, some twenty-five race riots occurred, most of them in the south. One response was the founding of the Commission on Interracial Cooperation in Atlanta in 1919. Within a few years, about eight hundred interracial committees were functioning across the south, and they would continue to do so for the next two decades. White participants saw themselves as offering help and understanding, with the goal of preserving racial segregation while ameliorating some of its inconveniences and insults.[4] But such efforts could not prevent the 1921 riot in Tulsa.

In the first decade of the twentieth century, Tulsa (located in Oklahoma Territory until that region achieved statehood in 1907) became an oil-driven boomtown whose population grew from 1,390 in 1900 to 72,075 in 1920.[5] Members of various women's clubs in Tulsa had attempted to interest Carnegie in funding a library building for the city, but there was no progress on that front until the intervention of Joseph G. Masters, the superintendent of schools and a member of the Commercial Club's library committee. In late November 1909, he wrote to Carnegie asking for a building grant and reporting that the city would appropriate funds to maintain a Carnegie library. At the same time, a local clubwoman whose husband was a wealthy oilman traveled to New York to pay a visit to the Carnegie offices. By the end of the month, Bertram had responded to Masters with an offer of $35,000 for a building if the city would promise an annual appropriation of $3,500. But it was not until 1916 that the Carnegie building was completed. By that point the corporation's pledge had increased to $55,000, in recognition of the city's rapid growth and thanks to the prompting of First National Bank of Tulsa president Grant R. McCullough, who had visited Carnegie in New York in 1915.[6]

In the interim, beginning in 1912, the Tulsa Library Association installed a public library in two rooms of the county courthouse. Access to its largely donated collection was supported by a membership fee of $1 for each library user and a $100 monthly appropriation from the city. In December of that year, the association's board of trustees hired Alma Reid McGlenn, an Ohio native and trained librarian who had headed the South Side Branch of the Carnegie Library of Pittsburgh, to run Tulsa's library. Known as a "strict disciplinarian" and "a lady of broad and liberal culture," she shaped users' library experiences until she retired in 1939. Even as she encouraged children to use the library, she steered them gently away from adult to juvenile material and kept what she considered "daring fiction" behind the desk.[7]

Most blacks in Tulsa lived in Greenwood, an area along and around Greenwood Avenue, where by 1920 about 1,100 African Americans resided. They owned and supported numerous businesses, a hospital, an elementary and a secondary school, two theaters, churches, and other neighborhood establishments.[8] Among these community members was A. J. Smitherman, who had begun publishing a weekly newspaper in Muskogee but had since relocated to Tulsa, where he published the *Tulsa Star* from his newspaper office at 501 North Greenwood. He was also active in the local Democratic party at a time when most African Americans were Republicans loyal to the party of Lincoln.[9]

Smitherman helped establish a public library in Greenwood, which included a reading room and space for meetings.[10] In the summer of 1913, Levada Williams began to serve as the librarian but left the post in less than a month.[11] Despite this precarious beginning, some community members took a strong interest in preserving the fledgling institution. For instance, as a fundraising event for the library, a Professor Woods gave a lecture there in the fall of 1913.[12] Then early in February 1914, a Professor Hughes gave a talk about securing the funds the city had voted to supply in support of the library, and J. B. Stradford and attorneys with the last names of Martin and Jones participated in the discussion.[13] For the next two weeks, the *Tulsa Star* ran a paragraph noting that many people were unaware of the existence of the library and asserting that, when they discovered it, they enjoyed reading books, periodicals, and newspapers there.[14]

On February 21, 1914, the *Tulsa Star*'s front page announced that meeting participants had elected a board of managers to set policy and oversee the library. J. B. Stradford was elected president and treasurer and a Miss V. L. Johnson was secretary. Additional board members included A. J. Smitherman and nine other men and women. They announced their intention to hold a fundraising campaign and urged everyone to donate.[15] By that summer the library had moved into space at the back of the sixty-six-room Stradford Hotel at 301 North Greenwood, and Smitherman himself was now the librarian, once again using the newspaper to publicize the collection.[16]

The front page of the *Tulsa Star* included repeated notices from the librarian asking that overdue books be returned: the collection was small and keeping books for longer than the two-week loan period meant that others in the community could not use them.[17] Smitherman placed a series of ads requesting the donation of books, including a Bible, and reported that the facility was "a very popular place for the young people" and that ladies and teachers also used the library.[18] He reported on other cities where African Americans had access to library collections and services. In September 1913, he ran a brief story about the cornerstone-laying ceremony marking the establishment of Louisville's second branch library for African Americans.[19] He printed a letter from Stradford reporting on his tour of Kansas City in May 1915 and the existence of a city-funded public library in a building on Garrison Square in an African American neighborhood. Smitherman also lamented the lack of city funding for the library he had helped create and maintain in Greenwood.[20]

In the fall of 1915, Smitherman, in a spirit of competitive civic pride, ran a front-page story about the public library in Muskogee that served African Americans. That library had received book donations from libraries in New York, Saint Louis, and Bloomington, Indiana, and now planned to ask the city and the Carnegie Corporation for funds to construct a building.[21] By 1920, the Greenwood library had moved into a building that Smitherman owned at Archer and Frankfort streets, where he continued to serve as librarian, with his wife working as assistant librarian. They oversaw numerous activities and volunteers, including Mrs. F. R. Williams, who organized a children's "Sunshine Club," whose members met at the library every Sunday afternoon for a story hour followed by a short horizon-broadening ride in Mrs. Williams's car.[22]

In his newspaper Smitherman reported that he and his wife had installed a heating stove and that he had been pointing out to city officials how inferior the facility was compared to the whites-only library in downtown Tulsa. The Smithermans hoped the city would provide funds sufficient to pay the utility bills and build a collection of works by African American authors.[23] Instead, the public library that Democrat Smitherman had helped to found struggled after Republican T. D. Evans took office as mayor in 1920 and discontinued the city's small appropriation for the Greenwood facility.[24]

In the summer of 1920, Tulsa's head librarian, Alma Reid McGlenn, wrote to Carnegie's secretary, Bertram, telling him, "We are organizing work among our colored population." She thus ignored African Americans' efforts to create their own library in an environment of overwhelming white hostility. McGlenn continued, "[The people] number ten thousand, the library is in temporary quarters, [a] small building unsuited to needs, located on city grounds, is centrally located and available for a permanent building. We are asking for an appropriation of twenty-eight hundred maintenance fund for the coming fiscal year. Is there any possibility of our getting a small appropriation from the Carnegie Corporation to build a building for these people?" Bertram replied:

I regret . . . that the condition of matters in regard to the keeping of pledges—pledges given to secure such library buildings as this on behalf of which you write—was found to be so unsatisfactory that the Board of Trustees of the Corporation were led to suspend for the present the giving of such library buildings in the State of Oklahoma. In any event, the Trustees of the Corporation some time ago decided that no applications for the erection of library buildings would be considered while the abnormal conditions prevail which have been created by war."[25]

This was the lesson the Carnegie Corporation had learned from Atlanta, where white resistance to black advancement took many forms, including delaying tactics that wasted Bertram's time and thwarted local African Americans' efforts.

At the end of May 1921, a white female elevator operator in downtown Tulsa accused a young black man named Dick Rowland of accosting her on the elevator. He was arrested. Although the operator later declined to press charges, the city's white-owned newspaper announced that Rowland would be lynched. On the night of May 31, between 1,500 and 2,000 whites, many of them armed, went to the courthouse where he was held. African American businessman J. B. Stradford and newspaper owner A. J. Smitherman enlisted other black men to intervene. Gathering their guns, they drove to the courthouse, where they did prevent the lynching. Nonetheless, a scuffle at the scene quickly erupted into a gun battle that moved into the Greenwood neighborhood.[26]

The next morning, the National Guard arrived to restore order. Marauding whites had looted Greenwood homes and office buildings and set the district on fire, destroying thirty-six square blocks of homes, churches, and other structures. Thousands of African Americans were rounded up and taken to holding areas while whites stole their property and burned their undefended homes. The mob torched Smitherman's home and his newspaper operation, valued at $40,000 in the 1920s.[27] Also destroyed were Stradford's hotel, home, and other holdings, which were valued at close to $125,000. Their beloved library, its collection, and any logs of registered borrowers, accessions, or circulation were also destroyed. Whites accused Stradford and Smitherman of inciting the riot, and both fled the state, never to return. Yet later developments and investigations revealed that city officials and a white business cabal had been looking for ways to confiscate land in the Greenwood area, which they wanted to turn into an industrial complex because of its proximity to the railroad. They had shaped the white reaction to the Rowland incident to suit their own purposes.[28] Although the library seems to have been a victim of collateral damage rather than a deliberate target, its destruction represents the extreme end of a continuum. In the Jim Crow era, a few African American libraries failed through neglect or outright destruction, a few achieved modest success, but most were engaged in continuing struggles for sustainability. As black residents were clearing the debris and erecting tents and wooden huts on the ashes of Greenwood, McGlenn wrote to Bertram: "Our negro branch library building, books and equipment was [sic] burned during our race riot. If we were to make formal application would we stand any chance of being granted a small appropriation to help rebuild? any help you could give would be appreciated." Later that fall, she tried again, writing to Bertram "at the request of a negro society." He answered with a reiteration that the Carnegie Corporation had ceased to give grants for library buildings.[29]

Historians of the Tulsa riot have documented the city's almost total abandonment of Greenwood. The district's residents did not receive insurance payments for their losses because insurers claimed that their policies specified riot exclusions. The Red Cross did offer help in the form of food, clothing, and some shelter; and the organization collaborated with the National Guard to provide medical care for the wounded. But for the most part, the revitalization of Greenwood depended on the hard work and sacrifice of residents who had lost almost everything.[30]

Nonetheless, historians have not noticed an important exception to official white Tulsa's abandonment of Greenwood: the public library and its growing determination to extend its collections and services throughout the city. In 1923, McGlenn opened Tulsa Public Library's first deposit station, located in a school and intended to serve children who found it difficult to go to the central library. Soon the Celia Clinton, Lowell, Kendall, Jefferson, Emerson, Whittier, Lee, and Mark Twain elementary schools all had public library stations. As part of this extension effort, the library rented a building in Green-wood, establishing a branch with five hundred volumes and hiring Luenda Meadows as librarian (fig. 3). Children were heavier users of the collection than adults were. In 1930, 20,000 of the library system's 45,000 registered borrowers were children, and the librarian asserted that the economic depression had resulted in more visits to the library and more worn-out books. Later that year, the city voted for a $75,000 bond issue that resulted in the construction of four branch buildings designed by architect Donald McCormick. One was for Greenwood, and it was constructed at the corner of Greenwood Avenue and Oklahoma Street on a site it shared with the George Washington Carver School. By 1938, Christine Carey was the branch librarian, and the facility continued to serve the neighborhood until 1967, when it closed and the new Seminole Hills Branch opened.[31]

Flush from the oil boom of the 1920s, other towns in Oklahoma also began offering library services to African Americans. The state's oldest library for blacks, the Excelsior in Guthrie, continued to operate even during an era when the chief librarian and board members of the town's whites-only Carnegie library were rumored to belong to the Ku Klux Klan. A complaint was lodged when they expressed a desire to remove Catholic material from the main library's shelves. (In the 1920s it was common for Klan members in southwestern states to be anti-Catholic and anti-Semitic as well as anti-black.)[32]

Okmulgee, about forty miles south of Tulsa, had fewer than 2,500 residents in 1907 when Oklahoma became a state; but by the early 1920s it had five oil refineries and a population of 35,000. A city bond issue for a public library system included a main building for whites and a branch for blacks, and in 1923 Okmulgee constructed the Dunbar Branch, the state's first and largest purpose-built library—and, at $18,000, the most expensive—for African Americans. By the late 1930s, when the city's population had dropped by half, Maude J. Carter was in charge of the Dunbar Branch and its 5,000 or so volumes. The circulation rate was about 32,000 among a black population of about 3,600.[33]

Muskogee had a library that African American women had created in 1914. It functioned for a time as a branch of the city's library system; but in 1928, when it was operating under the auspices of the

Figure 3. Beginning in 1923, the Tulsa Public Library provided African Americans with a five-hundred-volume collection in a rented storefront. The Greenwood Branch building opened in the early 1930s. Courtesy of the Oklahoma Department of Libraries.

Frances Harper Club, a fire damaged the building and the collection. The city repaired it and reopened it as a branch.[34] Along with the Excelsior in Guthrie and a small library in the all-black town of Boley, the branches in Tulsa, Oklahoma City, Okmulgee, and Muskogee were the only ones occupying their own buildings in the 1920s. Other cities provided library collections for their black residents but housed them in public schools, where students rather than adults were more likely to use them. In 1922, the Booker T. Washington School in Enid began serving as the site of a branch (open during school hours) of the Garfield County Library, with the county board of education providing the books. At about the same time, the Booker T. Washington High School library in Sapulpa opened year round as a public library branch under the direction of Mrs. N. C. Day. About 70 percent of its users were children. In 1926, the Lincoln School in Chickasha provided a library that functioned as a branch. Even during summer vacation, when a dedicated teacher, Grace Dorsey, kept it open, most of the users were children. A year or so later, the Ponca City Library established a branch collection at the Attucks School. In 1929, the Lincoln Elementary School in Tahlequah became a city branch with 219 volumes.[35]

The Carnegie library in Oklahoma City followed a familiar path to opening. Members of the Philomathea Club, a women's organization with a member serving as president of the Federation of Women's Clubs of Oklahoma, began in 1898 to organize a public library. It soon had a pledge of $25,000 from Carnegie, and the building opened in 1901. Only eight years later, Carnegie gave another $35,000 for a building addition. Mabel Peacock became head librarian in 1919 and served into the 1930s.

In 1921, soon after an African American Episcopalian priest, Father Kilpatrick, attempted to use the library, the city established the separate Dunbar Branch in rented quarters, which were located in what the Oklahoma Library Commission called "a brick building in the business district." The building apparently had been a pool hall, and replacing that form of amusement with a presumably more wholesome and certainly more literary one reinforced white middle-class perspectives about proper forms of recreation.[36] Seven-year-old Ralph Ellison, who would later write the iconic novel *Invisible*

Man, competed with friends to see who could read through the meager collection fastest. In a memoir, he recalled the thrown-together library as "something of a literary chaos. But how fortunate for a boy who loved to read!"[37] Librarians Lillian Youngblood and Alphenia Young organized and staffed the facility, and in 1925 city librarian Mabel Peacock oversaw the construction of two branch buildings. The Dunbar Branch moved into one of them in 1926. The city had appropriated $5,000 for the building, and African American women's clubs had donated a lot on Fourth Street. By 1937, the new library had about 3,600 volumes for approximately 15,000 black residents and a circulation rate of 22,256.[38]

Throughout the south, towns and cities were experiencing growth as rural people moved into them, and many libraries began offering segregated collections and services in the relatively prosperous years after the end of World War I and before the economic disaster of the 1930s. The models for library segregation had been established in the prior two decades, and this approach expanded during the 1920s. The impetus was more than an increase in tax revenue or the growing number of African Americans in southern municipalities. Civil rights violations grew notably during this decade, and they included the continuing assault on voting rights and the further hardening of residential segregation. In Texas, the 1919 law that enabled the establishment of county libraries included a racial segregation provision. As head of the Gainesville Public Library, Lillian Gunter had been behind the creation of the law because she thought it was essential that libraries distribute more reading material in rural areas. When county commissioners previously had objected to a designated Negro reading room in her town library's basement, she realized that racial segregation was an integral aspect of library "progress." The county library law advanced reading at the expense of social justice.[39]

In the middle of the decade, the American Library Association sent questionnaires about "Negro library service" to thirty-four public libraries in the south, midwest, and northeast. A document summarizing their replies shows that Durham, North Carolina, circulated the most books to the smallest number of registered borrowers and that Louisville, Kentucky, with its two well-known branches, had more than 7,100 registered borrowers and an annual book circulation

of more than 126,000 among the city's African American population (table 1).[40] In the early 1920s, the library association had been
involved in the creation of the Hampton Institute Library School,
which offered the only degree program in the south open to African
Americans, and at least some of the motivation behind the survey was
to gauge the willingness of southern white librarians to support the
effort by hiring the graduates to staff their Negro branches.[41]

TABLE 1. BLACK LIBRARY HOLDINGS, BORROWERS, AND CIRCULATION BY CITY, 1925

CITY	NUMBER OF VOLUMES	REGISTERED BORROWERS	CIRCULATION, LATEST YEAR
Atlanta, GA	n/a	5,834	18,091
Birmingham, AL	5,948	6,425	48,139
Chattanooga, TN	n/a	1,691	16,984
Durham, NC	4,428	680	9,894
Evansville, IN	n/a	1,035	10,114
Greenville, SC	n/a	600	*
Houston, TX	n/a	2,831	18,000
Jacksonville, FL	n/a	770	7,298**
Knoxville, TN	n/a	2,954	8,947
Little Rock, AR	2,000	N/a	***
Louisville, KY (2 branches)	n/a	7,141	126,922
New Orleans, LA	n/a	2,979	31,299
Norfolk, VA	n/a	1,450	11,998
Savannah, GA	n/a	822	3,386
Tampa, FL	n/a	825	5,171

Source: American Library Association, *Negro Library Service* [Chicago, 1925].
*"Annual per capita circulation estimated at 0.6 [of estimated 10,000 black population]
as compared with 4 per capita for white population." (Without the number of volumes
available to each group, this comparison is meaningless and possibly even intentionally
misleading.)
**"Average circulation for 19 years ending 1924."
*** Circulation reported as "500 volumes per week average," but the number of weeks the
library was open each year is unstated.

In her survey response, Lela May Chapman, vice-director of the
Birmingham Public Library in Alabama, said that she was happy with
the head of her black branch, whom she described as the "wife of a
prominent insurance man, graduate of Talladega College, with no

previous library training or experience but industrious, interested, and tactful." But she worried that there was no ready pool of potential replacements. Expressing her belief that African Americans were better able to serve other African Americans, Chapman wrote that the white librarian at Talladega College was considering offering a training course for black women interested in running school libraries and asserted that Birmingham would provide partial payment to a staff member who took a leave to study at a library school. Nora Crimmins in Chattanooga, Tennessee, also thought her library would provide leave and pay for a staff member to attend library school courses, as it had previously done for the librarian who had received apprenticeship training from Thomas Blue and Rachel Harris in Louisville. Librarians at the Jacksonville (Florida), Greenville (North Carolina) and Norfolk (Virginia) libraries were also willing to allow a staff member to take a leave of absence to attend school.[42]

But some respondents were more negative. Henry Gill of New Orleans indicated that his library could not afford to send staff to a library school and that their low salaries meant that they would not be able to afford such training themselves. Some respondents said that black librarians and assistant librarians had received training in the main library, apparently alongside whites, who were receiving apprenticeship-style practical instruction instead of attending library school. Mary D. Pretlow, head of the Norfolk Public Library reported that the librarian and the assistant librarian at the Blyden Branch for African Americans, both of whom were college graduates, had received training at the main library. But their training was not as thorough as that provided to whites because they were not allowed to work at the public service desks, where they would have encountered white library users. Some respondents wrote that cataloging, classification, and acquisition were conducted at the main library, suggesting that it was possible to get by with a branch head who had no grasp of the theory or practice behind library operations.[43]

Several of the librarians answering the questionnaire asserted that a library school for African Americans was needed, but Mary Rothrock of the Lawson McGhee Library in Knoxville was wary. Any library school for Negroes would have to prepare them for the south's dismal financial support for public libraries. It was hard enough for northern-trained white librarians to adjust to southern realities, she said. But it was impossible for her to imagine a black librarian trained in the north, on the assumption that she would work in the north, who would be able to accept the working conditions at a segregated southern library. If one of the functions of professional education was to socialize students into the customs and practices of the profession, then a southern library school for blacks would need to manage the expectations of students who, as public librarians, could expect to work part time at low pay with little support for collection building or outreach.[44]

According to survey data, most white library directors were content with the performance of their African American staff. Little Rock Public Library director Beatrice Prall wrote that the librarian who ran the segregated branch, located in a rented room in a building in the African American section of town, was a "colored woman of about 40 years of age, well liked and trusted, not of the 'pushy' variety." Joseph Marron, a librarian in Jacksonville, described the black woman who oversaw the separate room for African Americans at the main library as a former teacher who was "very ambitious and resourceful." From New Orleans, Gill reported that his African American staff members were "college graduates from two of the best Negro schools . . . chosen on recommendation . . . by presidents of their schools." In Greenville, the librarian was a "colored college graduate and ordained Baptist preacher." From Chattanooga, where the branch was located at Howard High School, Nora Crimmins described the branch librarian as a former teacher who was "amiable, pleasing in manner and a good executive" but whose night assistant knew more about literature. Rothrock wrote that her branch librarian in Knoxville was a college-educated man previously employed at the YMCA in Cincinnati and that his assistant was "good, faithful, simple, lacking in initiative, [and] incapable of further development in library work."[45]

In addition to training almost forty of the head librarians of blacks-only branches, Louisville's Blue and Harris involved themselves in the establishment of library services for African Americans elsewhere in the south. For example, in 1914, Harris gave an address at the opening ceremony for the Cherry Street branch of the Evansville Public

Library in Indiana. In a speech later published as "The Advantages of Colored Branch Libraries," she underscored the importance of cooperation between the white library's administration and staff and that of the black branch. Harris also served as a consultant to black librarians hired to run new branches, including those in Georgetown, Kentucky, and Roanoke and Lynchburg, Virginia.[46]

In 1913, Chattanooga opened a branch library in the Howard School, beginning with a collection of about three hundred books. When the school and the branch moved into a new building in the early 1920s, the Chattanooga Public Library directors voted to acquire 4,000 new books for the collection. Blue spoke at the opening ceremony on October 11, 1922. Apparently one of his former trainees (presumably Kate Brown) was now the branch librarian.[47] In a fourteen-paragraph address, Blue devoted three paragraphs to congratulating and praising whites for their generosity in providing library services for African Americans. He recognized the "spirit of fairness, the spirit of liberality, the spirit of 'charity for all'" that animated library and school officials in Chattanooga and noted the same qualities in Louisville's white officials. Mentioning that he had attended the most recent annual meeting of the American Library Association in Detroit, he reported on the Work with Negroes Round Table session, where, he acknowledged, southern whites had not all agreed on how to provide library services to African Americans. But, he noted, there was consensus that black southerners deserved library services and that white library officials were obligated to provide them. Blue also emphasized that the library could open the doors of opportunity, but only if African Americans chose to visit it, consult its reference collection for information, and check out its books for education and recreation.[48]

While other major southern cities were constructing buildings and creating collections and services for both white and black readers, library advocates in Richmond, Virginia, were engaged in a long-term campaign to convince their fellow taxpayers and the city council to support a public library. Finally, in 1922, the success of a $200,000 bond issue led to the opening of a main public library in 1924. In the following year, the Richmond Public Library's Negro branch opened at the Phillis Wheatley YWCA, which provided two rooms at no cost to the library or the city. Its name, the Rosa D. Bowser Branch Library, honored a revered teacher and clubwoman.[49]

As the twenties waned, the Rosenwald Foundation became a new source of philanthropic support for African American libraries. Then, after the 1929 stock market crash diminished the foundation's available funds, the federal government stepped in, offering work-relief programs for women that began to include book repair and library service projects. These two funding sources coincided with the profession's increasing interest in establishing county libraries that would extend collections and services beyond municipal boundaries. An early example was the creation of the Harris County Library in the early 1920s, which extended the service area beyond that of the thriving Houston Public Library.

County libraries seemed to hold special promise in the south, which remained largely agrarian and rural until after World War II. Rural areas generally had much less access to reading material than urban areas did; and because more African Americans lived in the country, their lack of access was pronounced. County libraries were an opportunity to reach out to the least served: African Americans living in rural poverty. The provision of federal dollars might seem to suggest the possibility that local bigotry could be transcended. But as Louise Robbins reported in her study of Rosenwald and Works Progress Administration library projects in Oklahoma, the WPA's reliance on local whites precluded the potential for change. Only the Rosenwald projects, with their determination to serve African Americans, attempted to shift the racialism of the library landscape.[50] Influenced by Washington's work with the Tuskegee Institute, Rosenwald decided to donate a large percentage of his fortune to building schools for African Americans in the south. He eventually became aware that his schools needed libraries and that, more broadly, the rural counties where the majority of his schools functioned needed collections and services.[51]

Julius Rosenwald was born in Springfield, Illinois, in 1862. After a brief but unsuccessful foray into the retail clothing and tailoring industry in New York City, he moved to Chicago, where he created a successful clothing factory that began to sell to the newly founded mail-order firm Sears, Roebuck. Rosenwald became a major stockholder in Sears and in 1896 became an employee of the company, ascending in 1908 to president and chief executive officer. His net worth by the mid-1920s was approximately $150 million.

In Chicago he belonged to Temple Sinai, where Rabbi Emil Hirsh led a Reform Judaism congregation interested in ethical living and charitable giving.[52] Rosenwald had earned his millions a bit later than contemporaries such as John D. Rockefeller, who in 1902 had created the philanthropic General Education Board with the purpose of promoting "education within the United States without distinction of race, sex or creed."[53] This model influenced Rosenwald, as did another philanthropic organization, the Anna T. Jeanes Foundation. With the help of Booker T. Washington, Philadelphia Quaker Anna Jeanes had established the Rural Negro School Fund in 1907. The fund hired African Americans, mostly women teachers, to serve as consultants to small black schools throughout the south. Known as Jeanes teachers or Jeanes supervisors, they traveled countless miles, visiting schools, advising teachers on their classroom methods, delivering books to tiny library alcoves in one-room schoolhouses, and generally making the most of the meager educational resources available to southern blacks in the first half of the twentieth century. Jeanes teachers also worked across the color line to engage officials in state departments of education, particularly those with responsibility for rural schools. As their reputation for competence and commitment grew, Jeanes teachers came to act as supervisors of black rural schools, with the blessing of white county superintendents.[54]

Jeanes teachers were highly influential. In the late 1920s and early 1930s, black parent-teacher associations in North Carolina (where the state spent $3 per capita for white students and $1 per capita for black students) raised money to buy the small circulating collections that Jeanes teachers carried from school to school. In South Carolina, a teacher named Justine Wilkinson, who had taken a library science course at Spelman College in Atlanta, began her career at a Rosenwald school in Belton. In the early 1930s, while teaching in Pendleton, she helped organize a Faith Cabin library. She left her position at Pendleton in 1936 to become a Jeanes supervisor in Aiken County, where, as was typical in the south, schools for blacks were more crowded and had lower-paid teachers and fewer school days than did schools for whites. Like other Jeanes teachers, she probably cobbled together collections of reading material gathered from white schools. Many went so far as to clip articles out of periodicals and reassemble them as scrapbook-like readers, which students used in lieu of real textbooks.[55]

As it had done for Carnegie, Washington's memoir *Up from Slavery* introduced Rosenwald to the suffering and aspirations of black southerners. In 1910, his friend Paul J. Sachs, of the Goldman Sachs investment firm, had sent him the book, along with a biography of William H. Baldwin, Jr., who had served on both the General Education Board and Tuskegee's board of trustees until his death in 1905. Rosenwald was inspired by Baldwin's philanthropic activities, including his role in effecting Carnegie's $600,000 donation to Tuskegee, and decided to "endeavor to emulate" him, especially his efforts to address "the Negro problem along common-sense, helpful lines."[56]

When the general secretary of the Chicago YMCA, Wilbur Messer, approached Rosenwald for a donation to build a black YMCA in the city, Rosenwald made a counter offer: any city able to come up with $75,000 for a black YMCA building would receive $25,000 from him. As African Americans in several cities took up the challenge, Messer had a chance meeting with Booker T. Washington and recommended Rosenwald as a potential candidate for Tuskegee's board. In the spring of 1911, Messer arranged a lunch meeting between the two, along with other Chicago businessmen. Immediately afterward, Washington asked Rosenwald to serve on Tuskegee's board. Rosenwald declined. But after he made a trip with Messer and others to tour the campus that fall, he accepted Washington's second invitation and become a trustee of Tuskegee Institute. His acquaintance with Washington blossomed into friendship and Rosenwald began, under Washington's guidance, to visit black high schools and colleges in the south and donate funds to them. In 1911 he began giving money to the NAACP, and in 1912 he agreed to serve on the board of the association's newly established Chicago chapter. (Board members also included Hull House founder Jane Addams.) In that same year he was instrumental in convincing Temple Sinai to host the NAACP's annual meeting in Chicago.[57]

Washington and Rosenwald and their respective secretaries,

Emmett Scott and William Graves, began exchanging correspondence and visits, and the Rosenwalds invited Washington and his wife socially to their home. In the fall of 1912, Washington proposed using some of the money that Rosenwald had donated to Tuskegee to construct schoolhouses in small communities in the south, on the condition that local people donate matching funds and provide the labor. Rosenwald assented. In the summer of 1914, Washington wrote to Rosenwald, describing his visit to four schools built with Rosenwald money and local labor and saying that residents were grateful for the help and optimistic about the future. Washington refined the donation plan on paper so that interested communities would understand that Rosenwald would give $350 only if the local community matched or exceeded his contribution and if public school officials were involved. He also positioned Tuskegee's extension department as administrator of the program.[58]

Influenced by Washington and by those in Washington's circle, including various General Education Board and Jeanes Fund officials, Rosenwald adopted this model for rural school development, which would scale up considerably when he founded his philanthropic foundation a few years later. The first such school building, a one-room wooden structure near Tuskegee Institute, was funded with $300 from Rosenwald, $360 from local whites, $150 from African Americans (who purchased the lot), as well as in-kind donations of work worth $133, for a total cost of $943. In addition, the state of Alabama and Macon County committed to accepting the new institution as part of the existing school system and promised to keep it open.

With the creation of the Rosenwald Foundation in 1917, the rural school building initiative grew. By June 30, 1928 (the end of the foundation's 1927–28 fiscal year), 4,138 school buildings had been erected in fourteen southern states. Public monies had footed 60 percent of the total cost, with African Americans donating 19 percent, Rosenwald and his foundation 16.5 percent, and whites 4.5 percent. A total of $20,307,380 had been spent on schools that served some 8,685,585 black southerners.[59] But fund officials decided to discontinue the school building program at the end of the 1931–32 fiscal year, when the proportion of giving had shifted slightly, with taxes contributing 64 percent, African Americans donating 17 percent,

Rosenwald 15 percent, and white contributions 4 percent. All told, the collaboration resulted in the construction of 4,977 school buildings, 217 homes for teachers, and 163 industrial workshops. The multimillionaire and his foundation had given a total of $4,366,519, an enormous amount but still less than the $4,725,871 donated collectively by southern blacks, a chronically impoverished group. By 1932, the state with the most Rosenwald schools was North Carolina, whose 813 buildings had seats for 114,210 students. Mississippi had the second-highest number of buildings, 633, with a capacity of 77,850 students (table 2).[60]

TABLE 2. ROSENWALD PUBLIC SCHOOL BUILDINGS AND PUPIL CAPACITY, 1932

STATE	BUILDINGS	PUPIL CAPACITY
Alabama	407	40,410
Arkansas	389	46,980
Florida	125	22,545
Georgia	261	37,305
Kentucky	158	18,090
Louisiana	435	51,255
Maryland	153	15,435
Mississippi	633	77,850
Missouri	4	1,260
North Carolina	813	114,210
Oklahoma	198	19,575
South Carolina	500	74,070
Tennessee	373	44,460
Texas	527	57,330
Virginia	381	42,840
Total	5,357	663,615

Source: Edwin R. Embree, Julius Rosenwald Fund: Review of Two Decades, 1917–1936 (Chicago, 1936), 23.

The Rosenwald Foundation's library service program operated from 1927 to 1936. Rosenwald had begun by cooperating with local school systems and local people, all of whom contributed funding so that school buildings could be erected. As that early phase of his philanthropy developed, Rosenwald and his foundation officials noticed a dearth of reading material. During the 1927–28 fiscal year, the fund began contributing money for small collections, with books purchased at a discount through the power of Sears's volume buying. The fund provided one-third of the cost of the books; the other thirds came from public money and black communities. During that fiscal year, the fund spent $301,341 on school buildings compared to $6,429 on library collections for 140 Rosenwald schools. Depending on the level of local funding, the school collection could be a small $75 library or a larger $105 library. Both collections included titles recommended by Florence Rising Curtis, the white director of the Hampton Institute's library school; representatives of the American Library Association; and selected school librarians. Just as the Carnegie Corporation had standardized public library building design, the Rosenwald Foundation had developed architectural plans for a two-classroom building and a ten-classroom building, but only the latter was spacious enough to include a fourteen-by-sixteen-foot room to the left of the entrance, across from the school office, for the library.[61]

By the end of the next fiscal year, 419 rural schools housed Rosenwald collections. During 1928–29 the fund contributed its customary one-third toward collection building at twenty-two African American colleges and normal schools for training teachers. But that year the foundation also began to look outside the schoolhouse for ways to extend libraries countywide, where they could serve everyone no matter their color or where they lived in the county. Demonstration projects were designed to prove the value of libraries and inspire local governments to continue supporting them.[62]

Ultimately, the foundation's educational activities included contributions to county library demonstration projects in seven southern states; support for state library commissions in Alabama, Arkansas, South Carolina, and Tennessee; donations to the white library school at Emory University in Atlanta and the black one at Hampton Institute; funding for forty-three libraries at African American colleges and for public libraries serving African Americans in Atlanta, Mobile, Richmond, and New York; support for an extension service project at the Charleston (South Carolina) Museum; institutes and conferences on southern libraries; and funding for a southern library field representative. The four urban public libraries serving African Americans received a total of $18,077. The forty-three college libraries, in sixteen states, received $54,975 for books. In contrast, the library demonstration project involving extension efforts to whites and blacks in eleven counties in Alabama, Louisiana, Mississippi, North Carolina, South Carolina, Tennessee, and Texas cost $456,775.[63] The amount donated to each county varied, as did the number of whites and blacks living in each county (table 3). The Rosenwald schools added to their importance in rural communities by serving as the sites for collections accessible to blacks in and out of school.

TABLE 3. DOLLAR AMOUNTS CONTRIBUTED TO LIBRARY DEMONSTRATION PROJECTS BY THE ROSENWALD FOUNDATION, AND WHITE AND BLACK RESIDENTS BY COUNTY, 1930

COUNTY	ROSENWALD FOUNDATION	WHITES	BLACKS
Charleston (South Carolina)	80,000	46,238	54,812
Coahoma (Mississippi)	10,200	10,469	35,858
Davidson (North Carolina)	16,833	42,630	5,235
Hamilton (Tennessee)	74,152	123,342	36,155
Jefferson (Texas)	12,000	100,369	33,022
Knox (Tennessee)	24,374	136,704	19,198
Mecklenburg (North Carolina)	40,000	89,948	38,023
Richland (South Carolina)	68,750	49,540	38,127
Shelby (Tennessee)	58,500	179,158	127,324
Walker (Alabama)	37,147	51,632	7,813
Webster Parish (Louisiana)	34,819	16,368	13,090
Total	**456,775**	**846,383**	**408,672**

Source: Edwin R. Embree, *Julius Rosenwald Fund: Review of Two Decades, 1917–1936* (Chicago, 1936), 42; Louis R. Wilson and Edward A. Wight, *County Library Service in the South: A Study of the Rosenwald County Library Demonstration.* (Chicago: University of Chicago Press, 1935), 23, tab. 1.

The Walker County Library in Alabama opened in June 1931. In 1933 the library closed for about five months after political infighting left it with no appropriation, and tensions over strikes at area coal mines added to the library's difficulties. Nevertheless, the library established branches and stations in schools and other locales throughout the county. The demonstration library opened a branch for African Americans in a vacant building but then relocated that collection to the library room of the six-teacher Walker County Training School in Patton, one of 389 Rosenwald schools in the state and one of nine constructed in the county in the early 1920s. Patton was a mining area about fifty-five miles northwest of Birmingham. A small town, Oakman, was about five miles away, and a larger town, Jasper, was about seventeen miles away. Students would leave their homes in other parts of Walker County and stay with local Patton families while school was in session. Because African Americans were spread out over the 792-square-mile county and most of the collections were in schools, rural county residents had trouble reaching a deposit station. Consequently, librarians expected students to take books home to their parents. But that was not an option for students at Walker County Training School who were living away from home, although they supposedly could take books to the relatives or friends with whom they lodged during the school year. Until the end of the demonstration project (when the county system's book truck began weekly delivery), the school librarian drove her own car from Patton to transport books to and from various deposit stations at county schools serving rural African Americans.[64]

Louisiana's Webster Parish had no library until the fall of 1929, when it opened a Rosenwald demonstration facility in Minden, about thirty miles from Shreveport. The overwhelmingly rural parish—which had consolidated many small schools into ten for whites (including two high schools) and thirty-four for blacks (including one high school)—established eleven branches for whites and nine for blacks. A book truck delivered reading material to the Central Consolidated School for African Americans and other stations across the 609-square-mile parish. On the truck was a sign reading, "Webster Parish Library / Books. Service Free to All." In the spring of 1930, parish library director Mary Walton Harris told attendees at the Louisiana Library Association's annual meeting in Monroe about cooperative school-library efforts but acknowledged that adults were reluctant to use collections housed in schools. Many adults whose education had taken place in one-room schools were intimidated by larger schools and felt conspicuous standing in line with students at the circulation desk.[65]

Even more discouraging were the library's attempts to reach adults who lived so far away that their children (some 65 percent of the parish's students) had to commute by truck or bus to school. The library staff member could send books home but had no real sense of what an unseen and unheard group of readers might want. Harris reported that one undaunted librarian automatically handed a child another book to take home whenever one was returned to the library. She did not mention (although others had noticed) that custodians of small, far-flung library collections had little, if any, knowledge of the main library's holdings. In the age of the centralized card catalog, they had no way to quickly or easily discover those holdings, a situation that further hampered their ability to recommend relevant books to particular readers. Most teachers had no library training, although Harris said that a few had attended summertime teacher-library training programs and that two of the African American teachers planned to do so.[66]

Over the course of the demonstration, however, most of the teachers at the dozen or so schools for African Americans that housed county collections received library instruction at the Webster Parish Training School, a five-building, thirty-acre facility on the outskirts of Minden. Constructed in 1922, the school included a library built with donations from the Rosenwald and Slater foundations and the General Education Board. Local African Americans had provided the labor for the parish's only purpose-built library for blacks. The director of the Webster Parish Library hired and supervised an African American man, who worked from the training school library to provide teacher instruction, drive the book truck to stations throughout the county, and run the library at the school.[67] In 1933 the parish's economic condition worsened, and the demonstration library's three main sources of financial support—the town of Minden, the parish board of education, and the Rosenwald Foundation—all cut funding. The Carnegie Corporation and the Louisiana Library Commission took up the shortfall until 1934, when local public funding was restored.

Between 1921 and 1936, Edwin Sanders Richardson, Sr., served as the parish's superintendent of schools, and he focused on standardizing parish-wide school equipment, policies, and practices. In 1933, during the American Library Association's annual conference, he gave a talk about the parish's collaboration between schools and libraries at a joint meeting of the League of Library Commissions and the association's County Libraries and Trustees section. Richardson noted that people in Minden had wanted to start a public library but that some—whom he referred to as "the more democratic element"— were against it unless it would include service to the whole parish. Apparently he counted himself among this element because, under his tenure, the school board provided equal educational opportunities throughout the parish and would not support anything less when it came to library services. Richardson particularly specified that, by "the whole parish," he meant black and white residents.[68]

Like Webster Parish, Richland County in South Carolina had no countywide service before the Rosenwald demonstration project began. The state capital, Columbia, located in the county, did have a public library. It had begun as a subscription-based library established by the private Columbia Library Association, was open only to whites, and had only a few hundred members. In 1924 the municipal government and the Community Chest began providing some funding, which made the private library more public. In 1927 the county created a $30,000 fund for library maintenance, and in 1930 the Rosenwald Foundation committed to giving the library association $75,000 for a five-year demonstration project. The library created a separate collection for extension service to white schools and deposit stations throughout Richland County. It also opened a branch for African Americans in Columbia that provided extension service to black schools in the county.[69]

In Charleston, representatives of the Rosenwald Foundation worked with local organizations to create demand for a public library in the city and with county and state officials to create an appropriation to support county-wide services. The fund doubled its usual match, offering $2 for every $1 provided by the city and county during the first two of the five years. The Charleston Free Library occupied a wing of the Charleston Museum and it received $35,000 from the Carnegie Corporation for purchasing books over the five-year demonstration period. The library established branches for whites throughout Charleston County and two for African Americans in the city of Charleston, although one soon closed. The remaining branch sent books to some of the African American schools in the county. Other schools continued to receive small collections of donated books that the county's Jeanes supervisor had been storing at her home until she could deliver them to classrooms. The city's white library moved into its own building in 1935, and the county supported it with appropriations after the demonstration period and Rosenwald funding ended.[70]

Charleston's local interracial committee had a hand in creating the branch library for African Americans out of an existing reading room. The secretary of the county library board, a wealthy white woman named Celia P. McGowan, was an influential member of the committee. She had an attitude of patronizing superiority toward the black committee members and saw herself as better equipped to represent their interests than they were themselves. As a result, she blocked the potential appointment of any African American to the library board.[71]

McGowan had learned of the Rosenwald Foundation in 1925, when she was attending a meeting of the Commission on Interracial Cooperation in Atlanta. She shared information about the fund's interest in libraries with the local committee members, among them Susan Dart Butler. In 1927, Butler created a library for Charleston's African Americans out of her Baptist minister father's private collection and housed it in Dart Hall, a building her father had constructed as a private school because the public school system could or would not accommodate all the school-age blacks in Charleston. Susan Butler staffed the reading room, which was open for a few hours on Monday, Wednesday, and Friday evenings. Some sympathetic whites donated books; those donors included McGowan and another wealthy woman, Louisa Stoney, who gave the reading room a number of volumes after she and her husband sold their Medway Plantation in Mount Holly.[72]

With an infusion of Rosenwald money, Dart Hall Library moved into three rooms on the second floor and in July 1931 opened with a collection of 3,600 books as part of the Charleston Public Library. The county rented the space from the Dart family for $1 a year until 1952, when it bought the building. Butler worked under a trained librarian named Julia McBeth. In the summer of 1932, Butler took library science classes at Hampton Institute in Virginia. With McBeth's departure after a year of service, Butler became the head librarian at the branch, a position she held until her retirement in 1957.[73]

In Texas, two city libraries, in Beaumont and Port Arthur, cooperated to provide services throughout Jefferson County, with Beaumont's Tyrrell Public Library operating an extension service to manage the effort. In 1930, the Rosenwald Foundation pledged $12,500 to the five-year Jefferson County Library Service demonstration project. The service maintained a separate collection for community book deposit stations located in the black school in Port Arthur and at other black schools throughout the county.[74]

In Clarksdale, Mississippi, the only town in Coahoma County, a Carnegie public library began operating with a city appropriation in 1915 and received an additional county appropriation beginning in 1917. In 1923, the library bought a truck to deliver books and began operating deposit stations in rural schools for whites. At some point, the Clarksdale library began allowing African Americans to read library books in a small basement room. That service was discontinued when it became too popular (from the white librarian's perspective). Instead, the library opened a small station in the county agricultural high school and training school and experimented unsuccessfully for about a year with home-based stations. Library trustees refused to extend collections and services any further to African Americans, who constituted about half the city's population and about three-quarters of the county's, because they had decided that their limited resources should be dedicated to whites. In 1929, after city voters passed a $30,000 bond issue for an addition to the Carnegie building, the board of education, the city council, and local African Americans cooperated on the construction of a branch library building to serve Clarksdale's 5,000 black residents. An estimated 30,000 African Americans elsewhere in Coahoma County continued to have access to the station in the agricultural high school. In 1930, Rosenwald gave $17,500 to expand the collection in the high school over the five-year demonstration. By 1932, however, the city and the county were no longer able meet their obligation to the library, and the Rosenwald Foundation withdrew its support from the Coahoma County project.[75]

In North Carolina, African Americans in Mecklenburg County

had public library access only through the Brevard Street Library in Charlotte, despite a twenty-year period of white library expansion and extension.[76] The Rosenwald Foundation pledged $80,000 to the county to spend on a five-year demonstration project, on the condition that the independent Brevard Street Library would become a branch of the public library system. It did so, and by 1931 stations in thirty-seven county schools for African Americans were operating, all in keeping with Rosenwald's commitment to a "unified system, under a single administrative head, combining service to the community and to the schools, both white and Negro."[77] In 1932, however, when the deepening Depression forced the county to reduce its library budget by one-third and its staff from twenty-eight to eleven, Rosenwald dropped the project.[78]

The Rosenwald demonstration project in Tennessee involved three municipal public libraries that extended services countywide after passage of the state's County Library Law of 1929. The Cossitt Library in Memphis began serving Shelby County, the Lawson McGhee Library in Knoxville began serving Knox County, and the Chattanooga Public Library began serving Hamilton County (fig. 4).[79] After the end of the five-year Rosenwald project, Chattanooga carried on its efforts to extend library services. By the late 1930s, the public library was offering black city and county residents a collection of about 15,000 volumes dispersed among four branches in city schools, four branches in county schools, and two additional locations. The city high school for African Americans held about 11,000 of those volumes, which it circulated to city and county schools that did not have a branch library.[80]

After its southern demonstration projects had ended, the Rosenwald Foundation hired two researchers from the University of Chicago's Graduate Library School, Louis R. Wilson and Edward A. Wight, to evaluate the program. They not only analyzed data generated by library operations and collected by library staff but also asked thousands of county residents to log their reading practices for one week. Wilson and Wight reported the statistics and experiences of whites and blacks separately, so it is possible to get a picture of the impact of the Rosenwald-funded county libraries on both urban and rural African Americans.[81]

Figure 4. During the Depression, Chattanooga and Hamilton County Public Library used a bookwagon to extend collections to rural African Americans. Courtesy of the Chattanooga and Hamilton County Public Library.

Wilson and Wight noted that women were much heavier users of the libraries than men were and that white professional men were heavier users than black working-class men were: "From these data it is apparent that the objective set up by the libraries of *equal service to all* is difficult of attainment and can be achieved, if at all, only by careful analysis of the population and special effort to meet the needs of the various groups in each service area." Simply looking at the low ratio of books to persons itself suggests the inadequacy of the collections accessible to African Americans (table 4). More than 10,000 volumes were available to African Americans in Tennessee's Knox County, or 0.55 per capita. The lowest per capita ratio was 0.07, in South Carolina's Richland County, where only about 2,600 library books were circulating among black residents.[82]

The percentage of adult versus juvenile holdings varied widely. An astounding 86 percent of the 10,540 volumes circulating to African Americans in Mecklenburg County, North Carolina, were intended for young readers. At the other, less extreme, end of the spectrum was

TABLE 4. ROSENWALD DEMONSTRATION LIBRARY BOOKS AVAILABLE TO
AFRICAN AMERICANS, BY VOLUMES PER CAPITA, 1934

COUNTY	VOLUMES	% OF TOTAL COLLECTION	% OF POPULATION BLACK	VOLUMES PER CAPITA
Knox (Tennessee)	10,463	7.7	12	0.55
Webster Parish (Louisiana)*	3,869	17.6	44	0.30
Mecklenburg (North Carolina)*	10,540	9.9	30	0.28
Hamilton (Tennessee)	10,230	6.9	23	0.28
Walker (Alabama)	2,004	10.5	13	0.27
Coahoma (Mississippi)	9,637	16.7	77	0.27
Jefferson (Texas)	5,205	4.8	25	0.16
Charleston (South Carolina)	8,287	24.1	54	0.15
Richland (South Carolina)	2,628	5.6	43	0.07

Source: Louis R. Wilson and Edward A. Wight, *County Library Service in the South: A Study of the Rosenwald County Library Demonstration* (Chicago: University of Chicago Press, 1935), 86, tab. 9; U.S. Census Bureau, *Census of Population and Housing, 1930,* vol. 3, *Reports by States,* http://www.census.gov. Data for Davidson County, North Carolina, and Shelby County, Tennessee, are not available.
* Only 1933 figures are available.

the collection in Knox County, Tennessee, with 45 percent catego-
rized as juvenile works. Somewhat more than half of the smallest
collection, in Alabama's Walker County, was considered juvenile,
meaning that local black children had access to only 1,182 volumes.
Their adult relatives and neighbors had access to about 500 works of
fiction and about 320 works of nonfiction (table 5).

Each of Rosenwald's library-related efforts had at least some
influence on the availability of reading material, but the county
library demonstration project had the greatest direct impact on
black southerners because it delivered books to small out-of-the-way
schools and deposit stations. In four of the demonstration counties,
African Americans outnumbered whites in the rural areas: Coahoma, Mississippi; Charleston and Richland, South Carolina; and
Shelby, Tennessee. In Coahoma and Charleston counties, the number of rural blacks was so high that, combined with the number in
urban areas, they formed the majority. In Coahoma County, African Americans contributed more than three times the amount that
Rosenwald or their white neighbors gave, yet the county, the city,

TABLE 5. PERCENTAGE OF ADULT AND JUVENILE BOOKS IN ROSENWALD
DEMONSTRATION COLLECTIONS ACCESSIBLE TO AFRICAN AMERICANS,
BY TOTAL NUMBER OF VOLUMES, 1934

COUNTY	VOLUMES	% ADULT FICTION	% ADULT NONFICTION	% JUVENILE
Mecklenburg (North Carolina)*	10,540	9	5	86
Knox (Tennessee)	10,463	26	29	45
Hamilton (Tennessee)	10,230	n/a	n/a	54
Coahoma (Mississippi)	9,637	9	18	73
Charleston (South Carolina)	8,287	19	16	65
Jefferson (Texas)	5,205	13	8	79
Webster Parish (Louisiana)*	3,869	7	35	58
Richland (South Carolina)	2,628	32	21	47
Walker (Alabama)	2,004	25	16	59

Source: Louis R. Wilson and Edward A. Wight, County Library Service in the South: A Study of the Rosenwald County Library Demonstration (Chicago: University of Chicago Press, 1935), 88, tab. 10.
* Only 1933 figures are available.

and the fund ultimately gave up on them.[83] Although not all of the projects were successful in the long run, they did demonstrate both people's hunger for books and the challenges involved in feeding that hunger.

Even as the Rosenwald library demonstration projects were making their own "free to all" claims, extending segregation and insufficient collections in the late 1920s, blacks in the border state of West Virginia won a victory for integrated service when the Charleston Public Library's separate branch for African Americans opened on Shrewsbury Street in 1927. The plan was to locate the library in a new building that would also house the Garnett High School for blacks. After declaring that both the main and branch libraries were part of the school system, the school district told the head of the Charleston Public Library to refuse service to African Americans and send them to the Garnett branch instead. But in 1928, Anderson H. Brown, E. L. Powell, and William W. Sanders, all African American residents of Charleston, sued the district's board of education on the grounds that it had no authority to take over the tax-supported public library system. The three men were represented by Attorneys T. G. Nutter and C. E. Kimbrough. Nutter had founded the NAACP in West

Virginia in 1914 and had fought for black civil rights for decades.[84] Indeed, the year before he took the library case, he had tried to convince the school board to allow local black architect John C. Norman to design the Garnett High School building, which Norman had offered to do for free. Instead, the board gave the contract to a local white firm, without asking for bids.[85]

In the library case, Nutter pointed out that the Garnett branch was inadequate, with a collection and services far inferior to those of the Charleston Public Library, which his clients, who were city taxpayers, were helping to finance. Kanawha County judge Arthur P. Hudson sided with the board of education, whose attorney acknowledged that black residents were taxpayers but argued that the state had a policy of segregation. He also said that blacks at the Garnett branch could request books from the main library and that a courier would pick them up while they waited. A Baltimore newspaper, the *Afro-American,* reported the decision and predicted "a bitter fight" when it was appealed.[86]

With help from the NAACP, Nutter filed the appeal, and the West Virginia Supreme Court reversed the lower court's decision, noting that state law allowed for segregation in schools but not in public libraries and that the board of education's involvement in a public library did not make it a school library.[87] Louis Shores, a librarian at Fisk University, mentioned the case as an example of whites' attempt to use branch libraries as a way to deny service at the main library.[88] But his article appeared in the *Journal of Negro Education,* which was probably not on most librarians' professional reading lists. They hardly noticed the decision.

Ten years would pass before southern blacks made another legal challenge to library segregation. It would come in the neighboring state of Virginia, and it would not be a victory. In the interim, the Great Depression intervened, and existing black libraries struggled to maintain deteriorating collections.

CHAPTER 4

Faltering Systems

The Great Depression was an era in which large numbers of unemployed people increasingly used library services, collections, and reading rooms, filling their days by perusing newspapers, magazines, and books inside a public building. This influx of users coincided with a dramatic decrease in financial support for local public services as budgets tightened or disappeared altogether during the economic downturn.[1]

While public library branches for African Americans suffered along with their larger library systems, their struggles with inadequate funding predated the economic crisis. When the stock market crashed in 1929, the rural south was still largely black and largely devoid of schools, books, and libraries. In the Deep South and especially in rural areas, books and libraries remained scarce, despite the best efforts of the Rosenwald Foundation and its partners. But county-wide services were rare everywhere in the United States. In 1932, only 231 (7.5 percent) of the 3,072 counties in the nation had library systems that extended service county-wide through deposit stations, bookmobiles, and other methods.[2]

Private and public money for library collections and services had supported the creation of such systems in rural areas where blacks had never before had access to libraries. In combination with the Great Migration into urban areas with existing libraries, the push for county-wide services led to incremental improvements in African Americans' access to reading material. Yet in his study of Alabama,

Toby Graham argues that President Roosevelt's Depression-era New Deal programs were "missed opportunities" to improve library access for African Americans in the state, and his argument holds true for the entire south.[3] Between 1930 and 1937, average total per capita spending on book collections, bindery services, and periodical subscriptions for African Americans ranged from 0.007 in Nashville to 0.013 in Atlanta and Houston to 0.07 in Danville, Virginia. In 1937, seven black branches, including Oklahoma City, spent $100 or less on acquisitions, binding, and subscriptions. Along with Oklahoma City, Birmingham, Dallas, Nashville, and New Orleans clustered toward the bottom in per capita expenditures that year, spending less than one cent per African American resident to maintain collections.[4]

New Orleans offers an example. In March 1932, local attorney and book collector E. A. Parsons became head of the city's public library. Like his three predecessors, he had no formal education or training in either library administration or library science; and by early 1935, local newspapers were editorializing about his incompetence and dishonesty. In January of that year, the Inter-Organization Committee on the Public Library, representing the New Orleans Central Trades and Labor Council, the Parent-Teachers Association, the Public School Teachers Association, the Council of Jewish Women, an organization of business and professional women, and a host of other civic groups, mobilized to improve library collections and services. The committee recommended hiring outside consultants to survey the situation and suggest improvements. A month later, the library board agreed to immediately ask the American Library Association to arrange for the appointment of outside consultants "so that the said survey may be conducted and completed within the shortest possible time consistent with a fair, impartial and thorough investigation of the affairs of the New Orleans Public Library."[5]

Two directors of large urban public libraries agreed to investigate and report on the New Orleans Public Library: Joseph Wheeler, the head of the Enoch Pratt Free Library in Baltimore, and Jesse Cunningham, the head of the Cossitt Library in Memphis. Their fifty-four-page report, based on their April 1935 visit to the city, criticized E. A. Parsons on every criterion used to judge the efficiency and effectiveness of the public library. As a book collector, he had failed to understand the city's diverse public at the very time that the needs and desires of public library users were increasing in response to the Depression. As a political appointee, he had found nothing wrong with hiring his own relatives for library jobs, despite their lack of education and training. He had remodeled his own office even though the branch buildings needed both exterior and interior paint. A practicing attorney, he had met with clients and appeared in court during regular business hours, when other library directors were meeting with staff and handling administrative responsibilities.

Under such precarious management, all the branches suffered. Staff everywhere were burdened with a "heavy service load," calculated as average book circulation per employee. Wheeler and Cunningham pointed out that the national average for book circulation per public library employee was 18,927. At the Canal Branch there were 158,221 book circulations per employee in 1934. The system's lowest service load was at the Algiers Branch, which had 62,627 book circulations per employee. The Dryades Branch fell between those two extremes, with 113,947 book circulations per employee. Yet this was still more than six times the national average.

Unlike the other branches, each of which had one full-time assistant to the head librarian, Dryades had two full-time assistants because, during the week, it was open three hours a day longer than the other branches were. Even on Sundays, Dryades was open from two to six. Although the surveyors recommended specific ways to economize, they did not suggest eliminating the second full-time assistant position at Dryades, noting that, as the only public library open to blacks in New Orleans, it functioned as a central library offering both reference services and a circulating collection. The staff probably did not experience the level of frustration of the single assistant at the Nix Branch, who, according to the survey, was charging out one book per minute for most of the time the library was open, not to mention checking in returned books and tending to other tasks. Individuals who wanted to borrow books sometimes had to wait as long as twenty-five minutes at the circulation desk.[6] When compared to the other branches, Dryades seems to have fared relatively well during these hardships. But there was one key difference.

White library users always had the option of visiting other branches or the main library. Blacks did not.

During the 1930s, public libraries became linked to the adult education movement. Just as southern library service for African Americans lagged behind that for whites, adult education activities in public libraries were practically nonexistent for southern blacks. One exception was an experimental program at the Auburn Avenue Branch of the Atlanta Public Library. With funding from the Carnegie Corporation and the Rosenwald Foundation, the American Adult Education Association and the American Library Association worked with local staff to set up two adult education programs for African Americans: one in Harlem at the 135th Street Branch of the New York Public Library, the other at the Auburn Branch. An adult education worker, Mae C. Hawes, moved to Atlanta in 1931 to run the program, which ended in 1934. Its varied activities included lectures by Spelman College and Atlanta University faculty members, the American Library Association's Reading with a Purpose program, the formation of reading and discussion groups, and musical presentations.

But everything that was wrong with the Auburn Avenue Branch—lack of funding, inadequate staff, and a resulting absence of collaboration with other community agencies—carried over to the adult education effort, as Atlanta University sociologist Ira D. Reid asserted in his book *Adult Education among Negroes*. For adult education in public libraries to be effective, the public library itself had to be effective, and that required more money than cities such as Atlanta were willing to dedicate to services for African Americans.[7] Eliza Gleason quoted Reid in her own book, *The Southern Negro and the Public Library*, and then suggested that public libraries should rise to the challenge. Gleason believed that their collections, public service orientation, and neutrality made them the best institutions for such efforts.[8] Reid apparently disagreed, for he created a partnership with W. E. B. Du Bois to found an Atlanta University offshoot known as People's College, for which he served as director. People's College was staffed by Atlanta University faculty, who offered their services gratis to teach night classes. They were attended mainly by literate African American workers and cost ten cents per course.[9]

Municipal libraries found it difficult to serve the residents within their growing cities' boundaries, and administrators turned their attention to counties and the provision of county-wide collections. Federal New Deal dollars began helping existing city and county libraries serve more people, and government funds also went toward establishing new county libraries. For the first time, some county libraries began to serve rural African Americans in the south. White library officials saw the extension of service as progress and spoke highly of libraries that served whites and blacks. But on closer inspection, libraries, even those using federal funding, were serving whites and blacks separately and thus extending segregation along with collections and services. Many rural African Americans who had received no library service before the Depression could now use small deposit stations. Although they offered few titles and little actual service, such collections made it possible for white officials to claim they were creating new library supporters. Yet in some places, collections for rural African Americans were more substantial and came with a knowledgeable librarian for reference consultations and reading suggestions. Overall, improvements were incremental and uneven.

Librarians who wanted to extend collections and services to rural populations understood that they were engaged in a marketing effort as they tried to create demand among people struggling to survive agricultural and economic reversals in a region with few cultural or educational opportunities. Two studies from the period, both conducted in Mississippi, draw a stark picture of African American country life. In the 1930s, sociologist John Dollard spent five months observing black and white life in a small delta town, Indianola, in Sunflower County, where 70 percent of the population was black. In "Southerntown" (Dollard's pseudonym for Indianola in his study) and throughout the region, the schooling offered to African Americans was "caste education" designed to train black students for the menial jobs that would be available to them as adults. Given the attitude of whites, Dollard found it remarkable that black literacy levels and school attendance were as high as they were. He noted the presence of a high school for African Americans in Southerntown, pointed out that such facilities were still uncommon in the region, and asserted that the only way for most blacks to enter the middle class was by attending high school and college. He wrote that schools for African American children were deliberately sub par because whites feared that educated blacks would be "unfit . . . for their caste and class roles." That schools even existed was the result of "the fervor of Negro belief in education as a means of advancement."[10]

Farther south in the state, Allison Davis, Burleigh Gardner, and Mary Gardner studied "Old City," surrounding "Old County," and neighboring "Rural County." "Old City" was later identified as Natchez. In the 1930s, the rural areas outside Natchez were 80 percent African American, and most people in the country were tenant farmers who grew cotton.[11] Davis and the Gardners reported that tenant farmers had enough to eat after the fall sale of their cotton crops and from spring to midsummer when they raised some vegetables and borrowed money from the landholder. However, "during the other four to six months of the year, most tenant-families in Old County, between 1933 and 1935, lived in semistarvation."[12] Like Dollard, the researchers reported on the "markedly inferior" schools available to blacks and cited Horace Mann Bond's statistical analysis showing that, in predominately black counties, whites had much to gain by diverting tax dollars disproportionately to white schools. Black schools were in buildings not constructed for that purpose. While counties supplied white schoolhouses with equipment and books, they usually did not provide them to black schools. Under such circumstances it is not surprising that the researchers concluded that the estimated 70 percent literacy rate among African Americans overstated their ability to read beyond the minimum they needed to function as agricultural or domestic workers.[13] Neither study mentioned the availability of a library; but the struggle for food, clothing, shelter, and education mitigated against library use, even if collections had been available.

Going without cash, food, new clothes, decent housing, and convenient transportation was a new experience for many whites during the Depression but not for most southern blacks, particularly in rural areas. Elderly southern whites interviewed by Kenneth J. Bindas's history students in the early 1990s recalled the Depression as a time when it was difficult to find a job, make money, and have enough to eat, and they asserted that everyone was poor together. But they also remembered having black sharecroppers or tenants on their farms and cooks in their kitchens. Bindas points out that whites tended not to recognize how much more they owned than their black workers and neighbors did. Their lack of empathy was systemic, rooted in the ideology of white supremacy and the practice of segregation.[14] Whites who were high school age in the 1930s recalled being unable to purchase books and either making low grades or leaving school altogether. In contrast, a black interviewee recounted her long days as a child farm laborer for whom school was never an option.[15]

Studies of Rosenwald Foundation and federal programs for library projects in Oklahoma, South Carolina, Alabama, and several Tennessee Valley states highlighted both the need for outside money to support a wider distribution of books and periodicals and the continuing control of local whites over that distribution process. The situation in Oklahoma, documented by Louise Robbins, serves as an illustration. Between 1928 and 1936, about 150 elementary and high schools in the state received small collections of books purchased at a discount from Sears, with Rosenwald underwriting one-third of the cost, the school one-third, and the community one-third. For most of these schools, this was the first and only collection available to students, who did not receive free textbooks as part of their schooling in Oklahoma. A few of the high schools opened their collections to the public; these were the only libraries available to African Americans in Canadian and Grady counties. Rosenwald collections (some of which also went to white high schools) included titles such as Washington's *Up from Slavery*, Du Bois's *The Souls of Black Folk*, and other books written by and about African Americans.

Rosenwald also helped colleges and universities expand their libraries. For instance, the foundation gave $2,000 (with matching amounts from the state and alumni) to augment the collection at the Colored Agricultural and Normal University in the all-black town of Langston. This marked a sharp increase in the library's materials budget in 1929–30.[16] Nevertheless, when the university began to undergo the accreditation process a few years later, the library did not meet standards for the region.[17]

The Oklahoma Library Commission published a report in 1937

acknowledging the paucity of library collections and services for black residents. Seventy towns had white libraries, but only ten extended some form of service to blacks. The commission reported that three counties had used Works Progress Administration money to open reading rooms for black Oklahomans and that more would be established with future expected funds.[18] Thanks to an infusion of WPA money between 1938 and 1947, separate African American libraries in Oklahoma doubled in number from eight to sixteen, including libraries in the black towns of Boley and Taft. Additional deposit stations with small rotating collections served African Americans who had access to no other library. Although not all of the WPA libraries remained open after federal funding ceased, most continued to serve African Americans until desegregation.[19]

Not surprisingly, an influx of federal funding did not translate into equitable library service. Because the federal government hired local people to supervise its WPA projects, the result was an extension of existing patterns. African Americans who had previously had no access to library books did begin to have some access, but collections for whites were far larger and services more extensive.

The situation in South Carolina illustrates the point.[20] When the WPA began offering library service projects in the state in 1935, its library agency was not functioning because the legislature had never appropriated funds for it. Although book collections were available in some areas, fully tax-supported public libraries were rare, and a 1932 survey found that only fifteen relied solely on public funding. South Carolina's total per capita spending on libraries was 0.10 at a time when the national average was 0.37, and its library holdings were 0.12 volumes per capita when the national average was 0.82. On Louis Round Wilson's "Index of Library Development," the state was tied with Arkansas at next-to-last. (Mississippi was in last place.)[21]

Wilson reported that four of the fifty-three public libraries in South Carolina in 1935 served 15 percent of the state's African American residents: 122,117 people out of a total of 793,681.[22] In some other states, active libraries had used WPA resources to strengthen and extend existing collections and services in selected regions. But South Carolina's library leaders had decided to bring book collections to every county of the state. The result was that towns with as few as 1,500 residents received collections in reading rooms or deposit stations. For example, in 1939, Jasper County, on the Georgia border, opened a reading room with a collection of forty-five books and a list of ninety-eight registered borrowers. Two years later, the county had a collection of 1,600 volumes, but it is not clear that black residents, who far outnumbered whites, had access to any of them.

Unsatisfied with the inadequacy of such efforts, WPA officials began to collaborate with self-selected local sponsors to send book-mobiles all over the state, delivering a changing selection of titles to deposit stations in existing buildings, mostly schools. They also created two regional demonstration libraries meant to convince locals of the value of libraries and persuade them to support their continuation with tax dollars. Because so many of South Carolina's counties were too small and poor to support full-service public libraries, regional libraries working across county boundaries offered at least a chance for sustainability after the demonstration ended.[23]

Colleton and Dorchester counties, with about 25,000 African Americans out of a total population of about 46,000, had three libraries (at least one of which depended on private subscriptions) that held about 9,800 volumes. By 1941, with the addition of loaned books from the WPA, the total approached 15,000; and bookmobiles were stopping at sixty different locations in the two counties. Apparently, this collection was available only to whites because a different collection, donated by "a Negro philanthropist of Washington, D.C.," circulated to deposit stations in schools for black South Carolinians. When the demonstration project ended, residents of the counties chose not to spend their meager public monies on a permanent regional library.[24]

More successful was the demonstration project involving Marion, Georgetown, and Horry counties, which had 15,000 volumes owned by only three local libraries, two of which relied on private revenue. Each county had used WPA funding early in the program to try to expand county-wide library services, but by 1940 they understood the futility of small-scale and necessarily underfunded efforts and decided to collaborate on a regional demonstration project. A year later, their stock of books had doubled, bookmobiles were crossing county boundaries to stop at 286 locations, and the system had four public and fifteen school libraries as well as four reading rooms. Nearly 30,000 volumes, 2,500 of which were on loan from the WPA, were offered to the 62,142 whites in the three counties. White local sponsors and WPA officials decided not to include African American residents in the demonstration project. As the University of Chicago doctoral student who studied the situation explained,

> Service to the 46,000 Negroes who comprise 42 per cent of the region's population has been deliberately postponed by those in charge of the demonstration. Since such service as these folk receive throughout the state is characteristically extended from agencies which were established to serve the white population, it was deemed expedient to concentrate first on developing a strong and permanent regional system, without forcing the racial issue. With such great differences as exist in these counties in the proportion of Negroes to white persons, this issue might well have become a serious point of contention among the participants to the demonstration, had it been raised when contracts were being considered. It might even have caused the entire undertaking to fail.[25]

Saying that service to African Americans had merely been postponed suggests that the researcher's sources preferred to position themselves as acting in the greater good—sacrificing, but only temporarily, the rights of blacks for the benefit of whites. They kept local white southerners happy by ensuring that their black neighbors would not share the same access to information. At the same time, they reassured northern whites that they were concerned about providing access to African Americans as soon as that was practicable. If any of them had noticed that they were using federal funds to suppress information and stymie increased literacy, they did not acknowledge it.

The annual report of the South Carolina WPA statewide library project for the fiscal year between July 1938 and July 1939 included a two-and-a-half-page section titled "Negro Libraries" that reveals the attitude of at least one white official toward service to African Americans. Written by project supervisor Agnes D. Crawford, the section opened with a mention of "the high percentage of illiterates within this race" and the "lack of real leadership within the communities that can afford a library."[26] Crawford reported that, with the addition of seven "Negro units" during the fiscal year, South Carolina now had a total of twenty-nine collections accessible to African Americans, of whom 20,022 were borrowers. Most of the units operated out of existing African American schools or deposit stations housed in a variety of settings. The Jeanes teachers helped distribute the boxes of books comprising the collections. In 1938–39, statistics for school libraries and for those public libraries established after the creation of the WPA (all receiving financial assistance from it) had a total of 314,927 volumes, with 32,238 in Negro units, and a total circulation rate of 1,765,048, with 157,110 among black borrowers. African American library aides paid by the WPA oversaw twenty-four of the units, and at least one of those aides had taken library training courses in preparation for regular employment as a teacher-librarian.

Crawford closed her account with a tale of two WPA supervisors, presumably white women, who delivered the first collection of books to a school in Jonesville, in Colleton County. Until the WPA began extending services in the spring of 1939, no African Americans had been able to use a public library in the county. The two supervisors stayed for the flag-lowering ceremony conducted at the end of the school day and teared up during the reciting of the Pledge of Allegiance. One reported her realization that "although our races were not the same, one flag and one government was ours, we share alike its privileges, we fight together its problems. Long may we be 'book friends' to this race."[27] Her assertion that "we share alike its privileges" was deluded at best and added a dose of condescension to an official federal agency report that had already begun by citing lack of literacy and leadership as two chief causes of the dearth of library collections and services for rural blacks. Crawford seems to have had a shallow understanding of the factors that comprised the reasons behind denying tax-supported services to African Americans. A sense of willful ignorance underlay her paternalistic pride at delivering a box of books to a rural black school.

At the end of February 1940, 790 whites and 29 blacks on relief were working for the South Carolina statewide library project. Between July 1, 1939 and February 29, 1940, 13,329 books in the

Figure 5. A young woman mends books as part of the WPA Library Project during the Depression. Courtesy of the National Archives and Records Administration, College Park, Md.

Negro collection had been repaired, compared to 156,005 in the white collection (fig. 5). In April 1940, 8,006 white library books and 434 black library books were repaired, about the same as in July of that year. Circulation of books during those eight months totaled 2,030,789 for the white collection and 80,713 for the black collection. In April 1940, 419,258 white and 18,373 black library books circulated. Of the total collection available in South Carolina (443,222 volumes), the WPA had purchased 18,640 but left no information about how the total was divided between black and white collections. At the end of February, 2,215 bookmobile stations were open to whites, while none was open to blacks.[28]

Blacks in Alabama also experienced blatant discrimination. For instance, some two hundred blacks in the town of Luverne had signed up as borrowers at a hypothetical library they hoped would be created with WPA funds. But their representative and chief letter writer, Dalzie M. Powell, was stymied by federal, state, and county officials, who either denied their power to act or ignored her altogether.[29] African Americans in Luverne did not need a demonstration project to convince them of the value of public libraries; more than two hundred of them just wanted some books to read. Had they been white, county WPA representatives and local librarians would have organized them into a citizens committee to advocate for more library funding. Instead, their support was squandered.

Next door, in Mississippi's Jackson County, a black school, Jackson College, used WPA funds to provide county-wide library services. In 1940, the college became a state school for training African American teachers and changed its name to the Mississippi Training School for Negroes. Late in 1942, an official with Mississippi's WPA program wrote to Florence Kerr, the federal agency's assistant administrator, asking whether the Mississippi Library Commission could turn over maintenance of 27,000 books paid for with federal dollars to the county libraries that the WPA had helped create and to the Mississippi Negro Training School, which had been functioning as a de facto county library. According to the official, the school had used WPA money to create an extension collection, and he wanted to support the continuation of that service by lending federally owned books to the school and to the county libraries in exchange for their commitment to provide "housing and personnel for the widest possible use of the material." The request was approved.[30]

Like other federal programs, the Tennessee Valley Authority put whites first in its wide-ranging economic development program in the seven states fed by the waters of the Tennessee River—a region in which blacks accounted for 23 percent of the population. The TVA's library program was headed by Mary Utopia Rothrock, who had worked at public libraries in Memphis and Knoxville. As in other southern counties, Jeanes teachers pitched in; for example, a Jeanes supervisor in Scottsboro, Alabama, helped Reverend Horace Snodgrass, a WPA relief worker, find a building to use as delivery headquarters for small rotating collections in Alabama's Jackson County.[31] Rothrock and the TVA's black supervisor of Negro training, J. Max Bond, were in general agreement that integration made sense. Nevertheless, TVA libraries offered segregated collections, when they were offered at all. The Watts Bar Dam site near Dayton provided an important test case for Rothrock's vision of regional libraries across multiple county boundaries. Based out of the Lawson McGhee Library in Knoxville, the regional service maintained sixty-nine collections in four counties, and a least a few were for African Americans. The community building for black workers and their families at Watts Bar also held a library collection.[32]

Eliza Atkins Gleason's book, *The Southern Negro and the Public Library,* provides the best snapshot of southern library conditions for African Americans in the late 1930s. The book is based on her dissertation, "The Government and Administration of Public Library Service to Negroes in the South," which she completed in 1940. Both works report data that Gleason compiled from questionnaires she had sent to public, college, and secondary-school libraries serving African Americans and from visits to public libraries that served African Americans in separate structures from those that served whites.[33] In 1939, about 20 percent of the African Americans living in thirteen southern states had "some degree of library service." Ninety-nine public libraries in the south served African Americans in some manner, and twenty-four had been established in the five years before her survey.[34] Between 1900 and 1934, about seventy-five public libraries for blacks were established, and another twenty-four were added between 1935 and 1939. The increasing number of libraries resulted in a growing proportion of African Americans with access to library collections and services: from 10.46 percent in 1926 to 21.39 percent in 1939.[35]

The acceleration of the rate of foundings is surprising, given the fact that the country was in the midst of an economic depression. The growth underscores a significant change in library support, from tax funding at the local level and private philanthropy at the local and national levels to federal intervention through various economic relief and recovery programs. Although the Rosenwald Foundation contributed to southern library growth in the 1930s, additional impact came from federal dollars. When the WPA offered to pay a librarian's salary if a black branch were created, the public library in Pine Bluff, Arkansas, "donated" books from its collection, and members of a Negro executive committee collected community donations to raise the librarian's only spending money.[36]

Libraries continued to restrict use to whites only. As Gleason documented, almost 2 million southern blacks lived in areas with public libraries that refused them service. Notwithstanding the increased activity in state library extension during the Depression, Gleason found that only half of the ten extension agencies in existence provided collections and services for African Americans, and then only on a small scale. In Florida, Oklahoma, and Virginia, no county library branches served African Americans, although seven municipalities in Florida, five in Oklahoma, and ten in Virginia had library branches serving them. Alabama, Arkansas, Georgia, Kentucky, Louisiana, and Mississippi each had one county system that included branch service to African Americans, and a few towns and cities in each of those states also provided branch service. A dozen branches in nine Texas municipalities served African Americans; three of those cities also provided county-wide service, and another four counties had small stations rather than branches.[37]

In his 1940 report on the Rosenwald Foundation's activities, Edwin Embree wrote:

> Among the weaknesses of our democracy is our treatment of Negroes. Our attitude toward this race, which makes up one tenth of our entire population, more than one quarter of the historic region of the South, is a threat to the whole theory and practice of democracy. . . . Consideration for the Negro rests not merely on the grounds of humanity and charity; it rests on the solid base of enlightened selfishness. It is a question not only of the rights of the Negroes themselves: it is a question of the total health and strength of the nation.[38]

Embree's message of enlightened self-interest had little immediate impact on library collections and services for African Americans. But by the late 1930s, African Americans had begun to include libraries in their quest for civil rights. For example, attorney James Nabrit, Jr., who had moved to Houston in 1930 to practice law and was engaged in bringing cases designed to overturn the state's whites-only election primaries, began vocalizing his objections to the paltry public library collection accessible to African Americans, pointing out that only 6,000 of the library system's 300,000 volumes were available to blacks.[39]

It was in Virginia, however, that blacks put their bodies on the line for physical access to libraries. One of the first recorded southern desegregation efforts occurred in 1939 in Alexandria, where the whites-only public library had opened in 1937. A young local attorney, Sam Tucker, had earned his undergraduate degree at Howard University at the same time that Charles Houston was shaping the university's law school into a tool for desegregation. Tucker's home was near the new Alexandria Public Library, but neither he nor any of the other 5,000 African Americans in town were allowed to use it. Tucker decided to take action, and in March 1939 he escorted retiree George Wilson, an army veteran, to the library's desk and filled out the form requesting a library card. The staff refused to issue the card on the basis of Wilson's race. Tucker took the library to court, and Charles Houston helped him ready his case. At proceedings in July, the judge agreed that the library was a tax-funded institution that should be open to all, but he also asserted that Wilson's form had not been filled out properly. On that basis, he said, Wilson could be denied a library card. The judge delayed making a final decision on the case to give city and library officials time to develop a strategy to prevent integration.[40]

Meanwhile, in August, five young black men who had been coached by Tucker occupied the library in what newspapers, borrowing the language of labor, called a "sit-down strike." William Evans, Edward Gaddis, Morris Murray, Clarence Strange, and Otto Tucker walked one by one to the circulation desk, asked to be issued a borrower's card, waited for the clerk to say that colored persons were not allowed to use the library, and then picked a book off a shelf and sat down—each at a different table—to read. After about an hour, the police showed up and ushered them outside and, in front of a crowd of onlookers and reporters whom Tucker had invited as witnesses, arrested them on charges of disorderly conduct, despite the fact that the men and the officers had been polite throughout the encounter. As in the Wilson case, the judge delayed, giving the city and the library's board time to ponder their options.

In 1937, the board had briefly entertained the notion of creating a separate library for blacks. Now, after Tucker's direct actions, it moved swiftly to build a segregated branch. The main library began honoring blacks' requests for library cards, but their cards could only be used at the new branch, which opened in April 1940. Sam Tucker refused to patronize it.[41] White librarians praised Alexandria's library system because, true to the profession's sense of itself as a purveyor of democracy, it offered collections and services freely to all. This perspective was self-serving, perhaps even self-deceiving. African Americans such as Tucker, Wilson, and the five men who staged the sit-in already understood what the Supreme Court would declare in 1954: that separate, by definition, was unequal. The 1930s would prove to be the last decade in which public libraries continued their unalloyed commitment to racial segregation.

CHAPTER 5

—⸺—

Change and Continuity

Eliza Atkins Gleason's 1941 book, *The Southern Negro and the Public Library*, was ahead of its time in pointing out the inefficiency and ineffectiveness of racially segregated municipal services. Gleason's call to action appeared at a transition point between the Depression-era commitment to expand libraries' geographic and demographic reach and the post–World War II intensification of the struggle for black civil rights. In the 1930s, a version of service to all could be accomplished within a segregated system, but this was not so certain in the 1940s. A few public libraries began to move toward desegregation in the 1940s, perhaps not so much on the basis of Gleason's call to be reasonable but more as a result of local encounters with African American taxpayers who were attempting to use a municipal service.[1] It would take another two decades, a civil rights movement, and federal legislation for the last southern public libraries to jettison segregation and begin openly serving black and white together.

In 1944, Atlanta University's School of Library Service, where Gleason served as the first dean, declared in a recruiting brochure that the southern branch library model had failed African Americans who were denied access to the main library and to branches available to whites only.[2] Along with Gleason, a few other scholars and activists began to include segregated public libraries in their analyses of the state of American race relations. Among them was sociologist Charles S. Johnson, director of Fisk University's Department of

Social Sciences, one of twenty scholars invited in 1938 to provide information to Gunnar Myrdal when he began his research on black Americans.[3]

With funding from the Carnegie Corporation, Myrdal had temporarily left his job at the University of Stockholm to move to the United States, but the developing war forced his return home before the project was complete. He eventually came back to the United States and finished his research, issued in two volumes as *An American Dilemma: The Negro Problem and Modern Democracy* (1944). The report incorporated some of Gleason's findings, noting the lack of library collections available to southern blacks.

Even before Myrdal was able to complete his project, the Carnegie Corporation had decided to publish some of the information he was compiling. Charles Johnson's contributions were among that released material. Johnson had been working with interviewers who were gathering data to document what he called "social behavior in interracial contact situations in selected areas of the United States."[4] The result was his book, *Patterns of Negro Segregation.*

Categorizing public libraries, along with parks and playgrounds, under the heading "Recreation," Johnson wrote, "Public libraries represent an area of extreme racial distinction, since these publicly supported institutions sometimes make no provision for Negroes."[5] He noted the lack of libraries in the rural south and reported that, when bookmobiles and libraries did exist, everyone assumed they were for whites only. A white librarian in Johnston County, North Carolina, claimed she had never considered what to do if a black person were to enter the library and try to use the books, until one of Johnson's interviewers asked her. In her response, she made a class distinction, saying that she might let "the colored teachers" use the library's books if they asked to but that she would be reluctant to let others.[6]

Johnson reported three cases in which African Americans were allowed to use a bookmobile or a library through white mediation. A bookmobile librarian told an interviewer that a white woman's black cook had found a book she wanted to read while her employer was browsing among the shelves, and the librarian had checked it out using the white woman's card. The wife of a black school principal reported getting library books with the intervention of "a white lady friend," who pretended the books were for herself. A servant mentioned that her employers sent her to the library to get books for them and said that she, too, read the books.

Johnson observed that southern cities were more likely than small towns were to have a separate branch for African Americans, even without an ordinance or law requiring library segregation, because urban whites had assumed it was necessary and expected. There were variations in service levels: some main libraries were willing to send books to branches when requested, and others allowed blacks to use only what was in the Negro branch's collection. Johnson asserted that segregation was not the norm in libraries in the north and in some border states such as Maryland.[7]

Gleason's book was highlighted in the opening sentence of Anna Holden's January 1954 report on the Southern Regional Council's survey of library services for African Americans. Holden noted that, since 1941, "Negro use of the main library has grown from an isolated phenomenon to an increasingly acceptable practice in certain areas of the South." Whereas Gleason had identified only four communities that offered full library services for black residents, Holden found fifty-five. Yet access to the main library did not automatically mean access to all branches. In fact, Holden's data suggest that southern libraries had anything but a standardized approach to serving African Americans. Some allowed what they called "full service," although they wouldn't serve black children. Some allowed blacks to browse among the shelves, borrow books, and consult the reference collection but not enter or sit down in the reading rooms. Some served blacks passively, answering reference questions and lending books for those bold enough to ask, but did not proactively offer services and collections.[8]

Historians of the American south have documented the paradoxical persistence of racial segregation during and immediately after World War II.[9] Change occurred incrementally, if at all, until the middle of the 1940s, when returning black GIs reignited their domestic commitment to the wartime Double V campaign for democracy abroad and at home. A decade before the Supreme Court's 1954 *Brown v. the Board of Education* decision declared separate but equal

an unattainable fantasy, it was becoming clear that southern municipalities could no longer afford segregation. African Americans, particularly those who had moved to urban areas during the Depression
and the war, were continuing to increase their educational levels and
their expectations; and some white southerners were coming around
to Gleason's view that maintaining the myth of separate but equal
was a luxury they could not afford. As Holden reported just months
before the *Brown* decision, "the task of providing two reference centers with special collections, films, and records seems too costly an
undertaking for serious consideration."[10]

Public libraries almost never desegregated for that reason alone.
Local action by African American residents was necessary. The fact
that some libraries refused to desegregate until after passage of the
Civil Rights Act of 1964 reveals the uneven patterns of change in
southern institutions that were under local rather than national control. In the 1940s, even as a few libraries were desegregating, new
segregated libraries were still opening for business.

Despite the activity of the 1920s and 1930s—the construction of
buildings, the creation of collections, and the extension of library
services for African Americans—the situation in the south remained
dismal in the 1940s. But there were cracks in the foundation. While
many new libraries continued to open on a segregated basis (as in
Alexandria), a few began life as integrated public services. A further
indication of change was the desegregation of a few libraries that had
long operated on a segregated basis. For example, as Alexandria was
adjusting its public library policies in response to pressure from African American residents, Louisville was experiencing pressure from
local black residents who were interested in using the entire library.
Among the first to offer segregated services to African Americans,
Louisville was also one of the first to desegregate its public library,
after years of local pressure. During the war, African American residents of Evansville, Indiana, (north of the Ohio River but south and
west of Louisville) began to use collections and services in branches
beyond segregated Cherry Street.[11] In the 1950s, the Cherry Street
building was sold, and the city used the $15,000 in proceeds to
acquire a bookmobile.[12]

Murray Atkins Walls was a key figure in desegregating the Louisville library. A native of Indiana, she had taught school in Indianapolis and had taken summer courses at Columbia University. She had married a Louisville physician, John Walls, in 1935 but did not move permanently to the city until 1940, when she took a job there in public housing. Both she and her husband were active in the local chapter of the NAACP and in various civic organizations, including interracial ones.

One day in the spring of 1941, Murray Walls went to the main building of the Louisville Free Public Library to do some research for a speech she was preparing to give at Louisville Municipal College, the African American arm of the University of Louisville. She found that she was not welcome at the main library or at any branches other than the Western and Eastern ones. She decided to send a letter to Joseph Rauch, who had moved to Louisville in 1912 to become rabbi at Congregation Adath Israel. He had served on the library's board since 1922 and had been its president for much of that time.[13] In her letter Walls wrote, "I, like many other Negroes in Louisville, find it almost unbearable not to be able to visit the Main Library or any convenient Branch." She asked the board to open the library to all in support of democracy and out of a sense of fairness.[14]

Rauch did not answer her letter, but library director Harold F. Brigham did respond a few weeks later. Although he said that the library administration was unwilling to go against traditional patterns of race relations, he did acknowledge that the two colored branches were inadequate for the educated black elite and that all African Americans had the right to have access to everything in the library's collection. Encouraged, Walls wrote more letters and, with a committee of supporters, visited the library board, asking to use the library on the same basis as whites. Board members dismissed their request without discussion.

On Bill of Rights Day in December 1941, Walls and other NAACP members went to the main library's auditorium to hear President Roosevelt's radio address. At first, the woman in charge tried to discourage them from entering; but after a quick call to Brigham, she allowed group members to seat themselves and listen to the radio broadcast alongside white library users. Walls later called it one of the first sit-ins of the civil rights movement. In 1948, after more activism, the board desegregated Louisville's main library; and in 1952, it opened all the branches to African Americans.[15] Louisville was quickly joined by Nashville, which in 1948 sold the Negro branch building to a plumbing company for $42,000. Branch librarian Ophelia E. Lockert organized a library improvement committee, whose members included Arna Bontemps, a writer and head of the Fisk University library, and Calvin McKissack, an architect whose brother Moses had been passed over when the Negro library was being planned. The committee recommended that a new branch be situated in the Hadley Park neighborhood, that a bookmobile be acquired to extend services beyond the library building, and that the main library be opened to African Americans. While Lockert worked in temporary quarters housing the old Negro branch's collection, library officials quietly desegregated the library in 1949. The Hadley Park Branch opened in 1952.[16]

In 1949, the Tennessee cities of Knoxville and Chattanooga both decided to allow African American adults to use the main library, and a year later Chattanooga also began allowing children to use it, although the restrooms remained off limits. Apparently the change in Chattanooga occurred after the city commission fielded a request for the funding of a new branch library for African Americans. Although some whites complained about having to share space and collections with blacks, others apparently agreed with or at least accepted the decision to save money with a single service. Days after the library board decided to desegregate, the local black-owned newspaper printed an editorial congratulating the board on its sound decision.[17] That same year, San Antonio, Texas, opened its main library to African Americans. Librarian Julia Grothaus, board president M. M. Harris, and board member John McMahon (the president of a local Catholic women's college) secured the policy change and then relied on Prudence Curry, head of the Carver Negro Branch, to spread the word "without fanfare." By 1953, the board included an African American trustee, Stonewall Davis.[18]

However, with most new libraries and branches, it was business as usual. Gaffney, South Carolina, opened a branch for blacks in 1942 and a second branch for them as late as 1961. In 1945, Stillwater, Oklahoma, appropriated $1,000 to establish a public library for

African Americans in an annex of the Booker T. Washington School, where all grades were taught.[19] North Little Rock, Arkansas, opened its library with a separate Negro branch in 1947. In Montgomery, Alabama, the Union Street Branch for Negroes opened in 1948.[20]

Five years after the public library in Macon, Georgia, opened to whites in 1923, a collection of about five hundred books became available to African Americans in a "branch" that was open for a few hours a day. It occupied three different buildings but never increased in size and was finally abandoned in 1949. By then, Macon's public library was serving whites throughout Bibb and Twiggs counties. In 1953, the Macon Federation of Colored Women's Clubs was able to convince the city library to add a branch for African Americans with its own staff, budget, and board. In Columbus, Georgia, the public library used WPA funds to support a summer reading program at the black high school in the late 1930s. After WPA funding ended in 1941, the high school library stayed open an extra hour after classes ended to serve the public. The collection included the WPA books and new bestsellers that the school librarian purchased with a $10-a-month budget from the public library. In 1945, the public library opened a branch with five hundred books in a public housing project. Not until 1953 did African Americans in Columbus have a purpose-built public library branch.[21]

By 1944, twelve of the thirteen southern state library agencies had acknowledged the dearth of collections and services for urban and rural blacks and were offering some form of service to African Americans statewide.[22] In Louisiana, statewide service was centered at Southern University, a black land-grant college in Baton Rouge. Established in June 1943 and headed by Carrie C. Robinson, a graduate of the library school at Hampton, the service answered reference questions, mailed books and booklists to black adults on request, and issued certificates to those who read twelve specified books in a year. The service did not lend novels or children's books. During its first year of operation, the service oversaw 4,500 transactions with residents from most of the parishes in the state.[23]

In the late 1930s, when she was gathering data for her dissertation, Gleason identified four southern library systems that served African Americans on a segregated basis. By 1944, that number had jumped by at least twenty, with North Carolina and Texas offering the most service and Alabama and Arkansas the least.[24] At the same time, a new model was being put in place. For instance, when Newland, North Carolina, established its first public library in 1942, officials seem to have leveraged the novelty of a free circulating collection to provide the additional innovation of integrated service. As a report put it, "library service was new to all citizens and all were privileged to make use of it at the same time."[25] Five years later, Hazard, Kentucky, opened its new Bobby Davis Memorial Library, which (along with the park in which it sat) had been donated by Mr. and Mrs. L. O. Davis in honor of their son, who had died during World War II. Although African Americans were not allowed to attend the library's Great Books discussion program, they were able to use the collection alongside all other Perry County residents.[26]

Yet even as some new libraries were opening to all, their counterparts elsewhere were experiencing the obstructions and delays so common during the previous decades. Progress in a few places was overshadowed by the continuing widespread ban on total access for African Americans. In some places, racial segregation of southern public libraries not only persisted but grew. One such case occurred in the East Texas city of Tyler. In the 1940s, Tyler's population was about 26 percent African American, and the surrounding Smith County's about 30 percent. When the Negro Public Library opened in 1941, it served approximately 20,000 people.[27] After decades of being denied access to the central library, black residents finally had public library services; and the facility remained open until 1968, when desegregation of the municipal library finally made it redundant. In contrast to the agitation that led to the opening of Alexandria's separate library, the mood was quieter in Tyler, where African Americans worked in collaboration with paternalistic whites.

In 1898, Tyler, the county seat, had been the site of a Texas Federation of Women's Clubs meeting in which the statewide group followed the national organization's decision to focus on establishing public libraries. Inspired, the Tyler chapter began planning and raising funds, and in the spring of 1899 it opened a library of 235 volumes to members who paid $1 for a borrower's card. In 1901, the chapter converted the members-only institution to a free public library, and by 1903 the city had received Carnegie's pledge for a building. When it opened in 1904, the Carnegie library officially became the property and responsibility of the city of Tyler.[28]

By 1941, when whites and blacks came together to form the provisional board of a new Negro library, the city's African American population had been denied access to the public library for forty years. By calling their committee "provisional," they indicated their belief that the city, as funder, would have the right to appoint a permanent board or that the main city library might found it as a branch library under the supervision of the library director and board. White members of the provisional board included Lillian Peek, coordinator of family education for the Tyler public schools; Lucy Marsh, secretary of her father's estate; attorney H. B. Marsh, who chaired the Negro library's budget committee; and Woman's Forum member Lenora Woldert, whose late husband had been an important area businessman. Among the African American members was E. E. Neal, who taught sociology at Texas College and served as the publicity chairman for the local NAACP chapter.[29] The provisional librarian was Bessie Davis Randall, who in the 1930s had been the librarian at all-black Emmett Scott School, which served all grades during her time there.[30]

In 1940, a local group known as the Tyler Community Council for Family Living had organized into committees to help improve nutrition among poor families, with a focus on school lunches, home gardening and canning, house and property upkeep, and school guidance counseling. Coordinator Lillian Peek was working to involve existing volunteer associations in this task. She had approached black leaders in Tyler to let them know about the council's work, and the result was the creation of the Negro Community Council. At a January 1941 meeting at the Emmett Scott School, black council members identified several necessary projects, including hot lunches for schoolchildren, crime prevention, street paving, a vocational training program for boys, and a library. Peek invited Oscar Burton, vice-president and general manager of Gulf States Telephone Company, to head the white council's new race relations committee and serve as an adviser to the Negro Community Council. Peek told him that the first order of business would be the Negro library, which had "reached a stage where it needs your help right now." The white council was transforming its library committee into a broader race relations committee, and Burton agreed to serve. He seemed especially interested in Peek's point about the council's commitment to democracy and self-sufficiency, which he understood to mean making people less dependent on Depression-era federal aid.[31]

Burton convened a meeting of the Race Relations Committee at the Chamber of Commerce; but according to Peek's account, only whites spoke. She herself reported on the creation and activities of the Negro Community Council, and Lucy Marsh reported on the library project. Marsh said that the Negro Community Council had set two goals: not only the creation of a library but the establishment of "a large active white committee" to support it. Ina Roberts, the librarian at the white Tyler Junior College, reported that the Negro library had received lumber and furnishings from several companies and that the labor of preparing the room was provided by local black carpenters and students from the black Texas College. Even the library's sign involved free black labor because a Texas College faculty member had designed and lettered it.[32]

By June 1941, Randall had accessioned 731 books and cataloged 100 of them. All were gifts; the library also had on hand a little more than $400 in cash donations.[33] Lenora Woldert attended the city commission meeting that month, giving a report that emphasized the role of Tyler's churches in helping establish a reading room for Negroes. She asked the city to add a $100 "donation" to the money already raised. City manager G. D. Fairtrace recommended giving that money from the existing library fund, and the commission did so.[34]

On July 23, 1941, Tyler's Negro library, represented by Mrs. A. B. Gertz in her role as chairman of the board of directors, entered into an agreement with the seven trustees of Bethlehem Baptist Church to use its basement as the site for the newly formed library's collection and services. They agreed that the library would supply a partition, shelving, tables, chairs, and other furnishings and books, all of which would remain the property of the library and "all of which will be available to and for the use of the members of said church and all of the colored children who reside in the vicinity thereof and who may avail themselves of the advantages thereof."[35]

In August, however, Marsh reported that she had discovered that city commission members, who had spoken in favor of the project, were not interested in supporting it financially. Perhaps she had heard that the Tyler Public Library board had voted to write a letter to the city commission saying that, if the commission appropriated funds for the Negro library, it should also appoint a separate board under the commission's supervision. In other words, the public library's board had no interest in administering a branch for local African Americans.

Seeking another source of support, Marsh contacted the Carnegie Corporation, only to discover that it was not making such grants anymore.[36] But the provisional board did begin to receive help from an outside source, the extension division of the Texas State Library. Division head Dorothy Cotton Journeay had logged many miles in her own car and at her own expense to visit and offer advice to the state's far-flung libraries.[37] She visited Tyler's Negro library in December 1941 and then made a return visit in January to give her report and attend the board meeting. Journeay recommended simplifying book cataloging by dropping Cutter numbers, reshelving daily and leaving every third shelf only half full, and making the library a branch of the Tyler Public Library under the supervision of its head librarian.[38] She apparently was unaware that the white library had already rejected that option. Journeay recalled her December visit to the library as "exhilarating," especially as compared to her visits to long-standing, middling white libraries. Her report on her second visit concluded with the observation that Texas did not provide sufficient library collections and services for its black population and expressed a hope that Tyler would inspire others throughout the state to establish libraries for African Americans.[39]

At her meeting with the provisional board in January 1942, Journeay met three new white members: not only Burton but also Reverend Meade Brown, an Episcopal pastor, and Gus F. Taylor, president of Citizens Bank. Taylor agreed to chair the finance committee, telling his new colleagues to think of him as "an agitator" committed to the library project. Burton chaired a committee charged with securing support from the city commission, but he informed his fellow board members that his committee would "act cautiously in approaching the Commission for reasons best known to committee."[40]

It was summer before Burton attended a commission meeting to discuss the library. With him were businessmen E. P. McKenna and J. H. Calhoun as well as Lenora Woldert and Lillian Peek. Burton asked the commission to appropriate $100 a month for the fiscal year beginning on July 1. The $1,200 annually would almost cover the $1,450 the library had budgeted for the year's operations. He also asked that the appropriation be formalized by law and that the city take responsibility for the library management. This could be done, he suggested, by delegating authority to the existing public library's board, which might in turn appoint a board to update and advise them about the Negro branch's operations. Woldert spoke in favor of the appropriation, saying that the city "should help the negroes help themselves." She also informed the commission that the Negro library's provisional board would take responsibility for providing a permanent site for the institution. In support of Woldert, McKenna said that she was largely responsible for the creation and maintenance of the library, and he invited the commissioners to visit the church basement to see for themselves what had been accomplished. Calhoun echoed Woldert's sentiments, saying that the city fathers had an obligation to provide the leadership that Negroes expected from them.[41]

The white-owned *Tyler Courier-Times* occasionally published news stories about the library and its plans. In January, the paper covered the board meeting that Journeay had attended, noting that she had described the operations of the library for African Americans in Waco. The paper also reported that the library was planning to raise funds by holding a movie night, that black organizations such as the Chauffeurs Association were selling tickets, and that whites had bought tickets to give to their black servants and employees. The article also summarized the librarian's report to the board, identifying her as "Bessie Randall, Negress." During the summer, the paper published a brief announcement that a budget for the library would be under consideration at the next commission meeting and asserted that the library was "under the direction of Tyler women who have been raising money for its support."[42]

A *Courier-Times* editorial advocated for the city commission to appropriate an annual budget for the library, stating, "This is a reasonable request. The Negroes of the community are taxpayers and are entitled to this service since they have shown that it is a service that they appreciate and will take advantage of." In other words, it was not enough to be a taxpayer; an African American had to earn the right to use a tax-supported library that, in the white-owned newspaper's formulation, "white citizens have sponsored for the educational and social good of the Negroes." The editorial asserted that the Tyler Community Council for Family Living and the work of Woldert and fellow provisional board member Mrs. J. W. Smiley had overseen the establishment of the library. The writer claimed that Tyler's whites were "liberal" toward blacks, had given four-fifths of the cash raised for the library, and were working with blacks for the betterment of local Negroes.[43] Anyone reading the local newspaper could not have missed the implication that a library accessible to African Americans was not a right but a privilege bestowed by patronizing whites.

In July Burton attended a second city commission meeting, where he was assured that commissioners would consider including the Negro library in the coming year's budget.[44] In September, the commissioners were ready to act. Three of the four present at the meeting voted to appropriate $1,200 for the library, but there was no discussion or vote regarding the idea of making it a branch of the Tyler Public Library.[45] During the same month, ticket sales for a benefit musical concert in the Texas College auditorium yielded close to $90, and the provisional board members made personal donations to round the figure up to $100. The library also received an influx of books when the city manager had 2,000 volumes transferred from Smith County's old rural library to the Negro library. Only three hundred were sturdy enough to be added to the collection.[46]

Tyler's white residents believed that they had taken the leadership role and raised most of the money to establish the library. Librarian Bessie Davis Randall had a different perspective. In an April 1943 article in the Texas Library Association's *News Notes,* she referred to the library only as "the outgrowth of the Negro Community Council."[47] Randall reported that it had received $500 and 2,500 books as donations, that it subscribed to two newspapers and twenty-one magazines, and that she was hoping that the city's appropriation of $1,200 would soon be significantly increased. Tyler's Negro library had joined the state's fifteen public library branches and twenty-three county library branches (none of them in Smith County) that, she wrote, "contribute to the educational, moral and civic uplift of the Negroes of Texas."[48]

Randall resigned in the fall of 1943 to pursue a year of further education; and although the board invited her to return as librarian when she was done, she did not go back to the Tyler library. Sara Jackson replaced her until January 1944, when she was replaced by Julia Warren. When Warren resigned in September 1947, the board hired Willie Mae Kelley.[49]

At the end of 1946, Bethlehem Baptist Church's pastor, Reverend J. M. Stewart, asked to have his basement back for expanded church programming. For years, the provisional board had been looking for a site and raising funds to construct a building of its own. Now Pastor Stewart had given board members a deadline. The board met twice about the matter in January 1947. Woldert reported having $5,500 worth of bonds donated from various sources for a building. She also summarized the history of the library, giving Peek much of the credit for leading the effort. The board wanted the city to take over management of the library and purchase a site, at which time the board would sign over the bonds for the building. One possibility was to purchase a building from Camp Fannin, a defunct World War II army training and prisoner-of-war center outside the city. Meanwhile, the board's secretary wrote a letter thanking the church and asking for more time.[50]

During the summer of 1947, the city paid $2,500 for the army building. It was given sixty-seven days to remove it from Camp Fannin; but without a site, the city had to ask for an extension of the deadline. The next spring, board members informed the city manager that they had found a lot on Lollar Street. In late October 1948, almost two years after Pastor Stewart had tried to dislodge the library from the church basement, a new pastor, Reverend Robert L. Rowe, wrote to the city manager, pointing out that the church had asked at the beginning of the year for its basement back and that it now expected $25 a month in rent until the space was vacated. At its meeting in late October, the library's provisional board voted to start paying rent.

By February 1949, the city had acquired the lot on Lollar Street, and the city engineer was receiving approval from the commissioners to construct the library from materials salvaged from the Camp Fannin building. The library board signed over the bonds to the city to pay for the construction crew. Within a year, the library began operating out of the building on Lollar Street.[51] While the library was an improvement over the complete lack of publicly accessible collections and services that had previously existed in Tyler, it came nowhere near equal in the separate-but-equal formulation.

About the same time that Tyler's library was moving into its own building, the Southeastern Library Association was publishing the results of a survey conducted in nine states—Alabama, Florida, Georgia, Kentucky, Mississippi, North Carolina, South Carolina, Tennessee, and Virginia—in 1946 and 1947. The last chapter of the book-length report was titled "Library Service for Negroes." Of 597 southeastern public library systems, a total of 188—102 county, 67 municipal, and 19 regional—provided some kind of service to African Americans. The survey had left out another thirty-seven reported elsewhere, including five independent libraries, bringing the total to 225, or a little over a third of southeastern public libraries. The report gave a rough estimate of about 550,000 of the 8.5 million books in the region's public libraries available to the approximately 6.8 million African Americans living there. The authors considered this "far from adequate" but portrayed the situation as "rapidly improving," asserting that "the public library is a distinctly public institution . . . nurtured in the American tradition of equal opportunity." Even though a Negro Advisory Committee was listed in an appendix, the report did not advocate taking a step toward equalizing opportunities by desegregating libraries.[52] Whites apparently had a hard time imagining such a step.

CHAPTER 6

Erecting Libraries, Constructing Race

Library buildings, like the books they shelter, have many uses. They are workplaces, storehouses, and community spaces. But they also have symbolic importance, one that involves not only the attributes of the physical building but also the ways in which people interact—or don't interact—with it. The residents of Greensboro, North Carolina, put a great deal of time, thought, action, and money into contesting and then creating a library building that opened with only 150 books on its shelves. In 1916, a newspaper in Nashville, Tennessee, described the new home of that city's Negro branch as "a handsome structure, designed upon the most approved library plans and . . . elegantly furnished and equipped." Yet ten years later an outside consultant stated that the branch's small collection was inadequate and worn out.[1]

The Carnegie Corporation gave building grants; it was up to the locals to put books on the shelves. The result, all too often, was a building that was more symbolically than literally useful. For example, after moving from rented space to an expensive and impressively ornamented central building, the Chicago Public Library faced years of inadequate operating budgets doled out by city officials who were content with symbolism rather than service. Budgetary constraints sometimes forced the library to curtail collection development and cut Sunday hours, undermining its ability to attract working-class readers. In her study of the cultural elite's influence on Chicago at the end of the nineteenth century, Helen Horowitz demonstrates that a magnificent library building designed to inspire its visitors might conflict with the institution's intention to serve the popular taste for literature. In the words of the fictional Irish immigrant to Chicago, Mr. Dooley, "a Carnaygie libry is archytechoor, not litrachoor."[2]

For the most part, African American library buildings were small, with inadequate collections and funding. Nevertheless, they were significant, both as physical places in the urban landscape and as symbolic spaces in the lives of local black communities. Purpose-built structures had a greater visual impact than did more modest services set up in basements of public libraries (as in Jacksonville, Florida) or in rooms of high schools (as in Galveston, Texas). Separate public library buildings loomed large in their neighborhoods. With their classical columns, brick construction, and stone trim, they projected stability and opportunity.

In *The Production of Space*, French sociologist Henri Lefebvre posits three useful concepts. First is *perceived spatial practice*—that is, the idea that every society creates its own distinctive space. Thus, the spatial practice of the New South included racial segregation and gender-specific roles designed to create appropriate places for black men, black women, and white women, and to keep those places separate from and subordinate to the place of white men.

Second is his notion of *conceived space*, the sort of design an urban planner, an engineer, or an architect might devise. In the Carnegie years, the space that eventually became a library always received attention from library trustees and community backers, who searched for the ideal building site; from librarians, architects, and city engineers, who envisioned the space; from Carnegie's secretary, James Bertram, who obsessively collected and distributed floor plans; and from construction contractors and subcontractors, who focused on the library as a jobsite.

Third is Lefebvre's concept of *space as it is lived*, in which users appropriate a physical space for their own imaginative and symbolic purposes. Geographers have argued that public space can be used to reify cultural categories and to undermine them. Historians of Richmond, Virginia, have pointed out that a city's black residents may recall their neighborhood as a space of their own making, rather than the city's, a conceptualization that allows them to construct it as "a place of congregation as well as segregation." As library historian Phyllis Dain has pointed out, public libraries may have opened with an elitist, uplift-the-masses attitude, but in operation they were tools that visitors put to various unpredictable uses.[3]

According to architectural historian Abigail Van Slyck, libraries were "always cultural artifacts whose meanings varied with the intentions and experiences of a diverse group of users." She argues that large, imposing, and elaborately ornamented central libraries conveyed the cultural elite's view of the buildings as institutions fostering their own values, interests, and belief systems. The creation of more modest and welcoming branches in residential neighborhoods reflected the impulses of professional librarians, who wanted to situate branches close to working-class homes, and of middle-class club women, who wanted to secure public space for their intellectual pursuits. When it came time to build those branches, however, library governing boards tended to take less interest in the projects, delegating more of the decision making to librarians, who sought to make these neighborhood buildings attractive to working-class visitors, particularly immigrant children.[4] The exception to that pattern was the attitude toward branches for African Americans. In those cases, library boards actively engaged in discussions, as did city officials, librarians, local blacks, and, in the early years, Booker T. Washington's Tuskegee machine. They negotiated building sites, architect selection, public and private funding, exterior and interior designs, and the ways in which the building's symbolic and literal value would be celebrated when construction began or ended.

Van Slyck demonstrates that public library design and construction both influenced and were influenced by ideas about culture, class, gender, and race. She documents the case of Gainesville, Texas, where librarian Lillian Gunter planned to use Carnegie's 1913 grant to extend services to African Americans by including a Negro reading room in the basement of her new Carnegie library, where it (and the toilet facilities) would be out of sight. Yet she took no responsibility for the collection, believing that African Americans should themselves donate whatever books and periodicals would be on offer. In any event, the city council rejected Gunter's proposed use for the room, and Gainesville's blacks had to wait for another decade before a reading room became available to them in the Gainesville Colored School.[5] The whites in Gainesville ascribed a very different meaning to cultural space than did the blacks who were shut out of it.

Newspaper descriptions of black libraries emphasized the material nature of the structures and their modern conveniences—such as electric lights and steam heat—which not all southern blacks had access to in their schools and homes. Detailed descriptions helped readers imagine themselves occupying the spaces designed to support individual and community literacy. An Evansville, Indiana, newspaper described a new library in precise detail:

> The building fronts 56 feet on Cherry street and runs 40 feet on Church street. The main entrance and vestibule are of white stone. The balance of the exterior, up to the first floor transom level, is of a brown pressed brick. Above the transom level the exterior walls are of brick covered with white stucco. The building is very attractive. The roof is glazed tile. There is a full size basement in which are . . . a men's meeting room and toilets. On the first floor are two reading rooms, each 17 by 30 feet, and a room for the librarian. The building is electrically lighted and will have Public Service steam heat. The vestibule has a tile and wood panelled wainscoating. The stairways are ornamental cast iron.[6]

A reporter described Knoxville's new branch building in similar detail:

> There is one large, well lighted hall, one end of which is to be used as a general reading room. A portion of the other end is railed off for research and study work. Open book cases line the wall and there are racks and shelves for magazines and newspapers. . . . The librarian's desk is in the center of the room facing the main door. In the basement or ground floor is an auditorium which can be used for lectures, meetings and entertainments. The building is furnace heated and has all modern improvements.[7]

The availability of money and the willingness to spend it always prefigured and influenced the construction of libraries. In contrast to other communities, Louisville received a disproportionately high share of Carnegie dollars. The corporation pledged $250,000 for the central building and another $200,000 for eight branches. The city supplemented the central library grant using various methods and spent $435,000 for the site, structure, and furnishings of the main library. Opened in July 1908, the two-story T-shaped facility was built of gray limestone and featured a third story over the central section as well as a basement. The front portion of the structure was 274 feet wide by 42 feet deep, while the back section measured 74 by 77 feet. About 125,000 volumes were housed in the new building, and the open stacks room alone held 20,000 volumes in a "magnificent" space measuring 38 by 98 feet. The exterior and the lobby were designed in Louis XVI style, with two-story fluted columns at the entrance and in the lobby. Etched into the spaces between the interior columns were names associated with the western canon: Shakespeare, Bacon, and other famous writers. The lobby was flanked on both sides by marble staircases with ornamental iron railings; they led to the second floor, where an art room and a children's room were situated.[8]

Louisville's Western Colored Branch Library opened a few months later. It held 3,000 volumes in a one-story Carnegie building, which measured seventy-seven by forty-five feet and cost $43,343 to build and equip. This was considerably more than most Carnegie library buildings cost; about two-thirds came in below $20,000.[9] The branch had been established in 1905 in rented space on the first floor of a private residence in a predominately black neighborhood on the city's west side. The new branch building, still on the west side, was just blocks from the central library. The building's exterior was brick with stone trim. On the first floor were an adult reading room and a children's reading room. In the basement were two classrooms and an auditorium.[10] The Eastern Colored Branch Library, also Carnegie funded, opened in 1914 in a sixty-by-eighty-foot building, with the library and an auditorium on the first floor and classrooms and a playroom in the basement.[11]

In Louisville, an abundance of Carnegie money and local white good will precluded the arguments over library location that erupted in other cities and towns, where only one library was available to serve the entire black population. For example, in Nashville, where some white library leaders were skeptical about the wisdom of providing a branch for blacks, black library leaders disagreed about where the branch should be built. Likewise, in Greensboro, some worried that a location on Bennett College's grounds would discourage a broad swath of the public from visiting the library.

As separate branches for African Americans were being constructed, segregated YMCAs and YWCAs were also appearing on the urban landscape. These recreation centers cost less to construct than libraries did. Louisville had a YMCA whose building and lot totaled $10,000; New Orleans's cost $6,400, Knoxville's $2,000. W. E. B. Du Bois called them "monuments to a miserable unchristian and unmanly prejudice," and his criticism could be applied to libraries as well: "the good accomplished is no excuse for the insult offered."[12]

The injection of Carnegie funds and the requisite annual city appropriation for maintenance might have fed into the black economy, providing design and construction projects for African American architects, engineers, contractors, and trades workers. Instead, local black professionals and skilled workers received little or no benefit from these important building projects in their neighborhoods. Even in a staunchly independent community such as Savannah's, the black library's architect, Julien de Bruyn Kops, was a white employee of the city. Kops adapted plans from a library in Sheridan, Indiana, that Bertram had sent him.[13]

At the beginning of the twentieth century, few blacks had the courage or the means to enter the architecture profession. Even those who were interested in the career faced the expense of attending a northern college, where architectural programs were deeper and stronger than those in the south. But even if they were able to conquer that hurdle, discrimination would limit their commissions and thus their ability to earn a livelihood.[14]

At the time the Carnegie buildings were going up, Tuskegee Institute was the only college for African Americans that offered an architecture program. Howard University did not establish its architecture curriculum until 1919, Hampton Institute not until 1940.[15] Because the building trades were among the practical industrial arts that Booker T. Washington emphasized, Tuskegee-trained students had long been learning to repair and construct buildings and make bricks. The training had the added advantage of providing the school with affordable labor, an important consideration for Washington, who spent half of each year soliciting funds to keep the institute open. It also provided work for destitute students, who traded their labor for an education at Tuskegee, and discouraged vandalism because students who had constructed campus buildings took pride in them.

By the 1890s, the field of architecture was becoming professionalized. Yet even in the white world, it was difficult to convince potential customers of the advantages of hiring an architect. The difficulty was even more extreme in the black world. African American architects faced many of the same barriers that black physicians and business owners did: racial prejudice not only from whites but sometimes even from middle-class blacks, who preferred to take their business to white professionals. Such behavior prompted local business leagues and newspapers to launch campaigns to encourage African Americans to support each other and to keep their dollars in their own segregated neighborhoods. However, the architecture profession was particularly problematic. As the field split off from the other building trades and became more professional, artistic, and exclusive (and less backbreaking), it drew white men in a way that bricklaying and other construction work did not.

This tension was reflected in Washington's choice of Robert T. Taylor, a graduate of the Massachusetts Institute of Technology, to head Tuskegee's new architecture program. In addition to teaching and mentoring students, Taylor also designed campus buildings, including Tuskegee's Carnegie library. Unlike the other manual arts teachers, he had a college degree and thus had more in common with the teachers in the school's academic division, who had graduated from Fisk, Harvard, and other colleges. But his curriculum mixed design with manual skills, with the goal of creating a fallback for a graduate who could not land contracts in a world primed to ignore him.[16]

At the time, Tuskegee was still an industrial school whose architecture program could not compete with those at colleges and universities. It was inadequate for someone as ambitious as William Sidney Pittman, the future architect of Houston's Negro library. After working his way through the institute, the Alabama native moved to Philadelphia to study architecture at Drexel Institute, receiving financial aid from Booker T. Washington in exchange for his promise to come back to Tuskegee to teach.

In 1900 Pittman returned to the institute in time to participate in the planning of Tuskegee's Carnegie library, providing the water-color perspective sketch of the structure.[17] Alongside him on the faculty was John A. Lankford. Raised in Missouri, Lankford had studied mechanical drawing, carpentry, and engineering at Lincoln Institute before moving to Tuskegee in 1896 to study under Taylor. Among his early commissions was the design and building of Palmer Hall on the campus of the Agricultural and Mechanical College in Normal, Alabama.

Lankford moved to Washington, D.C. in 1902 to design and oversee construction of the headquarters of an African American fraternal organization, the United Order of True Reformers.[18] At the grand opening, Grand Worthy Master Dr. W. L. Taylor (whose house Lankford would design in 1909) described the building's brief history, noting his determination to employ a black architect and black tradesmen because "we wanted this building put up to the credit of the Negro Race."[19] In addition to standing as a monument of accomplishment in the American city with the largest number of African American residents at the time, the building launched Lankford's career in Washington and "revolutionized the building trade among the Negroes of the District of Columbia" because he insisted on hiring black workers in the building trades.[20] In an address to the National Negro Business League in 1905, Lankford asserted that the structure "stands out to the civilized world as . . . an example of what the Negro can do and has done with his brain, skill and money."[21]

Washington, D.C., was home to many skilled African American workers, including bricklayers, carpenters, and painters.[22] For architects, it was a promising milieu; so in 1905, Pittman, unhappy working under Taylor at Tuskegee, moved there to work as a draftsman for Lankford. He designed the segregated YMCA building and in 1907 created the Negro Building at the Jamestown Tercentennial. After marrying Booker T. Washington's daughter, Portia, he remained in Washington until 1913, when the couple moved to Dallas.[23]

Pittman was the first black architect in Dallas. During his tenure there, he built not only the Colored Carnegie Library in Houston but also Houston's Wesley Chapel, which served members of the African Methodist Episcopal church. He also built AME churches in other Texas towns. Three years after completing the library in Houston, Pittman designed the Texas headquarters of the Grand Lodge of the Colored Knights of Pythias, "the most distinctive building in Deep Ellum," which was Dallas's main black neighborhood and business district.[24]

Washington's son-in-law was an ambitious "race man" who insisted on hiring black tradesmen wherever possible. For example, his design for the Saint James AME Temple, which opened in 1921 in Dallas, was built by black contractors and construction workers. The black-owned *Dallas Express* newspaper ran a photograph of the new structure, saying in the caption that "every Negro should feel a measure of genuine pride in this building as it proves that there is no color in the line of the building art—that the black man can do anything, if given a chance, anyone else can do."[25] Yet a decade earlier, Pittman may have had trouble finding such skilled workers in urban Texas. A 1902 report indicates that there were four black carpenters/contractors in Houston and two white contractors who had segregated work crews. At the time Houston did not have a black plumber, a black brick contractor, or a black plasterer.[26]

Like other designers of Carnegie library buildings, Pittman often found himself caught among the expectations of librarians, James Bertram, and community officials and leaders. Yet his connections could also work in his favor. For instance, Washington's assistant, Emmett J. Scott, intervened in the case of his hometown, Houston, urging the library committee to hire Pittman as architect for the new building.[27] By April 1911, Pittman had the job, thanks not only to Scott's interest but also to the work of local library advocate J. B. Bell.[28]

Although Bertram routinely sent his "Notes on the Erection of Library Bildings" with the letter confirming a Carnegie grant, his pamphlet somehow lost its way to Houston. Consequently, Pittman sketched plans for the library without having seen the Carnegie guidelines, which recommended reserving as much space as possible for reading rooms and stacks, even if entrances, coat closets, and other such areas were cramped.[29] In July 1911, Pittman sent a set of

Figure 6. William Sidney Pittman designed Houston's Colored Carnegie Library building. In rainy weather, the unpaved street where it was situated became muddy and difficult to traverse. Courtesy of the Houston Public Library Collection, Houston Metropolitan Research Center.

his plans to Scott, explaining that the library committee had made specific suggestions about the design of the building and noting that he had given the project his fullest attention and effort.[30] True to form, however, Bertram criticized Pittman's design, suggesting that he reduce the size of the elaborate entrance and expand the space for books and readers.[31] When the library opened two years later, its foyer was so small that the local newspaper took note of it (fig. 6).[32]

Booker T. Washington kept his son-in-law informed about possible opportunities, telling him in 1907 that Howard University was expecting a Carnegie library building grant, in 1909 that the Normal School for Colored Students in Montgomery was planning a library, and in 1911 that both Meridian, Mississippi, and New Orleans were expecting Carnegie grants for libraries.[33] Yet even though he followed up on these leads, Pittman found it difficult to secure design contracts for libraries. The case of Savannah's Carnegie library for

African Americans suggests why. Apparently, officials in Savannah allowed only white architects to submit designs for consideration. Pittman and his old colleague Lankford protested, and Savannah Negro Business League members wrote to R. A. Franks, treasurer of the Carnegie Corporation, stating their preference for a black architect. But their efforts were too late; the selected white architect had already submitted his designs to Bertram for approval.[34]

In addition to meeting overt discrimination, black architects were stymied by more subtle methods of architect selection. It was customary for library trustees to assign additional branch designs to the same architects who had worked on previous branches.[35] When cities built library branches for white neighborhoods, using white architects, the practice favored those same white architects when library trustees turned their attention to branches for African Americans. Such was the case in Nashville. The city had hired the New York architectural firm Ackerman and Ross to design the expensive main library building. Bertram criticized them for wasting space and refused the board's subsequent request for a grant to enlarge the building. When the board was ready to begin the North branch project (for whites), they invited architects' bids rather than rehiring the New Yorkers. The job went to Clarence K. Colley, a local white architect, who in 1911 had designed the administration building at the new Middle Tennessee State Normal School in Murfreesboro. When the time came to choose an architect for the Negro branch, the Nashville board decided to avoid expense and delay and simply appointed Colley to the task because his work on the North branch had been satisfactory.[36] As a result, a local black architect, Moses McKissack III, had no chance to bid on the city's branch for blacks (fig. 7).

McKissack's father and grandfather had learned the building trades as slaves. After working with his father and others, McKissack moved to Nashville in 1905 and established himself as an architect-builder, designing and constructing homes for whites who worked at Vanderbilt University. He was responsible for the design and construction of the Carnegie library at Fisk University, which opened in 1908, five years before the Nashville library board decided to hire Colley.[37] McKissack would have been the logical choice for the public library branch, but he apparently was never considered.

Figure 7. Carnegie building projects did not always create jobs for black architects and other skilled trades workers. In Nashville, local white architect Clarence K. Colley designed the Negro Public Library, which opened in 1916. Courtesy of the Metropolitan Government Archives of Nashville and Davidson County.

In New Orleans the library board decided to follow the same procedure for the black Dryades branch that they had used to find an architect for the white Canal branch: architects would submit plans, and the committee would recommend one to the board for approval.[38] Early in 1914, the board sent circulars about the competition to the city's architects.[39] A month later, the board approved the building committee's recommendation that local architect William R. Burk's submission be accepted.[40] Burk and his partner Joseph J. Lagarde had also won the earlier competition to design the Canal branch, so the Dryades contest seemed rather like an exercise for the sake of appearances.[41]

By the second week of March, the board had selected the plans and sent them to the mayor and council so that bids could be requested for the construction work.[42] In June 1914, the board ran newspaper ads asking for construction bids, which the city opened on June 16. In August board members decided to go with the lowest bid,

$21,300, from E. Richarme.[43] It is not clear whether any of the city's black artisans or laborers were hired to work on the building, but they probably had some involvement. According to reports, African American tradesmen in New Orleans received jobs and pay comparable to those of white skilled workers, and they had constructed Tulane University's library in 1901–2.[44]

Beyond hands-on construction, a group of black residents in New Orleans was involved in the rituals around the library's construction. In many communities, cornerstone-laying ceremonies and grand-opening celebrations highlighted the significance of a new building. Among African Americans, opening-day ceremonies for their new Carnegie libraries evoked the past and the future. Speakers talked about the efforts that had gone into creating the libraries and the achievements of those who had persisted despite difficulties and opposition. They also discussed the potential that the new buildings represented and expressed their hopes that African Americans would put the libraries to good and frequent use. Local newspapers often covered such events, spreading the word beyond those who had attended the festivities.

Black library advocates in New Orleans—where even a funeral is an opportunity for a musical parade—wanted to celebrate their accomplishment. Early in 1915, library board president John Fitzpatrick (who as mayor had secured the use of the old courthouse for the city's first public library in 1896) met with a group who expressed interest in having a cornerstone-laying ceremony to launch the Dryades branch project. He replied that branch libraries never had such ceremonies but assured them that there would be "proper ceremonies" when the building was finished. Librarian Henry Gill reported that he had met with "Mr. Jones" (probably Reverend Robert E. Jones), who had asked for a library ceremony in time for Booker T. Washington's visit to New Orleans, but the board chose to wait until the building was completed. About a month before the building was scheduled to be finished, the board began planning the dedication ceremony. Ideas for speakers came and went. At the same time, the board decided to ask the city engineer to request bids on furnishings for the branch. Then, noticing they had spent almost all their money, members also decided to ask the city for a book acquisitions budget. The architect Burk offered to provide furniture, but the board managed to scrape together enough money to place an order.[45]

On the morning of Thursday, July 29, board members met at the new library. City engineer W. J. Hardee inspected the building and declared it to be satisfactory. Mayor Behrman then gave the building keys to the library board. "Owing to the fact that the receiving of the Building was precipitated by the letter of the City Engineer announcing that the Building was ready to be transferred on the following morning, the President suggested that as this Branch was now in the control of the Library Board for Library purposes, no other ceremonies were necessary. This suggestion of the President was approved by the Board." In other words, board members saw no reason to allow blacks in New Orleans to celebrate or congregate in observance of this important milestone in their history. The mayor intervened. At their September meeting, he told the board that a group of leading blacks had discussed the matter with him, and he suggested the board make arrangements for them to hold an opening ceremony. It was planned for mid-October, a few weeks after the expected arrival of the furniture.[46]

But problems arose. Shortly before the ceremony, a hurricane damaged the new library's roof; it needed repairing before the building could open. Then the furniture contractor defaulted on his promise to fill the library's order by October 3, which board members discovered three days before the opening ceremony. Consequently, the board contacted "the Committee of Colored People" to say that the opening would be postponed by a week, to Saturday, October 23. At the ceremony the city's acting mayor filled in for the absent mayor. Library board president John Fitzpatrick addressed the crowd, as did J. M. Vance, chairman of the board's arrangement committee. Members of the "Committee of Colored People" also spoke, including Reverend Robert E. Jones, chairman of the day; Mrs. S. F. Williams representing the schools; Rev. J. L. Burrell representing the churches; F. B. Smith and Dr. J. T. Newman representing the professions; S. W. Green representing fraternal interests; Albert Workman representing labor organizations; W. E. Cohen representing business interests; and Alfred Lawless, Jr., representing the universities.[47]

Branch library architects tended to follow their own earlier designs, with the result that African American library buildings differed little in their visual aspect from other branches.[48] For example, in Knoxville the library board chose Albert B. Baumann, who had also designed the Lawson McGhee Library, to design the African American library.[49] In New Orleans, Burk designed the Canal Branch exterior in Spanish Renaissance style with buff-colored brick and white terracotta trim, while the Dryades Branch's exterior was beaux-arts with red brick and Bedford stone trim. But each was a two-story building with a double staircase that required visitors to ascend to the main entrance on the upper floor. Over the front door of each building was an open book carved of stone. At Canal the book was flanked by two lamps representing enlightenment, while at Dryades two cornucopia representing the fruits of knowledge were carved on either side of the book. Inside, each library divided the main floor into separate reading rooms for adults and children. On the lower level, each building housed a lecture hall complete with stereopticon equipment.[50] Such similarities implied separate but equal services.

The Dryades Branch did more than provide a collection and the space in which to interact with it. It included meeting space for community groups. The nearby colored YMCA used the auditorium for meetings on Sunday afternoons, after assuring the board that they were not for religious purposes.[51] But in an unexpected twist, the branch was forced to give up library space to another municipal agency. Before the building had been open a year, the mayor had appropriated space in the basement to house the district's board of exemption.[52]

In addition to decorative symbols, branch buildings had inscriptions that contained messages for passersby. Some branches were named after their street or neighborhood location, such as the Auburn Avenue Branch Library in Atlanta and the Brevard Street Branch Library in Charlotte. Others were named after their donors or supporters. Over the door of the Houston and Evansville branch buildings were the words "Carnegie Library." In Greensboro, "Carnegie Negro Library" was carved over the entrance, distinguishing it from the Carnegie Library that served as the town's white library. In contrast, an inscription on a tablet at Knoxville's Negro library read, "This tablet is erected by the City Commissioners of Knoxville in recognition of the faithful efforts of Charles W. Cansler, who first conceived the idea of this library for his race, and who aided materially in securing it."[53]

The cornerstone of the Dryades Branch proclaimed that the library was "The University of the People." This was a common promotional term among public libraries all over the United States. As inscribed on a blacks-only library, however, the phrase suggested that the collection inside was meant to edify rather than entertain. It also implied that the collection was a solution to local schools' inadequate alternatives and that even people too poor to attend college or purchase books could find intellectual sustenance inside.

The buildings housed all the customary activities of early twentieth-century libraries: reference, reading, children's story hours, community and club meetings, book borrowing and returning. But in at least one case, the library served another purpose altogether. When the American Library Association met in New Orleans in April 1932, black attendees used the Dryades Branch auditorium as their headquarters during the conference. That was necessary because they were not allowed to participate in the conference activities that were scheduled at whites-only venues. Four years later, when the conference was held in another segregated city, Richmond, African Americans and some whites protested such treatment. In response, the library association established a policy not to meet in southern cities until all members were given equal access to all venues.[54]

Purpose-built structures housing libraries for African Americans loomed large on the urban landscape. They took their place near churches, schools, YMCAs, office buildings, and clubhouses constructed by and for blacks. They portrayed stability through the use of solid materials such as brick or stone. They symbolized African American activists' ability to attract both public and private financial support for library collections and services. They represented blacks' desire for intellectual stimulation, entertaining reading material, and educational opportunities for their children, who were relegated to separate and inferior public schools with no libraries or inadequate ones. Libraries also provided a secular social space where individuals and organizations could assemble for nonreligious purposes, an alternative to the church as an important congregating place. They offered a space in which their users could interact with the thoughts of whites recorded in books and periodicals without having to interact with actual whites who required them to act out their roles in the southern social hierarchy. African American libraries were part of a larger built environment that demarcated black areas of racially segregated cities and signified the activities, aspirations, and achievements of the residents of those areas. Nonetheless, they furthered the practice of racial segregation. Their separateness helped maintain the fiction of black inferiority and protected white readers from the knowledge of black readers. The libraries' diminutive size reassured whites that separate would not be equal. As a new form of cultural institution, they encompassed competing needs. As a racial project, they encoded white fears and black hopes in structures of paradoxical proportions.

In the 1920s, public library services for African Americans continued to be established, but often they were situated in existing rather than newly erected structures. William Pittman found it difficult to continue working as an architect, in part perhaps because his powerful father-in-law died in 1915, in part because of his own high expectations of others and high opinion of himself. He began taking more jobs as a carpenter and fewer as an architect. His marriage failed, and he reinvented himself as a publisher of a newspaper that relentlessly mocked and criticized black preachers and others whom he considered immoral. He was tried and acquitted of libel, but in 1937, when he was sixty-one, he was sent to Leavenworth Penitentiary after a conviction for obscenity in connection with articles he had published alleging extramarital affairs among certain African Americans. Incarcerated for several years, he served his time working at the prison library.[55]

CHAPTER 7

Books for Black Readers

B eyond the negotiating and navigating necessary to open library buildings for African Americans, the libraries' real promise lay in the collections they gathered and made available. Yet that potential was circumscribed by the kinds of reading material selected for acquisition and dissemination. Public librarians tended to shape local collections according to standards of taste and appropriateness that evolved over time. The result was a tension between the potential for change that a black library represented and the pressure toward stasis apparent in a collection that supported the status quo. In a homogeneous midwestern town, the collection offered at the "Main Street public library" might enhance "social harmony" among the small community of readers who regularly borrowed books.[1] But in a southern town with a substantial proportion of African American residents, the "Main Street public library" offered a collection to white readers, and a separate branch (if it existed) offered another collection to black readers. Even though the collections did feature some of the same books and periodicals, the only "social harmony" the arrangement supported was one designed to keep racist whites happy by barring blacks from so-called community space.

Throughout the Progressive era, urban public librarians identified with the reform movements of the period. They opened the shelves to browsers; established separate rooms for children's collections and services; developed bibliographies to help clubwomen read, write, and research; extended service through branches and deposit stations;

and purchased foreign-language materials for immigrants. In all such efforts, librarians voiced a dual need to both shape and serve their various publics. The shelves offered open access, for example, but the librarian's desk was positioned to aid surveillance lest such access foster misbehavior. Children's rooms provided literature to guide and entertain youthful minds in a setting far away from the adults who expected silence in their reading room. Foreign-language material was proffered as a temporary encouragement for people who were on the way to English-language literacy and thence to Americanization.[2]

Confronted with the prospect of African American readers, southern white librarians who chose to serve them retained their sense of responsibility for shaping their clients through a selection of the "best" literature. They sought to select materials that would answer the needs, as they understood them, of previously unserved readers. Librarians' book selections for the African American branches revealed their expectations and assumptions about their clientele and about their own values as members of the library profession.[3] Although expectations and assumptions differed somewhat between white and black librarians, the usually measly resources available for acquisitions thwarted their ability to shape collections for specific communities. As with buildings, much depended on the budget. Like good municipal bureaucrats everywhere, public librarians routinely asserted that they did not have enough funding to serve their clientele effectively; and among libraries set aside for African Americans, funding was especially thin.

The extent and nature of the collections available in African American public libraries suggest the ways in which library enthusiasts of the time conceptualized an institutional intervention into the reading practices and choices of black Americans. The collections offered at segregated branch libraries are difficult to interpret, however, and their existence raises a number of questions. For instance, did the existence of separate collections of reading material undermine the sharing of a common literature? Were there different expectations and assumptions when the readers were black instead of white? To what extent were books by and about African Americans included? How significant was the availability of the library's collection, given that it represented only a fraction of the printed matter in circulation? Were there differences in the selections of white versus black librarians? What about the library collections made up mainly of books donated by community members rather than handpicked by librarians?

Librarians themselves were puzzled. In 1913, William Yust, who had headed the Louisville Free Public Library when it established its Western Colored Branch in 1905, surveyed the literature on African American reading habits for his colleagues at an American Library Association conference, noting that "what the negro reads is in itself a large and interesting subject."[4] Among the research he cited was an article about the Marblehead libraries, which George Sherwood Dickerman had published in Hampton Institute's periodical, the *Southern Workman*. A wealthy resident of Marblehead, Massachusetts, James J. H. Gregory, had donated books that were distributed to African American communities in the south, with administration of the program run from Atlanta University's library. Dickerman had helped advise Gregory on which books to include in the Marblehead library collections. To determine the most popular books among students, he had surveyed officials from well-respected black colleges such as Atlanta, Fisk, Howard, Tuskegee, and Hampton as well as lesser-known schools in places such as Athens, Georgia, and Norfolk, Virginia. There was no overwhelming agreement about the most popular books. Fifteen schools, the survey's largest consensus, concurred on only two titles: a biography of Abraham Lincoln (presumably the one written by Henry Clay Whitney and published by Baker and Taylor in 1908) and Louisa May Alcott's novel *Little Women* (table 6). Daniel Defoe's classic novel *Robinson Crusoe*, came in third, followed by the author Paul Dunbar, whose poetry and prose, written in black dialect, were so well known that Dickerman did not bother to mention any of the titles. Harriet Beecher Stowe's novel *Uncle Tom's Cabin*, recommended by ten schools, was one vote behind Dunbar, while W. E. B. Du Bois's essay collection, *The Souls of Black Folk*, received nine votes, tying with Sir Walter Scott's novel *Ivanhoe*.[5]

The list was complicated by its mixture of fiction and nonfiction and of adult and juvenile literature, a reflection of the different grade levels taught at the thirty-five institutions surveyed. For example, eight respondents recommended a biography of Frederick Douglass (although Dickerman did not specify whether it was the one

TABLE 6. BOOKS RECOMMENDED BY THIRTY-FIVE AFRICAN AMERICAN
EDUCATORS, IN ORDER OF NUMBER OF RECOMMENDATIONS, 1913

BOOK	NUMBER OF RECOMMENDATIONS
Biography of Abraham Lincoln	15
Little Women	15
Robinson Crusoe	14
Paul Dunbar's works	11
Uncle Tom's Cabin	10
Ivanhoe	9
Souls of Black Folk	9
Ramona	8
Biography of Frederick Douglass	8
Uncle Remus	7
Alice's Adventures in Wonderland	6
Grimms' fairy tales	6
John Halifax, Gentleman	6
The Last Days of Pompeii	6
The Swiss Family Robinson	6

Source: George Sherwood Dickerman, "The Marblehead Libraries," Southern Workman
39 (September 1910): 490–500.

written by Frederic May Holland, Booker T. Washington, or Charles
W. Chesnutt) and Helen Hunt Jackson's young-adult novel Ramona,
a "plea for the Indian." Joel Chandler Harris's folktale collection,
Uncle Remus, received seven votes.[6] A popular Victorian rags-to-riches
novel, John Halifax, Gentleman, by Dinah Mulock Craik, received six
votes, as did Grimms' Fairy Tales. Surprisingly, Washington's Up from
Slavery did not receive enough recommendations to get a mention
from Dickerman, nor did any of Chesnutt's five works of fiction published between 1899 and 1905.

Dickerman found it difficult to summarize his survey results in a
way that would help Gregory decide which volumes to include in the
Marblehead collections. For advice he turned to Sarah Askew, a
white librarian who worked for the New Jersey Public Library Commission and was engaged in a promotional effort to increase libraries throughout the state. Ultimately, Gregory used Askew's recommendations to create his collections, privileging the opinion of a

northern white librarian over the collective opinions of thirty-five educators at black institutions.[7] According to Yust, Askew believed that, when it came to reading, "the colored people's tastes are for quick action, strong emotion, vivid coloring, and simplicity of narration." However, his report for the American Library Association does not provide a data source for her statement. Dickerman's article in the *Southern Workman* included a list of the forty-eight Marblehead titles sent to a school in Cartersville, Georgia, in the summer of 1910. All of the Marblehead collections apparently included the same titles, all recommended by Askew and purchased for distribution by Gregory. Few of them had been on the lists Dickerman had received from the black colleges and institutes. The Cartersville collection included no books about Lincoln or tales about Uncle Remus. Du Bois's *The Souls of Black Folk* did not make Askew's list, nor did Stowe's *Uncle Tom's Cabin*, although her novel *The Minister's Wooing* did. Likewise, Scott's *Ivanhoe* did not go to Cartersville, but his novel *Kenilworth* did. *Grimms' Fairy Tales* was not in Askew's collection, but *Aesop's Fables* was. The only books on both lists were a biography of Douglass (Askew specified Chesnutt's) and a book by Dunbar: she recommended a single poetry collection, *Lyrics of Love and Laughter.* [8]

As white librarians puzzled over African Americans' reading preferences, they tended to rely on facile generalizations rather than concrete evidence. In 1923, ten years after Yust reported on the Marblehead collections, Charles D. Johnston, the chief librarian at the Cossitt Library in Memphis, declared at the American Library Association's Work with Negroes Round Table, "that books in demand by negro readers should be supplied as far as practical, but the same care should be used as in selecting books for children."[9] Such opinions reveal that it was difficult, especially for white librarians, to draw conclusions about "what the Negro reads." That very phrase implied that librarians could comprehend and cater to a unitary, monolithic race-based taste. In fact, individuals displayed different predilections, preferences, and abilities honed by their varying circumstances of life.

In his 1913 report, Yust was extending a common conversation among librarians to include a relatively new group of library users. That conversation had arisen in the final quarter of the nineteenth century, when librarians had been discussing the nature of public library collections. They were particularly focused on non-literary fiction. A few extremists argued for its omission from public libraries on the grounds that it had no redeeming qualities, especially for working-class readers, who needed practical and uplifting material. Yet most librarians concentrated on selecting good fiction over bad. They eschewed dime novels, for example, and urged each other to be vigilant against immoral fiction, in which vice went unpunished; unrealistic novels, whether too optimistic or too pessimistic; and badly written books that failed to provide readers with examples of good grammar and usage. Their collection budgets revealed the depth of their ambivalence about fiction. In the 1890s public library collections tended to limit their fiction levels to 20 or 25 percent, although some librarians allowed higher proportions of fiction in the branches. But librarians were pitting themselves against their publics, whose demand for fiction accounted for a significant proportion of circulation. In a 1902 survey of public libraries, fiction represented 70 to 80 percent of the total circulation.[10] The question of fiction for children was even more troubling. Librarians generally seemed to think that they had a responsibility to help children develop the habit of reading, as long as it did not become an obsession, and the duty to lead children from the more sensational and unrealistic to the more refined—say, from Horatio Alger to George Eliot. They also seemed to understand the need to nurture not only children's intellectual development but also their emotional life and imagination.[11]

In city systems, neighborhood branch libraries catered more to children and teenagers than to adults; but because the black branches functioned as the only library open to their clientele, some of those collections tended to include more reading materials for adults than the white branches did. The variety of opinions about "what the Negro reads" reflected the continuing proliferation of publication during the late nineteenth and early twentieth centuries as well as educators' and librarians' confusion as they attempted to identify and recommend the "best" books. Librarians debated about whether they should acquire fiction and, if so, whether it should be high-quality work or high-demand work, for the categories could be mutually exclusive.[12] In essence, the question came down to whether municipal libraries should "fulfill the public's felt needs" or "culti-vate their tastes."[13] The need to cater to black readers' interests and desires conflicted with the librarian's own desire to socialize them into meeting mainstream America's expectations.

Nonetheless, Yust's report signaled librarians' recognition that African Americans formed a group of potential library users with dis-cernible, if variable, reading interests. When librarians had budgets for building their collections, selection was an art rooted in practice rather than theory or research. They were guided by the recommen-dations of experts who published lists of "best" books and by their own knowledge of what was actually leaving the library shelves. When librarians had no book-buying budget, selection hardly entered into the process of acquisition. Collection building involved the passive acceptance of donations, discards, and duplicates.

There was no standard collection size for segregated libraries. Librarians relied on city appropriations augmented with gifts for their collection budgets. Often, city appropriations were sufficient only to cover staff salaries, supplies, electricity, and heating fuel. Con-sequently, the number of volumes on the shelves of new libraries varied, from a low of 150 books in Greensboro, North Carolina, to a middling amount of 2,800 in Evansville, Indiana, to a high of 5,649 in New Orleans.[14]

Atlanta's Auburn branch opened on July 25, 1921, with a collec-tion of 2,000 books. In January board members of the city library had realized that the new building might open without any books because they had made no allocation from the central library's regular budget for the new branch's collection. So the board called a meeting with a group of African American leaders and asked them to put together a twelve-person "advisory committee" whose actual role would be to raise private money and donations for the collection. A year later, the board disbanded the committee when board members realized that it wanted to do more than simply donate books. Perhaps board members were also concerned about the nature of the donations, which included works on black history.[15]

Continuing budget shortfalls meant that collections usually did not grow rapidly or at a steady pace. Public libraries for African Amer-icans tended to house collections that were too small and too narrow for their potential users.[16] This was a problem even in Louisville, whose library system was well funded. While collections and services for the city's African Americans benefited from the financial support, the idea of providing a collection of books and periodicals for black readers still raised questions. Rachel Harris, writing for a white audience, recalled that local blacks were not readers, so those involved in creating the Western Branch wondered if the collection would be used.[17]

While the Carnegie building was under construction, the Western branch was housed in rented quarters with an estimated 1,400 books. By 1910, there were 7,533 volumes in the new building, which was designed to serve a community of 29,000 literate African Americans over the age of nine.[18] Blue and Harris were considered to be experts on appropriate material for libraries that served black readers. In 1921, the Louisville Free Public Library published the list of books by or about African Americans that they had added to the branch collections, along with a brief introduction by their white supervisor, system director George Settle. He wrote that the published list was a response to "repeated requests for lists of books in the Colored branches of interest to colored readers." Although he saw the publication as a form of outreach promoting the use of the library branches, the list had a wide audience. Its publication was announced in the *Bulletin of Bibliography and Dramatic Index, Public Libraries, Library Journal, Special Libraries,* and the *Cumulative Book Index.*

This was not the first such list. In 1900, Daniel A. P. Murray at the Library of Congress had produced his *Preliminary List of Books and Pamphlets by Negro Authors* to assist W. E. B. Du Bois as he was preparing an exhibit for the Paris Exposition. In 1903, the Library of Congress published *A Select List of References on the Negro Question;* a second issue came out in 1906. In 1905, Atlanta University issued *A Select Bibliography on the Negro.* The *Negro Year Book,* first published in 1913, included a bibliography of recent publications. The journal *Crisis,* which began publication in 1910, included book reviews and brief recommended reading lists.

Blue and Harris aimed their list at public librarians and their clients. It included 109 nonfiction books, 18 works of fiction, 26 pamphlets, 32 music items, 8 magazines, and 22 newspapers. Among the recommendations were six nonfiction works by Du Bois as well as his novel, *Quest of the Silver Fleece;* eleven books by Washington; and twelve books by Dunbar. It listed five works of Chesnutt's fiction and his biography of Douglass, as well as Douglass's autobiography. Ten songs by Harry T. Burleigh and ten by Samuel C. Taylor were included, as were compilations of Negro folk songs and jubilee and plantation songs. Harris and Blue recommended subscriptions to *Crisis, Southern Workman,* the *Journal of Negro History,* and the children's magazine the *Brownies' Book,* among others. They listed almost two dozen black-owned newspapers, including those from Baltimore, Atlanta, Birmingham, Chicago, Indianapolis, Nashville, New York, Pittsburgh, and Washington, D.C.[19]

Soon after this first list was published, the library released a supplementary list of twenty-eight items that had since been added to the black branches' collections. The new list included additional works by Carter G. Woodson and Washington; Claude McKay's 1922 poetry collection, *Harlem Shadows;* five more newspapers, including the *Savannah Tribune;* and three more magazines, including the National Urban League's magazine *Opportunity,* which began publication in 1923. The supplement also recommended twenty-four books about African Americans by white authors, including Ray Stannard Baker's *Following the Color Line,* George Washington Cable's *The Negro Question,* Lily Hammond's *In Black and White,* Mary White Ovington's *Half a Man,* Thomas Nelson Page's *Negro: The Southerner's Problem,* and Ulrich B. Phillips's *American Negro Slavery.*[20]

Louisville was an exception to the general approach to acquiring collections for African American libraries. It was obvious to black librarians and to black readers who used public libraries that white paternalism was no basis for collection decisions. Blue and Harris had the knowledge and the financial resources to shape collections for the communities their branches were designed to serve. Because they trained several of their counterparts who ran black branches in other cities, their influence extended beyond the library's walls and the city's boundaries.

Among those they influenced was Marian Hadley from Nashville. The Nashville Public Library archives includes a log of accessions for the Negro Library for the period 1915 to 1927.[21] An analysis of which specific books were acquired and which were not can enrich understanding of the mediating influence of librarians' selection practices on the choices available to readers. Nashville provides evidence that a white librarian's selections differed from a black librarian's, especially after the black librarian had received training in Louisville.

Nashville Public Library director Margaret Kercheval had her board's approval to spend $2,000 to stock the new branch. She hired Hadley, a local woman, to run the branch; and in the fall of 1915, Hadley spent two months at Blue and Harris's apprenticeship training course in Louisville. In her absence, Kercheval began spending the branch's collection budget. Between July 1915 and January 1916, she accessioned 1,778 volumes, including 379 volumes of juvenile fiction and 308 volumes of juvenile nonfiction. For adult readers, she acquired 409 volumes of fiction, and 241 of literature, with the remainder categorized as nonfiction, including 103 classed in the sociology category.[22]

Kercheval's approach was markedly different from Hadley's later patterns. She ordered multiple titles by standard authors, including twenty by Henry James, nineteen each by Sir Walter Scott and Mark Twain, sixteen by James Fenimore Cooper, fifteen by Rudyard Kipling, ten each by Louisa May Alcott and George Eliot, four each by Leo Tolstoy and Jane Austen. She ordered multivolume sets of works by poets James Russell Lowell and James Whitcomb Riley as well as twenty-three books by Thomas Nelson Page and eighteen by Joel Chandler Harris. She purchased eight copies of the Bible and bought Charles Darwin's *Descent of Man* and *Origin of Species* and William James's *Principles of Psychology* and *Pragmatism*. She ordered eight titles by Booker T. Washington but none by W. E. B. Du Bois, three by Paul Dunbar but none by Charles Chesnutt, even though works by Du Bois and Chesnutt were still in print.[23]

Black schoolchildren had access to fewer textbooks than white schoolchildren did, but what they did have carried the same messages about good morals and love of country.[24] A public library collection could offer children and teenagers many choices beyond what the schools exposed them to, so Kercheval ordered seven hundred juvenile books in time for opening day. Thirteen of the Joel Chandler Harris titles she ordered were recommended in the 1909 edition of the *Children's Catalog: A Guide to the Best Reading for Young People Based on Twenty-Four Selected Library Lists,* a standard guide for librarians who were building their collections. Some of the Thomas Nelson Page titles she acquired were also intended for the children's collection, and the *Children's Catalog* recommended most of them.[25] Kercheval's emphasis on children's reading material meant that the collection did not match the proportions—or the exact titles—recommended in the American Library Association catalogs published in the early twentieth century as guides for collection-building librarians (table 7).

TABLE 7. PERCENTAGE OF BOOKS LISTED IN TWO AMERICAN LIBRARY ASSOCIATION (ALA) CATALOGS (1904, 1911) AND THE COLLECTION OF THE NASHVILLE NEGRO PUBLIC LIBRARY (1916), BY DEWEY DECIMAL CLASS

CLASS	DESCRIPTION	ALA, 1904	ALA, 1911	NASHVILLE, 1916
0	General works	1.9	1.88	0.22
1	Philosophy	1.9	2.52	1.97
2	Religion	4.2	4.6	2.25
3	Sociology	8.0	10.28	5.79
4	Language	1.6	0.77	0.45
5	Natural science	6.2	5.4	2.30
6	Useful arts	6.0	10.8	3.20
7	Fine arts, music, sports	4.7	7.56	1.46
8	Literature	13.4	7.4	13.55
F	Fiction	16.3	10.8	23.05
9	History	13.3	7.19	2.70
910	Travel	9.1	10.28	1.74
B	Biography	13.5	10.2	2.70
JF/N	Children's	*	12.5	38.62

Source: Melvil Dewey, ed., *A.L.A. Catalog* (Washington, D.C.: Government Printing Office, 1904); Elva L. Bascom, ed., *A.L.A. Catalog, 1904–1911* (Chicago: American Library Association, 1912); "Condensed Accession Book: The Official Record of Each Volume Added to the Negro Branch of the Nashville Carnegie Library, 1915–27," Nashville Public Library Archives, Metropolitan Government Archives of Nashville and Davidson County.
* Not tabulated separately

Even with its emphasis on juvenile fiction and nonfiction, the opening-day collection in Nashville fell slightly short of what the librarians in Louisville recommended (table 8). While Kercheval was ordering multiple titles by Thomas Nelson Page, Hadley was probably learning from Harris and Blue that these books were not the best selections. In the Louisville Free Public Library archives is a typed "List of Books Selected from Titles in the Western Colored Branch of the Louisville Free Public Library Recommended for First Purchase," which apparently was used for apprentice training. Items on it date to 1919, meaning that Hadley would not have received a copy during her training in 1915. Nonetheless, it remains a good indication of Harris and Blue's opinion of Page. They recommended none of his works for the children's collection, although they did list his *The Negro: The Southerner's Problem* in their adult nonfiction section and his *Gordon Keith* and *In Old Virginia* in their adult fiction section. They also recommended Harris's *Uncle Remus, His Songs and His Sayings* for adults and children, *Uncle Remus and His Friends* for adults, and *Nights with Uncle Remus* for children. For the opening-day children's fiction collection, they listed two works by Helen Bannerman: *The Story of Little Black Sambo* and *The Story of Little Black Mingo.* After she returned to Nashville, Hadley added those two books plus Bannerman's *Little Black Quasha, Little Black Bobtail,* and *Little Black Quibba* to the Negro branch's collection. She had to reorder them later, apparently because they were in demand.[26]

TABLE 8. FIRST-PURCHASE RECOMMENDATIONS OF THE COLORED DEPARTMENT LIBRARIANS OF LOUISVILLE FREE PUBLIC LIBRARY, BY CATEGORY, NUMBER, AND PERCENTAGE, 1919

CATEGORY	NUMBER	%
Reference	51	5.23
Adult nonfiction	261	26.77
Adult fiction	222	22.77
Biography	26	2.67
Juvenile nonfiction	193	19.79
Juvenile fiction	222	22.77
Total	975	100

Source: "List of Books Selected from Titles in the Western Colored Branch of the Louisville Free Public Library Recommended for First Purchase" [1919], Nashville Public Library Archives, Metropolitan Government Archives of Nashville and Davidson County.

Such books were on recommended lists for elementary schools throughout the south, and Kristina DuRocher has asserted convincingly that their graphic depictions of racist stereotypes were part of a systematic socialization of children into a culture of white supremacy.[27] But black children may have experienced such works a bit differently. In particular, Hadley would have learned from Rachel Harris how to use such books in story hours, mediating between the text and the listeners and thereby managing their response to the stereotypically racist drawings that accompanied Bannerman's books. According to Harris, the principal of Louisville's Samuel Coleridge Taylor Colored Public School told an Uncle Remus story to a group of children and parents. She also reported that a student in a library-sponsored storytelling contest gave an account of Little Black Sambo. The experience of oral storytelling to an all-black audience was different from the experience of absorbing the books alone or with a racially mixed group.[28]

The *Brownies' Book* magazine for children, a short-lived collaboration between W. E. B. Du Bois and writer Jessie Fauset, was one of numerous efforts to transmit more realistic depictions of African American life and culture. Many well-known black authors were also writing for young people. For instance, Langston Hughes and Arna Bontemps published novels and poems for children in the 1920s and 1930s, and Carter Woodson's press, Associated Publishers, began issuing nonfiction works for children in the late 1930s. In 1941, a black librarian at the Chicago Public Library, Charlemae Hill Rollins, published *We Build Together: A Reader's Guide to Negro Life and Literature for Elementary and High School Use.* Her co-author on the third edition, issued in 1967, was New York Public Library's children's librarian and storyteller Augusta Baker. Both women called for the creation of more authentic depictions of black people. They were well aware that, in the first half of the twentieth century, it was impossible to build a library collection that did not include insulting images and characterizations of African Americans.[29]

There remained a dearth of good material, as children's book author Ellen Tarry (whose 1940s and 1950s writings were among the earliest to depict black urban life realistically) recalled.[30]

> In the juvenile field, when I started my teaching career, there were almost no books for young readers which showed the Negro as other than Uncle Remus or Little Black Sambo. Though Uncle Remus must

be reckoned as an outstanding contribution to the folklore of the world and Sambo is universal, as a steady, exclusive reading diet such books would have given children a stereotyped idea of the Negro.[31]

As Tarry pointed out, before she began writing, black urban experiences did not appear in children's literature: "Before that, all we had was Tobe, a little boy who was picking cotton somewhere. A beautiful child, lovely illustrations, but it was not the urban scene."[32] Yet one had to include such material in library collections while literary production slowly caught up with black readers' lives, needs, and interests.

In *Reading on the Middle Border,* Christine Pawley demonstrates that studying a small town's inhabitants' interactions with print reveals a community's local distinctiveness as well as its ties to a broader national culture. In the 1890s, the white, Protestant, middle-class clientele of the Osage, Iowa, public library had access to a collection that mirrored their tastes and interests, which, as Pawley notes, leaned toward the entertaining. Similar reading tastes, at least as reflected in public libraries, also seemed to exist farther south and among black Protestants. But there may have been certain categories of reading material that people did not look for in the local library. One may have been nonfiction books related to religious faith. Yet when white librarians thought about the reading interests of blacks, they assumed that religious books would figure in their collection acquisition plans. In 1906, George Utley, the white librarian in charge of the Jacksonville, Florida, public library, published an article titled "What the Negro Reads," which drew on evidence from local records at the basement circulation desk set aside for blacks. He expressed surprise that more books on poetry, religion, and music did not circulate, given what he considered the natural proclivities of African Americans.[33] But when stereotypes influence acquisition choices, the resulting low circulation should not come as a shock.

Nashville offers a good illustration of the relative importance of religious material to branch library users. Called the "Athens of the South," Nashville had a history of relatively moderate race relations (for the south) and a rich tradition of African American cultural expression. The city's First Baptist Church, founded in 1820, admitted blacks as well as whites; and in the early years, some, but not all, of the black members were slaves owned by white members. In the 1840s, two white church members taught several of their black counterparts to read and reported that their students were "greatly delighted with the privilege of reading the Bible."[34] As time passed, however, Nashville's white and black Baptists became increasingly separated. By the beginning of the Civil War, black churchgoers had their own pastor, procedures, and policies, although they were still considered a mission of white-controlled First Baptist Church. At the end of the war, the mission became a separate, independent entity, the First Colored Baptist Church.[35]

By 1874, the church's pastor, Nelson Merry, was serving as editor of the Negro Baptist Association of Tennessee's *Baptist Sunday School Standard,* one of several publications by and for African Americans founded in Nashville after emancipation. Local black-run newspapers (all with relatively short runs) included the *Colored Tennessean,* the *Tennessee Star,* and the *Citizen;* and Fisk University and the Fireside School also published their own newspapers. Nashville African Americans were also publishing books. For example, in the 1890s, the Sunday School Union of the African Methodist Church printed Daniel Payne's *History of the African Methodist Episcopal Church,* Sarah Early's *The Life and Labors of Reverend John Early,* and James Haley's *Thoughts, Doings, and Sayings of the Race: Afro-American Encyclopedia.*[36]

In 1895, black Baptists formed the National Baptist Convention, a response to their increasing marginalization in the white-dominated American Baptist Home Mission Society and the Southern Baptist Convention.[37] A key indicator of marginalization was the American Baptist Publication Society's refusal to publish the work of black religious leaders after members of the Southern Baptist Convention complained about its plans to do so.[38] Thus, in 1896, black Baptist leaders founded the National Baptist Publishing Board (NBPB), located in Nashville and destined to become the most successful African American publishing firm in the first half of the twentieth century. The moving force behind NBPB was Richard H. Boyd, a Nashville entrepreneur civil rights activist, and active Baptist. In addition to founding the press, he directed and in large part funded it.

Housed in its own building, with printing equipment in the base-ment, NBPB functioned as both a publisher and a printer; and the office was home to a number of offshoot activities. For instance, in 1905, Boyd and his associates founded a newspaper, the *Globe*, to publicize the protest they had organized against a recent ordinance requiring racial segregation on streetcars. The *Globe* remained active for decades, continuing to print news the white press ignored or misrepresented.[39]

By 1912 the NBPB was distributing some 8 million items annually to black Baptist congregations, who totaled almost 3 million members. Much of the material—Sunday school lessons, religious tracts, hym-nals, inexpensive Bibles, periodicals—was distributed to churches. But the NBPB also published books for individual purchase, including Harvey Johnson's *The Nations from a New Point of View* (1903), Thomas Oscar Fuller's *Twenty Years in Public Life, 1890–1910* (1910), Chester Arthur Eaton's *An Ounce of Prevention: A Practical Little Book to Be Used As a Health Guide for the Prevention of Diseases and Prolonging Life* (1915), and the *National Jubilee Melody Song Book* (1923).[40]

In 1915, a rift in the National Baptist Convention resulted in the formation of a separate organization, the National Baptist Conven-tion of America. Once again, publishing disagreements lay behind the rift, and Boyd's ownership and control of the NBPB were at stake. Boyd and his followers took the NBPB into the new organization. Meanwhile, the original National Baptist Convention incorporated and founded its own publishing body, the Sunday School Publish-ing Board, also based in Nashville. Although not as successful as the NBPB, it did have enough publishing and printing work to stay solvent.[41]

Yet another institution figured into Nashville's culture of print: the public library. Although secular, it, too, was racially segregated. The Carnegie Library of Nashville opened to whites in 1904 with Mary Hannah Johnson as director. Speaking before her colleagues at the American Library's 1903 conference, she had acknowledged that southern library development was lagging behind the rest of the nation's. But, she declared, southern whites would refuse to use any public library that admitted blacks, and any public library open to African Americans would be inundated by them. She concluded,

"The South needs a great many more public libraries and if they are to be established they must be libraries for white people. Afterwards, the question of negro libraries will be in order."[42] Johnson thus gave voice to white Tennessee's creed: in Lester C. Lamon's words, "black development had to proceed, if at all, at a respectful distance behind white progress."[43]

After much effort, Nashville's separate branch for African Americans opened in 1916. In anticipation of that opening, staff began placing book orders in the summer of 1915 and an accession book (dated from mid-1915 to the end of 1927) recorded the items received. A staff member would log each item on a separate line in the ledger, abbreviating information about author, title, place of publication, publisher, year, supplier, cost, Dewey Decimal class or genre code, and other related information.[44]

By the library's opening day, the accession book included records for 2,027 volumes. Fiction was the largest adult category, totaling about 40 percent of the collection, with a separate "literature" category accounting for another 17 percent. The nonfiction books in Dewey Decimal class 3, which included materials on sociology, law, education, and economics, formed slightly more than 7 percent. However, only forty books (2.25 percent) were classified as "religion."

By 1927 (the final year of documented accession records), the library housed 5,065 volumes. Nonetheless, only 3 percent of them were religious books. That sounds like a very small proportion, and a historian of public libraries might be justified in interpreting such small numbers as a sign that the secular institution of the library was not providing an appropriately balanced collection for its clientele—that library users were being denied access to a certain category of material. In contrast, a historian of print culture might consider the library's broader context. It is possible that the wealth of freely available and low-cost religious material in Nashville freed the public library to collect in other areas. By the time the public library opened in 1916, individuals in search of religious reading material may have become accustomed to relying on their churches and their own home collections.

Sacred reading was identified with the church and its publishing arm, whereas secular reading was identified with institutions such as schools and libraries. But black-church historians C. Eric Lincoln and Laurence H. Mamiya suggest that the situation was even more complicated: "The close relationship between the black sacred cosmos and black culture has often been missed by social analysts who impose sacred/secular distinctions too easily upon the phenomena of black culture. What is often overlooked is the fact that many aspects of black cultural practices and some major social institutions had religious origins."[45] As examples they cite the black church's role in the founding of "schools, banks, insurance companies, and low income housing" and note its nurturance of political activism and cultural expression.[46]

In the first two decades of the twentieth century, local church leaders and members occasionally worked with businessmen and educators to establish separate public library branches for African Americans. But often they did not. The Nashville library's most energetic supporters included James C. Napier, a lawyer, politician, and businessman with connections to Booker T. Washington and Andrew Carnegie, and undertakers Andrew N. Johnson and Preston Taylor, who pressured city hall. NBPB's Richard Boyd and fellow *Globe* founder Dock Hart unsuccessfully tried to convince city hall to build the branch near Fisk University, the city's black middle-class neighborhood—an involvement that seems to have been spurred by class affiliation rather than religious connection.[47] In short, it seems likely that black Nashville residents associated sacred reading with the church, and they expected to encounter secular reading elsewhere, including at their public library branch.

The library's staff seems to have held this view as well. Among the 152 religious books available by the mid-1920s, there were multiple copies of only one title: three copies of *The Book of Common Prayer* as well as a single copy of the Protestant Episcopal Tract Society's *Companion for the Book of Common Prayer.* The library had only one English-language copy of the Bible, but it did hold a German translation as well as the New Testament in French. A number of volumes were Bible-related, including Lyman Abbott's *Acts of the Apostles,* the International Bible Students Association's *Studies in the Scriptures,* and Mrs. Annie Russell Marble's *Women of the Bible.* Several of the Bible-related holdings were targeted for the educational market, including

Sunday School teachers—for instance, the American Tract Society's *Bible Text-book,* J. B. Shearer's *Bible Course Syllabus,* the Bible Study Publishing Company's series *Bible Study Union Lessons,* and the Uplift Publishing Company's *Happy Half Hours with the Bible.* Religious music was also represented in the collection, in the form of Scribner's *Hymns of Martin Luther,* Doubleday, Page's *Hymns That Every Child Should Know,* and the Bible Institute Colportage Association's *Revival Hymns.*

Some eighty different publishers were represented in the religious-book collection. In addition to those I have already mentioned, they included established New York firms such as Century; Dodd and Mead; Putnam's; Houghton Mifflin; Longmans, Green (which supplied William James's *Varieties of Religious Experience*); Macmillan; and Scribner's. Books from publishers in Boston, Philadelphia, and Chicago were also represented. Ten titles were produced by the religious publishing giant Fleming H. Revell, which had offices in New York and Chicago: *Jesus Is Coming, The Power of Prayer, "Forbid Him Not": Messages for Our Day and Time, Coronation Hymnal, Great Epochs of Sacred History and the Shadows They Cast, The Missionary Enterprise, What Does Christianity Mean?, The Cross at the Front, The College of Apostles,* and *The Eternal in Man.* Publications from sects with relatively few African American adherents also found their way into the collection. Among the publishers represented were the Presbyterian Committee of Publications, the American Unitarian Association, the Christian Science Publishing Society, Protestant Episcopal Tract Society, the Publishing House of the Methodist Episcopal Church South, the Methodist Book Concern, and the Jehovah's Witnesses' Tower Publishing Company.

On June 11, 1918, the library acquired eighteen titles published by Nashville's own NBPB, ten of which were songbooks or hymnals. Among the rest were Boyd's *Separate or "Jim Crow" Car Laws,* published in 1909 during the protest against the city's segregated streetcar ordinance; *The Baptist Church Directory; The National Baptist Pastor's Guide;* and *Ancient and Modern Sunday School Method.* Although the accession book lists the NBPB as the acquisition source, it records no prices for these titles, so it seems likely the publisher presented them as a gift.

Despite (or because of) the predominance of Baptists in Nashville, library staff built a collection that included a significant amount of material from other denominations, although it remained over-whelmingly Christian and Protestant in its orientation. Unfortu-nately, circulation records have not survived, so it is impossible to gauge the extent to which the religious books were borrowed. But given the much larger proportion of fiction and literature offered by the library and the thriving culture of religious print materials in the city, it seems safe to assume that few black residents used the library as their primary source for faith-based nonfiction.

The library's real problem was not a lack of religious material but its inability to compensate for inadequate school collections and essentially nonexistent private collections. In 1933, Benjamin Mays wrote about the need for better-educated pastors for black congrega-tions, but he could have been speaking of all black readers:

> In most sections of the South, library opportunities that are open to white ministers are closed to Negro ministers. In the few centers that provide library facilities for Negroes, they are grossly inadequate, and in many instances the kind of literature that is released to the Negro library is heavily censored. The Negro minister, therefore, needs a better academic background because his opportunity for self-im-provement is not equal to that of the white minister. The exceptional Negro pastor, who draws a large salary, may be able to build up an adequate library of his own; but the number who can do this is neg-ligibly small.[48]

Although the Nashville library had made a strong start, sustainabil-ity proved to be a problem (table 9). Over the next dozen years, it added about 3,000 volumes, yet those accessions were irregular: one year, only ninety volumes were added. By 1927, the branch owned about 5,000 volumes, but at least 2,000 of them were more than a decade old. They were intended to serve a population of about 32,000 literate African Americans age ten and over.[49]

Confederate veteran Gideon Baskette was president of the Nash-ville library system, even though he had no formal library science training. In his view, the Negro branch was a failure because it had only 240 annual circulations. He made no link between low circula-tion numbers and the fact that the branch had recently added only ninety volumes to its collection. After Baskette died in 1927, the

TABLE 9. NUMBER OF BOOKS ADDED ANNUALLY TO THE NASHVILLE NEGRO
PUBLIC LIBRARY, 1916-27

YEAR	BOOKS ADDED
1916	400
1917	225
1918	250
1919	300
1920	125
1921	90
1922	275
1923	175
1924	175
1925	250
1926	300
1927	465

Source: "Condensed Accession Book: The Official Record of Each Volume Added to the Negro Branch of the Nashville Carnegie Library, 1915-27," Nashville Public Library Archives, Metropolitan Government Archives of Nashville and Davidson County.

board invited C. H. Compton from the Saint Louis Public Library to assess the entire system and suggest improvements. Compton noted that Nashville was spending only 27 cents per capita on its library system, although the American Library Association's recommended standard was $1. Years of underfunding had sabotaged the library system and had been especially hard on the Negro branch, where Compton found a collection too small and too damaged to inspire much reading.[50]

In New Orleans, the Dryades Branch also functioned without adequate funding. In May 1915, city library director Henry Gill told the library board that he expected the new branch building to be completed in a month. He also pointed out that the branch had no budget for books. Rather than take money from the existing collections budget, the board sought additional funds from the city, but to no avail.[51] During these negotiations, the central ordering department of the New Orleans Public Library had nonetheless been acquiring books for Dryades and the other four branches.[52] On January 19, staff accessioned several copies of Alexander Pope's poem *The Rape of the Lock* for all five branches. Four received duplicate copies, but Dryades received only one. In March, the Algiers and Dryades branches received multiple copies of S. R. Smith's *Bunny Cotton-Tail Trail,* H. F. Simmerman's *Story of Two Kittens,* and Jennie Hall's *Viking Tales* for their children's collections. Most of the titles accessioned in April (229 volumes) and May (64 volumes) were for Dryades.

When the branch opened in October, Gill announced that it had the largest of the branch collections, with 5,000 volumes.[53] Yet according to an extant accession book of branch orders between 1911 and 1917, only 476 books were purchased for Dryades between January 1915 and August 1917. This suggests that much of the collection was made up of donations and discards. Of the books purchased, 11 were for reference use, 347 were for the adult collection, and 118 were for the juvenile collection. Because each book was assigned a Dewey Decimal Classification number, the accession log also reveals the subject matter of the purchases.[54] About 78 percent of the books intended for adults (270 volumes) were classified in the Dewey 800s for literature. Of the juvenile accessions, almost 63 percent (74 volumes) were also classed in the 800s. Another 19 percent of juvenile accessions (22 volumes) were assigned to the 300s category of fairy tales and folklore. The only other sizable group included the 17 percent of juvenile accessions (20 volumes) classified in the 900s category of history and geography.

At the branch's opening ceremonies in October 1915, attorney J. Madison Vance acknowledged blacks' gratitude for Carnegie's building grant but was concerned because the collection did not have more books by African American authors.[55] Accessions through August 1917 did not correct that imbalance: no books by African American authors appear in the accession records, nor did the library add any works by Joel Chandler Harris or Thomas Nelson Page or purchase any books with the keywords "Negro" or "slavery" or "plantation" in the title. Instead, staff added thirty-one titles by the popular author F. Marion Crawford, twenty-four by the crime novelist Wilkie Collins (some in duplicate), and sixteen by the historical novelist Klara Muller Mundt.

At a 1923 meeting of the Southwestern Library Association, "Henry M. Gill of the New Orleans Public Library outlined the policy of his library in its relation to the negro. The object in supplying books to negroes is not to furnish a veneer of culture but to aid in the development of useful citizens."[56] Yet some of the adult titles acquired in the Dryades Branch's early years offered neither a veneer of culture nor useful instruction. When the director of the newly created Louisiana Library Commission, fresh from California, later said publicly that illiteracy persisted among black Louisianans because the state could not afford two separate but equal school systems, Gill objected. In his view, segregation was not to blame. African Americans themselves were the cause of their own illiteracy, he said, because they "were not capable of education and did not want it."[57]

Despite Gill's attitude, the juvenile collection at Dryades appeared to support children's educational and entertainment needs, at least to some extent. It held duplicate copies of Katherine Devereux Blake and Georgia Alexander's *Graded Poetry*, a series of textbook readers for first through eighth grades. Other instructional texts included Franklin Thomas Baker's *First Year Language Reader* and *Second Year Language Reader*, Ida Coe and Alice Christie Dillon's *Story Hour Readers*, and Julia McNair Wright's *Seaside and Wayside*, designed to teach children about nature. Entertainment choices included versions of the fairy tales *Beauty and the Beast* and *Jack and the Beanstalk*, Lewis Carroll's *Alice's Adventures in Wonderland*, Beatrice Potter's *The Tale of Peter Rabbit*, and Ouida's *A Dog of Flanders*.

The Dryades collection grew at a faster pace than did the collections available to white residents at the main and other branch libraries, increasing by 25 percent (1,426 volumes) in its first five years of existence (table 10). The collection for whites grew by 18 percent during the same period. Between 1920 and 1925, the collection for blacks grew by 49 percent, compared to 24 percent for the collection for whites. In fact, the Dryades branch collection grew at a faster rate than did the population of its potential users. Between 1910 and 1920, as the white literate population increased by 21 percent, the black literate population increased by 18 percent.

Despite the collection's faster rate of growth, however, New Orleans's black residents had far less access to books than whites did. When the Dryades Branch opened, it housed 3.9 percent of the library books owned by the system. In 1920, it owned 4.1 percent, at a

TABLE 10. NEW ORLEANS PUBLIC LIBRARY BOOKS ACCESSIBLE
TO WHITES AND TO BLACKS, 1920 AND 1925

NEW ORLEANS WHITES-ONLY LIBRARIES (MAIN AND BRANCHES)			DRYADES BRANCH		
YEAR	NUMBER OF VOLUMES	% OF COLLECTION GROWTH	CITY'S WHITE POPULATION	NUMBER OF VOLUMES	% OF COLLECTION GROWTH	CITY'S BLACK POPULATION
1920	163,507 (0.57 per capita)	18	285,916 (74%)	7,075 (0.07 per capita)	25	101,930 (26%)
1925	202,947	24	n/a	10,570	49	n/a

Sources: "Accession Book A–Z (Branches)," 1911–17, New Orleans Public Library Archives; "Annual Report of the New Orleans Public Library, 1920" (New Orleans, 1921), 16–18; "Annual Report of the New Orleans Public Library, 1925" (New Orleans, 1926), 18–20; U.S. Census Bureau, Census of Population and Housing, 1920, vol. 3, Population: Composition and Characteristics of the Population by States, http://www.census.gov.

time when African Americans constituted 26 percent of the urban population. In 1925, the branch had increased its ownership to 5.2 percent of total library holdings. Using 1920 figures, I calculate that there was slightly more than half a book per white person in the city compared to less than a tenth of a book for each black person. Such comparisons indicate inequity, but for the individual reader they meant little. For library users and potential users, what mattered was that, by 1925, black citizens did not have access to the more than 200,000 volumes available to white taxpayers.[58]

Records of the branch's accessions between 1915 and 1917 suggest that gifts rather than purchases accounted for about 21 percent of the collection's growth. The most generous donor was Sylvanie F. Williams, principal of the Thomy Lafon School, who gave thirty of the ninety-nine gift volumes listed in the accession log.[59] In October 1915, she donated six titles by Charles Dickens, including *Great Expectations, Nicholas Nickleby, The Old Curiosity Shop, Oliver Twist, The Pickwick Papers,* and *The Uncommercial Traveler.* She also donated Edward Gibbon's five-volume *The History of the Decline and Fall of the Roman Empire,* Washington Irving's two-volume *Christopher Columbus* and four-volume *George Washington,* and a three-volume U.S. government publication titled *Documentary History of the Constitution of the United States of America, 1786–1870.*

Another important contributor was J. B. Bell, who contributed twenty volumes, including Francis Bacon's *The Advancement of*

Learning, Thomas Carlyle's two-volume *The French Revolution,* Emmanuel Kant's *The Critique of Pure Reason,* and Niccolo Machiavelli's *History of Florence,* among others. The evidence from New Orleans indicates that collection development was not guided by a knowledge of books by African American writers nor by a sense of any special interests or needs on the part of African American readers. Educated blacks such as Williams and Bell may have owned books by and about African Americans; but if they did, they were not giving them away.

Obviously, collection building can proceed without funding but not in the systematic, selection-driven way that librarians and library science educators were recommending during the professionalization process of the first half of the twentieth century. When trained librarians with a budget derived from local municipal taxes made acquisition decisions, they did so on the basis of accepted professional practices that, by 1930, had been codified in a textbook. The accrediting body for library science programs, the Board of Education for Librarianship, operated under the auspices of the American Library Association. In the 1920s the association produced seven textbooks in its Library Curriculum Studies series for use in library science programs. They covered core topics such as circulation, reference, and cataloging and classification and at the end of each chapter listed the sources used and added questions and exercises for students. The association chose a single expert to write each textbook but asked that author to move temporarily to Chicago to prepare the manuscript with help from an association-appointed committee and staff. Authors also traveled to libraries to observe and discuss their practices. Instructors in library schools piloted the draft manuscripts in courses and made suggestions for changes based on that experience. The American Library Association sent each draft to at least twenty-five librarians who were not affiliated with library science educational programs and asked for their comments. The final version thus represented a collective professional understanding of the topic.[60]

Librarian Francis K. W. Drury was the author of the textbook *Book Selection,* which the American Library Association published in 1930. He pointed out in the first chapter that selection involves three elements: "books, readers, and funds."[61] Because funds are always limited, the library staff, in consultation with the library's governing board, must choose which items to include in the collection.

According to Drury, readers' demand should guide the librarian, along with considerations such as the content of the books. Chapter 2, "Selection Based on Demand," suggests that public librarians should use a variety of methods to ascertain what taxpayers want: talking with individuals and members of civic organizations; evaluating information generated by circulation, borrower registration, reference transactions, and readers' requests; and conducting community surveys. Drury also recommended that librarians should consider the reading interests of what he called "special groups in the community" including the "foreign born" and Negroes: "Negroes are rightly proud of their literature and their artistic, musical, and literary contributions, and libraries do well to buy adequately along this line, and foster this excellent point of contact. Since a large percentage of the readers are children, there is a demand for juvenile literature which should be met as far as possible."[62]

At the end of chapter 2, Drury listed two sources for his paragraph on Negroes: a three-page discussion of "Library Service to Negroes," published in 1926 by the American Library Association's Committee on Library Extension; and librarian Louis Shores's article "Public Library Service to Negroes," published in *Library Journal* in 1930. Among the chapter's twenty questions and exercises for students is "Make up a list of books on Negro life and history written by Negroes."[63] It is difficult to imagine how students might have completed such a project successfully because the textbook does not discuss "Aids in Selection" until chapter 9 (although a footnote to the chapter's title does say that instructors can assign it whenever they see fit). An appendix at the end of chapter 9 listing periodicals that exclusively or routinely reviewed books includes only twenty-three titles, all of them mainstream white media such as the *Saturday Review of Literature,* the *Literary Supplement to the Times,* the *Atlantic Monthly,* and the *Yale Review.* A second appendix in the chapter recommends a few additional tools such as the *Cumulative Book Index,* the *Standard Catalog for Public Libraries,* and the companion *Children's Catalog.*[64]

Chapters 5 and 6 of the textbook focus on nonfiction and fiction respectively, but the specific selection aids listed in those chapters also fail to refer to lists of books by and about African Americans.[65] Nowhere do they mention the NAACP periodical, the *Crisis,* which reviewed books by and about African Americans; the lists of recommended books compiled by Blue and Harris in the 1920s; or any other black-focused selection aids such as the bibliographies routinely compiled by Monroe Nathan Work for Tuskegee Institute's *Negro Year Book.* Yet later, in chapter 10, Drury wrote:

> One of the privileges as well as one of the duties of the librarian is to lead and possibly to educate the public taste. . . . It is impossible to gratify every whim of every taxpayer. It is the whole taxpaying body, not each individual, which is to be considered. The librarian is put in charge to manage and direct, his hand is on the steering wheel and back seat driving is not to be regarded too seriously. He, therefore, must be the one to decide as to the combined value of demand and to provide for the good of all.[66]

As the century advanced, educators and practitioners continued to discuss and debate the basis of collection development. In 1939, for instance, the University of Chicago's Graduate Library School devoted its annual Library Institute to "The Practice of Book Selection." Carl B. Roden, the head of the Chicago Public Library, and Leon Carnovsky, an assistant professor at the Graduate Library School, both discussed the central question of collection development. As Carnovsky asked, "Shall the librarian shape his policy according to what people want or according to what they ought to want?"[67] Roden acknowledged Carnovsky's earlier work on the "demand theory" versus the "value theory" of book selection, noting that the financial strictures of the Depression were making it so difficult to meet demand that libraries were experiencing drops in their all-important circulation statistics, which tax-supported institutions used to prove they were serving their communities. He told his audience that "a very promising young student," Lowell Martin, had conducted a study to discover whether the Chicago Public Library system had acquired recent books about various social problems and had found the library's collection lacking. Roden questioned the need for all of the books on Martin's list, particularly for small branch libraries, but summed up the library's position this way: "for the present we must continue to confess ourselves as confirmed addicts to the theory of demand."[68]

Carnovsky, who had the luxury of being a faculty member rather than a public librarian, countered with the suggestion that librarians should provide collections of "important books" reflecting "established truths," although he knew they would not appeal to many readers of popular fiction and thus would reduce circulation.[69] Acknowledging "the cherished principle that the librarian should not permit his personal predilections to dictate his policy of book selection," he nonetheless argued for "a librarian whose predilections are for established truths and who then bases his book selection upon these truths."[70] The pitfall, of course, is that established truths can be disestablished. At one time, for example, scientific racism was seen as an established truth.[71] What if a white librarian has a predilection for mainstream white or even racist literature?

Yet Roden's addiction to demand also had its problems. What if the library-using public were comprised of whites who only wanted to read material by white authors who stereotyped, denigrated, or ignored African Americans? What if a black library were to open with no collection funds, a board filled with paternalistic whites, and book donors who included white board members, their friends, and well-educated African American residents? Libraries in the field were always more complex than the academic theories about them were.

During the Depression, many public libraries serving predominately or exclusively white clients lacked funding for collection development; but libraries for African Americans routinely dealt with this situation before, during, and after the 1930s. In Tyler, Texas, for example, the Negro Public Library (later renamed the Ella Reid Public Library) opened in the summer of 1941 in the basement of a Baptist church, but for several years the city did not appropriate funds for collection building. Consequently, most of the books were gifts from community members. A compilation of data drawn from the accession records indicates that, by 1968 (when the library closed), at least 70 percent of the volumes in the collection had been donated. Tyler's Negro library offers an example of collection building in which neither value nor demand played a part, at least not in the way in which Drury, Roden, and Carnovsky understood those concepts. Rather, it exemplifies supply-side collection development.

Yet one might argue that Carnovsky's conception of value was itself a supply-side approach, in which the library supplied the goods it thought people should want and thus created the demand. With a collection built primarily from donated books, the Ella Reid Public Library demonstrated supply-side collection development conducted by end users—(readers) rather than by intermediaries (librarians). When a library depends for its collection on gift books, the collection reflects the idiosyncratic choices of the donors: not only what they have personally acquired but also what they have chosen to get rid of. A thoroughly educated and socialized professional librarian might see the situation as a serious undermining of professional training. But in the case of segregated libraries, this seems to be the least compelling issue. In fact, the judgments of a white director trained in a white library school with a white-authored textbook that offers no concrete advice about selecting books by and about African Americans might do as much harm as good. Further, when some of the donations are duplicates or discards from the main library—in other words, books originally selected by whites for whites—the collection may be less idiosyncratic but no less skewed.

By the time Tyler's Negro library opened in 1941, more than one hundred public libraries for African Americans were operating. When African Americans were in charge of collection building, they selected from an increasing number of works published by and about blacks. In New York and Chicago, for instance, black librarians in branches that served predominately black clienteles were assembling special collections of Africana material. The Tyler library, as a latecomer to the field, might have been able to take advantage of this developing knowledge, if it had received sufficient financial and moral support from the city and its white library. But over the course of the library's twenty-seven years of existence, the total amount expended on books was less than $1,500, and the collection held fewer than 4,000 volumes, about 30 percent of which were designed for juvenile readers.[72] Many of the donated books were quite old. Among the recorded gifts were items that a librarian with an acquisitions budget and a mission to serve the whole community would not buy: outdated college algebra and grammar textbooks, R. Ball's 1900 *Elements of Astronomy,* and R. Millikan's 1906 *First Course in Physics.* Other old books included A. Ratzeberger's 1838 *Donkey Beads,*

Frances Hodgson Burnett's 1888 *Edith's Burglar,* A. F. Blaisdell's 1897 *Stories from English History;* Ouida's 1897 *The Massarene,* two copies of Lew Wallace's 1893 *The Prince of India,* Marie Corelli's 1900 *The Master Christian,* and H. Van Dyke's 1896 *Little Rivers* and 1898 *Story of the Other Wise Man.*

Although it was publicized as an exemplary interracial project, the library collection was largely overseen by whites, particularly in the early years. Its first 1,500 books were all gifts. About a hundred were weeded from Tyler's Carnegie Public Library. Others came from book drives conducted by the Boy Scouts, parent-teacher associations, churches, and schools. About three hundred were salvaged from the leftovers of a WPA-sponsored Smith County rural library system, which itself had begun in 1935 with donated books that relief employees had mended before distributing them throughout the county. At the suggestion of white board member Marguerite Merrick, the library wrote to Frank Glenn, owner of an antiquarian bookstore in Kansas City, to ask for donations. In addition to owning the bookstore, Glenn brokered deals to help university and research libraries acquire private libraries and thus establish or augment their special collections departments. His donations were likely non-rare books that his clients did not want. He sent at least two shipments, one of which contained forty-three volumes.[73] Ina Roberts, the librarian at Tyler Junior College, and Lucy Marsh, a wealthy Tyler resident, removed about 100 of the 1,800 volumes donated in the first year or so. They followed the University of Minnesota Library guidelines that Dorothy Journeay, Texas State Library's extension agent, had suggested. The Minnesota list advised librarians to steer clear of series books, although some made it to the Ella Reid Public Library's shelves anyway.[74]

Under such circumstances, community members who supported the existence of a library for African Americans might have been likely to donate better books. Tyler was home to Texas College, founded in 1894 under the auspices of the Colored Methodist Episcopal Church, and some of its faculty and alumni probably donated to the library. Among the gifts recorded in the accession book were Dunbar's *The Sport of the Gods,* Bontemps and Hughes's *Popo and Fifina,* Bontemps's poetry anthology *Golden Slippers,* as well as R. R.

Moton's *What the Negro Thinks*, and two copies of Mary White Ovington's *Half a Man*. The library owned nothing by Du Bois and only
Up from Slavery by Washington, although it is not clear whether this
was a purchase or a gift. Richard Wright's *Native Son* and James Baldwin's *Nobody Knows My Name* were also in the collection but were not
recorded as either gifts or purchases. Among the purchases were a
collection of Dunbar's poems edited by William Dean Howells, James
Weldon Johnson's *God's Trombones*, and Ken Smith's biography of
baseball star Willie Mays.

Among the gifts was Page's *Two Little Confederates*, the only book
by him in the collection. The library had two copies of Harris's *Uncle
Remus*, one purchased and the other of unknown origin; a copy of
Harris's *Uncle Remus, His Songs and His Sayings*, of unknown origin;
and a purchased copy of Harris's *Little Mister Thimblefinger*. Other gifts
included Edwin Embree's *Brown America*, written by the Rosenwald
Fund's president; G. P. Hamilton's *The Bright Side of Memphis*; DuBose
Heyward's *Mamba's Daughters*; Julie Peterkin's *Bright Skin and Black
April*; W. D. Weatherford's *Negro Life in the South*; and Lillian Smith's
Strange Fruit. Table 11 shows which of these gifts and purchases were
listed in the bibliographies of books by and about African Americans
issued periodically from the New York Public Library's 135th Street
Branch (renamed the Countee Cullen Branch in the early 1950s).[75]

Books that insulted and demeaned African Americans were in the
collection, including Thomas Dixon's 1902 racist version of southern history, *The Leopard's Spots*. (He would later be involved in D. W.
Griffith's pro-Ku Klux Klan film, *The Birth of a Nation*, which inspired
nationwide protests by African Americans and the NAACP.) *The Leopard's Spots* was a gift, possibly from an African American who wanted
other black readers to know about a writer whose 2004 biography
is titled *American Racist*. But given that many of the donated books
came from whites, it seems more likely that it had been gathering
dust on someone's shelves long after its initial controversial appear-
ance.[76] Perhaps the same person gave Margaret Mitchell's *Gone with
the Wind*, which the library also received as a gift. The library had six
titles in Inez Hogan's Nicodemus series, all but one of them gifts. In
1943, Charlemae Rollins, who worked at the Hall branch of the Chicago Public Library in a predominately black neighborhood, warned

teachers away from some of the Nicodemus books because they featured racist epithets, caricatures, and dialect.[77]

The library's purchases do reflect an awareness of important recent works. For example it bought two juvenile novels, Ovington's *Zeke* and Eva Knox Evans's *Araminta,* both recommended in the 1946 edition of the *Children's Catalog.* It also acquired Jane Dabney Shackelford's *The Child's Story of the Negro,* published by Woodson's Associated Publishers and reviewed by the *Crisis.* Eva Knox Evans's 1947 *All about Us,* also in the collection, had been recommended in the 1951 edition of the *Children's Catalog* by way of a quotation from the *Saturday Review of Literature:* "The object [of Evans's book] is to break down race prejudice."[78] The library also purchased Shirley Graham's book about Phillis Wheatley, recommended in the 1955 edition of *The Negro: A Selected Bibliography,* issued by the New York Public Library.[79]

Tyler's Ella Reid Public Library illustrates the state of information access in the age of Jim Crow. In terms of their interest to readers, the quality of titles was good. However, the library's small budget made it difficult to shape a dynamic collection featuring new titles or to replace old favorites with new editions. Tyler's situation was mirrored in libraries for African Americans across the south, whether they were branches of larger systems or independent entities.

TABLE 11. BOOKS BY AND ABOUT AFRICAN AMERICANS IN THE ELLA REID
PUBLIC LIBRARY, METHOD OF ACQUISITION AND DATE OF INCLUSION IN
THE NEW YORK PUBLIC LIBRARY'S (NYPL) NEGRO BIBLIOGRAPHY

AUTHOR	TITLE	METHOD OF ACQUISITION	DATE OF INCLUSION IN NYPL NEGRO BIBLIOGRAPHY
Brawley	*Negro Builders and Heroes*	unknown	1940, 1955
Brawley	*Negro Genius*	gift	1940
Embree	*Thirteen against the Odds*	purchased	1955
Franklin	*From Slavery to Freedom*	purchased	1955
Frazier	*The Negro in the United States*	unknown	1955
Graham	*Phillis Wheatley*	unknown	1955
Hare	*Negro Musicians and Their Music*	unknown	1940, 1955
Harris	*Uncle Remus, His Songs and His Sayings*	unknown	1940
Heyward	*Mamba's Daughters*	gift	1940
Holt	*George Washington Carver*	gift	1955
Howells	*The Complete Poems of Paul Laurence Dunbar*	purchased	1940, 1955
Hoyt Swift	*North Star Shining*	purchased	1955
Hughes	*Famous American Negroes*	purchased	1955
Johnson	*God's Trombones*	purchased	1940, 1955
Johnson	*The Book of American Negro Poetry*	unknown	1940, 1955
Kearns	*Blessed Martin de Porres, Saintly American Negro*	gift	1940
Knox Evans	*All about Us*	3 copies purchased	1955
La Farge	*Interracial Justice*	gift	1940
Moton	*What the Negro Thinks*	gift	1940
Ottley	*New World A-Coming*	gift	1955
Reid	*In a Minor Key*	gift	1940
Smith	*The Willie Mays Story*	purchased	1955
Sutherland	*Color, Class, and Personality*	gift	1955
Woodson	*The Negro in Our History*	1 gift; 2 unknown	1955
Wright	*Native Son*	unknown	1955

Source: Accession book, 1941–69, Ella Reid Public Library Collection, Pennsylvania Historical Society; *The Negro: A Selected Bibliography* (New York: New York Public Library, 1940); Dorothy R. Homer and Evelyn R. Robinson, *The Negro: A Selected Bibliography* (New York: New York Public Library, 1955).

CHAPTER 8

Reading the Race-Based Library

Public libraries offered collections of specific books and periodicals, and each of those collections represented potential and opportunity. In some cases, the potential and opportunity were truncated rather than realized. Two years after the American Library Association published its 1936 pamphlet *The Equal Chance: Books Help to Make It,* a researcher investigating the role of rural public libraries in adult education found evidence of censorship. The public libraries established in Louisiana's black schools tended to avoid adding "books that describe the emancipated Negro" to their collections. And Mississippi outlawed "the circulation of books that portray social equality between Negroes and whites."[1]

The reading material in a library tells the supply side of the story; that is, it indicates what the library staff thought should be actively acquired through orders and subscriptions and passively acquired through donations. The demand side of the story illuminates what readers have found worthwhile in the collection. Borrowing records register the names and addresses of community members with library cards and log the books that each cardholder took out of the library, thus revealing not only the books that circulated but also the number, frequency, and types of book loans for individual library users.[2] Ideally, all of the records of long-forgotten libraries are preserved in research archives. However, partial records are more typical, and some have not been saved at all. For example, it is not possible to learn how local people used the Ella Reid Public Library in Tyler, Texas, because, although the accessions book has survived, the borrowing log has not.

Circulation figures are easier to document because many public libraries kept track of circulation and recorded it in their annual reports. In the absence of individual borrower data, these figures offer important proxy information about library use. Circulation statistics aggregate data, recording the number of times a book was checked out in a given period. While they can indicate how heavily a collection was used and how use changed over time, they cannot tell us who read the borrowed books. For instance, did the original borrower read them, or were they intended for family members or friends? Nor can these statistics tell us how many unique titles circulated, which titles in particular circulated, how often they circulated, or which were available for home use but were never taken home. Likewise, they cannot indicate which books were used in the library and not taken outside the building. They usually cannot tell us how often current periodicals were read because, in many libraries, magazines did not circulate. Nor can they tell us which books were taken home but never read or which books were taken home and read aloud for the entertainment or education of family and friends, including those who could not read.

Another shortcoming of circulation counts is that they, like statistics about the number of volumes in a library and the number added during a given year, focus on library materials rather than library users. Statistics are affected by the freshness of the collection. If new reading material is not added regularly and if out-of-date or worn-out volumes are not weeded out, statistics will reflect static use or even decreases in the number of volumes borrowed. If there is no outreach or marketing of the library's services to non-users in the community, circulation statistics may stay steady as the branch continues to serve only a core of individuals accustomed to and comfortable with the building, the staff, and the organization of the collection.

As a measure of use, circulation statistics fall short. Nevertheless, they can be helpful for identifying patterns and trends, such as comparing one year to the next at a single library or for contrasting one library with another. They also give an overall sense of the community's involvement with the collection. To an extent, they can suggest the level of library-and-community or books-and-readers engagement. The individuals and groups that such data represent interact with texts in myriad ways that are both idiosyncratic and social.[3]

A striking example of one reader's use of books appears in the testimony of black educator Richard Wright, who in 1883 testified before the U.S. Senate Committee on Education and Labor about the status of black education in Georgia. Asserting the equality of blacks and whites, he cited classics of the western liberal tradition that documented the historic role of blacks in founding important religions, creating alphabetic writing, and originating branches of science. Historian James Anderson has interpreted Wright's defense of classical education for blacks as "not so much the imposition of an alien white culture that would make blacks feel inferior as it was a means to understanding the development of the western world and blacks' inherent rights to equality within that world."[4] The classics thus could be appropriated by different individuals and groups to serve their own needs and purposes.

The 1891–1902 records of the public library in Muncie, Indiana, illustrate how difficult it is to draw conclusions about collections and their uses. According to the *What Middletown Read* database, of the 413 books lent to the fifteen African Americans who were active borrowers, almost 85 percent were works of fiction; but they were not necessarily the same novels that the town's whites were reading. For example, blacks never borrowed Martha Finley's popular but overtly racist Elsie Dinsmore books.[5] Of the 149 Muncie library users who borrowed Thomas Nelson Page's nostalgic southern romance *Red Rock: A Chronicle of Reconstruction,* only one was identified as black: William Ball, a worker at the Findlay Rolling Mill. Of the ninety-nine people who borrowed Harriet Beecher Stowe's *Uncle Tom's Cabin* and who were identified by race, two were African American: William Ball and John Morin, a barber.

In the predominately white midwest at the end on the nineteenth century, African Americans may have experienced those novels differently from the way in which whites did. In other words, a public library's role in fostering a community's sense of a shared common

literary culture may be undercut by individual readers' interpreta-
tions inflected by sociocultural differences. Barbara Hochman has
pointed out that, well into the twentieth century, African Americans
read *Uncle Tom's Cabin* for a variety of reasons, including a desire to
learn about the slave past at a time when slavery was not generally
discussed and as a way to help them understand their own lives in
the racist present. For many, it was their first encounter with a story
about slavery, a past that many parents wanted to shield from their
children.[6]

Because public libraries often gave people their only access to
books, they attracted all kinds of readers. In 1913, the year that Houston's Colored Carnegie Library opened its new purpose-built structure, almost 1,800 residents registered as borrowers. They included
"porters, nurses, cooks and working girls and boys."[7] Similarly, in
1916, the first individuals to register at Nashville's newly opened
Negro Public Library included fifty-six teachers and a number of
other professionals and skilled workers, including physicians, nurses,
porters, pastors, businessowners, stenographers, clerks, bookkeepers,
hairdressers, cooks, and laundresses. Among 150 Nashville children
ages fifteen and under for whom registration data could be found,
only a handful were the offspring of teachers. About a quarter of
them were the children of laborers; others had parents who were
physicians, grocers, shoemakers, janitors, barbers, chauffeurs, and
cooks.[8]

The small, emerging black middle class and the tiny elite were
not measured by income alone but by involvement in education
and print culture.[9] Because separate libraries attracted working-class
and poor residents as well as their better-off middle-class neighbors,
library use might have been one marker of middle-class status, even
for someone employed as a housekeeper. Eleanor Holmes Norton,
an attorney who became the first female head of the federal Equal
Employment Opportunity Commission, remembered growing up in
the 1940s and 1950s in a striving middle-class family in Washington,
D.C. To her, "middle class" was a "cultural phenomenon" rather than
a literal economic category: "Even though [blacks] worked in white
folks' kitchens or their fathers were laborers, there was a cultural
striving that would separate them from people—white or black—who

conceived of themselves as being in their proper place. Blacks did not define their place by their work, or else all of us would have had to define ourselves as down-and-out. So you defined yourself by who you thought yourself to be."[10] Part of that definition, for some, involved visiting the library and taking a bit of it home, a few volumes at a time.

In 1909, before the Colored Carnegie Library in Houston opened in its own purpose-built locale, the city's white Carnegie Library opened a branch for African Americans in the Colored High School (later renamed Booker T. Washington High School). The opening-day collection included 356 books, about three-quarters of which had been weeded from the white library's collection. Of those, 144 volumes were adult fiction, 106 volumes juvenile fiction, 72 volumes adult nonfiction, and 34 volumes juvenile nonfiction. Issues of periodicals are included in the circulation records, among them *American Boy, Collier's, Crisis, Delineator, Ladies' Home Journal, Literary Digest, McClure's, Scientific American, Scribner's,* and the *Texas School Journal.*[11] Although a register of borrowers and an accession book have not survived, there are extant borrowing records for 1910–12.[12] It lists borrowers' numbers rather than names, so we cannot track the names of individuals who borrowed books. But a few notes in the margins do reveal names, so it is possible to learn some anecdotal information about how the collection was used.

The circulation log is a bound book of lined pages. The day's date is handwritten at the top of a page. The registered borrower's number appears in the lefthand column, the book title is abbreviated in the middle column, and its return date is stamped in the righthand column. Because these are borrowing rather than accession records, they reveal which titles in the collection circulated, not those that were only used in the library or that were part of the collection but not used at all. In addition to tracking every title that circulated, the log allows us to see how often it was borrowed. We can gauge the relative popularity of an item by how many times it circulated and by how many copies of a title the library held.

As I mentioned, the log recording the names, addresses, and identification numbers of registered borrowers no longer exists; but handwritten notes next to a few of the circulated titles reveal details about some of the library's users. For example, in January 1911, "Miss Brandon" checked out fourteen copies of Abbie Smith's dog story,

Bobtail Dixie. That same month, "Miss Blount" borrowed ten copies of *Stories of Great Americans for Little Americans,* and "Miss W. H. Blunt" borrowed twenty copies of a school textbook, *Hill's Readers.* In February, "Miss Blunt" borrowed ten copies of an elementary-level reader, *Baker's Action Primer.* In February and March, "Miss Blount, Gregory School" borrowed ten copies of a title noted only as *Second Reader.* (The Edgar M. Gregory School, founded during Reconstruction, had become the first public school open to blacks in Houston when it became part of the city's school district in 1876.)[13] Later in the spring, Miss Blount checked out eighteen copies of a book listed as *Roots and Stems,* which may have been Annie Chase's juvenile botany book, *Buds, Stems and Roots* or Brainerd Kellogg and Alonzo Reed's *Word Building with Roots, or Stems, and Prefixes and Suffixes.*

In 1911, borrower 939 repeatedly took out multiple copies of *Hill's Readers.* The year before, that borrower had also checked out *First Jungle Book, Arabian Nights,* and *Merry Animal Tales.* In March 1911, "Miss Bessie Neal" borrowed twenty copies of a volume recorded as *Whittier.* In April, "J. N. Dodson," the principal of Luckie Elementary School, took out twenty-one copies of the "South America" volume of *Carpenter's Geographical Reader* and twenty-one copies of *Rhymes of Woodland.* In November, he was back for fourteen copies of an unspecified volume of *Carpenter's Geographical Reader* and fifteen copies of the dog story *Rab and His Friends.* In June 1911, he took out twenty-one copies of *Our Schools Today.* In February 1911, "Mr. M. D. Haller" of the Douglass School borrowed twenty copies of *Christmas Stories.* An undated entry shows that he also took out twenty copies of *The Courtship of Miles Standish.*

Toward the end of April 1911, borrower 147 took out the *Eugene Field Reader,* a collection of Field's poetry for children, and renewed it in mid-May. At the end of the month he or she took out thirty copies of the same title. Between March 1910 and January 1912, 147 also borrowed a few issues of *McClure's,* the October issue of the *Ladies' Home Journal,* and fourteen books: *The Jungle Book, The Marrow of Tradition, Paradise Lost, Water Wonders, The Uncommercial Traveler, Works of Josephus, Stories to Tell to Children, How to Tell Stories to Children, Study in Scarlet, History of the Bible, Selections from the World's Orators, The Blue Flower,* a volume labeled only *Hawthorne,* and one labeled *Stories.* In January 1911, "Elaine Pearson" and "Miss Pratt" had also borrowed

How to Tell Stories to Children, as did "Mrs. W. B. Anderson" in March. Three different borrowers took out multiple copies of *Fifty Famous Stories Retold,* as did "Miss Baseley" from the Gregory School. *Longfellow* and *Merry Animal Tales* also went in multiple copies to borrowers associated with the Gregory School. In the spring of 1911, "Addie Green" took twenty copies of the *Progressive Road to Reading* as well as twenty-two copies of *Second Reader.*

Clearly, teachers used the library. Because it was located in the high school, it was especially convenient for teachers who worked in the building, yet that did not deter elementary school teachers from visiting and borrowing. Librarians' annotations indicate that most of their circulation activity did not involve ordinary one-visitor, one-title transactions but instead recorded the borrowings of teachers and principals who were supplementing the sparse reading material available at their schools.

Among the most popular items was Frank Carpenter's series of geographical readers. His 1910 volume on North America included descriptive tours of the tobacco and cotton lands of the south. In the section on Virginia, he noted the state's history of plantation slavery and mentioned that most African Americans had remained in the south after emancipation: "Our colored people are, as a rule, good citizens. Hundreds of thousands of them now own their homes and farms, many have learned trades or professions, and a large number have engaged in business of various kinds. Nearly all of them send their children to school, and not a few colored boys and girls are going to college."[14]

Carpenter's positive report glossed over the region's Jim Crow restrictions, their impact on the availability and quality of schooling, and the limited nature of the businesses and trades available to black citizens. The condescending phrase "our colored people" revealed a white writer's assumption that his audience was also white. Perhaps the teacher who carried multiple copies of this book from the library to her classroom helped her students recognize that Carpenter was nonetheless offering a positive depiction of African American accomplishment. He was not describing former slaves who happily continued to occupy the plantations but a motivated group of people who owned property and pursued education.[15]

Although many borrowing records were not annotated by name, they still revealed information about the collection and its use. In the log, the lowest borrower number is 2, the highest 2,197. No record of borrower 1's circulation transactions survives. Given that the library was in the high school, we can speculate that the principal, Charles H. Atherton, might have been the first person to register, perhaps for ceremonial rather than actual borrowing purposes. There are other gaps as well: no transactions were recorded for borrower 54, borrowers 79 to 81, or borrowers 995 to 2,196. This last range suggests a problem with the numbering system rather than the existence of more than 1,000 individuals who registered but then decided not to use their library cards. The total number of borrowers with recorded circulation transactions is 901. Among those who did borrow books, most had fewer than fifty transactions over the three-year period (table 12).

TABLE 12. CIRCULATION PATTERNS, HOUSTON COLORED CARNEGIE LIBRARY,
1910–12

NUMBER OF BORROWERS	THEIR CIRCULATION TRANSACTIONS
863	0–50
25	51–100
8	101–150
2	151–200
1	201–250
0	251–300
2	301–350
Total 901	

Source: Borrowing records, Colored Carnegie Library, 1910–12, Houston Public Library Collection.

The circulation log shows that several titles by African American authors were borrowed repeatedly. Sixteen different individuals checked out Du Bois's *The Souls of Black Folk*, including one who renewed it more than once and kept it from August 5 to October 4, 1912. Sixteen people also borrowed Du Bois's 1911 novel, *The Quest of the Silver Fleece*, which began circulating in February 1912. However, only three of the sixteen had also borrowed *The Souls of Black Folk*. One of them was borrower 208, who also checked out Chesnutt's

The Marrow of Tradition and *The House Behind the Cedars* but not *The Conjure Woman*. This person also did not borrow other works by African Americans, including Washington's *Up from Slavery*, *The Future of the American Negro*, *My Larger Education*, *The Negro in Business*, and *The Negro in the South;* Dunbar's *In Old Plantation Days* (the library had two copies), *The Strength of Gideon*, *The Life and Works of Paul Laurence Dunbar*, or *Poems;* or Matthew Henson's *A Negro Explorer at the North Pole* (the library had two copies) (table 13).

TABLE 13. BOOK TRANSACTIONS OF BORROWER 208, HOUSTON COLORED CARNEGIE LIBRARY, 1910–12

TITLE AS NOTED IN REGISTER	DATE BORROWED	DATE RETURNED
Blue Flower	2/8/10	2/18/10
Church Sociables and Entertainments	2/9/10	no record
Surrey of Eagle's Nest	2/18/10	2/26/10
Psychology	2/18/10	4/10/10
Marrow of Tradition	2/26/10	3/7/10
Psychology	4/9/10	4/12/10
Cruel as the Grave	4/11/10	4/19/10
Duke's Secret	4/19/10	no record
Oliver Twist and Other Stories	5/2/10	5/15/10
Oliver Twist and Other Stories	5/15/10	5/31/10
Textbook of Geology	6/14/10	7/12/10
Hundred Years of Missions	8/25/10	9/11/10
Textbook of Geology	9/5/10	10/17/20
Nedra	11/11/10	11/28/10
Human Body	11/11/10	11/23/10
Human Body	11/28/10	12/22/10
Human Body	12/22/10	12/27/10
Prodigal Son	1/5/11	1/12/11
Black Rock	1/12/11	1/26/11
Les Miserables	1/26/11	2/10/11
Robert's Rules of Order	2/7/11	2/21/11
Stories to Tell to Children	2/7/11	2/21/11
Old Norse Stories	2/7/11	2/21/11
Les Miserables	2/10/11	2/19/11
Les Miserables	2/19/11	2/28/11
Robert's Rules of Order	2/21/11	3/20/11
Teddy and Her Daughter	2/28/11	3/6/11
Little Minister	3/10/11	3/24/11
Robert's Rules of Order	3/20/11	4/10/11
Brewster's Millions	3/24/11	3/28/11
Beverly of Graustark	3/28/11	4/2/11

TABLE 13. (*Continued*)

TITLE AS NOTED IN REGISTER	DATE BORROWED	DATE RETURNED
Souls of Black Folk	4/2/11	4/11/11
Elizabeth Barrett Browning	4/6/11	no record
Elizabeth Barrett Browning	4/7/11	no record
Robert's Rules of Order	4/10/11	no record
Souls of Black Folk	4/11/11	4/24/11
Plain Tales from the Hills	5/17/11	5/31/11
Maid of Maiden Lane	6/26/11	6/29/11
Don Orsino	6/29/11	7/8/11
Old Mam'selle's Secret	7/3/11	7/10/11
Vanity Fair	7/10/11	7/17/11
Carhart and Chute Physics	7/10/11	7/31/11
Vanity Fair	7/17/11	7/28/11
He Fell in Love with His Wife	7/28/11	8/16/11
New Creations in Plant Life	7/31/11	8/14/11
Physics	7/31/11	8/14/11
House Behind the Cedars	8/14/11	8/21/11
Physics	8/14/11	8/21/11
He Fell in Love with His Wife	8/16/11	no record
Physics	8/21/11	9/13/11
Physics	9/13/11	9/28/11
Katrine	10/13/11	10/15/11
Infelice	10/25/11	11/6/11
Sherlock Holmes	1/26/12	2/6/12
Raffles	2/6/12	2/17/12
Rue with a Difference [sic.]	2/27/12	3/12/12
Highway of Fate	3/12/12	3/29/12
Quest of the Silver Fleece	5/8/12	5/16/12
Our Little Irish Cousin	6/3/12	no record
Child's Dream of a Star	6/9/12	6/10/12
Black Shilling	6/17/12	6/20/12
Monsieur Lecoq	7/2/12	7/8/12
Monsieur Lecoq	7/8/12	7/12/12
Monsieur Lecoq Part II	7/31/12	8/10/12
Monsieur Lecoq	7/31/12	8/10/12
Herb of Grace	8/9/12	8/22/12
Apache Princess	8/21/12	8/27/12
Story of Rhinegold	8/29/12	9/9/12
Tempest and Sunshine	9/9/12	9/12/12
Views in Africa	9/23/12	no record

Source: Borrowing records, Colored Carnegie Library, 1910–12, Houston Public Library, Houston Metropolitan Research Center.

TABLE 14. BOOK TRANSACTIONS OF BORROWER 682, HOUSTON COLORED
CARNEGIE LIBRARY, 1910–12

TITLE AS NOTED IN REGISTER	DATE BORROWED	DATE RETURNED
Jackanapes	3/31/10	4/5/10
Brewster's Millions	12/13/11	12/13/11
Lovely Mary	12/13/11	no record
Brewster's Millions	12/14/11	12/19/11
Helen's Babies	12/19/11	12/19/11
Monsieur Lecoq	12/19/11	1/2/12
Little Old Man and Other Stories	1/2/12	1/2/12
Aunt Jane's Nieces at Work	1/11/12	1/22/12
Physics	1/11/12	1/27/12
Monsieur Beaucaire	1/13/12	1/13/12
Self-raised	1/23/12	2/19/12
Physics	1/27/12	2/18/12
Story of Marco Polo	2/9/12	2/27/12
Quest of the Silver Fleece	2/17/12	2/18/12
Conquest of Canaan	2/18/12	3/12/12
Ben Hur	2/19/12	3/4/12
Story of Marco Polo	2/27/12	no record
Ben Hur	3/4/12	3/4/12
Conquest of Canaan	3/12/12	3/28/12
Ben Hur	3/18/12	no record
Story of Marco Polo	3/28/12	4/3/12
Conquest of Canaan	3/28/12	no record
Tale of Two Cities	4/28/12	no record
What a Young Woman Ought to Know	4/30/12	no record
Ben Hur	5/4/12	no record
Taking the Bastille	5/9/12	no record
King Arthur	6/18/12	7/4/12
Agriculture	6/22/12	7/6/12
Late Mrs. Neill	7/3/12	7/6/12
King Arthur and His Knights	7/5/12	7/17/12
Herb of Grace	7/6/12	7/17/12
Stories of Old Greece	7/8/12	7/11/12
Macbeth	7/11/12	7/25/12
Guy Mannering	7/12/12	7/25/12
Diplomatic Adventure	7/17/12	7/18/12
Rose of the River	7/18/12	7/23/12
Macbeth	7/26/12	8/7/12
Guy Mannering	7/26/12	8/7/12
Short History of English People	8/1/12	8/13/12
Souls of Black Folk	8/5/12	8/22/12
Souls of Black Folk	8/22/12	no record
Souls of Black Folk	8/28/12	9/18/12
Souls of Black Folk	9/18/12	10/4/12
Mrs. Wiggs of the Cabbage Patch	9/11/12	9/18/12
Lovely Mary	9/11/12	9/18/12
That's Why Stories	9/15/12	9/18/12

TABLE 14. (*Continued*)

TITLE AS NOTED IN REGISTER	DATE BORROWED	DATE RETURNED
Getting on in the World	9/30/12	10/8/12
Strength of Gideon	10/4/12	10/5/12
Heart of Oak (Book 3)	10/5/12	10/8/12
Story of the Greeks	10/8/12	no record
Sandy	10/8/12	10/21/12

Source: Borrowing records, Colored Carnegie Library, 1910–12, Houston Public Library, Houston Metropolitan Research Center.

Borrower 682, whose circulation pattern appears in table 14, was the second of the three library users who borrowed both of Du Bois's works. This person did not borrow anything by Washington, Dunbar, Henson, or Chesnutt. The third of the three borrowers was 1,215, whose relatively high number and short record indicates that he or she did not register to use the library until it had been open for a couple of years. Like 682, borrower 1,215 read Du Bois's novel first and then moved on to his nonfiction.

Borrowers 7 and 685 were the most active overall, with 335 and 324 circulation transactions, respectively. Each left a distinctive trail: borrower 7 checked out material that one might expect an educated adult to read, while borrower 685 took home items that an avid young reader might find appealing. The first circulation transaction for borrower 7 occurred on February 17, 1910. Within six months he or she had checked out twenty-five different books, including Chesnutt's *The Marrow of Tradition* and *The Conjure Woman;* Dunbar's *The Strength of Gideon* and *In Old Plantation Days;* and Du Bois's *The Souls of Black Folk.* Over the course of almost three years, borrower 7 took home classics such as Dante's *Divine Comedy* and Cervantes's *Don Quixote;* poetry by Elizabeth Barrett Browning and Henry Wadsworth Longfellow; novels such as William Makepeace Thackeray's *Vanity Fair* and George Eliot's *Silas Marner;* and a few juvenile books such as *Wigwam Stories Told by North American Indians* and *The Snow Baby.* In May and June 1911, he or she checked out and renewed *Oriental Literature, Village Life in China,* and *China and the Chinese.* Other transactions listed *Church Sociables and Entertainments;* the Koran; the works of Josephus; and a sprinkling of Christian fiction, including

Ralph Connor's *The Sky Pilot* and Marie Corelli's *The Master-Christian.* Borrower 7 also regularly read magazines and newspapers—not only the *Independent,* a black-owned newspaper published in Houston, but also *American Magazine, Review of Reviews, McClure's, Scientific American, Texas School Journal, Literary Digest,* and the *Crisis.*

In contrast, borrower 685 read very few magazines, checking out one issue each of *McClure's* and *Scribner's* and a few issues of *American Boy.* But his or her interests ranged far and wide, suggesting that 685 may have borrowed on behalf of a few other people. The first transaction, in February 1910, was Abbie Smith's dog story *Bobtail Dixie;* and the last book returned, in October 1912, was Daniel Defoe's *Robinson Crusoe.* Borrower 685 checked out James Otis's *Toby Tyler* three times (in July and October 1910 and in September 1911) and Mary Mapes Dodge's *Hans Brinker* three times (in February and October 1910 and in October 1911). Checked out twice was Page's *Two Little Confederates*—once in September 1910 and again in March 1911, when it was kept only overnight.

Borrower 685 checked out no works by African Americans and no issues of the *Independent* or the *Crisis.* He or she liked series books but didn't borrow them in the order in which they were published. For example, 685 checked out Mary Hazelton Blanchard Wade's *Our Little Indian Cousin* and *Our Little Canadian Cousin* in February 1910 but did not get around to borrowing books about the English, French, and Japanese cousins until the summer of 1911. On the other hand, 685 was a fan of the Motor Boys series, checking out three volumes in November 1910, another in February 1911, and reborrowing three titles in April. Other library users shared 685's enthusiasm for the series. The collection contained five different Motor Boys titles, which circulated a total of 117 times. Martha Finley's Elsie books were also popular: the library owned twenty-three different titles in the series, and they accounted for 327 circulations in three years. However, borrower 685 eschewed them.

In May 1911, he or she checked out Helen Nicolay's *A Boy's Life of Abraham Lincoln* and, after returning it, took home L. M. Montgomery's *Anne of Green Gables.* Borrower 685 read fairytales and folklore, which were in plentiful supply at the library, as well as Texas tales such as Edward Stratemeyer's *With Taylor on the Rio Grande* and *For the Liberty of Texas* and Kirk Munroe's *With Crockett and Bowie*. He or she was one of thirty-four borrowers who checked out Stowe's *Uncle Tom's Cabin*. Although 685, who was perhaps a boy or young man, did not borrow books by Paul Laurence Dunbar, Joel Chandler Harris, or Thomas Nelson Page, several other Colored Carnegie Library users did. Dunbar's *In Old Plantation Days* was as popular as *Uncle Tom's Cabin*, with thirty-four circulations. Thirteen black Houstonians borrowed Harris's *Uncle Remus*, while twenty-one borrowed *Nights with Uncle Remus*. Page's *In Ole Virginia* was borrowed only five times.

Borrower 706 was another active library user, one whose pattern of circulation can only be described as eclectic. Between February 7, 1910, and February 8, 1911, he or she was involved in 124 circulation transactions. Judging from the items in the log, borrower 706 liked war fiction and was interested in France. But he or she also checked out William Stoddard's *The Red Mustang, a Story of the Mexican Border*, a novel for young readers; *American Telephone Practice*, a technical tome originally published by the American Electrician Company; and the *Cruikshank Fairy Book*, which featured only four stories, among them "Jack and the Beanstalk" and "Cinderella." In addition, borrower 706 checked out periodicals, including issues of *American Boy, Ladies' Home Journal*, the *Delineator*, the *Crisis*, and *Hampton's Magazine*.

This pattern of borrowing raises a number of questions. Was 706 a teacher at the high school who could easily and regularly visit the library? If so, was he or she reading some of the books for pleasure and others to prepare for classes? Did 706's fairly broad range of interests actually reflect a small group's interests? Was he or she acting as an agent on behalf of family members or friends? Whatever the case, if 706 had not stopped borrowing books and magazines early in 1911, he or she would probably have been among the three most active library users during the period represented in the circulation log. But without concrete information about the library's registered borrowers, the comings and goings of books remain impressionistic.

The New Orleans Public Library produced annual reports that included circulation data for the Dryades Branch between 1916 and 1934. Both the size of the collection and the circulation increased during those years, although circulation did show fluctuations (table 15). In 1916, books circulated at an average rate of 2.8 times per year;

but in 1920, the rate had dropped to 2.7 times. By 1925 and 1930, book circulation had jumped to an average rate of almost four times per year; and in the Depression year of 1934, that rate had doubled to eight. In 1923, when the branch had 1,325 registered borrowers, the library owned 9,326 volumes, or seven books per borrower. In that year, there were twenty-three circulations per borrower, a rate higher than the circulations at large public libraries, which averaged 15.5 per user in 1921 and 21.6 in 1926.[16]

TABLE 15. BOOK STOCK AND CIRCULATION, DRYADES BRANCH LIBRARY, NEW ORLEANS, BY YEAR

YEAR	BOOKS IN STOCK	CIRCULATION	CIRCULATION PER BOOK
1916	6,187	17,533	2.83
1917	6,405	21,740	3.39
1918	6,535	22,565	3.45
1919	6,803	22,025	3.24
1920	7,075	18,907	2.67
1921	7,281	22,233	3.05
1922	8,403	26,188	3.12
1923	9,326	30,763	3.30
1924	10,079	31,299	3.10
1925	10,570	41,060	3.88
1926	11,221	42,448	3.82
1927	12,287	40,067	3.26
1928	12,585	36,997	2.94
1929	13,107	44,449	3.39
1930	12,907	50,509	3.91
1931	13,520	70,234	5.19
1932	13,779	89,599	6.50
1933	13,977	111,753	7.99
1934	14,087	113,947	8.09

Source: Joseph Lewis Wheeler and Jesse Cunningham, "Report of a Survey of the New Orleans Public Library" (1935), table between pp. 41 and 42.

The annual reports through 1927 also list the circulation of adult fiction, juvenile fiction, adult nonfiction, and juvenile nonfiction (table 16). In 1920, users borrowed 9,865 volumes of adult fiction and nonfiction, which formed 52 percent of total circulation. Circulation of juvenile fiction and nonfiction reached 9,042, or 48 percent of the total. This was higher than the 34 percent rate that was typical in the 1920s at public libraries in cities with a population of at least 200,000.[17]

TABLE 16. CIRCULATION, TOTAL AND BY CATEGORY, AT THE DRYADES
BRANCH LIBRARY, NEW ORLEANS, 1916–27

YEAR	TOTAL CIRCULATION	ADULT FICTION	JUVENILE FICTION	ADULT NONFICTION	JUVENILE NONFICTION
1916	17,533	5,240	1,689	5,557	5,031
1917	21,740	5,530	2,478	6,786	6,946
1918	22,565	5,826	2,634	6,651	7,454
1919	22,025	5,704	2,538	6,687	7,103
1920	18,907	2,789	2,263	7,076	6,779
1921	22,233	3,404	3,068	8,436	7,325
1922	26,188	4,340	4,488	8,933	8,427
1923	30,763	6,106	7,153	8,330	9,174
1924	31,299	6,529	7,507	7,940	9,323
1925	40,160	9,278	11,623	9,228	10,031
1926	42,448	9,985	12,086	10,009	10,368
1927	40,067	9,228	10,642	9,831	10,366

Source: "Annual Report of the New Orleans Public Library, 1916–1919" (New Orleans, 1920), 28–33; "Annual Report of the New Orleans Public Library, 1920" (New Orleans, 1921), 16–19; "Annual Report of the New Orleans Public Library, 1921" (New Orleans, 1922), 20–23; "Annual Report of the New Orleans Public Library, 1922" (New Orleans, 1923), 21–24; "Annual Report of the New Orleans Public Library, 1923" (New Orleans, 1924), 22–25; "Annual Report of the New Orleans Public Library, 1924" (New Orleans, 1925), 20–23; "Annual Report of the New Orleans Public Library, 1925" (New Orleans, 1926), 18–20; "Annual Report of the New Orleans Public Library, 1926" (New Orleans, 1927), 22–24; "Annual Report of the New Orleans Public Library, 1927" (New Orleans, 1928), 21–23.

Circulation statistics were different at the whites-only libraries in New Orleans. At the Canal branch, adult circulation in 1920 was 45,049, or 65 percent of the total. At the central library the difference was even more pronounced, with adult circulation in 1920 reaching 168,101, accounting for 77 percent of the total (table 17). The fact that more children than adults borrowed books at Dryades reveals much about the library's larger context. In general, more women than men used public libraries, but white women had more leisure time to spend there than black women did. Compared to white women, more than twice as many black women over the age of fifteen worked for pay in 1920.[18] Consequently, fewer had time to travel to the library or to linger among the stacks. Black adults also had lower literacy rates than their children did. Of the 84,314 blacks living in New Orleans in 1920, 13,234 (15.7 percent) were illiterate; and of the number who were illiterate, 12,317 (93 percent) were age twenty-one or older.[19] Children who had learned to read, even in underfunded, segregated classrooms, were able to find more books to read—and more fun books to read—at the library branch.

TABLE 17. CIRCULATION, TOTAL AND BY CATEGORY, AT THE CENTRAL LIBRARY AND TWO BRANCHES, NEW ORLEANS, 1920, 1925

LIBRARY	TOTAL CIRCULATION	ADULT FICTION	JUVENILE FICTION	ADULT NONFICTION	JUVENILE NONFICTION
1920					
Central	219,167	104,715	33,783	63,386	17,283
Canal	69,336	37,019	17,063	8,030	7,224
Dryades	18,907	2,789	2,263	7,076	6,779
1925					
Central	363,555	166,183	51,364	96,492	49,516
Canal	109,540	57,731	24,692	11,570	15,547
Dryades	40,160	9,278	11,623	9,228	10,031

Source: "Annual Report of the New Orleans Public Library, 1920" (New Orleans, 1921), 16–18; "Annual Report of the New Orleans Public Library, 1925" (New Orleans, 1926), 18–20.

African Americans with access to public libraries found the western classics in the stacks, but they discovered other reading material, too. They also used the public space of the library to support and augment their reading practices; for instance, adults and teens attended literary club meetings and scholarly lectures, and children participated in story hours (fig. 8). The Western branch in Louisville, for example, hosted reading clubs for young people in which members shared oral reports about books. Story hours at the branch drew 150 to 180 listeners every week.[20] At least one family relocated to Louisville so its children could have access to the library's collections and services (fig. 9).[21]

An untold number of library users were influenced by the books, newspapers, and magazines they borrowed and read; the story hours they attended; the staff members with whom they interacted; and the club activities they participated in. Anecdotes of that influence survive in individuals' published memoirs. For example, author Zora Neale Hurston recalled that a love of reading made her feel that she was different from other residents in Eatonville, Florida, where she lived until the age of nine. Her memoir, *Dust Tracks on a Road,*

Figure 8. Some high school students participated in the Douglass Debating Club, which met at the Western Colored Branch of the Louisville Free Public Library. Standing, left to right: S. R. Smith, assistant secretary; B. O. Wilkinson, treasurer; C. H. Parrish, Jr., critic; Clarence Marshall, chairman, program committee. Seated, left to right: William Downs, vice president; Frank Reid; unidentified. Courtesy of Louisville Free Public Library, Photographic Archives, University of Louisville.

Figure 9. Children's room, Western Colored Branch of the Louisville Free Public Library. Courtesy of Louisville Free Public Library, Photographic Archives, University of Louisville.

briefly recounts Eatonville's founding in 1886, when it became the first all-black town in the United States. Although Hurston noted that a library was established soon after the town's incorporation, "with books donated by the white community," she did not mention using the collection. Instead, her youthful encounters with books seemed to be somewhat random. She recalled a day when two northern white women visited her school and, after hearing her read aloud, gave her books, including an Episcopal hymnal, fairy and folk tales, Roman and Greek myths, Jonathan Swift's *Gulliver's Travels,* Rudyard Kipling's *The Jungle Book,* and Johann David Wyss's *The Swiss Family Robinson.* After a physical altercation with her stepmother, the teenaged Hurston fled her home. In another town she found a copy of John Milton's epic poem *Paradise Lost,* which someone had thrown into the trash. In her early twenties she befriended a singer who had attended Harvard and who lent her his books. Later, when she returned to high school at Morgan College, she worked for a white family and read from their library, whose holdings included poems such as Thomas

Gray's "Elegy Written in a Country Churchyard," Oscar Wilde's "The Ballad of Reading Gaol," and the *Rubaiyat of Omar Khayyam*. By then, she had read "hundreds of books," including dime novels and the pulp fiction of Horatio Alger.[22]

Although public libraries did not seem to influence Hurston's reading list during her formative years, they did contribute to Ralph Ellison's development. In his 1964 memoir, *Shadow and Act,* dedicated to long-time Tuskegee Institute librarian Morteza Sprague, he recalled reading T. S. Eliot's *The Waste Land* as a college sophomore and being "intrigued by its power to move me while eluding my understanding." He decided to read the works cited in the poem and, "for this, the library at Tuskegee was quite adequate and I used it." In the process, he discovered "Pound and Ford Madox Ford, Sherwood Anderson and Gertrude Stein, Hemingway and Fitzgerald."[23]

Those authors apparently were not available when, as a youngster, Ellison read everything in Oklahoma City's new public library branch for African Americans. Before the library opened, he was living in the parsonage of the Avery Chapel of the African Methodist Episcopal Church, where his mother worked for most of 1919. That same year, he began his education at the poorly equipped Douglass School, which served black students in grades 1 through 12. At the parsonage he read voraciously from a large and varied collection of books, which a succession of pastors and church members had amassed over time.

When Oklahoma City's Carnegie library opened the Dunbar Branch in a former pool hall in 1921, it became the first collection accessible to local African Americans. Ellison and his friends competed with each other to read all the books in the new but still small collection, which was composed of the Carnegie Library's discards and community donations. Because they read faster than the librarian could organize the books, the children were exposed to adult as well as juvenile books, including works by William Shakespeare, Theodore Dreiser, and Sinclair Lewis.[24]

In 1928, the Dunbar Branch moved into larger quarters on land owned by the Colored Women's Federated Clubs. But even then its collection consisted mainly of what Ellison's biographer describes as "used books and eclectic hand-me-downs." To extend his reading,

Ellison turned to the private libraries his teachers owned as well as one belonging to a friend's parents, who had been educated in the northeast and the midwest and owned works by George Bernard Shaw, Friedrich Nietzsche, and other authors not available at the Dunbar Branch.[25]

Like Ellison, Richard Wright used a white man's reading list to guide his self-education. In his 1937 essay "The Ethics of Living Jim Crow," he recalled using the whites-only public library while he lived and worked in Memphis in the mid-1920s. Because "it was almost impossible to get a book to read," he used the card of a white man he worked for. "I would write a note addressed to the librarian and sign the name of the white supervisor. I would stand at the desk, hat in hand, looking as unbookish as possible. When I received the books I would take them home." In his autobiography, *Black Boy,* Wright later elaborated on his encounter with a white librarian, a scene that scholars often cite and that has even been immortalized in a children's book. According to Wright's account, when he presented his first forged note, in which he asked for books by H. L. Mencken, the white woman at Cossitt Library's circulation desk asked, "You're not using these books, are you?" He replied, "Oh, no, ma'am. I can't read." In fact, having finished the ninth grade in Jackson, Mississippi, he *could* read. Nonetheless, he found Mencken's vocabulary and style challenging because he had never before encountered such sophisticated writing. Using Mencken's *A Book of Prefaces* as his guide to good reading material, Wright subsequently borrowed library copies of classics of western literature as well as works by important white modernist authors, including Sinclair Lewis's *Main Street* and Theodore Dreiser's *Sister Carrie.* When he came across unfamiliar words, he looked them up in a dictionary.[26]

Public libraries circulated both well-known classics and fresh new works, allowing borrowers with a preconceived list of authors and titles to discover new books as they browsed. But because Wright was not free to use the card catalog or browse among the stacks, the Memphis library did not help him discover books he might have wanted to read, especially those by African American authors. He was not even free to reveal an interest in reading but had to rely on deception and feigned ignorance.

Like the majority of blacks in Memphis, Wright was probably unaware that the library at LeMoyne Institute had, since 1903, provided space for a small collection weeded from Cossitt. It was intended to serve both campus and community, although LeMoyne's students were the main users. Nonetheless, the collection made it possible for Cossitt to claim that it was serving all. Dissatisfied with this situation, LeMoyne's president, A. J. Steele, approached the library board to open a separate off-campus branch, arguing that the public was reluctant to enter the private institute's library; but Cossitt made no move in that direction until the late 1930s.[27] The same issue had come up in Greensboro, but at least Bennett College had deeded land to the city and a separate Carnegie building had been constructed to encourage public use.

In the late 1920s, Cossitt Library's director, Jesse Cunningham, destroyed many of the worn-out books at LeMoyne and restocked the shelves to encourage more public use. But Cunningham severed the relationship a few years later after LeMoyne's new president, Frank Sweeney, unilaterally acquired additional books that the Cossitt Library board had refused to buy. Intent on securing accreditation for the college, he had declared that they were for the institution rather than the public.[28]

The Cossitt Library did not establish a separate branch for African Americans until 1939, well after Wright the obscure reader was on his way to becoming Wright the well-known author. The Vance Avenue Branch opened in an existing building and, by the early 1940s, had about 4,500 volumes on the shelves as well as 2,800 volumes that rotated as small classroom collections among the city's black schools. Cossitt also set up a public branch in Booker T. Washington High School, with a collection of about 2,200 volumes, but transferred the branch to the Board of Education in 1940. LeMoyne continued to serve the community, increasing its efforts after the Depression-era Federal Housing Authority funded LeMoyne Gardens, a large housing project across the street from the institution. By 1943, LeMoyne had 275 registered borrowers for its community collection, which included about 1,000 juvenile titles. Most of the borrowers were children, who took their selected books to the college library's circulation desk for checkout. The Vance Avenue Branch was "too far away to attract the children of LeMoyne Gardens," reported two of the college's librarians. "Therefore there is little cooperation and no conflict between the college library service and the public library."[29]

Neither LeMoyne's outreach nor the Vance Avenue Branch's establishment helped Wright. Moreover, although reading opened his mind to literature and the vast world it represented, it did not bring him pleasure. Instead, he remembered his early reading of library books as a desperate response to an otherwise stark intellectual and physical poverty. It isolated him from his fellow black southerners, whom he believed were uninterested in reading the kind of literature he found so compelling.[30]

Wright's contemporary, James Baldwin, was also drawn to collections that could educate him in the literary arts. Unlike Wright, however, he had grown up in the north, and his library experiences were different. Baldwin recalled that, by the time he was thirteen years old, he had read everything in the two Harlem-area branches of the New York Public Library. In his novel *Go Tell It on the Mountain*, his character John finds it difficult to enter the main library, whose scale far surpassed that of the branches, fearing that the whites inside would notice his inability to maneuver. John decides that the only way to build his confidence is to read everything in the branches first. Baldwin's descriptions, like Wright's, express a sensitivity to the forbidding atmosphere of the white library space.[31]

Not all library users who recorded their memories grew up to be famous novelists. Annie McPheeters was an assistant librarian at the Auburn Branch of the Atlanta Public Library between 1934 and 1936 and then served as head librarian until 1949. She recalled that young Martin Luther King, Jr., was one of the library's regular visitors. He apparently learned about Gandhi's passive resistance techniques (which King later deployed in his civil rights actions) by reading books that he had borrowed from the Auburn Branch. But the Gandhi books were in the adult section of the library, and King, a juvenile borrower, was not allowed to check them out on his library card. McPheeters solved the problem by issuing a library card to Martin Luther King, Sr., and allowing the son to check out the Gandhi books on his father's card.[32] In Memphis, Wright had deceived the librarian. In Atlanta, however, the librarian participated in the deception, bending the system to serve the readers.

McPheeters also recalled the visits of young Maynard Jackson, who later became Atlanta's first black mayor. Jackson's father would regularly bring his children to the library, where Maynard would fill a paper bag with books from the children's area. Then he would sit down to read, surreptitiously eating the food he had also hidden in the bag, until McPheeters would catch him and tell him to stop. Years later, Jackson's mother told McPheeters that he still loved to eat while reading.[33]

McPheeters influenced countless children, and the memories of various Atlanta residents corroborate and add to her accounts. A reporter for the *Atlanta Daily World* recalled how McPheeters worked to help improve his reading skills. Teacher George S. Rice remembered going to the library to create puppet shows. Rice's daughter, Saundra Murray Nettles, who grew up to be a librarian, a scientist, and an activist, met McPheeters at the new West Hunter Branch, where the librarian moved in 1949. Nettles recalled that McPheeters organized story hours, conversed with kids about the books they were reading in the library's summer reading program, corrected their diction, listened to them recite poetry, and told their parents when they had outgrown the children's books and were ready to tackle the adult collection. And, of course, she date-stamped the books they borrowed.[34] Nettles wrote, "I always looked for Mrs. McPheeters. Her presence, like a fresh, light perfume, filled the library. . . . Her body emanated agency—you could sense that she had just shelved a stray book left on a table, or realigned a chair. The reading rooms were quiet, Zen spaces where a child could close her eyes, one hand resting on the page just read, and follow the character into the life that beckoned from pictures and words."[35]

This was the kind of welcoming presence that Louisville's Rachel Harris had called for three decades earlier. As Harris affirmed, African American readers were better served by library staff members who looked like them and who exuded helpfulness rather than hostility. Black librarians would create "an atmosphere where welcome and freedom are the predominate elements," Harris suggested, implying that white librarians were creating quite a different atmosphere when African Americans entered the building. She wrote:

As far as grown people are concerned it would not make much difference, for we are experienced enough to know that if it were necessary to secure a book or an article on a certain subject we would not
let a frigid environment deter us from our object. But children are not
so constituted. Their sensitive natures cannot withstand unpleasant
conditions, and nine times out of ten their first visit under unfavorable
circumstances would be their last.[36]

In many white libraries, of course, discouraging black readers was
the point. In the small town of Lake City, South Carolina, for example, a white librarian called the police when a nine-year-old black boy
named Ronald McNair tried to borrow books in 1959. The police
refused to do anything, and the librarian relented and checked out
the books to McNair, who later grew up to become an astronaut.[37]
Journalist Carl Rowan recalled being locked out of the library when
he was growing up in McMinnville, Tennessee. "A wealthy white
woman" got involved, borrowing books by Jonathan Swift, Alexander
Pope, and Robert Burns for him. Rowan also wanted to read black
authors such as Langston Hughes and Richard Wright, but the library
didn't own them.[38]

Where they existed, libraries serving southern blacks supported
literacy in service to larger goals, including civil rights. John Lewis,
who became a long-serving U.S. congressman for the state of Georgia, remembered using public libraries to find works by Gandhi, Tho-
reau, and other writers who inspired nonviolent civil disobedience.
Reverend Dr. Joseph Lowery of Alabama, who served as president
of the Southern Christian Leadership Conference, recalled that
library collections offered information about black history and life
not found in state-approved textbooks.[39] Such stories suggest the
importance of information access as a component of empowerment
and achievement, fundamental to building literacy and learning.

Yet even when librarians encouraged and supported reading,
library use was hampered by low literacy skills, an outcome of state
and local policies that underfunded public education for African
Americans. The situation was particularly dire for people who could
not afford to move to towns with accessible libraries or to enroll in
private schools with longer academic years and adequate educational equipment. In such cases, improving literacy beyond mere

functionality was difficult. It helped to have books freely available.

In the early 1930s, circulation of library books among African Americans living in the eleven counties with Rosenwald demonstration projects increased dramatically. In five of those counties, there was zero circulation of library books among African Americans in 1930. In 1934, book circulation ranged from 15,545 in Richland County and 18,588 in Walker County to 38,471 in Charleston County, 43,905 in Shelby County, and 50,442 in Webster Parish.[40] Book circulation depends on the number of active library users and the number of volumes in the collection. For example, Richland County's number of books borrowed in 1934 was low as a result of a small number of active library users and a small collection. Almost 12 percent of African Americans in Columbia, South Carolina, which was served by the Richland County project, had registered to use the library by 1934, but the small number of volumes available to blacks, 2,628 (0.07 per capita) clearly dampened some individuals' enthusiasm. (The project did not serve rural blacks countywide.) On the other end of the scale was Webster Parish, where the per capita ratio of books to persons reached 0.30 and residents registered in greater numbers; almost 36 percent of urban and almost 23 percent of rural African American residents were registered borrowers.[41]

At almost every demonstration library, the largest category of individuals who borrowed books was students, ranging from a high of 97 percent of black library users in North Carolina's Davidson County to a low of 66 percent in Tennessee's Hamilton County.[42] Among employed black adults who used the county libraries, professional women were the largest occupational group, followed by men working in agriculture, then by men in the manufacturing and mechanical trades, and finally by women in domestic and personal service.[43]

In 1934, as they were assessing the Rosenwald demonstration project, Wilson and Wight gathered 2,559 reading reports from African American library users in the eleven counties. Students in grades 5 to 11 in urban schools reported reading 3,647 books, with younger students getting only about 6 percent of their books from public libraries and older students borrowing 14 percent of their books from libraries. Of the 325 books read by urban adults, 35 percent came from libraries. Rural students reported reading 1,333 books, with the older students getting 14 percent of their books from libraries.

Of the 730 books read by rural adults, 15 percent came from public libraries. School libraries were important sources of books for all categories of borrowers, except for urban adults.[44]

When students used public and school libraries to find fiction, they most often chose the standard fare that librarians agreed was appropriate for developing minds. When students read what they really wanted to read—that is, comic books (which Wilson and Wight called "cartoon books")—they had to buy or trade for them. Among male fifth and sixth graders in urban black schools, comic books accounted for 42 percent of their reading, but by the time they reached the eighth grade, that figure had dropped to 17 percent. For girls the percentage was lower, from 33 percent in fifth and sixth grade to 10 percent by eighth grade. In general, girls reported reading more books than boys did (686 versus 410). However, because the reading report forms were distributed at libraries, it may be more accurate to say that girls visited libraries more often and/or were more willing to report on their reading than boys were.[45]

Aggregated data can be helpful for an overview, but at the local level, readers display idiosyncrasies that make broad generalization challenging. A surviving report from one of the libraries offers additional data about local practices. On April 9, 10, and 11, 1934, the Chattanooga Public Library's Howard Branch for African Americans and its ten school-community branches for blacks throughout Hamilton County participated in gathering reader reports for Wilson and Wight. A total of 599 library users took part, 135 in the city's Howard branch and 464 in the county's branches. The top five occupations listed by participants were student (383), homemaker (83), farmer (31), laborer (28), and teacher (22). Students read a little more nonfiction than fiction, while homemakers read more fiction. About 57 percent of all the books read by farmers were fiction, while laborers read even more fiction.[46]

Table 18 shows the relative use of the library in the unincorporated town of Bakewell, twenty-three miles away from Chattanooga. Students made up 47 percent of the individuals who completed the reading reports over the three-day period but accounted for 55 percent of the circulation. They borrowed far more nonfiction (37 percent) than fiction (18 percent) and far more nonfiction than other readers reported. In city libraries serving whites, women typically outnumbered men, but that pattern did not hold among rural blacks in Tennessee. Homemakers accounted for only 13 percent of total library users, while farmers constituted 25 percent, even during three spring days when they might be expected to be busy in the fields. This doesn't necessarily mean that farmers read more than homemakers, of course, because anyone able to visit a library could borrow books on behalf of family members and friends. It may attest instead to the burdens and obstacles that restricted rural black women's opportunities for educational and recreational reading. Homemakers likely found it difficult to leave their domestic duties or to take their children with them to a distant library, while farmers may have had greater access to transportation over rural roads.

TABLE 18. READERS BY OCCUPATION AND PERCENTAGE OF TYPES OF BOOKS CIRCULATED, BAKEWELL SCHOOL-COMMUNITY LIBRARY, HAMILTON COUNTY, TENNESSEE, APRIL 9–11, 1934 (N=68)

READERS		% OF TYPES OF BOOKS CIRCULATED		
Occupation	% of people reporting that occupation	Nonfiction	Fiction	Total
Students	47.06	36.73	18.21	54.94
Homemakers	13.24	5.85	4.63	10.48
Farmers	25.00	10.5	11.11	21.61
Teachers	4.41	2.47	2.16	4.63
Laborers	10.29	4.02	4.32	8.34
Total readers	**100**	**59.57**	**40.43**	**100**

Source: Bertie Wenning, "Reading Survey of the Chattanooga Public Library and Its School-Community Branches, April 9–10–11, 1934" [1934], n.p.

Bakewell's library had the lowest percentage of student use of the ten libraries in the county (table 19). East Dale had the highest proportion of students using the library, almost 88 percent, and they accounted for 75 percent of the total circulation. As the percentage of students dropped, their relative importance as library users increased. For example, at the school-community library housed in the only high school that Hamilton County's African American residents could attend, Booker T. Washington, students accounted for 58 percent of registered borrowers and almost 62 percent of book circulation. In East Chattanooga, students were 47 percent of the borrowers who used the combined public and school library at the Roland Hayes School for grades 1 through 8 and were responsible for 56 percent of the total circulation.[47]

TABLE 19. LIBRARIES RANKED BY PERCENTAGE OF STUDENT BORROWERS, AND STUDENT BORROWING AS A PERCENTAGE OF ALL BORROWING, HAMILTON COUNTY, TENNESSEE, APRIL 9–11, 1934 (N=599)

LIBRARY*	% OF STUDENT BORROWERS	% OF NONFICTION BORROWED	% OF FICTION BORROWED	% OF TOTAL CIRCULATION
East Dale	87.5	57.5	17.5	75.0
Hixson	84.21	28.57	42.86	71.43
Howard (city)	76.29	22.77	47.03	69.8
Soddy	76.19	56.42	12.82	69.24
Lookout Mountain	73.69	21.21	36.37	57.58
Harrison**	71.4	10.34	68.96	79.3
Chickamauga	58.77	36.28	36.28	72.56
Washington	57.69	30.5	31.0	61.5
Roland Hayes	47.13	24.39	31.7	56.1
Bakewell	47.06	36.73	18.21	54.94

Source: Bertie Wenning, "Reading Survey of the Chattanooga Public Library and Its School-Community Branches, April 9-10-11, 1934" [1934]), n.p.
*Not listed is Pine Breeze Sanitarium where the only participants in the reading survey were ten students in the first through seventh grades.
** Harrison had only sixteen students in the school.

It is not surprising that library branches that purported to serve the whole community but were located in a school building drew disproportionate numbers of students as users or that students engaged in completing assignments used more nonfiction on the whole. At the twenty-year-old city branch, in Chattanooga's Howard School, 103 of the reading survey respondents were students, 90 of them in the eighth through twelfth grades. Somewhat counter to the nonfiction trend, those 90 students checked out 113 books during the three-day reading survey, with 78 (61 percent) classified as fiction. Twenty eighth graders borrowed thirteen works of fiction, eighteen ninth graders borrowed twenty-five works of fiction, and twenty-six tenth graders borrowed sixteen works of fiction. The ninth graders borrowed no nonfiction during the three days, so perhaps they were engaged in a literature assignment due that week. The maturity of the library in the Chattanooga community might also have made a difference because over the years individuals would have become accustomed to having a collection of fiction to use. The twelve schoolteachers who completed reading reports at the Howard branch reported borrowing nine nonfiction and thirteen fiction books, while the eight homemakers borrowed no nonfiction at all, instead taking home eighteen works of fiction. Two porters borrowed two works of fiction. The two unemployed readers reported borrowing three books of nonfiction and one of fiction.[48]

Metropolitan public libraries reported that their visitors during the Depression years increased significantly; circulation at the Dallas Public Library was up by 116 percent, in Memphis by 59 percent. Some who turned to the library for free recreation were not especially good at reading, and librarians were frustrated by the lack of easy-to-comprehend fiction and nonfiction suitable for adults.[49] Since the mid-1920s, the American Library Association and the American Association for Adult Education had been collaborating on studies of reading and advocating for the production of reading material for adults with low literacy. In 1935, with funding from the Carnegie Corporation, Chicago researchers William S. Gray of the University of Chicago and Bernice E. Leary of Saint Xavier College published their findings. Their book, *What Makes a Book Readable, with Special Reference to Adults of Limited Reading Ability: An Initial Study,* included a chapter on the reading abilities of adults, which the researchers had based on the results of reading tests given to 756 individuals in Illinois, Florida, Georgia, Kentucky, and South Carolina. The tests measured reading comprehension of fiction and nonfiction. Of those tested, 121 were African American students at the Model School of the Agricultural and Mechanical Arts College in Tallahassee, Florida: seventy-three in the senior high school grades and forty-eight in the junior high grades. According to Gray and Leary, the school served "young people and underprivileged adults of the colored race."[50] The researchers also administered tests to a larger sample that included an additional 151 farmers and villagers in Illinois; 121 indigent adults with little education in Columbus, Ohio; 125 "selected negro men" in Chicago; and 537 blacks living in eighteen Florida cities who participated in educational programs at the Agricultural and Mechanical Arts College.

G. T. Wiggins conducted the Chicago study, recruiting men from fraternal organizations such as the Elks Club. He approached 265 individuals, but many declined because they were illiterate or had low reading skills. The 125 Chicago residents he tested were mostly working men who had, on average, attended school through the eighth grade. Their mean score on the Monroe Standardized Silent Reading Test showed them to be reading at the eighth-grade level, whereas the mean for the Columbus group was at the fourth-grade level and the mean for the Florida group was at the fifth-grade level. Overall, Gray and Leary concluded, "approximately 70 per cent of the negroes tested are unable to engage intelligently in reading activities at the adult level."[51]

African Americans scored lower on all of the tests they took. While the mean score on the fiction comprehension test was 53.86 overall, it was 19.95 for students in the Agricultural and Mechanical Arts program. Likewise, while the mean score on the nonfiction test was 47.86 overall, it was 19.85 for the students. The researchers asserted that literacy improved when individuals stayed in school or in other adult education programs. Yet African Americans in the south often lacked such schools and programs, and the shorter school year for poor rural African American children, who had to work instead of go to school, was another barrier to literacy. But even when students such as those in the A&M program stayed in school, literacy suffered in the absence of reading material. As the researchers pointed out, the Florida students did not have a ready source of books so could not follow their own interests or desires when choosing what to read. They did not have access to public libraries where they could explore an array of fiction and nonfiction in books, magazines, and newspapers.[52]

Gray and Leary offered anecdotal evidence from readers in regard to the difficulty of the books they had read. With help from readers' advisers at forty unnamed large public libraries, the researchers amassed 170 reading reports from seventy-four men and ninety-six women. Although Gray and Leary did not indicate how many African Americans were among the readers, they did discuss one.[53] "A colored man, a freight-handler, who had left school in the fourth grade, declared that *Robinson Crusoe* was the best book he had ever read, because 'the words were so you could read right along.' "[54] According to the adviser's report, he was thirty years old and "reads everything that will 'learn him something.'" The man told the adviser, "Crusoe was like me, he made the best of everything."[55]

Using a variety of measures, such as how often the text used monosyllabic and polysyllabic words, the length of its sentences, and the variety of its vocabulary, Gray and Leary calculated the reading difficulty of both the original *Robinson Crusoe* and a later edition adapted for contemporary readers.[56] They rated the original as one of the hardest books to read and the adaptation as one of the easiest, noting that most adults with low literacy skills would be able to read it.[57] The freight handler had probably read the adapted version, given the adviser's description of it: "Written in first person singular. Short chapters. Proceeds without a break. Content—of primitive living, struggle for conquest, rich use of ingenuity. Lack of technical words. Short sentences. Good-sized print. Clear illustrations. Paragraph divisions. Subheads."[58] Yet the anonymous voice of this library user, mediated through the adviser's retelling, attests to the creative imagination that black readers could bring to texts.

Public libraries could indeed function as "zones of influence," to borrow Archie Dick's term. They were "dynamic spaces with many possibilities."[59] But for people to experience the library's influence, they needed both a physical space and a collection of things to read. Louisville's library system offered both, but in the early 1940s the branches for African Americans had become unable to serve the community to the extent needed. Using money from the Federal Housing Authority, created in 1937, the city constructed a 786-unit apartment building for low-income whites and an 808-unit building, Beecher Terrace, for blacks. The white project included a library, but Beecher Terrace was only a few blocks from the Western Colored Branch so did not include a library on site.[60]

In 1943, a graduate student completed a thesis on the reading habits of Beecher Terrace residents. She noted that Louisville's 47,000 African Americans (14.2 percent of the total population) could use the Eastern or Western libraries as well as a small subbranch run by the Western Branch staff. They could also request that books be sent to the branches from the main library. When material could not be sent to the branches, they could even, by appointment, go to the main library, but the white librarians would have to make arrangements to keep any black readers away from white readers. The Western Branch and its subdivision owned almost 17,000 volumes and had a total annual book budget of just under $1,700.[61]

The researcher visited 616 homes and discovered that 306 individuals had public library cards. About 38 percent of the cardholders were students, while about 20 percent were adults with at least a high school education. Most of the Beecher Terrace residents read fiction, and they named sixty-nine different titles they had borrowed from the library and read, only nine of them nonfiction. These works included popular books that any public library would offer, such as Pearl Buck's *The Good Earth*, Daphne DuMaurier's *Rebecca*, Richard Llewellyn's *How Green Was My Valley*, and Hans Christian Andersen's fairy tales. They read Joel Chandler Harris's *Uncle Remus* and Margaret Mitchell's *Gone with the Wind*. But they also named Radclyffe Hall's *The Well of Loneliness* and Richard Wright's *Native Son* as well as a novel from the Harlem Renaissance era of the 1920s, Jessie Fauset's *Plum Bun*. Among the handful of nonfiction works they reported reading were Washington's *Up from Slavery*, Benjamin Brawley's *Negro Genius*, and Willis Weatherford and Charles Johnson's *Race Relations*. The researcher concluded that the library should do more to encourage reading among the individuals who lived in the project's hundreds of households.[62]

By 1947, of the 597 public library systems operating in the southeast, 225 (38 percent) served African Americans. With only a few exceptions, however, that service took place in separate buildings and rooms. A survey of nine southeastern states in 1946 and 1947 revealed that every city with more than 50,000 African American residents—Memphis, Birmingham, Atlanta, Jacksonville, and Richmond—offered segregated library collections and services (table 20). Eight of the thirteen cities with 25,000 to 50,000 black residents provided collections and services. Fourteen out of thirty of the cities with 10,000 to 25,000 black residents gave them access to library books. The 7,685,977 African Americans living in urban areas of the nine states had access to 279,381 books in municipal libraries—0.03 volume per capita, or about one book for every twenty-seven people.[63]

TABLE 20. COMPARISON OF LOCAL BLACK POPULATIONS WITH
BLACK LIBRARY BUDGETS, VOLUMES, AND CIRCULATIONS,
RANKED BY PER-CAPITA BOOK CIRCULATION, 1946–47

CITY	BLACK POPULATION (PERCENTAGE OF BLACKS IN TOTAL POPULATION)	LIBRARY BUDGET IN DOLLARS	TOTAL VOLUMES (VOLUMES PER CAPITA)	TOTAL CIRCULATION (CIRCULATION PER CAPITA)
Louisville, Kentucky	47,158 (14.8)	22,969	38,160 (0.8)	104,502 (22.1)
Roanoke, Virginia	12,812 (18.5)	2,018	6,595 (0.5)	52,231 (7.9)
Savannah, Georgia	43,237 (45.0)	9,281	12,051 (0.3)	29,764 (3.2)
Danville, Virginia	10,168 (31.0)	2,100	4,799 (0.5)	24,232 (2.4)
Knoxville, Tennessee	16,094 (14.4)	5,852	5,923 (0.4)	23,307 (1.4)
Chattanooga, Tennessee	36,404 (28.4)	5,063	6,225 (0.2)	47,535 (1.3)
High Point, North Carolina	7,872 (20.4)	1,500	1,940 (0.2)	10,291 (1.3)
Clarksdale, Mississippi	6,672 (54.8)	780	5,130 (0.8)	8,863 (1.3)
Greenville, North Carolina	6,194 (48.8)	1,617	1,390 (0.2)	7,799 (1.3)
Asheville, North Carolina	13,435 (26.1)	2,900	5,919 (0.4)	11,623 (0.9)
Saint Petersburg, Florida	11,982 (19.7)	2,780	1,640 (0.1)	7,014 (0.6)
Winston-Salem, North Carolina	36,018 (45.1)	5,974	6,440 (0.2)	17,718 (0.5)
Petersburg, Virginia	13,483 (44.0)	1,883	3,882 (0.3)	6,305 (0.5)
New Bern, North Carolina	5,839 (49.4)	1,372	6,000 (1.0)	2,600 (0.4)
Richmond, Virginia	61,251 (31.7)	8,040	12,841 (0.2)	24,105 (0.4)
Norfolk, Virginia	45,893 (31.8)	3,747	7,768 (0.2)	18,918 (0.4)
Rome, Georgia	5,379 (20.8)	2,000	1,451 (0.3)	1,783 (0.3)
Miami, Florida	36,857 (21.4)	3,627	5,370 (0.1)	6,505 (0.2)
Portsmouth, Virginia	19,338 (38.1)	2,971	3,613 (0.2)	3,293 (0.2)

Source: Louis R. Wilson and Marion A. Milczewski, eds., *Libraries of the Southeast: A Report of the Southeastern States Cooperative Library Survey, 1946–1947* (Chapel Hill, N.C.: Southeastern Library Association, 1949), 253, 256–58, 260; tab. 104 appears on 259. My table only includes southeastern cities for which all data were available.

Post-War Standards for Public Libraries (1943) recommended two books per capita, and public libraries everywhere in the southeast fell short of this standard. For example, Portsmouth, Virginia, had a total population of 50,745 in 1940 and a total book stock of 19,323 in

1947, coming up short by 82,167 volumes. But even though the actual number of volumes per person was a dismal 0.4, this was still twice that available to African Americans in the city. In Louisville, with a population of 319,077 and a collection of 430,827 books in 1947, the overall per-capita book stock was 1.35, short of the standard but still more than the 0.8 available to the city's blacks.[64]

If we rearrange the figures by number of volumes available to the black population, we can speculate further about how readers experienced race-based libraries (table 21). For example, almost 49 percent of the population of Greenville, North Carolina, was African American. Those 6,194 individuals had access to 1,390 volumes—one volume for every 4.5 persons—and in a single year the volumes circulated 7,799 times. If every one of the volumes was borrowed an equal number of times, each went out 5.6 times. Of course, not every person used the library and not every book circulated. Nevertheless, access to such a small collection must have meant that some individuals read some books more than once and that library-based reading for many black southerners was an intensive rather than extensive proposition.[65]

If anyone was looking for ways to discourage people from using public libraries, they could find them in the segregated systems of the south. Provide too few books and a budget too small to maintain a usable collection. Many individuals who walked into libraries sparsely stocked with a collection of tattered, dirty, outdated books may have turned around and walked out again, never to return. Nonetheless, some must have read their way through the entire stock and then reread their favorites. Although small worn-out collections were not new enough, broad enough, or deep enough, they were still bigger than anything most readers had seen in anyone's home. After all, something was more than nothing. It was the most anyone could expect until public library systems desegregated.

TABLE 21. COMPARISON OF LOCAL BLACK POPULATIONS WITH BLACK
LIBRARY COLLECTIONS AND CIRCULATION, RANKED FROM LEAST TO MOST
VOLUMES AVAILABLE, 1946–47

CITY	BLACK POPULATION (PERCENTAGE OF BLACKS IN TOTAL POPULATION)	TOTAL VOLUMES (VOLUMES PER CAPITA)	TOTAL CIRCULATION (CIRCULATION PER CAPITA)
Greenville, North Carolina	6,194 (48.8)	1,390 (0.2)	7,799 (1.3)
Rome, Georgia	5,379 (20.8)	1,451 (0.3)	1,783 (0.3)
Saint Petersburg, Florida	11,982 (19.7)	1,640 (0.1)	7,014 (0.6)
High Point, North Carolina	7,872 (20.4)	1,940 (0.2)	10,291 (1.3)
Portsmouth, Virginia	19,338 (38.1)	3,613 (0.2)	3,293 (0.2)
Petersburg, Virginia	13,483 (44.0)	3,882 (0.3)	6,305 (0.5)
Danville, Virginia	10,168 (31.0)	4,799 (0.5)	24,232 (2.4)
Clarksdale, Mississippi	6,672 (54.8)	5,130 (0.8)	8,863 (1.3)
Miami, Florida	36,857 (21.4)	5,370 (0.1)	6,505 (0.2)
Asheville, North Carolina	13,435 (26.1)	5,919 (0.4)	11,623 (0.9)
Knoxville, Tennessee	16,094 (14.4)	5,923 (0.4)	23,307 (1.4)
New Bern, North Carolina	5,839 (49.4)	6,000 (1.0)	2,600 (0.4)
Chattanooga, Tennessee	36,404 (28.4)	6,225 (0.2)	47,535 (1.3)
Winston-Salem, North Carolina	36,018 (45.1)	6,440 (0.2)	17,718 (0.5)
Roanoke, Virginia	12,812 (18.5)	6,595 (0.5)	52,231 (7.9)
Norfolk, Virginia	45,893 (31.8)	7,768 (0.2)	18,918 (0.4)
Savannah, Georgia	43,237 (45.0)	12,051 (0.3)	29,764 (3.2)
Richmond, Virginia	61,251 (31.7)	12,841 (0.2)	24,105 (0.4)
Louisville, Kentucky	47,158 (14.8)	38,160 (0.8)	104,502 (22.1)

Source: Louis R. Wilson and Marion A. Milczewski, eds., *Libraries of the Southeast: A Report of the Southeastern States Cooperative Library Survey, 1946–1947* (Chapel Hill, N.C.: Southeastern Library Association, 1949), 259, tab. 104.

CHAPTER 9

Opening Access

Desegregation of public libraries occurred in two phases. Before the 1954 *Brown v. the Board of Education* decision, cities and towns such as Louisville and Nashville chose to quietly desegregate their libraries in response to local activism. After *Brown*, public libraries in communities that resisted desegregation delayed making changes until courts intervened. When Anna Holden of the Southern Regional Council published her survey of public libraries in 1954, she was under the impression that desegregating libraries would be simpler than desegregating schools and other institutions would be.[1] But whites' massive resistance to the *Brown* decision also affected libraries.[2]

Houston borrowed from both Louisville's incremental approach and Nashville's quiet method when it desegregated its library system in the 1950s. This was a deliberate strategy of the city's white commercial elite, who, expecting change, wanted to avoid federal intervention, maintain Houston's public image as a good place to do business, and keep segregation in place as much as possible.[3] The city's desegregation of public transportation, accommodations, and institutions took place in waves, which were set in motion by two significant civil rights victories in Texas. With the *Smith v. Allwright* decision in 1944, the federal Supreme Court outlawed the state's whites-only primary elections.[4] Then, in 1950, the Court's *Sweatt v. Painter* decision ruled that black students must be allowed to attend the University of Texas Law School because the hastily created separate law school for blacks did not provide educational resources equal to those at the university.[5]

Soon after the Court rendered its decision in *Sweatt,* influential blacks in Houston turned their attention to the central library. Apparently they believed that an effort to desegregate the public library would be historically significant, a logical next step in their long fight to secure citizenship rights and educational opportunities. In a letter to the library board, quoted by the *Houston Informer,* five African American leaders and activists, including Lonnie Smith of the *Smith v. Allwright* case, noted that they could probably win a lawsuit against the library if they chose to file. They said, however, that they preferred "a voluntary solution" because it "would go a long way toward establishing a better understanding and feeling between white and colored people of Houston."[6]

Working with the activists was attorney Herman Wright, who, with his partner, Arthur J. Mandell, had represented the Congress of Industrial Organizations in Texas in the 1930s and 1940s. In 1947, both had become members of the Houston branch of the NAACP.[7] As a member of that association's legal redress committee, Wright followed up on the group's letter after library board members failed to respond. Early in October 1950, he talked by phone with board president Mrs. Roy L. Arterbury about the possibility of arranging a meeting between the board and the legal redress committee. She apparently was noncommittal because on November 17 Wright sent her a letter stating that the committee would consider filing suit if the board did not arrange a meeting by November 27. Library director Harriet Dickson Reynolds promptly wrote back, saying that Arterbury and other board members were out of town and that a quorum could not be reached. She assured Wright that Arterbury would call him when she returned, although she did not say when that would be.[8] Reynolds's response was a classic case of "don't call us, we'll call you." Stalling for time, she sent Wright's letter and her own reply to assistant city attorney Herman W. Mead.

At the end of January 1951, Arterbury and another long-time board member, Mrs. R. L. Young, met with Mayor Oscar Holcombe to discuss ways in which to increase the library's budget. During their visit, Holcombe instructed them not to meet with the NAACP committee or to entertain the possibility of desegregating the library.[9] Holcombe, who had been mayor throughout the 1920s, had served off and on again during the next three decades. At one point, he had briefly been a member of Houston's Ku Klux Klan chapter, though he had decided to neither participate in nor interfere with the organization during its 1920s heyday.[10]

In February 1952, board president Arterbury and librarian Reynolds met with a white woman, Mrs. Newton Rayzor, and a black man, Charles Shaw, who were representing the Church Alliance Council. In a memo of the meeting, Reynolds noted that "Mr. Shaw pounded on the point of political equality. Mrs. Rayzor talked of Christian brotherhood." Rayzor and Shaw asked that Houston's black residents be allowed to use any of the city's libraries and that they also be given representation on the library board. Reynolds and Arterbury tried to appease them, pointing out that blacks could use the central library for reference work and could request that books from the central collection be sent to the Colored Carnegie Library for their use. Reynolds also suggested that the Colored Carnegie Library needed a Friends of the Library group to increase branch use and donor support.[11]

When Roy M. Hofheinz was elected mayor of Houston, the city's official treatment of African American residents began to change. Soon after taking office in early 1953, Hofheinz appointed Gould Beech, his executive assistant, to advise the library board. At their meeting in February, board members talked with Beech about strategies for increasing the library's budget. He broached the subject of desegregation, asking members for their opinions. Although board members Mrs. A. T. Carleton and Carl F. Stuebing were present, along with Arterbury and Reynolds, their responses were not recorded in the minutes of the meeting.[12]

In May, Mayor Hofheinz attended the library board's meeting and told members that he thought it was time to desegregate the library. He noted that Houston's black residents were taxpayers who should have access to the municipal services their taxes supported. He alluded to a court case to desegregate the city golf course, acknowledging that the city expected to lose and would not appeal. He reassured the board that Houston residents were ready to accept blacks in the library, emphasizing that those who would take advantage of the opportunity would be "serious minded and with good demeanor" and would follow the same library rules that whites did. Hofheinz told the board to desegregate quietly, making no announcements to the news media or the NAACP.[13] Neither Arterbury nor Young were present at the meeting. Arterbury, who had served on the board since her appointment in 1931, had resigned in March; and Stuebing had taken over as board president.[14] Young, a strong supporter of Mayor Holcombe, had died in late April.[15]

In June the mayor appointed Jack Valenti as Young's replacement. A native of Houston, Valenti had distinguished himself as a pilot during World War II and had earned a bachelor's degree from the University of Houston before completing a master's degree at Harvard in 1952. At the time of his appointment to the library board, he was a partner in the political consulting and advertising firm, Weekley and Valenti.[16]

At Valenti's first board meeting, on July 21, 1953, Billy B. Goldberg, chair of the board's expansion program committee, suggested that the library hire a consultant or work with staff in the city's planning department to create a coherent expansion program. The board agreed that he should work with the planning department on that study. Goldberg also raised the idea of selling both the Colored Carnegie Branch on Frederick Street and the Carnegie branch on Henry Street because circulation was decreasing at both locations. In the context of a proposed expansion program, members were interested in freeing themselves from the burden of upkeep on declining properties. In the past couple of years, they had approved more than $1,000 in roof repairs at the Colored Branch alone.

Although the issue did not come up at the meeting, board members probably also recognized that the demographics of the neighborhood around the branch had changed since World War II. The location was no longer convenient for many black Houston residents. And because other library buildings were off-limits to them, the consequences were pronounced. As their civil rights activism increased, many African Americans were disturbed by the decreasing level of library availability.

At the July 1953 meeting, the library board also discussed the matter of implementing the mayor's desegregation policy.[17] Library director Reynolds outlined the library's current policies and practices. Black readers were allowed to borrow books only at the Colored Carnegie Branch and at three deposit stations. If a black person asked for service at another location, the staff would refer that person to the Colored Branch. If a black patron needed to use reference materials or the card catalog, and they were not available at the branch, he or she would be served at the central library but only under certain conditions. The patron was not allowed in the front door but had to use a side entrance. The patron was not allowed to use the reading rooms or the card catalog but had to sit in a designated area of the mezzanine and wait for staff to bring the requested reference works or catalog drawers.[18]

Reynolds told the board that she was concerned about desegregating children's services. She pointed out that library services for children involved far more than the reference and circulation functions typically used by adults. They included story hours, clubs, and other group activities that could be construed as having a social component. Reynolds believed that white parents would object to such activities if black children participated in them. In her view, the library should take an incremental approach to desegregating service. Black adults should be allowed to use the central library's adult collection and reading rooms, but children's services should remain segregated.

The discussion that followed touched on issues such as whether whites and blacks would be allowed to use the same toilets, water fountains, and club rooms. Board members considered the definition of *adult* and talked about potential administrative problems in applying restrictions to some clients but not to others. Although board member Waldo Bernard moved that they approve Reynolds's recommendation to desegregate adult services, no one seconded the motion. Valenti moved that the issue be considered at a subsequent meeting, and everyone agreed.[19]

After the June meeting, when Mayor Hofheinz had told the board to desegregate the library, Reynolds had written to city attorney Will G. Sears for guidance. She asked if the library board could act alone or if the city council would have to approve its decisions. She asked if there were laws requiring segregation, either of the library itself or of facilities such as toilets and drinking fountains within the library. The attorney's reply is dated July 21, the day of the subsequent board meeting. Because the minutes do not refer to it, Reynolds probably had not seen it before the meeting took place. Sears told her that, according to the city code, the board had full authority and responsibility for governing and managing the library. He also noted that constitutional law required that all segregated facilities or services had to be "substantially equal."[20]

At the board's August meeting, Valenti moved "that all adult facilities at the central library be opened to Negroes; and, that for this purpose, an adult is defined as anyone of senior high school age and up." Waldo Bernard seconded the motion, and all seven board members approved. Mrs. Roland Ring, board secretary, recorded in the minutes that Valenti, Bernard, and Goldberg agreed that the board's decision represented progress and that they would monitor developments and consider expanding access later. Ring also noted that adult reading rooms, collections, and clubrooms would be open to African Africans as of August 21, 1953. In keeping with the mayor's wishes, the library would not announce the policy change to the public.[21]

On paper, the change made some 200,000 library books and the central and branch libraries available to Houston's black adults. But without a public announcement, African American residents were slow to learn the news. The first person to register, a student at Texas Southern University for Negroes, did so on August 28, a week after the official decision. When he asked to borrow books, he apparently expected to be turned away. Library staff reported that he was surprised when they issued him a borrower's card. Still, by the end of the year, fewer than fifty blacks had registered as borrowers at the central library; most were Texas Southern students. The library's annual report for 1953 noted that, with one exception, all of the African American borrowers returned their books on time.[22] Perhaps the librarian included this information because some white staff members had assumed that black readers would be irresponsible. But she may have offered these data in support of Mayor Hofheinz's assertion that whites had nothing to fear from opening the library to the kind of blacks who would be likely to use it.

Even the partial desegregation of Houston's main library put that agency ahead of many other institutions in the city. It was not until March 4, 1960, that black students in Houston, following the lead of activists in Greensboro, North Carolina, began to stage sit-ins and other forms of direct action that pushed restaurants, train stations, buses, hotels, and other private businesses and public accommodations to desegregate.[23] It was not until September 1960 that public schools in the city began incremental integration—six years after the *Brown* decision and a month after a federal district judge ordered desegregation of all first-grade classes.[24]

Despite the central library's 1953 policy change, the Colored Carnegie Branch continued to operate, emphasizing services for children and young adults. The branch librarian, Anita Sterling, visited four elementary schools and one senior high in her efforts to interest young people in using the library. She organized a reading club for teens, held story hours for children, and hosted a variety of activities in observance of Book Week. She also submitted columns and information to local newspapers to publicize the branch. As at the central library, Texas Southern students were relatively heavy users of the branch's collections and services.[25]

Meanwhile, Houston voters had approved a bond issue of $500,000 for the city library system, and the library's board and administration wanted outside guidance. At the time, Houston was spending only forty-two cents per capita on library collections and services, far less than the American Library Association's recommended $1.50 and significantly behind comparable cities such as Indianapolis ($1.81), Newark ($2.85), and San Francisco ($1.24). Houston's per-capita spending was even less than that of other notoriously underfunded libraries in southern cities, including New Orleans (fifty-five cents), Dallas (sixty-seven cents), and San Antonio (sixty-eight cents).[26]

In late October 1953, the central library hired Los Angeles Public Library director Harold L. Hamill to recommend improvements.[27] Hamill recommended that the system add six new branches, largely to serve the thriving middle-class families who were moving to expanding suburban residential areas. He also recommended increasing librarians' salaries; adding a branch coordinator, an additional cataloger, and a business manager; and establishing a system of financing to sustain an urban library capable of meeting the diverse recreational and educational needs of a growing populace. Additionally, Hamill recommended that the library buy another bookmobile to provide better service to the city's African American residents.

Although Hamill had considered recommending that one of the six new branches be situated in a predominately black area of town, he had not wanted to choose among several possible neighborhoods. In addition, he believed that many black adults tended not to use libraries because of their relatively low levels of education and income. Hamill apparently even considered recommending the closure of the Frederick Street Branch (as the Colored Carnegie Library was now called) because it circulated fewer than 10,000 volumes annually. However, he decided against that recommendation because the branch was inexpensive to operate and a "community asset to the Negro people."[28]

Importantly, Hamill urged the central library to serve African Americans regardless of age. "The public library has a special obligation to make its facilities as readily accessible to children as possible. The factors which discourage their parents from using the library do not necessarily affect the children with equal force, and the potential library use among Negro children is therefore much higher than among adults." He asserted that no "serious social problems would result" and that "the staff is willing to serve them."[29] However, his recommendation went unheeded.

During the next several years, African American children and their parents repeatedly requested service for youngsters at the central library. The 1954 annual report noted that "during the summer months we had many Negro children in the twelve to fifteen year age group (mostly boys) applying for cards and asking to go to the Norma Meldrum [Children's] Room. They were well behaved and went out quietly when told of our policy. We hoped that they went to Frederick Street for we assured them they needed their patronage."[30] In 1955, the central library's registration of African American borrowers doubled; most of them were university and high school students. But as new branches began to open and the city's elementary schools began to establish their own libraries, they siphoned off the central library's young white patrons. Nonetheless, despite a noticeable decline in use of the children's room, the central library policy was unchanged.

Although the library system's annual reports included one-page summaries about activity at the Frederick Street Branch, they did not note specific quantitative data. Thus, while we know that the branch's circulation, registration, and reference services increased at this time, we do not know by how much. In 1955, library assistant Anita Williams reported that the enrollment and completion rates in the summer reading program were "larger." In 1956, ninety children participated in the summer reading program. In 1958, branch librarian Addie Mae Henry reported that "the summer reading club really went over big this year."[31]

The library board, however, had more concrete data about the branch. In the mid-1950s, Frederick Street began cooperating with black schools, serving as a study hall for six classes of about sixty students each per day. The school system provided a teacher and a part-time librarian in exchange for the use of the building. The library system spent $9,000 a year to keep the branch open and to provide service at the Burrus and Emancipation deposit stations. In 1955, their total circulation reached 11,458, with an average daily circulation of twenty-four at the branch itself. In early 1956, the board decided to close the Burrus deposit station, downgrade the Emancipation station to a deposit collection, and buy fewer books for the Frederick Street Branch. The board also planned to lease the branch's main floor to the school system, with the goal of eventually moving the stacks to the basement and replacing the deposit stations with a bookmobile.[32] Within months, circulation dropped to half the rate of the previous year.

At a board meeting on May 18, 1956, Alice Stewart, supervisor of extension services, urged members to open the central library to all African Americans, telling them she suspected that frustrated residents were boycotting the segregated branch and stations. Instead, board members listened to children's librarian Ann Hornak, who argued against changing the policy. In her view, the numerous black children living in neighborhoods near downtown might put too many demands on children's services and collections and create "a problem in connection with story hours and toilets."[33]

At the same meeting, board member Stuebing reported that he

had consulted with the mayor's office and that adult African Americans were to be allowed to borrow books from any branch or library unit on a "special" basis. At the same time, he affirmed that staff should alert the library director or board president if any group of African Americans appeared to be preparing to protest at any library unit. Director Reynolds had already apprised city attorney George Neal of the decision, and the library board agreed at their May meeting that all policies regarding racial desegregation were now the responsibility of the mayor and city council.[34]

But African American residents had tired of this irrationality and discrimination. Board members listened to a letter sent to Reynolds by the father of a girl who had been turned away from the central library and told to go to the Frederick Street Branch instead. The writer was Henry Allen Bullock, who had earned a Ph.D. from the University of Michigan in 1942 and had served as head of the sociology departments at Prairie View A&M College in Waller County, Texas, and at Dillard University in New Orleans before becoming the head of sociology at Texas Southern in 1950.[35] Bullock noted that he had held a library card for the central branch since the summer of 1954. He mentioned that he was not the only Negro parent who wanted to encourage his children to read broadly from the larger collection available at the central library. Nor was he the only one who wanted to verify with the director that the desk clerk was correct in claiming that black adults but not black children were allowed to use the library.

Bullock stated that his daughter, who would be entering junior high in the fall, had been hurt by the encounter and the restriction. "Since the American Library Association has been one of the most sensible of all our educational institutions, I naturally hesitate to believe that a discrimination so illogical as that to which my child was exposed is an official policy." He concluded by asking that Reynolds send him the official policy statement.[36] The board appointed Waldo Bernard to contact Bullock, describe "the progress made in the library to date," and point out that the mayor and council, not the library, now made policy.[37] Subsequent minutes do not reveal the outcome of Bernard's and Bullock's discussion, but the library apparently did not fully desegregate until several years later.

Bullock was exactly what late nineteenth-century opponents of education for African Americans had feared: a black person who was willing to speak out when treated unfairly, willing to demand the rights due to him as a citizen, a taxpayer, and a human being. He also represented what supporters of education and libraries for African Americans had claimed would happen when blacks were given the same opportunities as whites. They would form a class of hardworking, responsible citizens who paid their taxes and a market of consumers who would contribute to overall economic growth. That second scenario occurred sooner than many whites, including those who ran Houston's public library, could accept.

Although the Frederick Street Branch continued to operate for a few more years, by the late 1950s it had outlived its usefulness, and not just because it was a relic of Jim Crow. The forty-year-old structure needed constant repairs, circulation was dwindling, and the outdated collection suffered from neglect and abuse. Reynolds and her director of extension services, Alice Stewart, recounted the "difficulties of service to Negroes and past experiences with heavy book losses, mutilation of materials, and vandalism at the Colored Carnegie Branch and on the [bookmobile known as] Traveling Branch #3," which served predominately black neighborhoods.[38]

There are different ways to interpret their report. Were conditions really this bad, or were whites' perceptions of these conditions influenced by their own racist stereotypes? Were some library users unable to return books because of problems with transportation, housing, or long work days? Did some express hostility to the separate and unequal library through pilfering or damage? Did whites' own long-term neglect of the building and its contents lead to the librarians' bleak assessment? Whatever the causes, the branch was clearly operating in an outdated building with an inadequate collection and inspired the pride of neither whites nor blacks.

Ultimately, the city's traffic problem led the board to sell the building and the buyer to tear it down. The branch sat in the path of a major street extension: one of downtown Houston's main arteries would pass through the site. In the summer of 1959, the mayor's office informed Reynolds that the extension project would begin in December, meaning that the building would need to be moved or demolished in the fall. The board wanted to sell the

Figure 10. Dedication ceremony at Colored Carnegie Library, Houston, 1913. Left to right: W. L. D. Johnson and small son; Nat Q. Henderson; W. E. Miller; E. O. Smith; Ora G. Lockett; J. B. Bell; L. H. Spivey; William Sidney Pittman, architect; Andy Parr; and John Atkins. Courtesy of the Houston Public Library Collection, Houston Metropolitan Research Center.

building and property, but they were unsure of their legal authority. An attorney in the city's legal department thought that if the building were no longer used as a library, it would have to revert to the ownership of the trustees of the Colored Carnegie Library Association. Reynolds checked the city directory and found that only two of the original trustees, W. L. D. Johnson and L. H. Spivey, were listed (fig. 10). She checked the deed and found no reversionary clause, merely the stipulation that the property was "for the use and benefit of the colored people of Houston." Reynolds asked the board to consider how to serve black readers once the branch was closed, and Stewart reported that the worn bookmobile also needed to be replaced.[39]

A few days later, Reynolds wrote a letter to Charles Easterling in the city's legal department, relaying some two dozen questions from the board regarding the fate of the branch. For instance, how would the library be compensated for the loss of the property, and how might that compensation be applied to other library services? How broadly could they interpret the phrase "for the use and benefit of the colored people"? Could they build a new integrated branch elsewhere and adhere to the spirit of a stipulation written when the end of racial segregation was nowhere in sight? How would they offer equivalent service to blacks once the branch designated for their use was gone? Board members expressed a desire to build another branch in a predominantly black neighborhood. But because funding for such a project was not in the library's budget, they wondered about the possibility of providing additional bookmobile service or renting space for the collections. Finally, they asked, "Will loss of [a] major branch for Negroes affect de-segregation of [the] library?"[40] Six years after token integration of the central library, the board understood the implication of closing the black branch. It would no longer serve as a way to divert black library users and keep most of them out of the system's other buildings.

In July 1959, three board members met with Easterling, who confirmed that there was no reversionary clause in the deed. However, the library did have to comply with the "for the use and benefit of the colored people" covenant. He urged them to ask the mayor and city council for full compensation for the loss of the building and property and authority to use that compensation as they saw fit, within the bounds of the covenant. The three members present passed a motion to implement Easterling's recommendations, and the four members not present assented by telephone. They were determined to realize the full value of the real estate under their authority and to retain control over spending that money.[41]

By August, board members had begun discussions about which predominately black neighborhood should be home to a new branch. In a five-year capital improvement plan, they included this and other proposed branches as well as work on existing buildings and construction of a storage facility.[42] In September, city voters agreed to a bond for library expansion. In an October board meeting, Reynolds reported on the availability of $312,000 in library bonds and another potential $550,000 when all of them had sold. She also reported that the city would grant the library $52,335 to compensate for the Frederick Street Branch.[43]

At a meeting in July 1961, the board voted unanimously to close the Frederick Street Branch as of July 31, with no public announcement.[44] Reynolds sent a memorandum of the decision to Mayor Lewis Cutrer, noting that the branch circulated a mere ten books daily. She assured him that a bookmobile would continue to visit predominately black neighborhoods regularly. Then she acknowledged the significance of the board's act: "With the closing of the Colored Carnegie Branch, the library system is for all practical purposes integrated."[45] It had taken almost a decade for Houston to desegregate its public library system completely. In February 1962, the city auctioned off the original Colored Carnegie Library building. The highest bidder demolished it immediately, saving only the cornerstone.[46] A photograph in the Houston Metropolitan Research Center shows L. H. Spiney and W. L. D. Johnson watching the destruction of the building they had worked so hard to create fifty years before (fig. 11).[47]

More than twenty libraries lifted racial restrictions between 1936 and 1953. By the time the Atlanta library system was moving toward desegregation in the late 1950s, libraries in Miami, Charlotte, New Orleans, and Baton Rouge had opened to all.[48] But just as Atlanta was slow to open a Negro branch, it was also slow to desegregate. According to Annie McPheeters, a librarian at the Auburn and later the West Hunter branches, local organizations such as the American Veterans Association and the Committee on Interracial Cooperation had tried but failed to desegregate the library in the early 1950s.[49] Then three people who would become essential in the fight to desegregate the Atlanta Public Library converged on the city: Whitney Young, Jr., Howard Zinn, and Irene Dobbs Jackson.

Figure 11. City councilman Robert T. Webb, Colored Carnegie Library founders L. H. Spivey and W. L. D. Johnson, and Ted Williams amid the rubble as the building was being demolished in 1962. Courtesy of the Houston Public Library Collection, Houston Metropolitan Research Center.

Young's father had been the first black principal and later president of the Lincoln Institute in Shelby County, Kentucky. The son earned a bachelor's degree from Kentucky State Industrial College in 1941 and, after service in World War II, a master's degree in social work from the University of Minnesota. In 1954 he became head of Atlanta University's School of Social Work. In the fall of 1956, Zinn, a working-class progressive historian, became chair of Spelman's history department and an adviser for the school's Social Sciences Club. Then in 1958, Jackson joined the college's French department after receiving a Ph.D. in French literature from the University of Toulouse. The daughter of an influential black Atlanta resident, she was the widowed mother of a son who, in the 1970s, would become the first black mayor of the city.[50]

After moving to Atlanta, Young worked with several civil rights and interracial organizations, including the NAACP and the Atlanta

Council on Human Relations (ACHR). In 1958 ACHR members petitioned the Atlanta Public Library's board of trustees, following a strategy that Young had drawn up for them. In preparing them for the petition, he had pointed out the inefficiency of separate but equal facilities and asserted that "any white person no matter how illiterate, dirty, or undesirable may use the main library, while the most learned, cultural and immaculate Negro citizen is denied."[51]

ACHR members included whites such as Reverend Edward A. Cahill of the local Unitarian Church, which Young attended. In their correspondence with the board and in meetings with library director John C. Settlemayer, the ACHR presented data they had gathered to make a rational argument for desegregation. Young pointed out that other cities had desegregated their public libraries. He noted that Atlanta's refusal to do so, while expecting some 150,000 residents to rely on the small branches designated for African Americans, undermined the progressive image of the city that Mayor William Hartsfield was promoting. Nevertheless, the library administration stalled.[52]

While the ACHR was chipping away at the library's stone wall, Zinn and other Spelman instructors began discussing with students in the Social Sciences Club the need for intellectuals to take a more active role in the civil rights movement. They decided to do something small but significant. As Zinn put it, "the enemy was weak and the possibility of gaining allies strong."[53] Because club members were frustrated by their need for books beyond those available in the college library and the public library's black branches, they decided that desegregating the library system was the perfect project.

Spelman students began going to the main library in downtown Atlanta. When they asked to borrow a book, white staff members said that it would be sent to one of the Negro branches or that the students could use it in the basement room set aside for Negroes. Still, the activists kept returning to the building and asking to borrow books. Zinn worried that Spelman's students, accustomed to the genteel atmosphere of a women's college, would find this "guerilla warfare" challenging. Over time, however, they appear to have grown bolder and their visits more frequent. Faculty members also participated in the action. For instance, in early May 1959, Earl Sanders, a violinist on the college's music faculty, was discovered browsing in the music collection on the second floor and was asked to leave the library.[54] Settlemayer was no longer able to ignore the steady stream of African Americans in the building. At a meeting on May 13, 1959, he told library board members that blacks were beginning to stay in the library, even after being asked to leave, and that city police officers were refusing to step in because no law specified that the library was a segregated space.[55]

Meanwhile, at some point during that month, Irene Jackson entered the main library and tried to become a registered borrower. In France, she had never been denied service at any library. Here, however, the clerk at the main circulation desk consulted with other staff members and then handed her a form to sign, saying they would contact her later. Jackson left the library assuming that she would never be contacted. When she told her father, John Wesley Dobbs, about the encounter, he suggested she sue. At the same time, Young and Zinn were working together to find two individuals willing to be plaintiffs in a lawsuit against the library. Jackson and a Morehouse theology student agreed to file. The library administration caught wind of the impending lawsuit. On May 19, board members had a closed meeting over lunch at a private club and decided to desegregate rather than face a lawsuit. They called Young to let him know and asked that Settlemayer be given a couple of days to inform and prepare his staff. As Zinn later wrote, the board members clearly understood that desegregation was inevitable. The only question was whether it would be quietly implemented by library officials or loudly broadcast by a judge deciding a lawsuit.[56]

On May 22, 1959, Jackson and Sanders became the first black Atlanta residents to borrow material from the main library. But its desegregation was not entirely quiet; the local newspapers carried the story. Settlemayer downplayed the significance of the new policy, telling the reporter that few blacks used the branches set aside for them and that consequently few would use the main library or the other branches newly available to them. Georgia governor Ernest Vandiver went so far as to assert that African Americans preferred to use only the branches designated for them. Mayor Hartsfield soothed worried whites, asserting that "a public library is a symbol of literacy, education and cultural progress. It does not attract troublemakers."[57] The news story in the Atlanta paper did attract a few troublemakers, however, because it mentioned Jackson by name and included her home address. For a time, she received harassing phone calls, and hecklers would park across the street from her home and jeer at her.[58]

By the time the library desegregated, the School of Library Service at Atlanta University had been operating for nearly two decades. Whites involved in the 1941 founding of the school had believed that the program was necessary for training African Americans to work in segregated academic and public libraries in the south. As the program became established, however, its faculty, under the leadership of Dean Virginia Lacy Jones, shaped a curriculum that went beyond mere training to include the design and execution of master's-level research projects.

In 1961, Jones wrote in the *Wilson Library Bulletin* (later excerpted in the *Crisis*), "that the terms 'segregated' and 'desegregated' mean different things in different communities." Noting that she had visited many southern public libraries, she tallied a spectrum of practices in "desegregated" libraries, from separate restrooms and separate entrances for white and black library users to requiring blacks to use separate reading areas. Some libraries still forbade blacks to use any of the reading rooms and made them use their books outside of the library instead.[59] In 1939, Eliza Gleason had found a similar range of local practices.

Lucretia Jeanette Parker and Bernice Lloyd Bell were both Atlanta University students who wrote theses updating Gleason's work. Parker released "A Study of Integration in Public Library Service in Thirteen Southern States," in 1953, and Bell followed up with "Integration in Public Library Service in Thirteen Southern States, 1954–1962" in 1963. In her introduction, Parker wrote that her goal was to document the libraries that had deviated from the segregated norm of the south. Yet later in the paper, she suggested a deeper purpose, declaring that her study would make sympathetic but timid librarians aware that many of their counterparts had already begun to dismantle segregation and that they should do so as well.

In 1939, Gleason had reported that a few cities in four southern states were allowing African Americans to use their main libraries

(Kentucky, Oklahoma, Texas, and Virginia). By 1953, Parker had identified cities in eleven southern states with integrated libraries. Among the Kentucky towns that had desegregated public libraries were Maysville (1936), Wheelwright (1942), Pikeville (1943), Carlisle (1947), and Hazard (1947). She found that San Antonio had desegregated before Houston, in 1949, as had Austin, in 1951.[60] Only Alabama and Georgia did not have cities on her list.[61] When collecting data, both Parker and Bell wrote to state libraries requesting a list of the public libraries that purportedly served whites and blacks at their central buildings. They then sent questionnaires to those libraries. When the state library reported no desegregated public libraries, Parker sent questionnaires to the public libraries in the state's five largest cities, while Bell sent them to the public libraries in the municipalities with the largest African American populations. When white librarians gave ambiguous answers to survey questions, Parker sometimes consulted staff at a city's African American branches or interviewed classmates who were from that city.[62]

Bell published her fifty-six-question survey as an appendix to her paper. General questions related to staffing, branches, collection size, and budget. She also specifically asked if black residents were allowed to use the main library. If so, was that availability generally known throughout the community, and did the library publicize it to African Americans? Bell (and apparently Parker) asked when and why the library was desegregated as well as whether restrooms, water fountains, entrances and exits, reading rooms, and public events such as story hours, film forums, and book reviews were segregated. For libraries that reported that they did not serve African Americans at their central buildings, Bell included a multiple-choice question: "What would you do if a Negro walked into the Library and requested service?" The answer choices were "(a) Serve him as any other patron would be served; (b) Inform him that Negroes are not served; (c) Call the police; (d) Refer him to the Negro branch."[63]

In her research, Parker discovered a welter of approaches to so-called integration. In Magnolia, Arkansas, the Columbia County Library began "integrated" service in 1947, agreeing to house a collection that local blacks had acquired and allowing them to use books from that collection or the county library's at a separate desk staffed by a black librarian. In Pine Bluff, Arkansas, African Americans used the separate Pullen Street Branch but could visit the main library if they needed a book not held by the branch. In 1951, Little Rock Public Library desegregated for adults ages sixteen and older, and in the early years the main users were students from Philander Smith College. Board member Mrs. David D. Terry supported the desegregation vote after meeting with representatives from the college and Dunbar High School as well as members of the local Urban League chapter. Apparently, Georg Iggers, a white teacher at the black college, had published a letter on the issue in the *Arkansas Gazette,* thus helping to convince the board to take the step. He pointed out that the college library collection was made up of mostly donated volumes and that the public library for African Americans had restricted hours and a small collection that was unsuitable for his students. Nonetheless, even after the board opened the library to African American adults, the restrooms continued to be segregated.[64]

Florida libraries reported a range of policies and practices. The Miami Public Library had opened in 1897 thanks to the efforts of local white clubwomen. It added the Dunbar Branch for African Americans in 1938.[65] In 1951, the city built a $1 million central library that was open it to all. Although the Dunbar Branch remained in service, African Americans could now use any public library building in Miami. Other Florida cities did not necessarily follow suit. According to Parker, Jacksonville still did not have integrated service in the early 1950s. Saint Petersburg was also not officially desegregated, but African Americans sometimes entered the building and received services anyway.[66]

In 1950, the board of directors of the New Orleans Public Library decided to open parts of the main library to African Americans ages sixteen and older. The library had closed stacks, but African American adults, like whites, could use the card catalog and borrow books. If they used the reading or periodicals rooms, however, they had to stay in separate areas marked "For Our Colored Patrons." All restrictions were removed in 1954.[67]

Although librarians at Nashville's public library did not complete Parker's questionnaire, she spoke to two African American acquaintances from the city. One reported a case in which an African American had made arrangements with library director Robert Alvarez to use the main library. The other said that she herself had borrowed books from the North Nashville Branch, situated in a white neighborhood.[68]

Many librarians did not answer Parker's survey; and among those who did, many left questions blank. Of eighty-seven surveys sent, forty-three were at least partially completed. Parker also received eighteen letters—some elaborating on the questionnaire, others offering information in place of the questionnaire. In all, Parker received information from thirty-five cities in which the main library offered at least some form of service to African Americans. State agencies reported thirty-nine such cities, and Gleason had earlier reported on nine additional cities not represented in Parker's study. Parker thus asserted that a total of forty-eight southern cities and towns were offering integrated services at their main libraries in 1953.[69]

Parker's method suffered from the shortcomings that all such questionnaires share. Individuals reported both facts and opinions. Some varnished the truth to make themselves or their communities seem more just than they really were. Some respondents reacted defensively, asserting that they had plans to desegregate someday or suggesting that Parker mind her own business. A few blamed the segregated situation on someone else: city officials, sympathetic but timid whites, the sponsors of book discussions held at the library.

Parker's informants described a wide range of attitudes among librarians. At one extreme were those who said their libraries did not offer service to African Americans and indicated no discomfort with that practice. At the other extreme were librarians who openly offered service to African Americans because they were taxpayers who deserved the same treatment as all other taxpayers. In the middle was a group presenting a number of variations on the theme of desegregation. Some didn't answer the questionnaire at all but wrote a letter instead because it gave them more control over their message. For instance, Ernestine Grafton, the director of extension at the Virginia State Library, wrote a letter that obscured reality, saying that, in general, "service to Negroes is given from the main libraries, branches, or bookmobiles," although she did not provide any concrete examples.[70]

Some survey respondents proudly reported that African Americans could enter the main library to borrow books but seemed to feel no shame when they explained that those same community members could not linger in an integrated reading room. Many librarians reported that they maintained segregated bathrooms, even when all other services and collections were available equally to blacks and whites. Most who reported some move toward total desegregation also acknowledged that African Americans had not been told of these policy changes. As one of Parker's informants in western Tennessee said, "colored people have been denied so much so long that they no longer expect to receive any consideration."[71]

In her analysis, Parker pointed out that Kentucky had the greatest number of integrated public libraries and suggested that its position as a border state meant that it was more influenced by northern attitudes than other southern states were. She speculated that cities near Kentucky, on the coast, or in some way geographically removed from the Deep South had more liberal policies. She also pointed out that states with lower proportions of African American residents were more likely to offer integrated services and that urban areas and small towns were more likely than middling cities to offer integrated services. Only twenty-six respondents had mentioned the year in which their libraries had jettisoned their segregation policies, and eighteen of them (69 percent) had listed a year after 1940.[72]

Like Parker, Bell had some trouble getting librarians to complete her survey. She sent 448 questionnaires to libraries in thirteen southern states and received 269 replies, an unspecified number of which were letters rather than completed surveys. She also sent questionnaires to each state library, whose responses were uneven. For example, in Alabama, where segregationist George Wallace had become governor in 1963, the state librarian provided no information via questionnaire or letter but merely mailed Bell a directory of libraries in the state. The librarians working in the Alabama cities with the highest proportion of African Americans failed to answer at all. The head of Arkansas's state library commission also responded to Bell's inquiry by sending her a directory of libraries in the state.[73]

Quiet desegregation continued to be libraries' preferred method. Public libraries in Florida (Panama City, Sarasota, Gainesville, Jacksonville, Dade City, and Fort Myers) and in Huntsville, Georgia, reported that they had desegregated, but none had announced that change to black residents. The library in Henderson County, North Carolina, reported that it had desegregated in the early 1950s but said that no African Americans had used it until 1959, when a few had entered the main building to see if they would be served. In Ocala, Florida, the public library decided in February 1959 to provide services to African Americans but made no specific announcement to that effect. In 1962, when Ocala's head librarian responded to Bell's request for information, staff members were continuing to encourage black children to attend story hours at the Madison Street branch in a predominately black neighborhood rather than go to the ones held at the main library. She wrote, "Although no negro will be turned away at any library, many do not go to them because they think they are not wanted." The librarian at the West Palm Beach Public Library claimed that the library had been integrated since its opening.[74]

Table 22 shows the greater number of desegregated libraries in 1963 as compared to 1953, by state. Bell found that, by 1963, almost every public library in Kentucky had been integrated. Louisville's head librarian, C. R. Graham, told her that the city's library system had desegregated in May 1948 out of a "desire to be just, fair and civilized." The library board added a Negro member in 1943; and by 1963, the system had 45 African Americans on its staff of 180. Two of them worked at the reference desk in the main library. Among the sixty-five Kentucky libraries that provided Bell with data, thirty-two said they had always been integrated, twenty-five said they had desegregated before 1950, and eight said they had desegregated after 1950.[75]

The North Carolina Library Commission reported that fifty-eight county libraries offered integrated service, up from the four Parker had found ten years earlier. (Bell received thirty-five surveys from North Carolina documenting only thirty-two integrated libraries.) Charlotte had quietly desegregated its audiovisual service in 1942 after African Americans who had read about the new service in the newspaper showed up to borrow media. Nonetheless, librarians made a point of working efficiently so that African American library users would be in and out of the building as quickly as possible. In 1952, a

TABLE 22. NUMBER OF CITIES REPORTING DESEGREGATED PUBLIC LIBRARIES,
BY STATE, IN 1953 AND 1963

STATE	1953	1963
Alabama	0	1
Arkansas	2	4
Florida	2	30
Georgia	0	8
Kentucky	13	67
Louisiana	2	9
Mississippi	1	6
North Carolina (counties)	4	32
Oklahoma	3	16
South Carolina	1	4
Tennessee	4	63
Texas	8	17
Virginia	8	33
Total	**48**	**290**

Source: Lucretia Jeanette Parker, "A Study of Integration in Public Library Service in Thirteen Southern States" (master's thesis, Atlanta University, 1953), 76–77, tab. 3; Bernice Lloyd Bell, "Integration in Public Library Service in Thirteen Southern States, 1954–1962" (master's thesis, Atlanta University, 1963), 99, tab. 5.

city bond issue funded a new main and nine branch buildings, and after 1955 (as each opened), they offered integrated service. When the main library opened on November 19, 1956, a local newspaper photographer documented the first person to check out a book: a black man, whose picture appeared in the next day's edition. However, city residents continued to use the Brevard Street Branch until urban renewal razed the building in the early 1960s.[76]

Eventually, library desegregation reached Virginia, where it received considerable publicity. In February 1960, African Americans in Petersburg refused to continue being relegated to the library basement, instead demanding access to the whole building. In a petition filed with the district court in Richmond, they said that having access only to the basement was "humiliating, embarrassing, unfair, nauseating and unconstitutional."[77] The decision to desegregate occurred after a nine-month struggle, during which the library closed temporarily. When African Americans tried to desegregate the library in Danville in April 1960, they sued and won after being denied service.

However, whites voted to close the library rather than comply with the desegregation decision. For a time, the city opened the library without chairs so that whites and blacks could not sit together, a tactic that came to be called "vertical integration."[78]

After *Brown,* Alabama was a flashpoint for massive resistance, and library desegregation occurred only after the kind of lawsuit that earlier quieter efforts had avoided. While Rosa Parks was working with the Montgomery NAACP in the 1950s, she encouraged students to try to use the main library because the separate Negro branch had a limited collection. They tried repeatedly and were always sent back to the branch.[79] In 1962, students won their suit to desegregate the Montgomery Public Library, prompting the librarians to deploy vertical integration. By late in the year, however, whites and blacks were using the library with tables and chairs restored. Mobile, Huntsville, Birmingham, and Anniston also desegregated in the 1960s.[80] One by one, public libraries officially opened their doors to all. The institution of reading had, finally, outlasted the institution of segregation.

Epilogue

As a teenager in 1953, Gloria Randle had walked among the shelves of books at Houston's main library after learning that it had desegregated. When she finished high school, she left her hometown to attend Indiana University on a scholarship. She earned a bachelor's degree in zoology in 1959, a master's degree in zoology in 1960, and a Ph.D. in higher education in 1965. After holding a number of positions in higher education, she became, in 1975, the first African American to serve as president of the Girl Scouts. In 1987, she moved to Greensboro, North Carolina, to serve as president of Bennett College under her married name, Gloria Dean Randle Scott. One of her achievements was to list the Bennett campus, including the Carnegie Negro Library, on the National Register of Historic Places, in 1992.[1]

Several years later, the library building was renovated for use as campus offices. As part of the reopening, the college organized a panel discussion featuring local Greensboro residents, who reminisced about the role of the Carnegie Negro Library in the community. Their comments conveyed pride in the library, reverence for reading, and gratitude for the welcoming librarians, although everyone in the room understood those narratives in the larger context of racial segregation.[2] As the discussion ended, Scott told a story of her own. She had lived in Greensboro earlier in her life, moving there in

1967 to take a position at the Agricultural and Technical College of North Carolina. After learning that the Carnegie Negro Library had closed only four years before, when the Greensboro Public Library had desegregated in 1963, she found it hard to understand how it could have been the only public library available to the area's black residents for so many years.

As a child, Scott had loved reading so much that she convinced a local bookstore owner to let her borrow books overnight for a small deposit so that she could read on the bus to and from school. She also recalled using the small Emancipation Park library, a segregated deposit station of the Houston Public Library, which occupied a room, not a whole building as the Greensboro Carnegie Negro Library did. She recounted her memory of riding the bus to what was to her an enormous library building in downtown Houston, after hearing that she would be allowed to enter and use it.[3]

Greensboro's public libraries desegregated a decade after the Houston Public Library had. In 1952, Leon Carnovsky had conducted a survey of the public libraries of Greensboro. In his report, he first discussed his findings regarding the main library. Then, in a separate section, he discussed the Carnegie Negro Library. Although he made several recommendations for improving both libraries, including the provision of a new building for each, he never considered the possibility that the two might merge or even cooperate. Instead, he recommended that the white library cooperate with other white libraries, mainly the one at the Woman's College in Greensboro, and that the black library work with the two other libraries in town serving African Americans: at Bennett College and at the Agricultural and Technical College.[4] As a white library expert acquainted with the work of Eliza Gleason, Carnovsky had an opportunity to influence events. But his visit seems to have been yet another missed opportunity in the history of segregated libraries.

Scott described her resentment and her confusion over restricted access to books, saying that keeping people away from education and reading made no sense.[5] Had Houston followed the same timeline as Greensboro, the future college president would have not used an integrated library until she moved to the midwest to attend Indiana University. Indeed, some of the people who were participating in the panel discussion had not used a library that was free to all until Greensboro's desegregated in 1963, a year after Houston had auctioned off its old Colored Carnegie Library building. The new owner had razed it, erasing from Houston's landscape a physical reminder that black residents' access had been restricted and that they had created ways to resist.[6]

In the late 1990s, Gloria Scott made a different decision regarding the Carnegie Negro Library in Greensboro. When the construction workers were taking down the wood that had covered and protected the stone where the name "Carnegie Negro Library" had been etched so many decades before, they asked if she wanted to revise or erase the outdated terminology on the sign. "No," she told them, "because that's what this is—a living monument." The building and its sign affirmed rather than denied history.[7] The Carnegie Negro Library sign and the stories told by the residents of Greensboro are reminders of a living past that remains connected to the present. Such memories and the narratives that communicate them can become "stories with socially transformative possibility," as Imani Perry has put it, but only if they are known and incorporated into the histories of "the American public library" that we construct.[8]

Many African American readers who used the public libraries designated for them appreciated the availability of reference works, circulating books, and newspapers and magazines as well as the opportunity to interact with a staff interested in their intellectual development. The potential of access was in and of itself powerful. Over time, however, that power dimmed as it became apparent that actual access could be diminished in many ways.

We might like to think that the history of racially segregated public libraries is part of a long-ago time and faraway place, with little relevance to the problems of today. But the fact that an early technology promising information access for all—the public library system— could be so deeply undermined by majority interests should make us think. Even as open source and open access are championed, their foes lobby for excludability. Others say that public libraries are no longer needed in the digital age, an assertion that ignores the obstacles rooted in class and race. Educational inequities, the "new Jim Crow" of mass incarceration, income and net-worth imbalances, and public library funding cuts persist.[9] As the twenty-first century demands new literacies and critical skills for full social, political, and cultural participation, barriers do not disappear. They merely shift with the times. Public libraries in the age of Jim Crow offer a history worth contemplating—a history of a time when information was not free, not for all.

Notes

INTRODUCTION

1. Yvonne Easton, ed., *I Dream a World: Portraits of Black Women Who Changed America,* rev. ed. (New York: Stewart, Tabori, and Chang, 1999), 122.
2. Sidney H. Ditzion, *Arsenals of a Democratic Culture* (Chicago: American Library Association, 1947); Nancy Kranich, ed., *Libraries and Democracy: The Cornerstones of Liberty* (Chicago: American Library Association, 2001); Redmond Kathleen Molz and Phyllis Dain, *Civic Space / Cyberspace: The American Public Library in the Information Age* (Cambridge: MIT Press, 1999).
3. John Willinsky, *The Access Principle: The Case for Open Access to Research and Scholarship* (Cambridge: MIT Press, 2005), 112–13.
4. Karla F. C. Holloway, *BookMarks: Reading in Black and White* (New Brunswick, N.J.: Rutgers University Press, 2006), 9.
5. Ibid., 10–11.
6. As late as 1934, states in the deep south had the lowest percentages of population with access to library service: for instance, only 45 percent of North Carolina's population and only 29 percent of Georgia's. See Louis R. Wilson, *The Geography of Reading* (Chicago: American Library Association and the University of Chicago Press, 1938), 13–14. For a study of reasons behind southern recalcitrance in the case of Carnegie libraries, see Donald G. Davis, Jr., and Ronald C. Stone, Jr., "Poverty of Mind and Lack of Municipal Spirit: Rejection of Carnegie Public Library Building Grants by Seven Southern Communities," in *Carnegie Denied: Communities Rejecting Carnegie Library Construction Grants, 1898–1925,* ed. Robert Sidney Martin (Westport, Conn.: Greenwood, 1993), 137–73.
7. Robert Darnton, "What Is the History of Books?" *Daedalus* 111 (Summer 1982): 67. Darnton's works reveal his interest in phenomena that are difficult to locate in his model of the circuit: censorship and suppression of information. For example, see Robert Darnton, *The Literary Underground of the Old Regime* (Cambridge: Harvard University Press, 1982); *The Forbidden Bestsellers of Pre-Revolutionary France* (New York: Norton, 1995); and *Censors at Work: How States Shaped Literature* (New York: Norton, 2014).
8. Darnton, "What Is the History of Books," 69.

9. Robert Darnton, "What Is the History of Books? Revisited," *Modern Intellectual History* 4 (November 2007): 495–508.

10. Thomas R. Adams and Nicolas Barker, "A New Model for the Study of the Book," in *A Potencie of Life: Books in Society*, ed. Nicolas Barker (London: British Library, 1993), 5–43.

11. Thomas Augst and Kenneth Carpenter, eds., *Institutions of Reading: The Social Life of Libraries in the United States* (Amherst: University of Massachusetts Press, 2007).

12. S. R. Ranganathan, *The Five Laws of Library Science* (London: Goldston, 1931), 299.

13. Geoffrey C. Bowker, *Science on the Run: Information Management and Industrial Geophysics at Schlumberger, 1920–1940* (Cambridge: MIT Press, 1994), 16.

14. Patterson Toby Graham, *A Right to Read: Segregation and Civil Rights in Alabama's Public Libraries, 1900–1965* (Tuscaloosa: University of Alabama Press, 2002), 131.

15. Important examples include Eliza Atkins Gleason, *The Southern Negro and the Public Library: A Study of the Government and Administration of Public Library Service to Negroes in the South* (Chicago: University of Chicago Press, 1941); E. J. Josey, ed., *The Black Librarian in America* (Metuchen, N.J.: Scarecrow, 1970); E. J. Josey, ed, *The Black Librarian in America Revisited* (Metuchen, N.J.: Scarecrow, 1994); Rosemary Ruhig Du Mont, "Educating of Black Librarians: An Historical Perspective," *Journal of Education for Library and Information Science* 26 (March 1986): 233–49; Rosemary Ruhig Du Mont, "Race in American Librarianship: Attitudes of the Library Profession," *Journal of Library History* 21 (June 1986): 488–509; James V. Carmichael, Jr., "Atlanta's Female Librarians, 1883–1915," *Journal of Library History* 21 (March 1986): 376–99; Dan Lee, "Faith Cabin Libraries: A Study of an Alternative Library Service in the Segregated South, 1932–1960," *Libraries and Culture* 26 (Winter 1991): 169–82; Lorna Peterson, "Alternative Perspectives in Library and Information Science: Issues of Race," *Journal of Education for Library and Information Science* 37 (Spring 1996): 163–74; John Mark Tucker, ed., *Untold Stories: Civil Rights, Libraries, and Black Librarianship* (Champaign: University of Illinois, Graduate School of Library and Information Science, 1998); and Graham, *A Right to Read*. Article-length historical surveys include Michael Fultz, "Black Public Libraries in the South in the Era of De Jure Segregation," *Libraries and the Cultural Record* 41 (Summer 2006): 337–59; and Cheryl Knott Malone, "African Americans and U.S. Libraries," in *Encyclopedia of Library and Information Science*, 3rd ed., ed. Marcia Bates and Mary Niles Maack (New York: Taylor and Francis, 2010), 1:42–50. A useful list of published sources appears in David M. Battles, *The History of Public Library Access for African Americans in the South, or Leaving Behind the Plow* (Lanham, Md.: Scarecrow, 2009).

16. Doris Hargrett Clack, "Segregation and the Library," in *Encyclopedia of Library and Information Science*, ed. Allen Kent, Harold Lancour, and Jay E. Daily (New York: Dekker, 1979), 27:184–204.

17. Peterson, "Alternative Perspectives," 163–69.

18. Lorna Peterson, "Review of John Mark Tucker, ed., *Untold Stories: Civil Rights, Libraries, and Black Librarianship*," Humanities and Social Sciences Net Online, June 1999, www.h-net.msu.edu. Some white librarians have acted heroically in race matters and been made object lessons to dissuade others. For example, see Louise S. Robbins, *The Dismissal of Miss Ruth Brown: Civil Rights, Censorship, and the American Library* (Norman: University of Oklahoma Press, 2001).

19. American Library Association, "Freedom to Read," www.ala.org.

20. Grace Elizabeth Hale, *Making Whiteness: The Culture of Segregation in the South, 1890–1940* (New York: Pantheon, 1998).

21. Shirley Schuette and Nathania Sawyer, *From Carnegie to Cyberspace: 100 Years at the Central Arkansas Library System* (Little Rock: Butler Center for Arkansas Studies, 2010), 28.
22. J. Douglas Smith, *Managing White Supremacy: Race, Politics and Citizenship in Jim Crow Virginia* (Chapel Hill: University of North Carolina Press, 2001), 259–70.
23. Jacqueline Dowd Hall, "The Long Civil Rights Movement and the Political Uses of the Past," *Journal of American History* (March 2005): 1235.
24. Glenda Elizabeth Gilmore, *Defying Dixie: The Radical Roots of Civil Rights, 1919–1950* (New York: Norton, 2008).
25. Michael J. Klarman, *From Jim Crow to Civil Rights: The Supreme Court and the Struggle for Racial Equality* (Oxford: Oxford University Press, 2006), 378; Aldon Morris, *Origins of the Civil Rights Movement* (New York: Free Press, 1986), 186–87.
26. Abigail A. Van Slyck, *Free to All: Carnegie Libraries and American Culture, 1890–1920* (Chicago: University of Chicago Press, 1998), 64–76.
27. James R. Grossman, *Land of Hope: Chicago, Black Southerners, and the Great Migration* (Chicago: University of Chicago Press, 1989), 3–4.
28. American Library Association, *Negro Library Service* (Chicago: American Library Association, 1925).
29. Ibid., 5.
30. Michele T. Fenton, "Way Down Yonder at the Cherry Street Branch: A Short History of Evansville's Negro Library," *Indiana Libraries* 30 (2011): 37–41; American Library Association, *Negro Library Service*, 15.
31. American Library Association, *Negro Library Service*, 6, 9–10, 16.
32. Grossman, *Land of Hope*, 4.
33. Frederic H. Robb, "Harsh, Vivian," in *1927 Intercollegian Wonder Book, or 1799—The Negro in Chicago—1927* (Chicago: Washington Intercollegiate Club of Chicago, 1927), 225; Dan R. Lee, "Harsh, Vivian Gordon (1890–1960)," in *Dictionary of American Library Biography*, 2nd supp., ed. Donald G. Davis, Jr. (Westport, Conn.: Libraries Unlimited, 2003), 3:129–31.
34. Grossman, *Land of Hope*, 4.
35. American Library Association, *Negro Library Service*, 15.
36. George Hutchinson, *The Harlem Renaissance in Black and White* (Cambridge: Belknap Press of Harvard University Press, 1995).
37. "Work with Negroes Round Table," *Papers and Proceedings of the Forty-Fourth Annual Meeting of the American Library Association* (Chicago: American Library Association, 1922), 362–66.
38. Ibid., 366.
39. Ibid.
40. W. E. B. Du Bois, letter to Morris Lewis, April 17, 1923; Ernestine Rose, letter to W. E. B. Du Bois, October 4, 1922; W. E. B. Du Bois, letter to Ernestine Rose, October 5, 1922; all are in Du Bois Papers, University of Massachusetts, Amherst, Libraries, http://credo.library.umass.edu.
41. "Work with Negroes Round Table," *Papers and Proceedings of the Forty-Fifth Annual Meeting of the American Library Association* (Chicago: American Library Association, 1923), 275.
42. "Interest Increases in Negro Literature: Miss Ernestine Rose Does Not Believe in Purely Colored Libraries," *New York Amsterdam News*, May 2, 1923, 1. On Du Bois's efforts to secure fair treatment for New York Public Library's African American staff, see Ethelene Whitmire, *Regina Anderson Andrews: Harlem Renaissance Librarian* (Urbana: University of Illinois Press, 2014), 88–92.

43. James V. Carmichael, Jr., "Southern Librarianship and the Culture of Resentment," *Libraries and Culture* 40 (Summer 2005): 327.
44. Douglas S. Massey and Nancy A. Denton, *American Apartheid: Segregation and the Making of the Underclass* (Cambridge: Harvard University Press, 1993): 26–42.
45. Janet Sims-Wood, *Dorothy Porter Wesley at Howard University* (Charleston, S.C.: History Press, 2014), 24.
46. A scholar should do for municipal libraries what Jeff Wiltse has done for municipal swimming pools—that is, focus on northern cases in the context of increasing racial segregation in the 1920s and later, after the Great Migration had begun in earnest. See Jeff Wiltse, *Contested Waters: A Social History of Swimming Pools in America* (Chapel Hill: University of North Carolina Press, 2010).
47. I am paraphrasing the famous sentence "Injustice anywhere is a threat to justice everywhere," in Martin Luther King, Jr., "Letter from Birmingham Jail," in *Why We Can't Wait* (New York: Signet, 1964), 65.
48. The following helped me formulate my own understanding of race: Jacques Barzun, *Race: A Study in Modern Superstition* (New York: Harcourt, Brace, 1937), reprinted as *Race: A Study in Superstition* (New York: Harper and Row, 1965); Peter L. Berger and Thomas Luckmann, *The Social Construction of Reality: A Treatise in the Sociology of Knowledge* (Garden City, N.Y.: Doubleday, 1966); and U.N. Educational, Scientific, and Cultural Organization, "Declaration on Race and Racial Prejudice," 1978, www.unesco.org.
49. George Lipsitz, *The Possessive Investment in Whiteness: How White People Profit from Identity Politics* (Philadelphia: Temple University Press, 1998), 1.
50. Joe Feagin, *Systemic Racism: A Theory of Oppression* (New York: Routledge, 2006), xiii.
51. Charles W. Mills, *The Racial Contract* (Ithaca, N.Y.: Cornell University Press, 1997), 19. The italics are his.

1. THE CULTURE OF PRINT IN A CONTEXT OF RACISM

1. U.S. Census Bureau, *Census Reports*, vol. 7, *Manufactures, Part I: United States by Industries* (Washington, D.C.: U.S. Census Bureau, 1902), cli. For documentation of the increase in book publication at the turn of the century, see Hellmut Lehmann-Haupt, *The Book in America: A History of the Making and Selling of Books in the United States* (New York: Bowker, 1951), 198–99, 321. On book publishers' increasing use of advertising and the public's hunger for fiction in the 1890s, see John Tebbel, *Between Covers: The Rise and Transformation of Book Publishing in America* (New York: Oxford University Press, 1987), 174–80.
2. U.S. Census Bureau, *Census Reports*, clii.
3. Carl F. Kaestle and Janice A. Radway, "A Framework for the History of Publishing and Reading in the United States, 1880–1940," in *A History of the Book in America*, vol. 4, *Print in Motion: The Expansion of Publishing and Reading in the United States, 1880–1940*, ed. Carl F. Kaestle and Janice A. Radway (Chapel Hill: University of North Carolina Press, 2009), 15.
4. Michael Winship, "The Rise of a National Book Trade System in the United States," and James L. W. West III, "The Expansion of the National Book Trade System," in *A History of the Book in America*, 4:56–77, 78–89.
5. James P. Danky, "Reading, Writing, and Resisting: African American Print Culture," in *A History of the Book in America*, 4:339–58.
6. William C. Welburn, "To 'Keep the Past in Lively Memory': William Carl Bolivar's Efforts to Preserve African American Cultural Heritage," *Libraries and the Cultural Record* 42 (Spring 2007): 165–79.

7. Elizabeth McHenry, "Reading and Race Pride: The Literary Activism of Black Clubwomen," in *A History of the Book in America*, 4:491–510.
8. Elizabeth McHenry, "'An Association of Kindred Spirits': Black Readers and Their Reading Rooms," in *Institutions of Reading: The Social Life of Libraries in the United States*, ed. Thomas Augst and Kenneth Carpenter (Amherst: University of Massachusetts Press, 2007), 99–118; Rosie L. Albritton, "The Founding and Prevalence of African-American Social Libraries and Historical Societies, 1828–1918: Gatekeepers of Early Black History, Collections, and Literature," in *Untold Stories: Civil Rights, Libraries, and Black Librarianship*, ed. John Mark Tucker (Champaign: University of Illinois, Graduate School of Library and Information Science, 1998), 23–46.
9. Louis Round Wilson, *The Geography of Reading: A Study of the Distribution and Status of Libraries in the United States* (Chicago: American Library Association and the University of Chicago Press, 1938), 14, 33. Here, "the south" includes Alabama, Arkansas, Florida, Georgia, Kentucky, Louisiana, Mississippi, North Carolina, South Carolina, Tennessee, Texas, and Virginia. Also see Eliza Atkins Gleason, *The Southern Negro and the Public Library: A Study of the Government and Administration of Public Library Service to Negroes in the South* (Chicago: University of Chicago Press, 1941), 76–77.
10. Rayford Logan, *The Negro in American Life and Thought: The Nadir, 1877–1901* (New York: Dial, 1954).
11. For works exploring urban segregation and its consequences, see W. E. B. Du Bois, *The Philadelphia Negro: A Social Study* (Philadelphia: University of Pennsylvania, 1899); St. Clair Drake and Horace R. Cayton, *Black Metropolis: A Study of Negro Life in a Northern City*, intro. Richard Wright (New York: Harcourt, Brace, 1945); Gilbert Osofsky, *Harlem: The Making of a Ghetto: Negro New York, 1890–1930* (New York: Harper and Row, 1966); Kenneth L. Kusmer, *A Ghetto Takes Shape: Black Cleveland, 1870–1930* (Champaign: University of Illinois Press, 1976); Albert S. Broussard, *Black San Francisco: The Struggle for Racial Equality in the West, 1900–1954* (Lawrence: University Press of Kansas, 1993); Douglas S. Massey and Nancy A. Denton, *American Apartheid: Segregation and the Making of the Underclass* (Cambridge: Harvard University Press, 1993); and Christopher Silver and John V. Moeser, *The Separate City: Black Communities in the Urban South, 1940–1968* (Lexington: University Press of Kentucky, 1995).
12. George Lipsitz, *The Possessive Investment in Whiteness: How White People Profit from Identity Politics* (Philadelphia: Temple University Press, 1998), 1–46.
13. William J. Gilmore, *Reading Becomes a Necessity of Life: Material and Cultural Life in Rural New England, 1780–1835* (Knoxville: University of Tennessee Press, 1989), 18–27.
14. Dorothy B. Porter, "The Organized Educational Activities of Negro Literary Societies, 1828–1846," *Journal of Negro Education* 5 (October 1936): 555–76.
15. Elizabeth McHenry, "'Dreaded Eloquence': The Origins and Rise of African American Literary Societies and Libraries," *Harvard Library Bulletin* 6 (1995): 32–56; Albritton, "The Founding and Prevalence of African-American Social Libraries," 23–46.
16. Ronald J. Zboray, *A Fictive People: Antebellum Economic Development and the American Reading Public* (New York: Oxford University Press, 1993), 133–35. See also Jesse H. Shera, *Foundations of the Public Library: The Origins of the Public Library Movement in New England, 1629–1855* (Chicago: University of Chicago Press, 1949).
17. Harvey J. Graff, *The Legacies of Literacy: Continuities and Contradictions in Western Culture and Society* (Bloomington: Indiana University Press, 1987), 340–66. Oral

information was equally important and similarly restricted. For example, southern abolitionists Angelina and Sarah Grimké had to leave their native South Carolina for the north, where at least some sympathetic residents supported their speaking tours. See Gerda Lerner, *The Grimké Sisters from South Carolina: Pioneers for Woman's Rights and Abolition* (Boston: Houghton Mifflin, 1967).

18. Janet Duitsman Cornelius, *"When I Can Read My Title Clear": Literacy, Slavery, and Religion in the Antebellum South* (Columbia: University of South Carolina Press, 1991); Carter G. Woodson, *The Education of the Negro Prior to 1861*, 2nd ed. (Washington, D.C.: Associated Publishers, 1919). White southerners' felt need to control communication and information persisted well into the twentieth century. See James W. Silver, *Mississippi: The Closed Society* (New York: Harcourt, Brace, and World, 1964).

19. William S. McFeely, *Frederick Douglass* (New York: Norton, 1991), 29–33; John Hope Franklin, *From Slavery to Freedom: A History of Negro Americans*, 3rd ed. (New York: Knopf, 1967), 202–3; Lynn E. May, Jr., *The First Baptist Church of Nashville, Tennessee, 1820–1970* (Nashville: First Baptist Church, 1970), 110.

20. Graff, *Legacies of Literacy*, 363.

21. James D. Anderson, *The Education of Blacks in the South, 1860–1935* (Chapel Hill: University of North Carolina Press, 1988), 4–32.

22. Paul M. Gaston, *The New South Creed: A Study in Southern Mythmaking* (New York: Knopf, 1970), 89.

23. Material on the role of philanthropists and educators in the southern education movement appears in C. Vann Woodward, *Origins of the New South, 1877–1913* (Baton Rouge: Louisiana State University Press, 1951), 396–408; Louis R. Harlan, *Separate and Unequal: Public School Campaigns and Racism in the Southern Seaboard States, 1901–1915* (Chapel Hill: University of North Carolina Press, 1958), 75–101; Anderson, *Education of Blacks*, 152–83, 206–37; and throughout James L. Leloudis, *Schooling the New South: Pedagogy, Self, and Society in North Carolina, 1880–1920* (Chapel Hill: University of North Carolina Press, 1996).

24. Anderson, *Education of Blacks*, 84; Henry Allen Bullock, *A History of Negro Education in the South from 1619 to the Present* (Cambridge: Harvard University Press, 1967), 89–116.

25. Andrew Carnegie, *The Negro in America: An Address Delivered before the Philosophical Institution of Edinburgh, 16th October 1907* (Cheney, Pa.: Committee of Twelve for the Advancement of the Interests of the Negro Race, 1907), 20.

26. Nicholas Lemann, *The Promised Land: The Great Black Migration and How It Changed America* (New York: Knopf, 1991), 3–58; Anderson, *Education of Blacks*, 98–101.

27. Anderson, *Education of Blacks*, 148–86.

28. Donald Franklin Joyce, *Gatekeepers of Black Culture: Black-Owned Book Publishing in the United States, 1817–1981* (Westport, Conn.: Greenwood, 1983), 24.

29. Ibid., 28.

30. Ibid., 28–29.

31. Penelope L. Bullock, *The Afro-American Periodical Press, 1838–1909* (Baton Rouge: Louisiana State University Press, 1981), 106–7, 226–27; Willard B. Gatewood, Jr., ed. *Slave and Freeman: The Autobiography of George L. Knox* (Lexington: University Press of Kentucky, 1979).

32. Anne Firor Scott, *Natural Allies: Women's Associations in American History* (Champaign: University of Illinois Press, 1991), 1–5, 112, 218 n. 22.

33. Theodora Penny Martin, *The Sound of Our Own Voices: Women's Study Clubs, 1860–1910* (Boston: Beacon, 1987), 3, 31–47; Scott, *Natural Allies*, 113, 119–22.

34. Anne Firor Scott, "Women and Libraries," *Journal of Library History* 21 (1986): 400–405.

35. Logan, *Negro in American Life*, 335–36.

36. Scott, *Natural Allies*, 12.

37. Jacqueline Anne Rouse, *Lugenia Burns Hope: Black Southern Reformer* (Athens: University of Georgia Press, 1989); Darlene Clark Hine, *When the Truth Is Told: A History of Black Women's Culture and Community in Indiana, 1875–1950* (Indianapolis: National Council of Negro Women, 1981); Cynthia Neverdon-Morton, *Afro-American Women of the South and the Advancement of the Race, 1895–1925* (Knoxville: University of Tennessee Press, 1989); Fannie Barrier Williams, "Club Movement among Negro Women," in *The Colored American from Slavery to Honorable Citizenship*, ed. J. W. Gibson and W. H. Crogman (Atlanta: Nichols, 1903), 197–232; and Paula Giddings, *When and Where I Enter: The Impact of Black Women on Race and Sex in America* (New York: Morrow, 1984).

38. Scott, *Natural Allies*, 112; Porter, "Organized Educational Activities," 555–76.

39. Jacqueline A. Rouse, "Atlanta's African-American Women's Attack on Segregation, 1900–1920," in *Gender, Class, Race, and Reform in the Progressive Era*, ed. Noralee Frankel and Nancy Schrom Dye (Lexington: University Press of Kentucky, 1991), 12–18; Stephanie J. Shaw, *What a Woman Ought to Be and to Do: Black Professional Women Workers during the Jim Crow Era* (Chicago: University of Chicago Press, 1996), 172, 316 n. 21; Josephine Washington, letter to Andrew Carnegie, November 16, 1908, Carnegie Corporation Records, Columbia University (hereafter cited as Carnegie Records); W. E. B. Du Bois, ed., *Efforts for Social Betterment among Negro Americans* (Atlanta: Atlanta University Press, 1909), 53, 117–19.

40. Du Bois, *Efforts for Social Betterment*, 47–64.

41. Earline Rae Ferguson, "A Community Affair: African-American Women's Club Work in Indianapolis, 1879–1917" (Ph.D. diss., Indiana University, 1997).

42. Deborah Gray White, *Too Heavy a Load: Black Women in Defense of Themselves, 1894–1994* (New York: Norton, 1999), 29.

43. Garrison, "The Tender Technicians: The Feminization of Public Librarianship, 1876–1905," *Journal of Social History* 6 (Winter 1972–1973): 131–59; Abigail Ayres Van Slyck, "The Lady and the Library Loafer: Gender and Public Space in Victorian America," *Winterthur Portfolio* 31 (Winter 1996): 221–42; Paula D. Watson, "Founding Mothers: The Contribution of Women's Organizations to Public Library Development in the United States," *Library Quarterly* 64 (July 1994): 233–69; Cheryl Knott Malone, "Women's Unpaid Labor in Libraries: Change and Continuity," in *Reclaiming the American Library Past: Writing the Women In*, ed. Suzanne Hildenbrand (Norwood, N.J.: Ablex, 1996), 279–99.

44. Orin Walker Hatch, *Lyceum to Library: A Chapter in the Cultural History of Houston* (Houston: Texas Gulf Coast Historical Association, 1965), 40–41.

45. Laurel Grotzinger, "The Proto-Feminist Librarian at the Turn of the Century: Two Studies," *Journal of Library History* 10 (July 1975): 195–213; Laurel Grotzinger, "Dewey's 'Splendid Women' and Their Impact on Library Education," in *Milestones to the Present: Papers from Library History Seminar V*, ed. Harold Goldstein (Syracuse, N.Y.: Gaylord, 1978), 125–54; Laurel A. Grotzinger, James V. Carmichael, Jr., and Mary Niles Maack, *Women's Work Vision and Change in Librarianship*, intro. Joanne E. Passet (Champaign: University of Illinois, Graduate School of Library and Information Science, 1994).

46. Garrison, "Tender Technicians," 132.

47. Joel Williamson, *The Crucible of Race: Black-White Relations in the American South*

Since Emancipation (New York: Oxford University Press, 1984), 111–39. See also Madelin Joan Olds, "The Rape Complex in the Postbellum South," in *Black Women in America*, ed. Kim Marie Vaz (Thousand Oaks, Calif.: Sage, 1995), 179–205; and Laurence Alan Baughman, *Southern Rape Complex, Hundred Year Psychosis* (Atlanta: Pendulum, 1966).

48. Peter L. Berger and Thomas Luckmann, *The Social Construction of Reality: A Treatise in the Sociology of Knowledge* (Garden City, N.Y.: Doubleday, 1966), 41.

49. Henry Louis Gates, "The Trope of a New Negro and the Reconstruction of the Image of the Black," *Representations* 24 (Fall 1988): 150–55.

50. Grace Elizabeth Hale, *Making Whiteness: The Culture of Segregation in the South, 1890–1940* (New York: Vintage, 1999).

51. Dewey W. Grantham, *Southern Progressivism: The Reconciliation of Progress and Tradition* (Knoxville: University of Tennessee Press, 1983), xvii.

52. William A. Link, *The Paradox of Southern Progressivism, 1880–1930* (Chapel Hill: University of North Carolina Press, 1992), 323–24.

53. Ibid., Grantham, *Southern Progressivism*, xx.

54. Morton Keller, *Regulating a New Society: Public Policy and Social Change in America, 1900–1933* (Cambridge: Harvard University Press, 1994), 259–60.

55. Ibid., Grantham, *Southern Progressivism*, xix–xxi.

56. Phyllis Dain, "Ambivalence and Paradox: The Social Bonds of the Public Library," *Library Journal*, February 1, 1975, 261–66.

57. Grantham, *Southern Progressivism*, 251, 253.

58. Marion Casey, "Efficiency, Taylorism, and Libraries in Progressive America," *Journal of Library History* 16 (Spring 1981): 265–79.

59. Abigail A. Van Slyck, *Free to All: Carnegie Libraries and American Culture, 1890–1920* (Chicago: University of Chicago Press, 1995), 64–76.

60. Louis R. Harlan, *Booker T. Washington: The Making of a Black Leader, 1856–1901* (New York: Oxford University Press, 1972), 218. The full text of the speech is reprinted in Louis R. Harlan and Raymond W. Smock, ed., *Booker T. Washington Papers* (Champaign: University of Illinois Press, 1972–1989), 1:73–77, with the manuscript version in 3:578–83.

61. Logan, *Negro in American Life*, 52, 76, 80. For Logan's explication of Washington's Atlanta Compromise speech, see 275–313.

62. Donald Gibson, "Chapter One of Booker T. Washington's *Up from Slavery* and the Feminization of the African American Male," in *Representing Black Men*, ed. Marcellus Blount and George P. Cunningham (New York: Routledge, 1996), 96–97.

63. W. E. B. Du Bois, *The Souls of Black Folk* (1903; reprint, Millwood, N.Y.: Kraus-Thomson, 1985), 41–59.

64. Earl E. Thorpe, *The Mind of the Negro: An Intellectual History of Afro-Americans* (Baton Rouge, La.: Ortlieb, 1961), 322–25.

65. August Meier, *Negro Thought in America, 1880–1915: Racial Ideologies in the Age of Booker T. Washington* (Ann Arbor: University of Michigan Press, 1963), 207–47. Conference paper titles appear in *A Guide to the Microfilm Edition of Records of the National Negro Business League* (Bethesda, Md.: University Publications of America, 1995).

66. W. E. B. Du Bois, "Petition of Negroes to Use the Carnegie Library," c. 1903, W. E. B. Du Bois Papers (MS 312). Special Collections and University Archives, University of Massachusetts Amherst Libraries, http://credo.library.umass.edu.

67. Harlan, *Making of a Black Leader*, 243–45.

68. Louis R. Harlan, *Booker T. Washington: The Wizard of Tuskegee, 1901–1915* (New York: Oxford University Press, 1983), 134.

69. Harlan and Smock, *Washington Papers*, 8:3.

70. David Kaser, "Andrew Carnegie and the Black College Libraries," in *For the Good of the Order: Essays in Honor of Edward G. Holley*, ed. Delmus E. Williams (Greenwich, Conn.: JAI Press, 1994), 121–29; Harlan, *Booker T. Washington*, 181–82.

71. Michael Bieze, "Booker T. Washington: Philanthropy and Aesthetics," in *Uplifting a People: African American Philanthropy and Education*, ed. Marybeth Gasman and Katherine V. Sedgwick (New York: Lang, 2005), 50–51.

72. Alice B. Kroeger, "Report on the Congress of Women Librarians at Atlanta," *Library Journal* 21 (November 1896): 57–58.

73. Atlanta's and Philadelphia's "upper ten" are discussed in Willard B. Gatewood, *Aristocrats of Color: The Black Elite, 1880–1920* (Bloomington: Indiana University Press, 1990), 91–92, 10–11, 96–103.

74. For an account of Wallace's role in keeping the topic of library services for African Americans off the 1899 conference program, see James V. Carmichael, Jr., "Southern Librarianship and the Culture of Resentment," *Libraries and Culture* 40 (2005): 336–37.

75. Anne Wallace, "The Southern Library Movement," in *Papers and Proceedings of the Twenty-Ninth Annual Meeting of the American Library Association held at Asheville, N.C., May 23–29, 1907* (Boston: American Library Association, 1907), 62–77.

76. Ibid., 68.

77. U.S. Department of the Interior, Bureau of Education, *Public Libraries in the United States of America: Their History, Condition, and Management* (Washington, D.C.: Government Printing Office, 1876), 890.

78. Charles A. Seavey, "Public Libraries," and Arthur P. Curley, "Boston Public Library," both in *Encyclopedia of Library History*, ed. Wayne Wiegand and Donald G. Davis, Jr. (New York: Garland, 1994), 85–86, 518–28; Jesse H. Shera, *Foundations of the Public Library: The Origins of the Public Library Movement in New England, 1629–1855* (Chicago: University of Chicago, 1949), 170–99; Walter Muir Whitehill, *Boston Public Library: A Centennial History* (Cambridge: Harvard University Press, 1956).

79. Wayne A. Wiegand, *The Politics of an Emerging Profession: The American Library Association, 1876–1917* (Westport, Conn.: Greenwood, 1986).

80. William I. Fletcher, *Public Libraries in America* (Boston: Roberts Brothers, 1894), 100–102; Philip Arthur Kalisch, *The Enoch Pratt Free Library: A Social History* (Metuchen, N.J.: Scarecrow, 1969).

81. Stanley Rubinstein and Judith Farley, "Enoch Pratt Free Library and Black Patrons: Equality in Library Services, 1882–1915," *Journal of Library History* 15 (Fall 1980): 445–53; Rosemary Ruhig Du Mont, "Race in American Librarianship: Attitudes of the Library Profession," *Journal of Library History* 21 (Summer 1986): 489–90; Charles S. Johnson, *Patterns of Negro Segregation* (New York: Harper and Brothers, 1943), 29.

82. George S. Bobinski, *Carnegie Libraries: The History and Impact on American Public Library Development* (Chicago: American Library Association, 1969), 43–44, 57–63.

83. The "New North" is discussed in Logan, *Negro in American Life*, 215–38.

84. In Texas, the establishment of public libraries relied on both the work of the Texas Federation of Women's Clubs and the wealth of Andrew Carnegie. See Donald G. Davis, Jr., "The Rise of the Public Library in Texas, 1867–1920," in *Milestones to the Present*, 166–83.

85. Robert M. Lester, *Forty Years of Carnegie Giving* (New York: Scribner's, 1941), 92–93; Bobinski, *Carnegie Libraries*, 13–17, 159, 209, 221, 225–26, 228–29. The states that built the most Carnegie public libraries were Indiana (165); California (142); Illinois, New York, and Ohio (106 each); and Iowa (101). In the southeast, Georgia built the most (24), Tennessee was in the middle (13), and Virginia had the least (3). See Theodore Jones, *Carnegie Libraries across America: A Public Legacy* (New York: Preservation Press and Wiley and Sons, 1997), 128–30.

86. American Library Association, Committee on Library Extension, *Library Extension: A Study of Public Library Conditions and Needs* (Chicago: American Library Association, 1926), 74.

87. Patterson Toby Graham, *A Right to Read: Segregation and Civil Rights in Alabama's Public Libraries, 1900–1965* (Tuscaloosa: University of Alabama Press, 2002), 6–25.

88. Louise S. Robbins, "Changing the Geography of Reading in a Southern Border State: The Rosenwald Fund and the WPA in Oklahoma," *Libraries and Culture* 40 (Summer 2005): 353–67; Dan R. Lee, "Faith Cabin Libraries: A Study of an Alternative Library Service in the Segregated South," *Libraries and Culture* 26 (Winter 1991): 169–82; Dan R. Lee, "From Segregation to Integration: Library Services for Blacks in South Carolina, 1923–1962," in *Untold Stories*, 95; Ethel Evangeline Martin Bolden, "Susan Dart Butler, Pioneer Librarian" (master's thesis, Atlanta University, 1959).

89. Thomas Jesse Jones, *Negro Education: A Study of the Private and Higher Schools for Colored People in the United States,* Bureau of Education Bulletin 1916, no. 38 (Washington, D.C.: Government Printing Office, 1917), 173.

90. American Library Association, *Library Extension,* 10–13, 73.

91. Wilson, *Geography of Reading.*

92. Howard W. Odum, *Southern Regions of the United States* (Chapel Hill: University of North Carolina Press, 1936), 5–11.

93. Ibid., 15–19.

94. Ibid., 105, 119–20.

95. Wilson, *Geography of Reading,* 16, 33–34.

96. Ibid., 326, 352, 423.

97. Ibid., 423.

98. Eliza Atkins Gleason, *The Southern Negro and the Public Library: A Study of the Government and Administration of Public Library Service to Negroes in the South* (Chicago: University of Chicago Press, 1941), 74–88, 67–68.

99. Ibid., 188.

100. The inspiration for this assertion comes from poet and musician Benjamin Zephaniah. In a videotaped interview displayed on the Freedom and Enslavement Wall at the International Slavery Museum in Liverpool, England, Zephaniah points out that whites were so proud of themselves for emancipating the slaves when in fact all people have the right to be free. It is not and should not be a privilege granted by whites to blacks.

101. William F. Yust, "What of the Black and Yellow Races?" *Bulletin of the American Library Association* 7 (January–November 1913): 165.

102. James Vinson Carmichael, Jr., "Tommie Dora Barker and Southern Librarianship" (Ph.D. diss., University of North Carolina, 1988), 16–17.

103. C. Vann Woodward, *Thinking Back: The Perils of Writing History* (Baton Rouge: Louisiana State University Press, 1987), 87.

104. Roger Chartier, *Forms and Meanings: Texts, Performances, and Audiences from Codex to Computer* (Philadelphia: University of Pennsylvania Press, 1995), 96.

105. Van Slyck, *Free to All*, xxvii.

106. Leon F. Litwack, *Trouble in Mind: Black Southerners in the Age of Jim Crow* (New York: Knopf, 1998), xiv.

2. CARNEGIE PUBLIC LIBRARIES FOR AFRICAN AMERICANS

1. C. Vann Woodward, *Origins of the New South, 1877–1913* (Baton Rouge and Austin: Louisiana State University Press and the Littlefield Fund for Southern History of the University of Texas, 1951), 107–53, 396–428.

2. Kenneth E. Carpenter, "Libraries," in *A History of the Book in America*, vol. 2, *An Extensive Republic: Print, Culture, and Society in the New Nation, 1790–1840*, ed. Robert A. Gross and Mary Kelley (Chapel Hill: University of North Carolina Press and the American Antiquarian Society, 2010), 273.

3. Paul M. Gaston, *The New South Creed: A Study in Southern Mythmaking* (Montgomery, Ala.: New South Books, 2002), 109–13.

4. George Bobinski, *Carnegie Libraries* (Chicago: American Library Association, 1969), 209, 215, 218, 221, 225, 229, 232.

5. Alvin S. Johnson, "A Report to Carnegie Corporation of New York on the Policy of Donations to Free Public Libraries" (New York, 1916), 50–55.

6. Bobinski, *Carnegie Libraries*, 13–17, 159, 209, 221, 225–26, 228–29.

7. Donald G. Davis, Jr., and Ronald C. Stone, "Poverty of Mind and Lack of Municipal Spirit: Rejection of Carnegie Public Library Buildings by Seven Southern Communities," in *Carnegie Denied: Communities Rejecting Carnegie Library Construction Grants, 1898–1925*, ed. Robert Sidney Martin (Westport, Conn.: Greenwood, 1993), 137–73.

8. Carolyn Hall Leatherman, "Richmond Rejects a Library: The Carnegie Public Library Movement in Richmond, Virginia, in the Early Twentieth Century" (Ph.D. diss., Virginia Commonwealth University, 1992), 147–71.

9. Edwin R. Embree, *Brown America: The Story of a New Race* (New York: Friendship Press, 1936), 112–17; James D. Anderson, *The Education of Blacks in the South, 1860–1935* (Chapel Hill: University of North Carolina Press, 1988), 15–27.

10. John Hope Franklin, "History of Racial Segregation in the United States," *Annals of the American Academy of Political and Social Science* 304 (March 1956): 7–9.

11. Martha Watkins Flournoy, *A Short History of the Public Library of Charlotte and Mecklenburg County* (Charlotte, N.C.: Public Library of Charlotte and Mecklenburg County, 1952), 2–3; Patricia Ryckman, *Public Library of Charlotte and Mecklenburg County: A Century of Service* (Charlotte, N.C.: Public Library of Charlotte and Mecklenburg County, 1989); Louis R. Wilson and Edward A. Wight, *County Library Service in the South: A Study of the Rosenwald County Library Demonstration* (Chicago: University of Chicago Press, 1935), 47–48; "Charlotte Mecklenburg Library History," www.cmlibrary.org; Eliza Atkins Gleason, *The Public Library and the Southern Negro* (Chicago: University of Chicago Press, 1941), 20, 81.

12. *Oklahoma Libraries, 1900–1937: A History and Handbook* (Oklahoma City: Oklahoma Library Commission, 1937), 167; Stephanie J. Shaw, *What a Woman Ought to Be and to Do: Black Professional Women Workers during the Jim Crow Era* (Chicago: University of Chicago Press, 1996), 138, 140, 222; "Along the Color Line: Social Uplift," *Crisis* 5 (February 1913): 163; "First Ladies of Colored America—No. 6," *Crisis* 50 (February 1943): 48.

13. *Oklahoma Libraries, 1900–1937*, 167.

14. Rosenberg Public Library Board of Directors, minute book, March 30, 1904, 1:83, Rosenberg Public Library Collection, Galveston.

15. Ibid., July 30, 1904, 1:107; October 7, 1904, 1:111.

16. Glynell Shadelford Barnes, "A History of Public Library Service to Negroes in Galveston, Texas, 1904–1955" (master's thesis, Atlanta University, 1956), 20.

17. "Negroes Insisted upon Admission to Rosenberg Library," *Galveston Daily News*, January 23, 1905, 8; Henry Noble, Jr., "The Colored People of Galveston Misrepresented and Will Not Be Forced to Act Wrong," *City Times*, January 28, 1905, 2.

18. Lorenzo J. Greene, "Sidelights on Houston Negroes As Seen by an Associate of Dr. Carter G. Woodson in 1930," in *Black Dixie: Afro-Texan History and Culture in Houston*, ed. Howard Beeth and Cary D. Wintz (College Station: Texas A&M University Press, 1992), 154.

19. Betty Irene Young, "Lillian Baker Griggs: Pioneer Librarian," *Durham Record* 1 (1983): 28–29.

20. Beverly Washington Jones, *Stanford L. Warren Branch Library: 77 Years of Public Service* (Durham, N.C.: Durham County Library, 1990), 20–21, 48–49; E. Franklin Frazier, "Durham: The Capital of the Black Middle Class," in *The New Negro: An Interpretation*, ed. Alan Locke (New York: Boni, 1925), 333–40; Leslie Brown, *Uplifting Black Durham: Gender, Class, and Black Community Development in the Jim Crow South* (Chapel Hill: University of North Carolina Press, 2008), 172–73; Janice Radway, "The Library As Place, Collection, or Service: Promoting Book Circulation in Durham, North Carolina, and at the Book-of-the-Month Club, 1925–1945," in *Institutions of Reading: The Social Life of Libraries in the United States*, ed. Thomas August and Kenneth Carpenter (Amherst: University of Massachusetts Press, 2007), 258–63.

21. Bobinski, *Carnegie Libraries*, 80–82; Thomas Jesse Jones, *Negro Education: A Study of the Private and Higher Schools for Colored People in the United States* (Washington, D.C.: Government Printing Office, 1917), 173–76; and the Carnegie Records. The count includes only those libraries that began as branches of white-run libraries or eventually became branches of library systems. Not included, for instance, was the planned Carnegie library in Mound Bayou, an African American town in Mississippi, which could not open "for want of books." See Neil R. McMillen, *Dark Journey: Black Mississippians in the Age of Jim Crow* (Champaign: University of Illinois Press, 1990), 324 n. 43.

22. Jesse H. Shera, *Foundations of the Public Library: The Origins of the Public Library Movement in New England, 1629–1855* (Chicago: University of Chicago Press, 1949), 200–237.

23. William J. Gilmore, *Reading Becomes a Necessity of Life: Material and Cultural Life in Rural New England, 1780–1835* (Knoxville: University of Tennessee Press, 1992), 181–82.

24. Michael Harris, "The Purpose of the American Public Library: A Revisionist Interpretation." *Library Journal*, September 15, 1973, 2509–14.

25. Elizabeth McHenry, *Forgotten Readers: Recovering the Lost History of African American Literary Societies* (Durham, N.C.: Duke University Press, 2002), 189.

26. Ibid., 10.

27. Bobinski, *Carnegie Libraries*, 22; Mary Edna Anders, "The Contributions of the Carnegie Corporation and the General Education Board to Library Development in the Southeast" (master's thesis, University of North Carolina, 1950), 97.

28. James M. SoRelle, "Race Relations in 'Heavenly Houston,' 1919–45," in *Black*

Dixie, 188–89; Tracy E. K'Meyer, *Civil Rights in the Gateway to the South: Louisville, Kentucky, 1945–1980* (Lexington: University Press of Kentucky, 2009), 1.

29. Reinette F. Jones, *Library Service to African Americans in Kentucky, from the Reconstruction Era to the 1960s* (Jefferson, N.C.: McFarland, 2002), 153–54.

30. "History of Kenton County Public Library, www.kentonlibrary.org; Lucretia Jeanette Parker, "A Study of Integration in Public Library Service in Thirteen Southern States" (master's thesis, Atlanta University, 1953), 37.

31. Parker, "A Study of Integration in Public Library Service," 79–99, 116–18; Cheryl Knott Malone, "Louisville Free Public Library's Racially Segregated Branches, 1905–1935," *Register of the Kentucky Historical Society* 93 (1995): 159–79.

32. Jones, *Library Service to African Americans in Kentucky*, 156.

33. "The Record of Albert Ernest Meyzeek," *Negro History Bulletin* 10 (May 1947), 186–87; "Events of the Past Week," *Indianapolis Freeman*, November 6, 1909, 1; April 11, 1908, 1; April 18, 1908, 1.

34. George C. Wright, *Life behind a Veil: Blacks in Louisville, Kentucky, 1856–1930* (Baton Rouge: Louisiana State University Press, 1985), 5–6.

35. "Events of the Past Week," *Indianapolis Freeman*, January 15, 1910, 1; photograph of Western Branch reading room, with caption, *Crisis* 1 (February 1911), 31; George B. Utley, letter to Thomas F. Blue, August 5, 1914, in Wright, "Thomas Fountain Blue," 21; George T. Settle, "The Louisville Free Library," *Southern Workman* 44 (October 1914), 540.

36. Luther Adams, *Way Up North in Louisville: African American Migration in the Urban South, 1930–1970* (Chapel Hill: University of North Carolina Press, 2010), 40–46, 82–84; George C. Wright, "Oral History and the Search for the Black Past in Kentucky," *Oral History Review* 10 (1982): 82.

37. Booker T. Washington, letter to James Bertram, August 28, 1909, in Booker T. Washington Papers, Library of Congress, microfilm reel 35.

38. Orin Walker Hatch, *Lyceum to Library: A Chapter in the Cultural History of Houston* (Houston: Texas Gulf Coast Historical Association, 1965), 43–48, 57–59, 61–62.

39. Howard Beeth and Cary D. Wintz, "Historical Overview," in *Black Dixie*, 88. Information about the Houston case is covered in Cheryl Knott Malone, "Autonomy and Accommodation: Houston's Colored Carnegie Library, 1907–1922," *Libraries and Culture* 34 (Spring 1999): 95–112.

40. Ibid., 88–92; Bruce A. Glasrud, "Jim Crow's Emergence in Texas," *American Studies* 15 (Summer 1974): 54–55; U.S. Census Bureau, *Census of Population and Housing, 1910*, vol. 1, *Population: General Report and Analysis*, www.census.gov.

41. [E. O. Smith], speech [September 27, 1911?], 2–3; E. O. Smith, "Library History," typescript of a speech [1939]; Houston Public Library Collection, Houston Metropolitan Research Collection (hereafter cited as HPLC), box 8, 2–3.

42. Charles F. Smith, "Negro Boy Contributed Most Books," *Houston Post*, April 19, 1914, 48.

43. "Memorandum to the Honorable Ben Campbell, Mayor, and Commissioners of the City of Houston," n.d., HPLC, box 8. Internal evidence suggests that this unsigned and undated memo was written in May 1914 by E. O. Smith. Also see "Annual Report of J. B. Bell, Treasurer, Colored Carnegie Library," in *City Book of Houston* (Houston, 1916).

44. American Library Association, *Negro Library Service* (Chicago: American Library Association, 1925), 13.

45. Neloweze Williams Cooper, "The History of Public Library Service to Negroes

in Savannah, Georgia" (master's thesis, Atlanta University, 1960), 19; editorial, *Savannah Tribune*, March 22, 1902, 2.

46. Minutes, Board of Curators, Savannah Colored Library Association, February 26, 1906, Savannah Public Library Collection; Cooper, "The History of Public Library Service to Negroes in Savannah," 21; *Goette's Savannah City Directory for 1906* (Savannah, Ga.: Goette, 1906), 533, 545, 647; *Goette's Savannah City Directory for 1907* (Savannah, Ga.: Goette, 1907), 216, 279, 340, 388, 477.

47. [Editorial], *Savannah Tribune*, March 22, 1902, 2.

48. Cooper, "Public Library Service to Negroes in Savannah," 22.

49. A. L. Tucker, "Annual Report of the Colored Library," in *Report of George Tiedeman, Mayor of the City of Savannah, for the Year Ending 1909 to Which Is Added the Treasurer's Annual Report* (Savannah, 1910), 395–97.

50. "Ibid.," 396; "History of the Carnegie Colored Library," *Savannah Tribune*, October 3, 1914, 4.

51. "Mammoth Concert in Savannah Theatre for Carnegie Library," *Savannah Tribune*, April 13, 1912, 1; "Carnegie Library Is Assured," *Savannah Tribune*, May 3, 1913, 1; "Carnegie Library Curators Make Appeal," *Savannah Tribune*, July 12, 1913, 1; Cooper, "Public Library Service to Negroes in Savannah," 23.

52. American Library Association, *Negro Library Service*, 4.

53. "Carnegie Library Provides Services for Negro Patrons," *Savannah Morning News*, January 15, 1950, n.p., clipping in the files of the Catham Effingham Liberty Counties Regional Library; Cooper, "Public Library Service to Negroes in Savannah," 23.

54. Helen Arthur Manint, "A History of the New Orleans Public Library and the Howard Memorial Library" (master's thesis, Tulane University, 1939), 12–13.

55. Ibid., 19–21; New Orleans city ordinance no. 10,254, February 2, 1894, in *Flynn's Digest of the City Ordinance* (New Orleans, 1896), 20.

56. Manint, "History of the New Orleans Public Library," 23–24.

57. Collin Bradfield Hamer, Jr., "New Orleans Public Library," in *Encyclopedia of Library and Information Science*, ed. Allen Kent and Harold Lancour (New York: Dekker, 1976), 19:354–55.

58. Minutes, Board of Directors, New Orleans Public Library, June 10, 1912, New Orleans Public Library Collection.

59. Dan R. Frost, "Dillard, James Hardy," in *American National Biography Online*, www.anb.org; Benjamin Brawley, *Doctor Dillard of the Jeanes Fund* (1930; reprint, Freeport, N.Y.: Books for Libraries Press, 1971); Valinda Littlefield, " 'To Do the Next Needed Thing': Jeanes Teachers in the Southern United States, 1908–34," in *Telling Women's Lives: Narrative Inquiries in the History of Women's Education*, ed. Kathleen Weiler and Sue Middleton (Buckingham, U.K.: Open University Press, 1999), 130–46.

60. Minutes, Board of Directors, New Orleans Public Library, September 11, 1912.

61. Ibid., November 14, 1912.

62. Ibid., February, 13, 1913.

63. Ibid., March 12, 1913.

64. Ibid., August 13, 1913.

65. Ibid., April 14, 1915.

66. "Annual Report of the New Orleans Public Library, 1921" (New Orleans, 1922), 14–15; minutes, Board of Directors, New Orleans Public Library, September 10, 1919; August 11, 1921.

67. Minutes, Board of Directors, New Orleans Public Library, January 11, 1922.

68. Don H. Doyle, *Nashville in the New South, 1880–1930* (Knoxville: University of

Tennessee Press, 1985), 148–50, 168; "Baskette, Gideon Hicks," in *National Cyclopaedia of American Biography* (New York: White, 1900), 8:475; "Claxton, Mary Hannah Johnson (Mrs. Philander P. Claxton)," *Who Was Who in America* (Chicago: Marquis, 1960), 3:162; Charles Lee Lewis, *Philander Priestley Claxton: Crusader for Public Education* (Knoxville: University of Tennessee Press, 1948), 122, 169–71; James L. Leloudis, *Schooling the New South: Pedagogy, Self, and Society in North Carolina, 1880–1920* (Chapel Hill: University of North Carolina Press, 1996), 146–49; Mary Hannah Johnson, "Southern Libraries" [speech], n.d., Nashville Public Library Archives, Metropolitan Government Archives of Nashville and Davidson County, "Library History" box, "Speeches" folder.

69. Cheryl Knott Malone, "The Adult Collection at Nashville's Negro Public Library, 1915–1916," in *Libraries to the People: Histories of Outreach*, ed. Robert S. Freeman and David M. Hovde (Jefferson, N.C.: McFarland, 2003), 148–56.

70. Minutes, Board of Directors, Nashville Public Library, February 2, 1915, and April 6, 1915, Nashville Public Library Archives.

71. Lester C. Lamon, *Black Tennesseans, 1900–1930* (Knoxville: University of Tennessee Press, 1977), 219–21.

72. "Deed to Library Is Given to City," and "Presenting Deed to City of Knoxville, Col. Tyson Recites History of Library," *Knoxville Sentinel*, January 10, 1917, n.p., clipping in McClung Collection, Knox County Public Library System, Knoxville, Tennessee, "Knoxville, Tenn.—Libraries" folder.

73. "Presenting Deed to City of Knoxville."

74. "Mayor John E. McMillan Accepts Splendid Library In Behalf of City of Knoxville," *Knoxville Sentinel*, January 10, 1917, n.p., clipping in McClung Collection,"-Knoxville, Tenn.—Libraries" folder.

75. Charles W. Cansler, *Three Generations: The Story of a Colored Family of Eastern Tennessee* (Kingsport, Tenn., 1939), 149.

76. S. G. Heiskell, letter to Andrew Carnegie, March 16, 1916, reprinted in "Ten Thousand Dollar Public Library for Negroes of Knoxville," *Journal and Tribune*, May 17, 1916, n.p., clipping in McClung Collection, "Knoxville, Tenn.—Libraries" folder.

77. Michael J. McDonald and William Bruce Wheeler, *Knoxville, Tennessee: Continuity and Change in an Appalachian City* (Knoxville: University of Tennessee Press, 1983), 34.

78. James Bertram, letter to S. G. Heiskell, March 28, 1916, Carnegie Records.

79. S. G. Heiskell, letter to James Bertram, March 30, 1916; James Bertram, letter to Heiskell, April 4, 1916; both in Carnegie Records.

80. S. G. Heiskell, letter to James Bertram, April 8, 1916, Carnegie Records.

81. James Bertram, letter to S. G. Heiskell, May 15, 1916, Carnegie Records.

82. S. G. Heiskell, letter to James Bertram, May 23, 1916, Carnegie Records.

83. "Site for Library for the Negroes," *Knoxville Sentinel*, November 7, 1916, n.p., clipping in McClung Collection, "Knoxville, Tenn.—Libraries" folder.

84. "New Library for the Negroes Is Dedicated," *Journal and Tribune*, May 7, 1918, n.p., clipping in McClung Collection, "Knoxville, Tenn.—Libraries" folder.

85. Mary Mallory, "The Rare Vision of Mary Utopia Rothrock: Organizing Regional Library Services in the Tennessee Valley," *Library Quarterly* 65 (January 1995), 62–88.

86. "Address of Professor Charles W. Cansler," [May 6, 1918], McClung Collection, Knox County Public Library System, Knoxville, Tennessee, folder labeled "Knoxville, Tenn.—Libraries."

87. Walter M. Kelley, letter [1] to Andrew Carnegie [October 1898?], Carnegie Records.

88. Walter M. Kelley, letter [2] to Andrew Carnegie, October 1898, Carnegie Records.

89. Ibid.

90. Hoke Smith, letter to Andrew Carnegie, November 2, 1898, Carnegie Records.

91. Alma Hill Jamison, "Development of the Library in Atlanta," *Atlanta Historical Bulletin* 4 (April 1939): 103–8.

92. Carrie E. Young, letter to Andrew Carnegie, February 23, 1899, Carnegie Records.

93. R. M. Cheeks, letter to Andrew Carnegie, February 27, 1899, Carnegie Records.

94. J. W. E. Bowen, letter to Andrew Carnegie, March 6, 1899, Carnegie Records.

95. "Mr. Carnegie's Gift to Atlanta," *Southern Christian Recorder*, n.d., n.p., clipping in Carnegie Records.

96. "Petition of Negroes to Use the Carnegie Library" [1903?], Du Bois Papers, University of Massachusetts, Amherst, Libraries, http://credo.library.umass. edu; William F. Yust, "What of the Black and Yellow Races?," *Papers and Proceedings of the Thirty-Fifth Annual Meeting of the American Library Association held at Kaaterskill, N.Y., June 23–28, 1913* (Chicago: American Library Association, 1913), 164.

97. J. R. Nutting and Thomas J. Day, letter to Andrew Carnegie, August 9, 1904, Carnegie Records; James Bertram, letter to J. R. Nutting, November 15, 1904, Carnegie Records.

98. Yust, "What of the Black and Yellow Races?," 164.

99. W. E. B. Du Bois, letter to Virginia Lacy Jones, December 19, 1950, Du Bois Papers.

100. Louis R. Harlan, *Booker T. Washington: The Wizard of Tuskegee, 1901–1915* (New York: Oxford University Press, 1983), 295–304; David Levering Lewis, *W. E. B. Du Bois: Biography of a Race, 1868–1919* (New York: Holt, 1993), 333–36; Charles Crowe, "Racial Massacre in Atlanta, Sep. 22 1906," *Journal of Negro History* 54 (April 1969): 150–75; David Fort Godshalk, *Veiled Visions: The 1906 Race Riot and the Reshaping of American Race Relations* (Chapel Hill: University of North Carolina Press, 2005).

101. Delia Foreacre Sneed, letter to James Bertram, October 28, 1914, Carnegie Records; James Bertram, letter to Delia Foreacre Sneed, October 30, 1914, Carnegie Records; James Bertram, note in files, n.d., Carnegie Records; Godshalk, *Veiled Visions*, 188–89.

102. From the Carnegie Records: Tommie Dora Barker, letter to James Bertram, April 29, 1916; James Bertram, letter to Tommie Dora Barker, May 5, 1916; Tommie Dora Barker, letter to James Bertram, May 8, 1916; James Bertram, letter to Tommie Dora Barker, May 15, 1916; Tommie Dora Barker, letter to James Bertram, May 23, 1916; James Bertram, letter to Tommie Dora Barker, May 26, 1916; Tommie Dora Barker, letter to James Bertram, May 31, 1916; James Bertram, letter to Tommie Dora Barker, June 5, 1916; Tommie Dora Barker, letter to James Bertram, September 13, 1916; James Bertram, letter to Tommie Dora Barker, September 15, 1916; James Bertram, letter to Tommie Dora Barker, November 9, 1916. Barker's role in overseeing the provision of library services for black Atlantans is discussed in James V. Carmichael, Jr., "Tommie Dora Barker and the Atlanta Public Library, 1915–1930: A Case Study in Female Professionalism," *Atlanta History* 34 (Spring 1990): 31–32.

103. "A Just Claim," *Atlanta Constitution,* February 26, 1917, 4.
104. From the Carnegie Records: Tommie Dora Barker, letter to James Bertram, November 20, 1918; James Bertram, letter to Tommie Dora Barker, November 26, 1918; Office of City Clerk, Atlanta, Resolution, March 1, 1920; Tommie Dora Barker, letter to James Bertram, March 17, 1920; Tommie Dora Barker, letter to Delia Foreacre Lee, April 15, 1920; James Bertram, letter to Delia Foreacre Lee, April 25, 1920; Tommie Dora Barker, letter to James Bertram, June 9, 1920; James Bertram, letter to Tommie Dora Barker, June 18, 1920; Tommie Dora Barker, letter to James Bertram, September 28, 1920.
105. From the Carnegie Records: James Bertram, letter to Tommie Dora Barker, October 5, 1920; Tommie Dora Barker, letter to James Bertram, October 1, 1920; Tommie Dora Barker, letter to James Bertram, March 4, 1921; Tommie Dora Barker, letter to James Bertram, June 15, 1921; James Bertram to Tommie Dora Barker, June 20, 1921.
106. E. P. Wharton, letter to Andrew Carnegie, April 7, 1905, Carnegie Records. For an account of the library's history, see Julia A. Hersberger, Lou Sua, and Adam L. Murray, "The Fruit and Root of the Community: The Greensboro Carnegie Negro Library, 1904–1964," in *The Library As Place: History, Community, and Culture,* ed. John E. Buschman and Gloria J. Leckie (Westport, Conn.: Libraries Unlimited, 2006), 79–100.
107. James Bertram, letter to E. P. Wharton, April 11, 1905, Carnegie Records.
108. E. P. Wharton, letter to James Bertram, April 22, 1905, Carnegie Records.
109. James Bertram, letter to E. P. Wharton, November 23, 1905, Carnegie Records.
110. E. P. Wharton to James Bertram, November 27, 1905, Carnegie Records.
111. James Bertram, letter to E. P. Wharton, December 1, 1905, Carnegie Records.
112. Watson Law, J. Elmer Dellinger, D. C. Suggs, and W. L. McNair, "Letter to the Public: Real Facts in the Library Case Are Stated," *Greensboro Daily Record,* March [1916], n.p., clipping in Carnegie Records.
113. T. J. Murphy, letter to secretary of the Carnegie Library Fund, August 9, 1915, Carnegie Records.
114. James Bertram, letter to T. J. Murphy, September 29, 1915, Carnegie Records.
115. Watson Law, letters to the Carnegie Corporation, March 10, 1916, and March 22, 1916, Carnegie Records.
116. "People of City Talking of a Referendum on Judgment of City Commission on Library," *Greensboro Daily Record,* March 11, 1916, n.p., clipping in Carnegie Records.
117. James Bertram, letter to E. J. Stafford, May 14, 1920, Carnegie Records; E. J. Stafford, letter to James Bertram, May 27, 1920, Carnegie Records.
118. James Bertram, letter to E. J. Stafford, June 1, 1920, Carnegie Records.
119. James Bertram, letter to E. J. Stafford, September 29, 1920, Carnegie Records.
120. Notes from a Carnegie board meeting [October 1920?], Carnegie Records.
121. James Bertram, letter to Robert R. Moton, December 15, 1920, Carnegie Records; James Bertram, letter to James H. Dillard, December 15, 1920, Carnegie Records.
122. James H. Dillard, letter to James Bertram, January 11, 1921, Carnegie Records.
123. From the Carnegie Records: James H. Dillard, letter to James Bertram, March 18, 1921; James Bertram, letter to James H. Dillard, March 21, 1921; James H. Dillard, letter to James Bertram, March 25, 1921; James Bertram, letter to James H. Dillard, March 28, 1921.
124. James H. Dillard, letter to James Bertram, April 4, 1921, Carnegie Records.

125. James Bertram, letter to Mayor Emory J. Stafford, April 21, 1921, Carnegie Records.

126. James Bertram, letter to W. B. Windsor, January 13, 1922, Carnegie Records.

127. W. B. Windsor, letter to James Bertram, February 25, 1922, Carnegie Records.

128. Charles H. Ireland, letter to James Bertram, February 27, 1922, Carnegie Records.

129. I. Garland Penn, letter to James Bertram, March 7, 1922, Carnegie Records.

130. From the Carnegie Records: James Bertram, letter to I. Garland Penn, March 16, 1922; I. Garland Penn, letter to James Bertram, March 20, 1922; James Bertram, letter to I. Garland Penn, March 24, 1922; I. Garland Penn, letter to James Bertram, March 28, 1922.

131. Charles H. Ireland, E. P. Wharton, F. A. Weston, E. J. Stafford, and Frank Trigg, letter to James Bertram, April 11 1922, Carnegie Records.

132. James Bertram, letter to Charles H. Ireland, April 13, 1922, Carnegie Records.

133. W. B. Windsor, letter to James Bertram, April 18, 1922, Carnegie Records.

134. W. B. Windsor, letter to James Bertram, September 27, 1922, Carnegie Records.

135. I. Garland Penn, letter to James Bertram, October 3, 1922, Carnegie Records.

136. From the Carnegie Records: Charles H. Ireland, letter to James Bertram, October 4, 1922; James Bertram, letter to I. Garland Penn, October 6, 1922; James Bertram, letter to Charles H. Ireland, October 10, 1922; Hersberger, Sua, and Murray, "Fruit and Root," 93–95.

3. SOLIDIFYING SEGREGATION

1. Jessie Carney Smith and Carrell Peterson Horton, eds., *Historical Statistics of Black America* (New York: Gale, 1995), 1532–33, 1536–37.

2. Eliza Atkins Gleason, *The Southern Negro and the Public Library* (Chicago: University of Chicago Press, 1941), 91; Louis Shores, "Library Service and the Negro," *Journal of Negro Education* 1 (October 1932): 374–80.

3. Louise S. Robbins, "Changing the Geography of Reading in a Southern Border State: The Rosenwald Fund and the WPA in Oklahoma," *Libraries and Culture* 40 (Summer 2005): 355.

4. George B. Tindall, *The Emergence of the New South, 1913–1945* (Baton Rouge: Louisiana State University Press, 1967), 150–56, 176–81; Cameron McWhirter, *Red Summer: The Summer of 1919 and the Awakening of Black America* (New York: Holt, 2011); David Fort Godshalk, *Veiled Visions: The 1906 Atlanta Race Riot and the Reshaping of American Race Relations* (Chapel Hill: University of North Carolina Press, 2005), 264–67.

5. Scott Ellsworth, *Death in a Promised Land: The Tulsa Race Riot of 1921* (Baton Rouge: Louisiana State University Press, 1982), 9.

6. Mildred Ladner Thompson, *Tulsa City-County Library, 1912–1991* (Tulsa, Okla.: Lion and Thorne, 1992), 1–72.

7. Ibid.

8. Ellsworth, *Death in a Promised Land,* 14–16.

9. Frank Lincoln Mather, "Smitherman, Andrew Jackson," in *Who's Who of the Colored Race* (Chicago, 1915), 250.

10. W. L. McKee, "Notice," *Tulsa Star,* September 19, 1913, 1; "News around the City," *Tulsa Star,* November 28, 1914, [5].

11. "Miss Williams in Charge of Library," *Tulsa Star,* July 1, 1913, 1.

12. "Local News in and around Town," *Tulsa Star,* September 19, 1913, [4].

13. "Local Bus. Men to Hold Own Doings," *Tulsa Star,* February 7, 1914, 1.
14. Untitled, *Tulsa Star,* February 14, 1914, [9]; February 21, 1914, [5].
15. "Public Library Organized," *Tulsa Star,* February 21, 1914, 1.
16. "News around the City," *Tulsa Star,* July 11, 1914, [5].
17. "Notice to Library Patrons," *Tulsa Star,* August 27, 1915, 1.
18. "News around Town," and "Star Want Ads," *Tulsa Star,* February 27, 1915, 4; "Star Want Ads," *Tulsa Star,* February 15, 1915, 4; "Star Want Ads," April 3, 1915, 4; "Star Want Ads," May 1, 1915, 4; "Public Library," *Tulsa Star,* December 12, 1914, 1.
19. "Afro-American Cullings," *Tulsa Star,* September 5 1913, [7].
20. "Stradford Visits Points of Interest on Way to New York," *Tulsa Star,* June 5, 1915, 1.
21. Delia Blanton, "Muskogee Public Library to be Enlarged," *Tulsa Star,* October 30, 1915, 1.
22. "'Sunshine Club' Is Organized," *Tulsa Star,* March 27, 1920, 10.
23. "Tulsa Colored Library Made Attractive," *Tulsa Star,* March 20, 1920, 7.
24. Mary E. Jones Parrish, *An Eye-witness Account of the 1921 Tulsa Race Riot* (1923; reprint, Tulsa, Okla: John Hope Franklin Center for Reconciliation, 2009), 76–77.
25. Thompson, *Tulsa City-County Library,* 33.
26. Ellsworth, *Death in a Promised Land,* 45–61; James S. Hirsch, *Riot and Remembrance: The Tulsa Race War and Its Legacy* (Boston: Houghton Mifflin, 2002), 77–92.
27. Parrish, *Eye-witness Account,* 79.
28. Hirsch, *Riot and Remembrance,* 153–55.
29. Thompson, *Tulsa City-County Library,* 34.
30. Hirsch, *Riot and Remembrance,* 130–34.
31. Thompson, *Tulsa City-County Library,* 35–37, 47–50, 72, 139.
32. George S. Bobinski, *Carnegie Libraries: The History and Impact on American Public Library Development* (Chicago: American Library Association, 1969), 165; Charles C. Alexander, *The KKK in the Southwest* (Lexington: University of Kentucky Press, 1965).
33. Maxine Bamburg, "Okmulgee," in *Encyclopedia of Oklahoma History and Culture,* http://digital.library.okstate.edu; *Oklahoma Libraries, 1900–1937: A History and Handbook* (Oklahoma City: Oklahoma Library Commission, 1937), 168–69; U.S. Census Bureau, *1940 Census of Population and Housing,* vol. 1, *Number of Inhabitants,* www2.census.gov.
34. *Oklahoma Libraries,* 167–68.
35. Ibid., 165–70.
36. Christine Pawley, "Better Than Billiards: Reading and the Public Library in Osage, Iowa, 1890–1895," in *Print Culture in a Diverse America,* ed. James P. Danky and Wayne A. Wiegand (Champaign: University of Illinois Press, 1997), 173–99.
37. Ralph Ellison, *Shadow and Act* (New York: Random House, 1964), 155.
38. Lawrence Jackson, *Ralph Ellison: Emergence of Genius* (New York: Wiley, 2002), 42–43, 95; *Oklahoma Libraries,* 168.
39. Alwyn Barr, *Black Texans: A History of African Americans in Texas, 1528–1995,* 2nd ed. (Norman: University of Oklahoma Press, 1996), 141; Abigail A. Van Slyck, *Free to All: Carnegie Libraries and American Culture, 1890–1920* (Chicago: University of Chicago Press, 1995), 158–59, 196–97; Margaret Irby Nichols, "Gunter, Lillian," in *Handbook of Texas Online,* www.tshaonline.org.
40. American Library Association, *Negro Library Service* (Chicago, 1925).
41. Robert Sidney Martin and Orvin Lee Shiflett, "Hampton, Fisk, and Atlanta: The Foundations, the American Library Association, and Library Education for Blacks, 1925–1941," *Libraries and Culture* 31 (Spring 1996): 299–308.

42. American Library Association, *Negro Library Service*, 1, 11.
43. Ibid., 5, 14.
44. Ibid., 1–2, 5, 10–14.
45. Ibid., 2, 5, 10–12.
46. Cheryl Knott Malone, "Quiet Pioneers: Black Women Public Librarians in the Segregated South," *Vitae Scholasticae* 19 (Spring 2000): 64–65.
47. Newspaper clipping, n.d., Thomas Fountain Blue scrapbooks on microfilm, Louisville Free Public Library.
48. "Address Delivered by Thos. F. Blue," n.d., Thomas Fountain Blue scrapbooks on microfilm, Louisville Free Public Library.
49. Carolyn H. Leatherman, "Richmond Considers a Free Public Library: Andrew Carnegie's Offer of 1901," *Virginia Magazine of History and Biography* 96 (April 1988): 181–92; Carolyn Hall Leatherman, "Richmond Rejects a Library: The Carnegie Public Library Movement in Richmond, Virginia, in the Early Twentieth Century" (Ph.D. diss., Virginia Commonwealth University, 1992); "Richmond Public Library History," www.richmondpubliclibrary.org.
50. Robbins, "Changing the Geography of Reading," 353–67.
51. Alfred Perkins, *Edwin Rogers Embree: The Julius Rosenwald Fund, Foundation Philanthropy, and American Race Relations* (Bloomington: Indiana University Press, 2011), 102–4.
52. Milton Goldin, "Rosenwald, Julius," in *American National Biography Online*, www.anb.org; Peter Max Ascoli, *Julius Rosenwald: The Man Who Built Sears, Roebuck and Advanced the Cause of Black Education in the American South* (Bloomington: Indiana University Press, 2006), 73; Stephanie Deutsch, *You Need a Schoolhouse: Booker T. Washington, Julius Rosenwald, and the Building of Schools for the Segregated South* (Evanston: Northwestern University Press, 2011), 38–39.
53. *The General Education Board: An Account of Its Activities, 1902–1914* (New York, 1916), 3.
54. Louise Anderson Allen, "Anna T. Jeanes Foundation," in *Encyclopedia of the Social and Cultural Foundations of Education*, ed. Eugene F. Provenzo, Jr., and Asterie Baker Provenzo (Los Angeles: SAGE, 2009), 1:48–49; Valinda W. Littlefield, "'I Am Only One, but I Am One': Southern African-American Schoolteachers, 1884–1954" (Ph.D. diss., University of Illinois at Urbana-Champaign, 2003), 74–85.
55. Ibid. For a discussion of scrapbooks as texts, see Ellen Gruber Garvey, *Writing with Scissors: American Scrapbooks from the Civil War to the Harlem Renaissance* (New York: Oxford University Press, 2012), 131–71.
56. Ascoli, *Julius Rosenwald*, 78–79.
57. "Lauds Rosenwald for Aid to Negro," *New York Times*, January 17, 1932, N3; Ascoli, *Julius Rosenwald*, 88–95; Deutsch, *You Need a Schoolhouse*, 107.
58. Ascoli, *Julius Rosenwald*, 137–43; Deutsch, *You Need a Schoolhouse*, 115–30.
59. Edwin R. Embree, *Julius Rosenwald Fund: A Review to June 30, 1928* (Chicago, 1928), 24–29. The number of African Americans is based on the 1920 U.S. Census. The figure is given for the total black population rather than "school-age" population since African Americans of all ages would attend at a time when illiteracy rates remained high. See U.S. Census Bureau, *Census of Population and Housing, 1920*, vol. 1, *Population, 1920*, www2.census.gov.
60. Edwin R. Embree, *Julius Rosenwald Fund: Review of Two Decades, 1917–1936* (Chicago, 1936), 23; Deutsch, *You Need a Schoolhouse*, 116–27.
61. Embree, *Review to June 30, 1928*, 23, 29–30, 35.

62. Edwin R. Embree, *Rosenwald Fund: A Review to June 30, 1929* (Chicago, 1929), 23–24, 31–32.

63. Embree, *Review of Two Decades, 1917–1936*, 42–43.

64. Pat Morrison, *Walker County, Alabama* (Charleston, S.C.: Arcadia, 2004), 64; Wilson and Wight, *County Library Service*, 30–32. For a detailed account of Walker County's library system, see Patterson Toby Graham, *A Right to Read: Segregation and Civil Rights in Alabama's Public Libraries, 1900–1965* (Tuscaloosa: University of Alabama Press, 2002), 27–32.

65. John Agan, *Webster Parish* (Charleston, S.C.: Arcardia, 2000), 73; Mary Walton Harris, "Cooperation of the County Library with Schools," *Peabody Journal of Education* 8 (September 1930): 90–93; *Louisiana: A Guide to the State* (Baton Rouge: Louisiana Library Commission, 1941), 486; Wilson and Wight, *County Library Service*, 32–35.

66. Harris, "Cooperation of the County Library with Schools," 90–93.

67. Ibid.

68. Wilson and Wight, *County Library Service*, 32–35.

69. Ibid., 37–39.

70. Ibid., 39–41.

71. Edwin D. Hoffman, "The Genesis of the Modern Movement for Equal Rights in South Carolina," in *The Negro in Depression and War: Prelude to Revolution, 1930–1945*, ed. Bernard Sternsher (Chicago: Quadrangle, 1969), 198–99.

72. Ethel Evangeline Martin Bolden, "Susan Dart Butler, Pioneer Librarian" (master's thesis, Atlanta University, 1959).

73. Ibid.

74. Wilson and Wight, *County Library Service*, 41–44.

75. Ibid., 45–47.

76. Martha Watkins Flournoy, *A Short History of the Public Library of Charlotte and Mecklenburg County* (Charlotte, N.C.: Public Library of Charlotte and Mecklenburg County, 1952), 2–3; Patricia Ryckman, *Public Library of Charlotte and Mecklenburg County: A Century of Service* (Charlotte, N.C.: Public Library of Charlotte and Mecklenburg County, 1989); Wilson and Wight, *County Library Service*, 47–48. Biddle University for African Americans (now Johnson C. Smith University) built its Carnegie library in 1912, but the facility was presumably for students and faculty. See "History," http://library.jcsu.edu.

77. Flournoy, *Short History of the Public Library*, 3. The "unified" quotation is from Wilson and Wight, *County Library Service*, 48.

78. Flournoy, *Short History of the Public Library*, 3.

79. Wilson and Wight, *County Library Service*, 28.

80. Ernest I. Miller, "Library Service for Negroes in Tennessee," *Journal of Negro Education* 10 (October 1941): 636.

81. Wilson and Wight, *County Library Service*, 110–12.

82. Ibid., 207–8 and tab. 9.

83. Louis R. Wilson and Edward A. Wight, *County Library Service in the South: A Study of the Rosenwald County Library Demonstration* (Chicago: University of Chicago Press, 1935), 23; Embree, *Review of Two Decades, 1917–1936*, 42.

84. "W. Va. NAACP Leader Passes," *Chicago Daily Defender,* June 30, 1959, 5. Among his other victories, Nutter would go on to desegregate the Montgomery, West Virginia, municipal swimming pool in the 1940s. See Jeff Wiltse, *Contested Waters: A Social History of Swimming Pools in America* (Chapel Hill: University of North Carolina Press, 2007), 159–65.

85. "Citizens' Demands Ignored in W. Virginia," *Chicago Daily Defender,* December 10, 1927, 1.

86. *Brown v. Board of Education* (1928), *Report of Cases determined by the Supreme Court of Appeals of West Virginia from September 11, 1928, to February 19, 1929* (Charleston, W.V.: Jarrett, 1929), 106 W. Va. 476; "W. Va. Library Case to Supreme Court," *Baltimore Afro-American,* April 21, 1928, 10; "W. Virginians Battle Segregated Library," *Chicago Daily Defender,* June 2, 1928, 12.

87. *Brown v. Board of Education* (1928).

88. Shores, "Library Service and the Negro," 374–80.

4. FALTERING SYSTEMS

1. Eric Novotny, "'Bricks without Straw': Economic Hardship and Innovation in the Chicago Public Library during the Great Depression," *Libraries and the Cultural Record* 46 (August 2011): 258–275; Robert Scott Kramp, "The Great Depression: Its Impact on Forty-Six Large American Public Libraries. An Analysis of Published Writings of Their Directors" (Ph.D. diss., University of Michigan, 1975), 65–68; Margaret M. Herdman, "The Public Library in Depression," *Library Quarterly* 13 (October 1943): 310–34.

2. Richard H. Hart, "Public Libraries: Modern Library Systems," in *Encyclopaedia of the Social Sciences,* ed. Edwin R. A. Seligman and Alvin Johnson (New York: Macmillan, 1930–1935), 12:661.

3. Patterson Toby Graham, *A Right to Read: Segregation and Civil Rights in Alabama's Public Libraries, 1900–1965* (Tuscaloosa: University of Alabama Press, 2002), 27.

4. Eliza Atkins Gleason, *The Southern Negro and the Public Library: A Study of the Government and Administration of Public Library Service to Negroes in the South* (Chicago: University of Chicago Press, 1941), 123–29.

5. Joseph L. Wheeler and Jesse Cunningham, "Report of a Survey of the New Orleans Public Library," April 16–24, 1935, 5, typescript, University of California at Berkeley Library.

6. Ibid., 42–43.

7. Ira D. Reid, *Adult Education among Negroes* (Washington, D.C.: Associates in Negro Folk Education, 1936), 28–29.

8. Gleason, *Southern Negro and the Public Library,* 151.

9. W. E. B. Du Bois, *The Correspondence of W. E. B. Du Bois,* ed. Herbert Aptheker (Amherst: University of Massachusetts Press, 1997), 2:391, n. 1.

10. John Dollard, *Caste and Class in a Southern Town* (New Haven: Yale University Press, 1937), 188–204.

11. Allison Davis, Burleigh B. Gardner, and Mary R. Gardner, *Deep South: A Social Anthropological Study of Caste and Class* (Chicago: University of Chicago Press, 1941), 3, 267.

12. Ibid., 379.

13. Ibid., 417–21.

14. Kenneth J. Bindas, *Remembering the Great Depression in the Rural South* (Gainesville: University Press of Florida, 2007), 28–36.

15. Ibid., 72, 35.

16. Louise S. Robbins, "Changing the Geography of Reading in a Southern Border State: The Rosenwald Fund and the WPA in Oklahoma," *Libraries and Culture* 40 (Summer 2005): 356–60.

17. Oklahoma Library Association, "Langston University Library History," www.199.164.253.25/centennial.

18. *Oklahoma Libraries, 1900–1937: A History and Handbook* (Oklahoma City: Oklahoma Library Commission, 1937), 170.

19. Robbins, "Changing the Geography of Reading," 362–63.

20. For a case study of South Carolina, see Edward Barrett Stanford, *Library Extension under the WPA: An Appraisal of an Experiment in Federal Aid* (Chicago: University of Chicago Press, 1944), 141–244. Additional details are in Robert M. Gorman, "Blazing the Way: The WPA Library Service Demonstration Project in South Carolina," *Libraries and Culture* 32 (Fall 1997): 427–55.

21. Louis Round Wilson, *The Geography of Reading: A Study of the Distribution and Status of Libraries in the United States* (Chicago: American Library Association and University of Chicago Press, 1938), 186.

22. Ibid., 33.

23. Stanford, *Library Extension,* 164–66.

24. Ibid., 168–69.

25. Ibid., 176–78.

26. Agnes D. Crawford, *Annual Report, Statewide Library Project, Works Progress Administration, South Carolina, July 1938–July 1939* (Columbia, S.C., 1939), n.p.

27. Ibid.

28. "WPA Statewide Library Project No. 4673, Summary and Production Report, February 1, 1940 thru February 29, 1940"; "Production Report, Statewide Library Project, South Carolina, Month of May 1940"; "Production Report, Statewide Library Project, South Carolina, Month of June 1940"; "Production Report, Statewide Library Project, South Carolina, Month of July 1940," typescripts, Records of the Work Projects Administration, National Archives and Records Administration, College Park, Md.

29. Graham, *Right to Read,* 35–36.

30. Jackson State University, "History," www.jsums.edu; "Jackson State University," in *Historically Black Colleges and Universities: An Encyclopedia,* by F. Erik Brooks and Glenn L. Starks (Santa Barbara, Calif.: ABC-CLIO, 2011), 79–80; J. M. Bryant, letters to Florence Kerr, December 18, 1942, and December 23, 1942, Records of the Work Projects Administration, National Archives and Records Administration, College Park, Md.

31. Graham, *Right to Read,* 37–40.

32. Mary Mallory, "The Rare Vision of Mary Utopia Rothrock: Organizing Regional Library Services in the Tennessee Valley." *Library Quarterly* 65 (January 1995): 79–80.

33. Gleason, *Southern Negro and the Public Library,* 6–7.

34. Ibid., 90–91; Louis Round Wilson, "Education for Librarianship: A New Opportunity in the South," in *Library Conference Held under the Auspices of the Carnegie Corporation of New York and the General Education Board: March 14–15, 1941* (Atlanta: Atlanta University, 1941), 13.

35. Gleason, *Southern Negro and the Public Library,* 91.

36. Ibid., 78–79.

37. Ibid., 73–77.

38. Edwin R. Embree, *Julius Rosenwald Fund: Review for the Two-Year Period, 1938–1940* (Chicago, 1940), 3.

39. Howard Jones, *The Red Diary: A Chronological History of Black Americans in Houston*

and Some Neighboring Harris County Communities—122 Years Later (Austin, Tex.: Nortex, 1991), 109; Merline Petrie, *In Struggle against Jim Crow: Lulu B. White and the NAACP, 1900–1957* (College Station: Texas A&M University Press, 1999), 21–23.

40. J. Douglas Smith, *Managing White Supremacy: Race, Politics, and Citizenship in Jim Crow Virginia* (Chapel Hill: University of North Carolina Press, 2002), 261–70.

41. Ibid.

5. CHANGE AND CONTINUITY

1. Eliza Atkins Gleason, *The Southern Negro and the Public Library* (Chicago: University of Chicago Press, 1941).

2. Atlanta University School of Library Service, *Libraries, Librarians and the Negro* (Atlanta, 1944), 19.

3. Gunnar Myrdal, *An American Dilemma*, vol. 1, *The Negro Problem and Modern Democracy* (New York: Harper and Brothers, 1944), x–xiv.

4. Charles S. Johnson, *Patterns of Negro Segregation* (New York: Harper and Brothers, 1943), xiii.

5. Ibid., 26.

6. Ibid., 26–29.

7. Ibid.

8. Anna Holden, "The Color Line in Libraries," in *Changing Patterns in the New South* (Atlanta: Southern Regional Council, 1955), 60–62. Holden listed fifty-nine "full service" libraries but noted that four of them did not serve children; my figure of fifty-five makes that adjustment.

9. Nell Irvin Painter, *Creating Black Americans* (New York: Oxford University Press, 2005), 219–38.

10. Holden, "Color Line," 62.

11. Darrel E. Bigham, *An Evansville Album* (Bloomington: Indiana University Press, 1988).

12. Herbert Goldhor, *The First Fifty Years: The Evansville Public Library and the Vanderburgh County Public Library* (Evansville, 1962), 4.

13. "Oral History Interview of Murray Atkins Walls and John Walls," transcript, July 27, 1977, http://digital.library.louisville.edu; "A Finding Aid to the Joseph Rauch Papers," http://americanjewisharchives.org.

14. Luther Adams, *Way Up North in Louisville: African American Migration in the Urban South, 1930–1970* (Chapel Hill: University of North Carolina Press, 2010), 106.

15. "Oral History Interview"; Adams, *Way Up North*, 105–7.

16. Earline H. Hudson, "Library Service to Blacks and Black Librarians in Tennessee," in *The Black Librarian in the Southeast*, ed. Annete L. Phinazee (Durham: NCCU School of Library Service, 1980), 108.

17. Lucretia Jeanette Parker, "A Study of Integration in Public Library Service in Thirteen Southern States" (master's thesis, Atlanta University, 1953), 55–57.

18. Ibid., 60.

19. Esther Mae Henke, "The History of the Public Libraries in Oklahoma" (master's thesis, University of Oklahoma, 1954), 130.

20. Bernice Lloyd Bell, "Integration in Public Library Service in Thirteen Southern States, 1954–1962" (master's thesis, Atlanta University, 1963), 71; "History: The William F. Laman Public Library System," http://lamanlibrary.org; Parker, "Study of Integration," 27.

21. Gwendolyn Lewis Redd, "A History of Public Library Service to Negroes in Macon, Georgia" (master's thesis, Atlanta University, 1961), 30–32; Juanita Louise Jones Crittenden, "A History of Public Library Service to Negroes in Columbus, Georgia, 1831–1959" (master's thesis, Atlanta University, 1960), 18–21.

22. *Libraries, Librarians and the Negro*, 16.

23. Dorothy G. Williams, "Adult Education in Public Libraries and Museums," *Journal of Negro Education* 14 (Summer 1945): 326.

24. *Libraries, Librarians and the Negro*, 17.

25. Parker, "Study of Integration," 49.

26. Ibid., 37.

27. Ibid.

28. Sarah H. Harper, *One Hundred Years of Library Service to Tyler, Texas* (Tyler: Friends of the Tyler Public Library, [1999]), 1–3.

29. List of board members, minute book, [1941–1949], Tyler Negro Library, Local History Collection, Tyler Public Library; "Branch News," *Crisis* (March 1940): 87.

30. "Emmett J. Scott High School, 1918–1970: Reunion 2000," http://files.usgwarchives.net/tx/smith/history/school/scott/esreu2000.txt.

31. Lillian Peek, *Team Work on the Home Front* (Austin: Hogg Foundation, 1943), 9, 11, 16, 23–26.

32. Ibid., 24–25.

33. Minutes, Tyler City Council, June 6, 1941, City of Tyler Archives.

34. Ibid.

35. Agreement, July 23, 1941, typescript, Ella Reid Public Library Collection, Pennsylvania Historical Society.

36. Minute book, Tyler Negro Library, August 25, 1941; minutes, Board of Directors, Tyler Public Library, August 14, 1941, Local History Collection, Tyler Public Library.

37. David B. Gracy II, *The State Library and Archives of Texas: A History, 1835–1962* (Austin: University of Texas Press, 2010), 91.

38. Dorothy Journeay, "Field Visit Report on the Negro Public Library, Tyler, Texas, December 30, 1941," 2, Local History Collection, Tyler Public Library.

39. Ibid., 1; Dorothy Journeay, "Memorandum Concerning Second Field Visit to Negro Public Library of Tyler," March 9, 1942, [2], Local History Collection, Tyler Public Library.

40. Minute book, Tyler Negro Library, January 16, 1942.

41. Minutes, Tyler City Council, June 19, 1942.

42. Undated newspaper clippings, Ella Reid Public Library Collection. At least one of the clippings is misidentified as being from the *Chicago Tribune*. The clippings correlate with discussions of *Tyler Courier-Times* coverage in the minute book, Tyler Negro Library, January 16, 1942; June 24, 1942.

43. Ibid.

44. Minutes, Tyler City Council, July 3, 1942.

45. Ibid., September 18, 1942.

46. Minute book, Tyler Negro Library, September 23, 1942; November 25, 1942.

47. Bessie Davis Randall, "Public Library Service for Negroes," *News Notes* 19 (April 1943): 14.

48. Ibid.

49. Minute book, Tyler Negro Library, January 20, 1944; July 24, 1944.

50. Ibid., December 18, 1946.

51. Ibid., January 8, 1947; January 14, 1947; March 24, 1948; September 24, 1948;

October 28, 1948; March 17, 1949. Also see minutes, Tyler City Council, March 31, 1947; July 4, 1947; September 24, 1948; February 4, 1949.

52. Louis R. Wilson and Marion A. Milczewski, eds. *Libraries of the Southeast: A Report of the Southeastern States Cooperative Library Survey, 1946–1947* (Chapel Hill: University of North Carolina Press, 1949), 253–56, 290, 8.

6. ERECTING LIBRARIES, CONSTRUCTING RACE

1. "To Open Negro Branch of Carnegie Library," *Nashville Tennessean,* February 6, 1916, 14B; C. H. Compton, "Survey of the Nashville Carnegie Library" (Nashville, Tenn., July 5–7, 1927), 15.

2. Helen Horowitz, *Culture and the City: Cultural Philanthropy in Chicago from the 1880s to 1917* (Lexington: University Press of Kentucky, 1976), 121–24; Lawrence W. Levine, *Highbrow/Lowbrow: The Emergence of Cultural Hierarchy in America* (Cambridge: Harvard University Press, 1990), 159.

3. Henri Lefebvre, *The Production of Space,* trans. Donald Nicholson-Smith (Oxford: Blackwell, 1991), 38–39. For an introduction to Lefebvre's work and significance, see Delores Hayden, *The Power of Place: Urban Landscapes As Public History* (Cambridge: MIT Press), 18–19, 317. Also see Susan Ruddick, "Constructing Difference in Public Spaces: Race, Class, and Gender As Interlocking Systems," *Urban Geography* 17, no. 2 (1996), 132–51; Elsa Brown and Gregg Kimball, "Mapping the Terrain of Black Richmond," *Journal of Urban History* 21, no. 3 (1995): 317; Phyllis Dain, "Ambivalence and Paradox: The Social Bonds of the Public Library," *Library Journal,* February 1, 1975, 266.

4. Abigail A. Van Slyck, *Free to All: Carnegie Libraries and American Culture, 1890–1920* (Chicago: University of Chicago Press, 1995), xxvii, 101–124.

5. Ibid., 65, 111, 158–59, 196–98.

6. "Fourth Library for Evansville," *Evansville Courier,* January 4, 1914, n.p.

7. "Negro Library Opening May 8," unidentified newspaper, April 25, 1918, n.p., clipping in McClung Collection, Knox County Public Library, Knoxville, Tennessee, "Libraries. Free Colored Library." folder.

8. William F. Yust, *The Louisville Free Public Library: An Address before the Richmond, Virginia, Education Association* (Louisville, 1912), 5; Works Projects Administration, *Libraries and Lotteries: A History of the Louisville Free Public Library* (Cynthiana, Ky.: Hobson, 1944), 108–11.

9. Donald E. Oehlerts, *Books and Blueprints: Building America's Public Libraries* (New York: Greenwood, 1991), 62.

10. Works Projects Administration, *Libraries and Lotteries,* 116.

11. Yust, *Louisville Free Public Library,* 10; Thomas F. Blue, "A Successful Library Experiment," *Opportunity* 2 (August 1924): 245.

12. W. E. B. Du Bois, ed. *Efforts for Social Betterment among Negro Americans* (Atlanta: Atlanta University Press, 1909), 95–96.

13. Robert Burke Walker, Jr., "Georgia's Carnegie Libraries: A Study of Their History, Their Existing Conditions, and Conservation" (master's thesis, University of Georgia, 1994), 70–72.

14. Richard K. Dozier, "The Black Architectural Experience in America," *AIA Journal* 65 (July 1976): 164.

15. Charles E. Brownell, Calder Loth, William M. S. Rasmussen, and Richard Guy Wilson, *The Making of Virginia Architecture* (Richmond: Virginia Museum of Fine Arts, 1992), 93.

16. Much of this discussion relies on Harrison Mosley Ethridge, "The Black Architects

of Washington, D.C., 1900–Present" (Ph.D. diss., Catholic University of America, 1979), 1–40.

17. William Sidney Pittman, letter to Booker T. Washington, March 16, 1901, Booker T. Washington Papers, Library of Congress, microfilm reel 3.

18. Ethridge, "The Black Architects of Washington, D.C."

19. W. P. Burrell, *Twenty-Five Years History of the Grand Fountain of the United Order of True Reformers, 1881–1905* (Westport, Conn.: Negro Universities Press, 1970), 321.

20. "Doing Something for the Race," *Washington Bee,* January 7, 1905, 1.

21. John A. Lankford, "Report of the Sixth Annual Convention of the National Negro Business League Held in New York City, August 16, 17, 18, 1905" (1905).

22. E. Franklin Frazier, *Black Bourgeoisie: The Rise of a New Middle Class* (Glencoe, Il.: Free Press, 1957), 197–98; W. E. B. Du Bois, *The Negro Artisan* (Atlanta University Press, 1902), 110–11.

23. Louis R. Harlan, *Booker T. Washington,* vol. 2, *The Wizard Of Tuskegee, 1901–1915* (Oxford: Oxford University Press, 1983), 18–120; biographical annotation, in Louis R. Harlan, ed., *Booker T. Washington Papers,* ed. Louis R. Harlan (Champaign: University of Illinois Press, 1972), 236–37; Ruth Ann Stewart, *Portia: The Life of Portia Washington Pittman, the Daughter of Booker T. Washington* (Garden City, N.Y.: Doubleday, 1977), 78; obituary of William Sidney Pittman, *Dallas Morning News,* February 19, 1958, n.p.

24. Brownell et al., *Making of Virginia Architecture,* 93; Alan Govenar and Jay Brakefield, *Deep Ellum: The Other Side of Dallas* (College Station: Texas A&M University Press, 2013), 37–38.

25. "The New Saint James A.M.E. Temple, Good and Florence Streets Will Celebrate Its Opening Exercises," *Dallas Express,* January 1, 1921, 2.

26. "Great Throngs Attend Dedication of New $50,000 St. James A.M.E. Church," *Dallas Express,* January 15, 1921, 1; Du Bois, *Negro Artisan,* 99–100.

27. William Sidney Pittman, letter to Emmett J. Scott, April 1, 1911, Booker T. Washington Papers, microfilm reel 3.

28. William Sidney Pittman, letter to Emmett J. Scott, April 11, 1911, Booker T. Washington Papers, microfilm reel 3.

29. A thorough discussion of Bertram's "Notes" appears in Van Slyck, *Free to All,* 35–40.

30. William Sidney Pittman, letter to Emmett J. Scott, July 2, 1911, Booker T. Washington Papers, microfilm reel 3.

31. The following are archived in the Carnegie Corporation of New York Records, Rare Book and Manuscript Library of Columbia University, microfilm reel 14: James Bertram, letter to H. B. Rice, December 12, 1911; James Bertram, letter to William Sidney Pittman, January 8, 1912; H. B. Rice, letter to R. A. Franks, June 30, 1911; J. B. Bell, letter to Emmett J. Scott, December 20, 1911; Emmett J. Scott, letter to R. A. Franks, December 23, 1911.

32. "Dedication Exercises at Colored Carnegie Library," *Houston Chronicle,* n.d., Houston Public Library Collection, box 8.

33. The following are archived in the Booker T. Washington Papers, microfilm reel 3: Booker T. Washington, letter to William Sidney Pittman, April 24, 1909; William Sidney Pittman, letter to Booker T. Washington, July 15, 1909; Booker T. Washington, letter to William Sidney Pittman, March 29, 1911; Booker T. Washington, letter to William Sidney Pittman, April 8, 1911; William Sidney Pittman, letter to William Burns Paterson, April 11, 1911; Booker T. Washington, letter to William Sidney Pittman, May 11, 1911. Also see Harlan, *Wizard of Tuskegee,* 119.

34. Walker, "Georgia's Carnegie Libraries," 72–73.
35. Van Slyck, *Free to All*, 112–13.
36. "Middle Tennessee State University," in *The Tennessee Encyclopedia of History and Culture*, http://tennesseeencyclopedia.net; minutes, Board of Directors, Nashville Public Library, August 28, 1913, and March 3, 1914, Nashville Public Library Archives, Metropolitan Government Archives of Nashville and Davidson County.
37. Dreck Spurlock Wilson, ed. *African American Architects: A Biographical Dictionary, 1865–1945* (New York: Routledge, 2004), 386–90.
38. Minutes, Board of Directors, New Orleans Public Library, August 13, 1913, New Orleans Public Library Collection.
39. Ibid., February 11, 1914.
40. Ibid., March 11, 1914.
41. Alcée Fortier, ed., *Louisiana: Comprising Sketches of Parishes, Towns, Events, Institutions and Persons, Arranged in Cyclopedic Form* (n.p.: Century Historical Association, 1914), 600.
42. Minutes, Board of Directors, New Orleans Public Library, March 11, 1914.
43. Ibid., August 12, 1914.
44. Du Bois, *Negro Artisan*, 127.
45. Minutes, Board of Directors, New Orleans Public Library Board of Directors, February 10, 1915; March 10, 1915; April 14, 1915; May 12, 1915; June 9, 1915.
46. Ibid., August 11, 1915; September 8, 1915.
47. Ibid., October 13, 1915; November 10, 1915.
48. Van Slyck, *Free to All*, 111–12.
49. Robert P. Williams, letter to Carnegie Corporation, August 23, 1916, Carnegie Corporation Records, microfilm reel 16.
50. Dryades branch architectural plans, William R. Burk Collection, Southeastern Architectural Archive, Tulane University; *Annual Report of the New Orleans Public Library, Fisk Library, Simon Hernsheim Library, 1911* (New Orleans, 1912), 17; *Annual Report of the New Orleans Public Library, Fisk Library, Simon Hernsheim Library, 1912* (New Orleans, 1913), illustration between 40 and 41.
51. Minutes, Board of Directors, New Orleans Public Library, November 14, 1917; December 14, 1917.
52. Ibid., August 8, 1917.
53. "Carnegie Library," photo and caption, 1929, clipping in Knoxville Public Library Archives.
54. Minutes, Board of Directors, New Orleans Public Library, May 11, 1932; Rosemary Ruhig Du Mont, "Race in American Librarianship: Attitudes of the Library Profession," *Journal of Library History* 21 (Summer 1986): 488–509; Jean L. Preer, " 'This Year—Richmond!': The 1936 Meeting of the American Library Association," *Libraries and Culture* 39 (Spring 2004): 137–60.
55. Stewart, *Portia*, 78–86; Roy L. Hill, *Booker T's Child: The Life and Times of Portia Marshall Washington Pittman*, rev. ed. (Washington, D.C.: Three Continents Press, 1993), 59–73; Carolyn Perritt, "The Dissident Voice: William Sidney Pittman," *Legacies: A History Journal for Dallas and North Central Texas* 16 (Spring 2004), http://texashistory.unt.edu.

7. BOOKS FOR BLACK READERS

1. Wayne A. Wiegand, *Main Street Public Library: Community Places and Reading Spaces in the Rural Heartland, 1876–1956* (Iowa City: University of Iowa Press, 2011), 186.

2. Rosemary Ruhig Du Mont, *Reform and Reaction: The Big City Public Library in American Life* (Westport, Conn.: Greenwood, 1977), 66–104; Wayne A. Wiegand, "Tracing the Concept of Freedom of Access to Information in American Library History," in *Buch und Bibliothekswissenschaft im Informationszeitalter*, ed. Herausgegeben von Engelbert Plassmann, Wolfgang Schmitz, and Peter Vodosek (Munich: Saur, 1990), 313–21.

3. Evelyn Geller, *Forbidden Books in American Public Libraries, 1876–1939* (Westport, Conn.: Greenwood, 1984), 99–108.

4. William F. Yust, "What of the Black and Yellow Races?" *Bulletin of the American Library Association* 7 (January–November 1913): 165.

5. George Sherwood Dickerman, "The Marblehead Libraries," *Southern Workman* 39 (September 1910): 490–500.

6. The Douglass biography is listed in Dickerman's survey as *Life of Frederick Douglass*. The only similar title then available was Douglass's own *The Life and Times of Frederick Douglass*.

7. Dickerman, "Marblehead Libraries," 493.

8. Yust, "What of the Black and Yellow Races?," 166; Dickerman, "Marblehead Libraries," 498–99.

9. "Work with Negroes Round Table," *Bulletin of the American Library Association* 17 (July 1923): 277.

10. Esther Jane Currier, *Fiction in Public Libraries, 1876–1900* (New York: Scarecrow, 1965), 28–30, 32–36, 44–135.

11. Ibid., 179–233.

12. Ibid., 2–29.

13. Lawrence W. Levine, *Highbrow/Lowbrow: The Emergence of Cultural Hierarchy in America* (Cambridge: Harvard University Press, 1988), 159.

14. Martha J. Sebastian, "History of the Carnegie Negro Library, Greensboro, North Carolina," speech, October 27, 1944, 3, Bennett College Archives; "Condensed Accession Book: The Official Record of Each Volume Added to the Negro Branch of the Nashville Carnegie Library from July 20, 1915," Nashville Public Library Archives, Metropolitan Government Archives of Nashville and Davidson County; Michele T. Fenton, "Way Down Yonder at the Cherry Street Branch: A Short History of Evansville's Negro Library," *Indiana Libraries* 30, (2011): 37; "Accession Book A–Z (Branches)," 1911–17, New Orleans Public Library Archives.

15. Tommie Dora Barker, letter to James L. Key, in minutes, December 5, 1921; minutes, January 4 and January 11, 1921, Atlanta Public Library Board of Trustees, Atlantic Public Library Archive.

16. Herbert Goldhor, *The First Fifty Years: The Evansville Public Library and the Vanderburgh County Public Library* (Evansville, Ind., 1962), 4; "Negro Library Opening May 8," unidentified newspaper clipping, April 25, 1918, McClung Collection, Knox County Public Library, "Knoxville, Tennessee—Libraries. Free Colored Library" folder; Fay Allen Schultz, "New Orleans Public Library in the Twentieth Century," *Louisiana Library Association Bulletin* 15, no. 2 (1952): 78–83; Leon Carnovsky, *The Public Libraries of Greensboro: A Survey* (n.p., [1952]), 15; minutes, January 4, 1921, and January 11, 1921, Atlanta Public Library Board of Trustees; Annie E. McPheeters, *Library Service in Black and White: Some Personal Recollections, 1921–1980* (Metuchen, N.J.: Scarecrow, 1988), 23–24.

17. Rachel D. Harris, "Work with Children at the Colored Branch of the Louisville Free Public Library," in *Library Work with Children*, ed. Alice I. Hazeltine (White Plains, N.Y.: Wilson, 1917), 379–82.

18. Ibid., 379; U.S. Census Bureau, *Census of Population and Housing, 1910,* vol. 2, *Population: Reports by States Alabama–Montana,* www.census.gov.
19. Louisville Free Public Library, "Some Books and Pamphlets, Music, Magazines and Newspapers by Negro Writers, Composers and Editors in the Colored Department of the Louisville Free Public Library" (Louisville, Ky., 1921).
20. Louisville Free Public Library, "Supplementary List [to 'Some Books and Pamphlets, Music, Magazines and Newspapers by Negro Writers, Composers and Editors in the Colored Department of the Louisville Free Public Library']" (Louisville, Ky., [1923]).
21. "Condensed Accession Book," Nashville Public Library Archives.
22. Cheryl Knott Malone, "The Adult Collection at Nashville's Negro Public Library, 1915–1916," in *Libraries to the People: Histories of Outreach eds.* Robert S. Freeman and David M. Hovde (Jefferson, N.C.: McFarland, 2003), 154.
23. Ibid., 148–55.
24. Leon Litwack, *Trouble in Mind: Black Southerners in the Age of Jim Crow* (New York: Knopf, 1998), 71; Bobby L. Lovett, *The African-American History of Nashville, Tennessee, 1780–1930: Elites and Dilemmas* (Fayetteville: University of Arkansas Press, 1999), 141.
25. *Children's Catalog: A Guide to the Best Reading for Young People Based on Twenty-Four Selected Library Lists* (Minneapolis: Wilson, 1909), 73–74.
26. "List of Books Selected from Titles in the Western Colored Branch of the Louisville Free Public Library Recommended for First Purchase," typescript, [1919], Nashville Public Library Archives; "Condensed Accession Book," Nashville Public Library Archives.
27. Kristina DuRocher, *Raising Racists: The Socialization of White Children in the Jim Crow South* (Lexington: University Press of Kentucky, 2011), 54–57.
28. Cheryl Knott Malone, "Books for Black Children: Public Library Collections in Louisville and Nashville, 1915–1925," *Library Quarterly* 70 (April 2000): 197.
29. Violet J. Harris, "From *Little Black Sambo* to *Popo and Fifina:* Arna Bontemps and the Creation of African-American Children's Literature," *Lion and the Unicorn* 14 (June 1990): 108–27; Holly G. Willett, *"Rifles for Watie:* Rollins, Riley, and Racism," *Libraries and Culture* 36 (Fall 2001): 487–505; Henrietta M. Smith, "An Interview with Augusta Baker," *Horn Book Magazine* 71 (May–June 1995): 292–96; Augusta Baker, "Guidelines for Black Books: An Open Letter to Juvenile Editors," in *The Black American in Books for Children: Readings in Racism,* eds. Donnarae MacCann and Gloria Woodard (Metuchen, N.J.: Scarecrow, 1972), 52.
30. In 2013, the Cooperative Children's Book Center at the University of Wisconsin counted sixty-seven books by and ninety-three about blacks among the 3,200 new books the center received (http://ccbc.education.wisc.edu).
31. Ellen Tarry, *The Third Door: The Autobiography of an American Negro Woman* (New York: McKay, 1955), 302.
32. Katharine Capshaw Smith, "From Bank Street to Harlem: A Conversation with Ellen Tarry," *Lion and the Unicorn* 23, no. 2 (1999): 281. The reference is to Stella Sharpe's *Tobe* (Chapel Hill: University of North Carolina Press, 1939).
33. Christine Pawley, *Reading on the Middle Border: The Culture of Print in Late-Nineteenth-Century Osage, Iowa* (Amherst, M.A.: University of Massachusetts Press, 2001): 91–105; George B. Utley, "What the Negro Reads," *Critic* 49 (July 1906): 28–30; Ron Blazek, "Utley, George Burwell," in *Dictionary of American Library Biography,* ed. George S. Bobinski, Jesse Hauk Shera, and Bohdan S. Wynar (Littleton, Colo.: Libraries Unlimited, 1978), 525–27.

34. Lynn E. May, Jr., *The First Baptist Church of Nashville Tennessee, 1820–1970* (Nashville: First Baptist Church, 1970), 110.

35. Mechal Sobel, "'They Can Never Both Prosper Together': Black and White Baptists in Antebellum Nashville, Tennessee," *Tennessee Historical Quarterly* 38 (Fall 1979): 306.

36. Bobby L. Lovett, *A Black Man's Dream, the First 100 Years: Richard Henry Boyd and the National Baptist Publishing Board* (n.p.: Mega, 1993), 65.

37. Paul Harvey, "'The Holy Spirit Come to Us and Forbid the Negro Taking a Second Place': Richard H. Boyd and Black Religious Activism in Nashville," *Tennessee Historical Quarterly* 55 (Fall 1996): 191–93.

38. C. Eric Lincoln and Lawrence H. Mamiya, *The Black Church in the African American Experience* (Durham, N.C.: Duke University Press, 1990), 33–34.

39. Lovett, *African-American History of Nashville*, 243–44.

40. Lovett, *Black Man's Dream*, 113; Harvey, *Holy Spirit*, 273.

41. Lincoln and Mamiya, *Black Church*, 33; Lovett, *Black Man's Dream*, 114.

42. Mary Hannah Johnson, "Southern Libraries," undated typescript of a speech, Nashville Public Library Archives. The speech was published as Mary Hannah Johnson, "Southern Libraries" *Library Journal* 28 (July 1903): 69–71.

43. Lester C. Lamon, *Black Tennesseans, 1900–1930* (Knoxville: University of Tennessee Press, 1977), 76.

44. "Condensed Accession Book," Nashville Public Library Archives.

45. Lincoln and Mamiya, *Black Church*, 7.

46. Ibid., 8.

47. Lovett, *African American History*, 115, 126.

48. Benjamin E. Mays, "The Education of Negro Ministers," *Journal of Negro Education* 2 (July 1933): 346.

49. Finance book, Negro library, Nashville Public Library Archives; minutes, Nashville Public Library Board of Directors, March 5, 1918, June 4, 1920, January 4, 1921, March 1, 1921, and April 3, 1923, Nashville Public Library Archives; U. S. Bureau of the Census, *Census of Population, 1930*, vol. 3, part 2, *Reports by States: Montana- Wyoming*, www. census.gov.

50. Charles H. Compton, *Survey of the Nashville Carnegie Library, Nashville, Tennessee, July 5–7, 1927* ([Nashville], 1927), 15.

51. Minutes, New Orleans Public Library Board of Directors, May 12, 1915, and June 9, 1915, New Orleans Public Library Archives.

52. "Accession Book A–Z," New Orleans Public Library Archives.

53. "Branch Library for Negro Race Ready for Use," *Times-Picayune*, October 24, 1915, 16B.

54. Dewey Decimal Classification, https://en.wikipedia.org.

55. "Branch Library for Negro Race Ready for Use," 16B.

56. E. W. Winkler, "Southwestern Library Association," *Library Journal*, May 15, 1923, 534.

57. Florence M. Jumonville, "Books along the Bayous: Reading Materials for Two Centuries of Rural Louisianians," in *Libraries to the People: Histories of Outreach*, eds. Robert S. Freeman and David M. Hovde (Jefferson, N.C.: McFarland, 2003), 22.

58. "Accession Book A–Z"; U.S. Census Bureau, *Census of Population and Housing, 1910*, vol. 2, *Population: Reports by States Alabama–Montana*, www.census.gov; U.S. Census Bureau, *Census of Population and Housing, 1920*, vol. 3, *Population: Composition and Characteristics of the Population by States*, www.census.gov.

59. *Soards' New Orleans City Directory for 1912* (New Orleans, 1911), 1184, 1416.
60. W. W. Charters, "Director's Introduction," in *Book Selection,* by Francis K. W. Drury (Chicago: American Library Association, 1930), ix–x.
61. Drury, *Book Selection,* 3–4.
62. Ibid., 8–21.
63. Ibid., 28.
64. Ibid., 281–83, 284–85.
65. Ibid., 164–65, 250, 281–85.
66. Ibid., 296.
67. Louis Round Wilson, ed., *The Practice of Book Selection: Papers Presented before the Library Institute at the University of Chicago, July 31 to August 13, 1939* (Chicago: University of Chicago Press, [1940]), 27.
68. Ibid., 15–16.
69. Ibid., 33–37.
70. Ibid., 34.
71. Nell Irvin Painter, *The History of White People* (New York: Norton, 2010), 327–42.
72. Accession book, 1941–69, Ella Reid Public Library Collection, Pennsylvania Historical Society.
73. "Circulating Library for County Homes to Operate Soon," *Tyler Journal,* December 13, 1935, 1; David Boutros, "From the Stacks: Research Center—Kansas City: Frank and Ardis Glenn and the Glenn Bookshop." *Missouri Historical Review* 107 (July 2013): 248–51.
74. Lillian Peek, *Team Work on the Home Front* (Austin, Tex.: Hogg Foundation, 1943), 24–25.
75. Accession book, Ella Reid Public Library Records; *The Negro: A Selected Bibliography* (New York: New York Public Library, 1940); Dorothy R. Homer and Evelyn R. Robinson, *The Negro: A Selected Bibliography* (New York: New York Public Library, 1955).
76. Anthony Slide, *American Racist: The Life and Films of Thomas Dixon* (Lexington: University Press of Kentucky, 2004).
77. Charlemae Rollins, "Children's Books on the Negro: To Help Build a Better World," *Elementary English Review* 20 (October 1943): 219–20.
78. *Children's Catalog* (New York: Wilson, 1946); *Children's Catalog* (New York: Wilson, 1951), 307.
79. Homer and Robinson, *The Negro;* accession book, Ella Reid Public Library Records.

8. READING THE RACE-BASED LIBRARY

1. Marion Humble, *Rural America Reads: A Study of Rural Library Service* (New York: American Association for Adult Education, 1938), 68.
2. I have been unable to find a complete set of records for a black public library that includes all three types of sources needed to construct a deep understanding of library use and users: accession or catalog records, a register of borrowers, and circulation transaction logs.
3. Stanley Fish, *Is There a Text in this Class? The Authority of Interpretive Communities* (Cambridge: Harvard University Press, 1980); Janice A. Radway, *Reading the Romance: Women, Patriarchy, and Popular Literature* (Chapel Hill: University of North Carolina Press, 1984); Christine Pawley, *Reading on the Middle Border: The Culture of Print in Late Nineteenth-Century Osage, Iowa* (Amherst: University of Massachusetts Press, 2001); Jonathan Rose, *The Intellectual Life of the British Working Classes* (New Haven:

Yale University Press, 2001); Elizabeth McHenry, *Forgotten Readers: Recovering the Lost History of African American Literary Societies* (Durham, N.C.: Duke University Press, 2002); Barbara Hochman, *"Uncle Tom's Cabin" and the Reading Revolution: Race, Literacy, Childhood, and Fiction, 1851–1911* (Amherst: University of Massachusetts Press, 2011), 249–50; and Archie Dick, *The Hidden History of South Africa's Book and Reading Cultures* (Toronto: University of Toronto Press, 2012), 100–111.

4. James D. Anderson, *The Education of Blacks in the South, 1860–1935* (Chapel Hill: University of North Carolina Press, 1988), 30; Leon Litwack, *Trouble in Mind* (Vintage, 1999), 75–76.

5. Frank Felsenstein and James J. Connolly, *What Middletown Read: Print Culture in an American Small City* (Amherst: University of Massachusetts Press, 2015), 127–28.

6. Hochman, *"Uncle Tom's Cabin,"* 231–51.

7. Charles F. Smith, "Negro Boy Contributed Most Books," *Houston Post*, April 19, 1914, 48; Cheryl Knott Malone, "Autonomy and Accommodation: Houston's Colored Carnegie Library, 1907–1922," *Libraries and Culture* 34 (Spring 1999): 95–112.

8. Cheryl Knott Malone, "Reconstituting the Public Library Users of the Past: An Exploration of Nominal Record Linkage Methodology," *Journal of Education for Library and Information Science* 39 (Fall 1998): 288–89.

9. Willard B. Gatewood, *Aristocrats of Color: The Black Elite, 1880–1920* (Bloomington: Indiana University Press, 1990), 7–30.

10. Yvonne Easton, ed. *I Dream a World: Portraits of Black Women Who Changed America*, rev. ed. (New York: Stewart, Tabori, and Chang, 1999), 151.

11. Minute book, Board of Directors, Houston Lyceum and Carnegie Library, June 8, 1909, Houston Public Library, Houston Metropolitan Research Center.

12. Borrowing records, Colored Library, 1910–12, Houston Public Library, Houston Metropolitan Research Center.

13. Houston Public Library, "History of the Gregory School and Freedmen's Town," www.thegregoryschool.org.

14. Frank G. Carpenter, *North America* (New York: American Book Company, 1910), 109.

15. Ibid., 311.

16. "Annual Report of the New Orleans Public Library, 1922" (New Orleans, 1923), 17; Douglas A. Galbi, "Book Circulation per U.S. Public Library User Since 1856," July 29, 2007, http://galbithink.org.

17. "Annual Report of the New Orleans Public Library, 1920/1921" (New Orleans, 1921), 16–19; Galbi, "Book Circulation per U.S. Public Library User Since 1856."

18. David M. Katzman, *Seven Days a Week: Women and Domestic Service in Industrializing America* (Oxford University Press, 1978), 79.

19. U.S. Census Bureau, *Census of Population and Housing, 1920*, vol. 3, *Population: Composition and Characteristics of the Population by States*, www.census.gov.

20. Cheryl Knott Malone, "Books for Black Children: Public Library Collections in Louisville and Nashville, 1915–1925," *Library Quarterly* 70 (April 2000): 195.

21. Stephanie J. Shaw, *What a Woman Ought to Be and to Do: Black Professional Women Workers during the Jim Crow Era* (Chicago: University of Chicago Press, 1996), 33.

22. Zora Neale Hurston, *Dust Tracks on a Road* (Philadelphia: Lippincott, 1942), 55–62, 135, 149, 156–57.

23. Ralph Ellison, "Hidden Name and Complex Fate: A Writer's Experience in the United States," in *Shadow and Act* (New York: Random House, 1964), 160.

24. Lawrence Jackson, *Ralph Ellison: Emergence of Genius* (New York: Wiley, 2002), 28–43.

25. Ibid., 70.
26. Richard Wright "The Ethics of Living Jim Crow" in Federal Writers' Project, *American Stuff* (New York: Viking 1937), http://newdeal.feri.org; Miles M. Jackson, Jr., "Books and Poverty Do Mix," *Negro Digest* (January 1967): 41–42; William Miller, *Richard Wright and the Library Card* (New York: Lee and Low, 1999); Karla F. C. Holloway, *BookMarks: Reading in Black and White* (New Brunswick, N.J.: Rutgers University Press, 2006), 45–51; Richard Wright, *Black Boy: A Record of Childhood and Youth* (New York: Harper, 1937), 217–18.
27. Reinette F. Jones, *Library Service to African Americans in Kentucky, from the Reconstruction Era to the 1960s* (Jefferson, N.C.: McFarland, 2002), 46–47.
28. Ibid.
29. Ernest I. Miller, "Library Service for Negroes in Tennessee," *Journal of Negro Education* 10 (October 1941): 635–42; Annie Mae Robinson and Francis W. Allen, "Community Service of a Negro College Library," *Journal of Negro Education* 12 (Spring 1943): 181–88; Carroll Van West, *Tennessee's New Deal Landscape: A Guidebook* (Knoxville: University of Tennessee Press, 2001), 146.
30. Holloway, *BookMarks*, 50.
31. Jordan Elgrably, interview, "James Baldwin: The Art of Fiction No. 78" www.theparisreview.org; James Baldwin, *Go Tell It on the Mountain* (New York: Dell, 1980), 35–36.
32. "Annie L. McPheeters Oral History Interview 1992 June 8," http://digitalcollections.library.gsu.edu.
33. Ibid.
34. Ibid.; Saundra Murray Nettles, *Necessary Spaces: Exploring the Richness of African American Childhood in the South* (Charlotte, N.C.: Information Age Publishing, 2013), 42–46, xvii; Annie L. McPheeters, *Library Service in Black and White: Some Personal Recollections, 1921–1980* (Metuchen, N.J.: Scarecrow, 1988), 78.
35. Nettles, *Necessary Spaces*, 43.
36. Rachel D. Harris, "The Advantages of Colored Branch Libraries," *Southern Workman* 44 (July 1915): 390.
37. "A Librarian Tried to Have a Genius Little Boy Arrested. The Cops Reacted the Same Way You Would," *Storycorps*, www.upworthy.com.
38. Ron Chepesiuk and Gale Teaster-Woods, "Making a Difference: African-American Leaders Rap about Libraries," *American Libraries* 26 (February 1995): 139.
39. Ibid., 140.
40. Wilson and Wight, *County Library Service*, 92.
41. Ibid., 90.
42. Ibid., 103.
43. Ibid., 102.
44. Ibid., 121.
45. Ibid., 115.
46. Bertie Wenning, "Reading Survey of the Chattanooga Public Library and Its School-Community Branches, April 9–10–11, 1934" [1934], n.p.
47. Ibid.
48. Ibid.
49. William S. Gray and Bernice E. Leary, *What Makes a Book Readable, with Special Reference to Adults of Limited Reading Ability: An Initial Study* (Chicago: University of Chicago Press, 1935), v, 225–27.
50. Ibid., 64.

51. Ibid., 75–76, 91.
52. Ibid., 70–85.
53. Ibid., 47–48.
54. Ibid., 48.
55. Ibid., 54.
56. Ibid., 183, 187, 189, 190.
57. Ibid., 200.
58. Ibid., 54.
59. Dick, *Hidden History*, 142.
60. Juanita Offutt, "Reading Materials Found in 616 Homes in a Negro Housing Project in Louisville, Kentucky" (master's thesis, University of Cincinnati, 1943), 31.
61. Ibid., 87.
62. Ibid., 93, 141–42.
63. Louis R. Wilson and Marion A. Milczewski, eds., *Libraries of the Southeast: A Report of the Southeastern States Cooperative Library Survey, 1946–1947* (Chapel Hill, N.C.: Southeastern Library Association, 1949), 253, 256–58, 260.
64. Ibid., 38–39.
65. On intensive and extensive reading, see Christine Pawley, *Reading on the Middle Border: The Culture of Print in Late-Nineteenth-Century Osage, Iowa* (Amherst: University of Massachusetts Press, 2001), 9, n. 1.

9. OPENING ACCESS

1. Anne Holden, "The Color Line in Libraries," in *Changing Patterns in the New South* (Atlanta: Southern Regional Council, 1955), 60–62.
2. On library desegregation in the 1960s, see Stephen Cresswell, "The Last Days of Jim Crow in Southern Libraries," *Libraries and Culture* 31 (Summer–Fall 1996): 557–73.
3. A version of the Houston section of this chapter appears in Cheryl Knott Malone, "Unannounced and Unexpected: The Desegregation of Houston Public Library," *Library Trends* 55 (Winter 2007): 665–74.
4. Darlene Clark Hine, *Black Victory: The Rise and Fall of the White Primary in Texas* (Millwood, N.Y.: KTO Press, 1979).
5. Merline Pitre, *In Struggle against Jim Crow: Lulu B. White and the NAACP, 1900–1957* (College Station: Texas A&M University Press, 1999).
6. "The Houston Library Fight," *Houston Informer*, March 25, 1953.
7. Pitre, *In Struggle*, 72.
8. Herman Wright, letter to Mrs. Roy L. Arterbury, November 17, 1950, and Harriet Dickson Reynolds, letter to Herman Wright, November 21, 1950, in minute book, Board of Directors, 1948–50, Houston Public Library, Houston Metropolitan Research Center.
9. Harriet Dickson Reynolds, letter to Herman W. Mead, November 24, 1950, in ibid.; "Board Members Visit Mayor," typescript, in minute book, Board of Directors, 1951–53, Houston Public Library, Houston Metropolitan Research Center.
10. W. H. Kellar, *Make Haste Slowly: Moderates, Conservatives, and School Desegregation in Houston* (College Station: Texas A&M University Press, 1999), 15.
11. Harriet Dickson Reynolds, typescript, in minute book, Board of Directors, 1951–53, Houston Public Library, Metropolitan Research Center.
12. Minute book, Board of Directors, February 20, 1953, in ibid.

13. Notes on Roy M. Hofheinz's talk, minute book, Board of Directors, May 18, 1953, in ibid.

14. "Mrs. Arterbury's Library Service," *Houston Post,* March 25, 1953, 1.

15. "Mrs. Young, Club Woman, Dies Here," *Houston Post,* April 29, 1953, sec. 1, p. 7.

16. Jack Valenti, *This Time, This Place: My Life in War, the White House, and Hollywood* (New York: Crown, 2008). Valenti met Lyndon Johnson in 1956 and later served under the president as his special assistant until 1966, when he resigned to become head of the Motion Picture Association of America, a post he held until mid-2004.

17. Minute book, July 21, 1953, Board of Directors, 1951–53, Houston Public Library, Houston Metropolitan Research Center.

18. Ibid.

19. Ibid.

20. Harriet Dickson Reynolds, letter to Will G. Sears, June 2, 1953, and Will G. Sears, letter to Harriet Dickson Reynolds, July 21, 1953, in ibid.

21. Minute book, August 21, 1953, and July 21, 1953, in ibid.

22. Minute book, July 21, 1953, and December 11, 1953, in ibid.; annual report of the Houston Public Library, 1953, Houston Public Library, Houston Metropolitan Research Center.

23. T. R. Cole, *No Color Is My Kind: The Life of Eldrewey Stearns and the Integration of Houston* (Austin: University of Texas Press, 1997).

24. M. Hurley, *Decisive Years for Houston* (Houston: Houston Magazine, 1966).

25. Anita Sterling, annual report of the Colored Carnegie Branch, 1953, Houston Public Library, Houston Metropolitan Research Center.

26. Harold L. Hamill, "Recommendations for the Houston Public Library," October 29, 1953, 1–2, 18, Houston Public Library, Houston Metropolitan Research Center.

27. The Los Angeles Public Library had hired its first African American librarian, Miriam Matthews, in 1927. By her retirement in 1960, she had risen from branch librarian to supervisor of twelve branch libraries. See Myrna Oliver, "Miriam Matthews," 97; Pioneering L.A. Librarian Was an Expert in Black History," *Los Angeles Times,* July 6, 2003, B16.

28. Hamill, "Recommendations," 8.

29. Ibid.

30. Annual report of Houston Public Library, 1954, Houston Public Library, Houston Metropolitan Research Center.

31. Annual reports of Houston Public Library, 1955, 1956, 1958, Houston Public Library, Houston Metropolitan Research Center.

32. Minute book, January 26, 1956, Board of Directors, 1956–57, Houston Public Library, Houston Metropolitan Research Center.

33. Minute book, May 18, 1956, ibid.

34. Ibid.

35. "Bullock, Henry Allen," *Handbook of Texas Online,* https://tshaonline.org.

36. H. A. Bullock, letter to Harriet Dickson Reynolds, April 26, 1956, minute book, May 18, 1956, Board of Directors, 1956–57, Houston Public Library, Houston Metropolitan Research Center.

37. Minute book, May 18, 1956, Board of Directors, 1956–57, Houston Public Library, Houston Metropolitan Research Center.

38. Minute book, February 23, 1962, Board of Directors, 1961–62, Houston Public Library, Houston Metropolitan Research Center.

39. Minute book, June 12, 1959, Board of Directors, 1958–60, Houston Public Library, Houston Metropolitan Research Center.

40. Minute book, June 12, 1959, Board of Directors, 1958–60, Houston Public Library, Houston Metropolitan Research Center.
41. Minute book, July 10, 1959, Board of Directors, 1958–1960, Houston Public Library, Houston Metropolitan Research Center.
42. Harriet Dickson Reynolds, letter to Lewis Cutrer, August 28, 1959, in ibid.
43. Minute book, October 14, 1960, in ibid.
44. Minute book, July 14, 1961, Board of Directors, 1961–62, Houston Public Library, Houston Metropolitan Research Center.
45. Harriet Dickson Reynolds, letter to Lewis Cutrer, July 22, 1961, in ibid.
46. Minute book, February 23, 1962, and October 13, 1961, in ibid.
47. Photographs, Houston Public Library, Houston Metropolitan Research Center.
48. Gary M. Pomerantz, *Where Peachtree Meets Sweet Auburn: The Saga of Two Families and the Making of Atlanta* (New York: Scribner, 1996), 246; Dennis C. Dickerson, *Militant Mediator: Whitney M. Young, Jr.* (Lexington: University of Kentucky Press, 1998), 110.
49. Annie L. McPheeters, *Library Service in Black and White: Some Personal Recollections, 1921–1980* (Metuchen, N.J.: Scarecrow, 1988), 86–87.
50. Howard Powell, "Howard Zinn, Historian, Dies at 87," *New York Times,* January 27, 2010, http:www.nytimes.com; and Pomerantz, *Where Peachtree Meets Sweet Auburn,* 246.
51. Nancy J. Weiss, *Whitney M. Young, Jr., and the Struggle for Civil Rights* (Princeton: Princeton University Press, 1989), 61.
52. Dickerson, *Militant Mediator,* 110.
53. Howard Zinn, "A Case of Quiet Social Change," *Crisis* 66 (October 1959): 472.
54. Ibid., 471.
55. McPheeters, *Library Service,* 87.
56. Zinn, "Case of Quiet Social Change," 474–75.
57. Pomerantz, *Where Peachtree Meets Sweet Auburn,* 247.
58. Ibid., 248.
59. "Segregation in Libraries," *Crisis* 68 (June–July 1961): 342–43.
60. Lucretia Jeanette Parker, "A Study of Integration in Public Library Service in Thirteen Southern States" (master's thesis, Atlanta University, 1953), 70.
61. Ibid., 76–82.
62. Ibid., 5–6; Bernice Lloyd Bell, "Integration in Public Library Service in Thirteen Southern States, 1954–1962" (master's thesis, Atlanta University, 1963), 21–22.
63. Bell, "Integration," 126–31.
64. Parker, "Study of Integration," 28–30; Karen Anderson, *Little Rock: Race and Resistance* (Princeton: Princeton University Press, 2010), 21.
65. Isaac R. Barfield, "A History of the Miami Public Library, Miami, Florida" (master's thesis, Atlanta University, 1958).
66. Parker, "Study of Integration," 31–33.
67. Ibid., 43; Bell, "Integration," 48.
68. Parker, "Study of Integration," 7.
69. Ibid., 71.
70. Ibid., 63.
71. Ibid., 59.
72. Ibid., 69–75.
73. Bell, "Integration," 24–26.
74. Ibid., 30, 32, 35, 60.
75. Ibid., 39, 41.

76. Ibid., 55, 59–60; Patricia Ryckman, *Public Library of Charlotte and Mecklenburg County: A Century of Service* (Charlotte, N.C.: Public Library of Charlotte and Mecklenburg County, 1989), 21.

77. Markus Schmidt, "After Sit-ins Come Protests, Court Cases, and Finally, Integration." www.progress-index.com.

78. Cresswell, "Last Days of Jim Crow," 558–60.

79. Rosa Parks, *Rosa Parks: My Story* (New York: Dial, 1992), 94.

80. Patterson Toby Graham, *A Right to Read: Segregation and Civil Rights in Alabama's Public Libraries, 1900–1965* (Tuscaloosa: University of Alabama Press, 2002), 69–98.

EPILOGUE

1. "Gloria Scott," *The History Makers,* www.thehistorymakers.com.

2. "Carnegie Library Conference," videotape, 1999, Bennett College Archives; Julia A. Hersberger, Lou Sua, and Adam L. Murray, "The Fruit and Root of the Community: The Greensboro Carnegie Negro Library, 1904–1964," in *The Library as Place: History, Community, and Culture,* eds. John E. Buschman and Gloria J. Leckie (Westport, Conn.: Libraries Unlimited, 2006), 97.

3. "Carnegie Library Conference."

4. Leon Carnovsky, "The Public Libraries of Greensboro: A Survey" [1952], 1–10, 15–17.

5. "Carnegie Library Conference."

6. Cheryl Knott Malone, "Unannounced and Unexpected: The Desegregation of Houston Public Library in the Early 1950s," *Library Trends* 55 (Winter 2007): 673.

7. "Carnegie Library Conference."

8. Imani Perry, *More Beautiful and More Terrible: The Embrace and Transcendence of Racial Inequality in the United States* (New York: New York University Press, 2011), 44.

9. Stephanie Ewert, "Racial Inequality in Expanded Measures of Educational Attainment," SIPP Working Paper No. 268 (Washington, D.C.: U.S. Bureau of the Census, Social, Economic, and Housing Statistics Division, August 2014); Michelle Alexander, *The New Jim Crow: Mass Incarceration in the Age of Colorblindness* (New York: New Press, 2010); Rakesh Kochhar and Richard Fry, "Wealth Inequality Has Widened along Ethnic, Racial Lines Since End of Great Recession," *FactTank,* December 12, 2014, www.pewresearch.org; American Library Association, "Public Library Funding Updates," www.ala.org.

Index